John Davidson,
First of the Moderns

John Davidson, First of the Moderns

A LITERARY BIOGRAPHY

——

JOHN SLOAN

CLARENDON PRESS · OXFORD
1995

Oxford University Press, Walton Street, Oxford OX2 6DP
Oxford New York
Athens Auckland Bangkok Bombay
Calcutta Cape Town Dar es Salaam Delhi
Florence Hong Kong Istanbul Karachi
Kuala Lumpur Madras Madrid Melbourne
Mexico City Nairobi Paris Singapore
Taipei Tokyo Toronto
and associated companies in
Berlin Ibadan

Oxford is a trade mark of Oxford University Press

Published in the United States
by Oxford University Press Inc., New York

British Library Cataloguing in Publication Data
Data available

Library of Congress Cataloging in Publication Data
Data available

ISBN 0 19 818248 1

1 3 5 7 9 10 8 6 4 2

Typeset by Best-set Typesetter Ltd., Hong Kong
Printed in Great Britain
on acid-free paper by
Bookcraft Ltd,
Midsomer Norton, Avon

For Betty

Preface

As long ago as 1917 Virginia Woolf expressed surprise that anyone as good as John Davidson should 'be so little famous'. Davidson's relative obscurity was to some extent his own doing. In the hasty, unwitnessed will he sent to his friend and publisher Grant Richards in the period of black depression some months before his suicide, he left two instructions: first, that 'no word, except of my writing, is ever to appear in any book of mine as long as the copyright endures'; and second, that 'no one is to write my life now or at any time'. The eccentric ban on future publication effectively ruled out the possibility of any new selected edition of his work for fifty years. Richards stuck loyally to Davidson's wishes, although he felt increasingly frustrated as he watched occasional flurries of interest in Davidson's work come to nothing.

One early upsurge of interest took place in 1917 with the publication of a study of Davidson's poetry and ideas by Hayim Fineman, a young American academic. It was on this occasion that Virginia Woolf reread Davidson in order to write a review of Fineman's book for the *Times Literary Supplement*. Anticipating modern judgements she decided that Davidson's later urban poetry, notably 'Fleet Street', 'The Crystal Palace', 'London Bridge', and 'Liverpool Street Station', were best. 'They are original without being prophetic', she wrote. Woolf's article might well have attracted attention to Davidson as a proto-modernist—1917 was the year in which T. S. Eliot's *Prufrock, and Other Observations* came out, and with it the phase of modern poetry can be said to have truly begun. But Davidson's work remained inaccessible except in first editions or in standard anthologies which invariably selected from his early lyrics. Arthur Quiller-Couch's *Oxford Book of English Verse* of 1900, for instance, included the song 'The Boat is Chafing at our Long Delay' and 'The Last Rose'. Although honoured at his inclusion Davidson had complained to Quiller-Couch at the time that these were unrepresentative pieces. Another missed opportunity occurred in 1918 when a young Aldous Huxley, recently down from Oxford, was commissioned to write a piece on

Davidson for the final volume of Thomas Humphrey Ward's *The English Poets*. Huxley's choice of 'Piper, Play' and 'A Ballad of Heaven' from Davidson's 1905 *Selected Poems* for John Lane did nothing to change the conception of him as a distinctive minor lyricist of the *Yellow Book* age.

Perhaps the most serious blow to Davidson's reputation was his omission from W. B. Yeats's *Oxford Book of Modern Verse* in 1936. Charles Williams, then an editor at the London office of the Press, suggested Davidson's name during the planning stages of the list. Yeats replied that he had withdrawn Davidson on finding that he had too much 'matter', although he conceded, 'I may have to restore him.' That he did not, many would attribute to his personal resentment over an anonymous review of *The Countess Kathleen* (1892) which he believed, mistakenly, to have been written by Davidson. Yeats was particularly stung by the sentence, 'There are no lines which go straight home and linger in the memory.' In his memoir 'The Tragic Generation' he was to conclude his highly unfavourable portrait of Davidson with a cruel echo of those words in, 'And now no verse of his clings to my memory.' It was a calculated revenge.

But other survivors of the 1890s had also written their memoirs, and the memory of Davidson's high standing among his contemporaries was kept alive. Max Beerbohm, who was one of his closest friends in his later years, wrote of him that he 'had what I think the other poets had not: genius (and a very robust genius)'. But the real sea change occurred in 1957 when both T. S. Eliot and Hugh MacDiarmid separately acknowledged their debt to Davidson on the centenary of his birth. For MacDiarmid, Davidson's importance lay in his ideas, particularly his interest in scientific material, while Eliot singled out Davidson's 'Thirty Bob a Week' as the poem which had provided him with a new poetic idiom for the 'dingy urban images' of his time. 'The personage that Davidson created in this poem has haunted me all my life,' he wrote, 'and the poem is to me a great poem forever.' Critics have found Eliot's choice of 'Thirty Bob a Week' odd, as Eliot's style and subject-matter seem closer to Davidson's later poetry, but Eliot's memory was not faulty. In *Ushant* (1952) Conrad Aiken recalls introducing Eliot and his other Harvard friends to 'Thirty Bob a Week' after a visit to England. Eliot at the time had discovered Krazy Kat, and Mutt and Jeff, but it was Davidson among other imports from the 'Old Country' that satisfied the need of the young Harvard men for the feeling of 'a double life—bi-lingual, bi-focal'. Like Eliot's J. Alfred Prufrock, Davidson's downtrodden, ignobly decent clerk is a man of acute self-consciousness who hears two voices singing in his head.

Recent criticism has established Davidson as a key presence in the process by which modernism emerged out of this 'duality of awareness'. Andrew Turnbull's 'Introduction' to *The Poems of John Davidson* (1973) and Mary O'Connor's *John Davidson* (1987) have stressed Davidson's anticipation of modernist methods, especially in his late poems where allusion and juxtaposition emphasize the fragmentariness, contingency, and unreality of the city scene. Kenneth Millard's *Edwardian Poetry* (1991) goes much further in locating the origins of Davidson's literary modernism, arguing that Davidson's cultural displacement from Scotland to England was 'a necessary stage in his literary development', aligning him 'with other Modernist outsiders to English culture and its London centre'. Robert Crawford's *The Savage and the City in the Works of T. S. Eliot* (1986) demonstrates the pervasiveness of Davidson's influence on Eliot's language, imagery, and theme—Davidson too saw something horrible and non-human, something savage in the city—while his more recent *Devolving English Literature* (1992) places Davidson in the tradition of bicultural 'British' writers such as Scott and Carlyle, whose work questions the Anglocentricity of 'English' literature. These significant critical contributions challenge persuasively those historians of Scottish literature who have argued that Davidson was wrong to pose himself against a background of English literature, or who would place him too narrowly in the context of the Spasmodic or Messianic traditions of nineteenth-century Scottish poetry. Perhaps an indication that Davidson has at last achieved the prominence he deserves as a modern is the choice of his poem 'Snow' from his posthumous collection of 1909 to open Douglas Dunn's *Faber Book of Twentieth-Century Scottish Poetry* (1992).

It is in the context of this renaissance of interest in John Davidson that the present literary biography appears. Several writers have been drawn to Davidson's life over the years.

Graham Greene was attracted to Davidson as the subject of a biography until he discovered that Davidson had put an embargo on anyone writing his biography. The taboo was broken in 1961 when J. Benjamin Townsend's *John Davidson: Poet of Armageddon* appeared. Townsend had access to a large collection of manuscripts in Princeton University Library, much of which had found its way there via Grant Richards. But Townsend lacked information about Davidson's early life, and since then a substantial amount of new material, including Davidson's personal correspondence with family, friends, and important figures of the period has been discovered.

The material contained much new factual information. Davidson's early life and early London years could now be filled in, including the ties which connect him to Robert Sherard's circle, to Oscar Wilde, Yeats, and the Rhymers' Club. It also provided a new perspective on Davidson's character and career, from his early unsettled life in Scotland to his years in London, struggling to reconcile the freedom to experience demanded by the artist in the age of the Decadence with the obligations of family; and to combine his ambitions as a poet with his need to survive in the commercial rough and tumble of Fleet Street, the theatre, and Paternoster Row. Davidson emerges not simply as a late-Victorian rebel, but as the 'first of the moderns' who, from his recovery from a breakdown in 1898 to his death in 1909, forged out a new idiom and subject-matter for twentieth-century English verse. My picture differs substantially from Townsend's portrait of him as a difficult, irascible Scotsman—a portrait based in large part on the impression he made on Yeats and others of the Rhymers' in his early days in London, on his business letters to John Lane and Grant Richards, and on his quarrels with his critics. The contentiousness of Davidson's character has to be seen in the context of a full understanding of the circumstances of his life and struggles as a poet, and in balance with the qualities of tenderheartedness and good humour which never left him in his final difficult years. Some of his friends gave evidence of this, but felt constrained by the stern injunction that his life should on no account be written. I have tried to use all the material that has become available to me to dispel the myths about John Davidson and tell his story as far as possible as it seemed to him and to his friends.

I wish to thank officials of the following institutions for making available material in their custody: the Beinecke Rare Book and Manuscript Library, Yale University Library; the Berg Collection, New York Public Library; the Bodleian Library, Oxford; the British Library; the Brotherton Collection, Leeds University Library; the William Andrews Clark Memorial Library, University of California; Columbia University; Glasgow University Library; the Huntington Library, San Marino, California; Merton College, Oxford; the Mitchell Library, Glasgow; Morrison's Academy, Crieff; the National Library of Scotland; Princeton University Library; the Harry Ransom Humanities Research Center, University of Texas at Austin; the Scottish Record Office; and the University of Reading. I should also like to thank the Rector of Kelvinside Academy, the staff of the Mitchell Library, Glasgow, and the Health Boards of Greater Glasgow and Lothian for patiently answering my enquiries.

I am also grateful to many individuals who gave help of various kinds during the preparation of this book. I am especially grateful to Roger Lonsdale, for his encouragement and his gift; Michael Rhodes, who generously passed on his knowledge; Pierre Coustillas, for our correspondence about Gissing; Walt and Marian Litz for the days at Princeton; my wife, Elizabeth, and Cathy Foot, who taught me about computers; and Carl Schmidt for the information that led me to the McCormick letters at Glasgow University. Finally I owe my deepest thanks to Val Cunningham for his magnanimity.

Contents

List of Plates

Abbreviations

Line references to the poems are to *The Poems of John Davidson*, ed. Andrew Turnbull (Edinburgh, 1973).

1

Early Life, 1857–1888

I

John Davidson was apt to deny the influence of his ancestors
in declaring his own freedom of mind, but the spirit of rebelliousness ran in his family. In 1784, Hugh Mitchell, his great-
grandfather on his father's maternal side, was 'exceedingly
unacceptable' as parish minister to the people of Eaglesham
in Lanarkshire, because he supported the French Revolution
and opposed state interference in the affairs of the Church.[1]
Mitchell, for some years Master of the first academy of Greenock, had served as tutor in the family of Archibald Nisbet of
Carphin after graduating from the University of Glasgow, and
in 1774 had married Nisbet's daughter Amelia. He was later
Master of an English and French academy in Glasgow, and on
the Peace of Amiens in 1802, visited France with his wife and
daughter, when all three were made prisoner by Bonaparte and
carried to Verdun before being liberated.

Jane Mitchell married John Davidson, a tenant farmer at
Craighead in the parish of Dailly in her father's native Ayrshire.
They had five sons and two daughters. The fifth son, Alexander,
was the father of the poet. He spent his boyhood in Ayrshire,
where he attended the local parish school, first at Kirkoswald,
where the mother and father of Robert Burns were buried, and
then at Girvan. But it was a time of great change in the farming
communities of Scotland, and his father, now elderly, and presumably with none of his sons willing to carry on farming, gave

---

[1] Although the genealogical record is incomplete, Hugh Mitchell can be identified from comments made in Fergus Ferguson's reliable 'Biographical Sketch' of
Alexander Davidson, in *Sermons by the Late Rev. Alexander Davidson* (Edinburgh,
1893), which also provides much of the information about Alexander Davidson and
Helen Crocket. Mitchell was the author of *Scotticisms, Vulgar Anglicisms and Gram-
matical Improprieties Corrected* (Glasgow, 1799). The main facts of his life are recorded
in Hew Scott's *Fasti Ecclesiae Scoticanae: The Succession of Ministers in the Church of
Scotland from the Reformation,* iii (Edinburgh, 1920).

up the tenancy of Craighead which had been in the family since the early eighteenth century, and retired to a cottage in Glasgow, on the south side of the river. Alexander was apprenticed to a draper, first in Lancaster and then shortly after in the coastal town of Wick, in the north-east of Scotland. At 17 he stood up in the town hall of Wick and gave a memorable temperance speech and was encouraged by the local Congregational minister to consider a career in the ministry. He went south to Glasgow the following year to begin his studies.

More than fifty years later John Davidson was to tell a magazine interviewer in London that his father was among the first to protest against the 'cruel, crude creed' of his ancestors.[2] In 1843, James Morison, one of the ablest young ministers in the Secessionist body, had persuasively challenged the Calvinist doctrine of election with a liberal theology based on free will and salvation for all men. Although this received little attention at the time, orthodox Congregationalism was shaken, and Morison and his supporters were driven out. Alexander Davidson, then 19, was one of the small band who followed him into the wilderness to form the Evangelical Union. It was a courageous step. For Alexander Davidson it meant the loss of financial support from the Congregationalists with whom he had intended to study. For the next six years he supported himself doggedly through university and theological hall on an average £1 a week he earned on Sundays as a supply preacher.

He was given his first church in 1849 in the remote northern fishing town of Frazerburgh. Two years later, on 5 June 1851, he married Helen Crocket. They had been members of the same congregation in Glasgow at the time of the disruption eight years earlier. She was an orphan. Her father, Alexander Crocket, had been parish schoolmaster at Bishop Mill in Elgin, but he had died in 1842 when he was only 45, and she had been sent south to Glasgow at the age of 7 or 8 to be brought up by relatives. Alexander and Helen Davidson spent the first two years of their married life in Frazerburgh. Their northern exile ended in the autumn of 1853 when Alexander was given a pastorship at the small manufacturing town of Barrhead, with a

---

[2] 'Mr. John Davidson', *Pall Mall Budget* (27 Dec. 1894), 16–17.

large Irish Catholic population, six miles south-west of Glasgow. It was here that John Davidson was born on 11 April 1857. Both his parents were 32.

It is generally assumed that Davidson's autobiographical poem, 'A Woman and her Son' greatly exaggerates the circumstances of his own life, but the words of the son to the mother— 'Eight times you bore a child, and in fierce throes, | For you were frail and small'[3]—would seem to be closer to the truth than has previously been supposed. John was the fourth child, but the first boy in the family. Of his three elder sisters, one had already died in infancy, and another was to die when he was 3 or 4. Euphemia, the third, was born at Barrhead in June 1855. After John came 'Lizzie', Alexander Davidson's favourite, also born in Barrhead in February 1859. Then there was a gap of five years before the birth of their youngest son, Thomas. There may well have been still births or miscarriages between. Large families and high infant mortality were commonplace in the middle-class Victorian family. Alexander Davidson was known as 'Papa' to the children. His salary was £80 a year, a meagre sum for a man with a family to support, but the 'manse', a small cottage in Lowndes street, was free.[4] There is no evidence that they were visited by Helen Davidson's two elder sisters, or by Alexander Davidson's numerous relatives, although Euphemia was named after his younger sister, and he seems to have kept in touch with his brothers, one of whom was a medical man.

John's only recollections of Barrhead as he later told an enquirer whom he felt made 'rather a myth of his childhood', were of 'the garden of the Evangelical Union manse, and a field with sheep and cows ajoining'.[5] Alexander Davidson was appointed assistant to James Morison at the North Dundas Street Church in Glasgow, and the family moved there in the summer of 1860 when John was 3. For Alexander Davidson it meant promotion, but sadly the improvement in the family situation was overshadowed by the death of John's eldest sister. Her burial plot in a Glasgow cemetery was to become the family

---

[3] 'A Woman and her Son', ll. 103–4.

[4] The salary of £80 a year at Barrhead is recorded in Harry Escott, *A History of Scottish Congregationalism* (Glasgow, 1960), 321.

[5] Davidson to 'Dear Sir', 20 Apr. 1905, Princeton.

grave. They had little opportunity to visit it. To the surprise of many, Alexander Davidson left Glasgow in the autumn of 1862 to become pastor of the church at Greenock, an industrial port at the mouth of the Clyde estuary. Characteristically, he exchanged material comfort for a church that had been without a pastor for a year because of differences among its members.

The family's first home was Alma Cottage, Ann Street, in the old part of town close to the chapel in Sir Michael Street. But in 1863 they finally settled at 3 Orangefield, a pleasant West End street built by David Reid in the 1820s.[6] John was to remember their servant, a good Christian woman called Mary Somerville, whom he nevertheless thought lazy because she used to boil the porridge at night and heat it up in the morning to save time.[7] His father was now well known in the town for his sermons and his impressive voice. John's own ambition as a child was to be a persuasive speaker like his father.[8] By the time they moved to Orangefield, the Sir Michael Street chapel was too small to hold all the people who arrived each Sunday to hear his father preach, and it was decided to build a new church that would draw people from the new West End as well as the old town. It was completed in the summer of 1865 at a cost of £2,600. It still stands, on the corner of Nelson Street and Nicholson Street, a monument to Victorian Gothic taste, with seating for 700 people. It was here in an atmosphere of revivals, prayer meetings and hymn-singing missions that John grew up.[9]

He was educated at home until he was 6 or 7. There was a widespread prejudice in Scotland at this time against children being sent to school before this age. The daily reading of *The Pilgrim's Progress* at the age of 6, which he recalled later, would have taken place under his mother's eye. His first school was George Square Academy, which was about a mile from his

---

[6] The architect of Orangefield is given in Eric Northey, 'The Poetry of John Davidson in its Social, Political and Philosophical Contexts', Ph.D. thesis (University of Newcastle, 1976).

[7] Davidson to Grant Richards, 13 Nov. 1908, Princeton.

[8] His memories of his father are in 'About Myself', *Candid Friend* (1 June 1901), 177–8.

[9] Information about Alexander Davidson's ministry is to be found in the denominational magazine, *The Day-Star* and in *Centenary Anniversary, 1846–1946. Nelson Street Evangelical Union Congregational Church, Greenock* (Greenock, 1946).

home.[10] Brutal caning was a daily occurrence there, the main victims being the poorest and most stupid boys. Parish schools in Scotland at that time were egalitarian places, with the boys from middle-class families mixing freely with those from poor homes. In John's class some of the boys were several years older than himself. He found a friend among them, a tall, raw-boned boy of 13 who protected him against those he could not fight. As the son of a Morisonian minister, he had to face hostility and being called names. He was soon moved to the Highlanders' Academy, which was at the west end of Roxburgh Street and closer to his home.[11] It provided a good education for the children of the middle classes of the town.

John was a precocious reader. Bunyan at the age of 6 had been followed at 7 by Scott's romances and Kingsley's *Hereward the Wake*, which he read every Sunday for several years in a bound volume of *Good Words*.[12] This may have been his way round the restrictions of the Sabbath. *Good Words*, which began publication in 1860, was considered to be safe religious reading as well as good literature. The Evangelical Union was believed to be more tolerant about Sunday observance. But many of the Morisonians practised a strict form of Sabbatarianism, and no one who worked in the license trade was allowed to be a member of their church. As was often the case in Scotland, left-wing theology went hand in hand with strict morality. Their official pamphlet on the 'Claims of the Sabbath' banned 'steam-boat trips and other Sunday excitements fashionable among clerks', and condemned families as 'self-debased whose members do not turn out, clean, and clad in their best, with their faces towards the house of God'.[13]

He remembered that his habit of writing verses began out of the sheer ennui of Sundays in his father's house. He wrote his first poem when he was 12—a heroic ballad on the religious

[10] George Square Academy is remembered in 'The Testament of a Juryman', *Westminster Gazette* (21 Jan. 1905), 2.

[11] The Highlanders' Academy is described in A. Williamson, *Views and Reminiscences of Old Greenock* (Greenock, 1891), which also provides other information about the town's history.

[12] His reading is recalled in 'Mr. John Davidson', *Bookman*, 7 (Nov. 1894), 48–9, and in 'About Myself', *Candid Friend*. His reading of *Hereward the Wake* is remembered in his 'Introduction' to *Godfrida*.

[13] 'Claims of the Sabbath: A Statement Issued by the Committee of the E. U. Conference' (Glasgow, 1855).

subject of 'The Defeat of the Moors by Ramiro, King of Spain'.[14] By then he had begun committing to memory Shakespeare's sonnets and Thomas Carlyle's *Sartor Resartus*. Together with Walter Scott's ballads, these were to be his earliest literary models. His poems seem to have attracted attention, for he was invited on walks by a young Greenock poet. He found his new friend 'magnetic', although with childhood candour he disdained his poetry, 'preferring Shakespeare'.[15] This early mentor, whose name is unknown, died of consumption. Their walks together may have resulted in the deepening responsiveness to his surroundings that Davidson associated with this time. In later life he described the walk along Shaw's water-cut above the town as 'the finest walk in the world. There is nothing even second to it.'[16] From the hills above the town he had views of industrial Greenock blending into the natural beauty of the Firth of Clyde, with its wooded slopes and mountain ranges visible across the estuary.

Greenock was at that time a thriving Victorian seaport, and as was often the case, an important centre for the foreign missions. Its main industries were shipbuilding and sugar-refining, but it also had engineering works, iron forges, cooperages, tanneries and cotton mills. Its population had almost doubled during the first thirty years of Queen Victoria's reign to nearly 40,000. As in other Victorian towns, prosperity and squalour were to be found together. There was a high incidence of alcoholism and violent crime. John's father—a well-known temperance reformer—may have been drawn there for this reason. Large numbers of men were to be found in Greenock at any one time—sailors from around the world, as well as immigrants from Ireland and the Western Isles who arrived looking for work. Davidson was sensitive to the squalid side of town life, but he seems to have been less moved by social concern than he was excited by the energy of the place and the beauty of its natural surroundings. For the youthful hero of 'A Ballad in Blank Verse of the Making of A Poet', these are parts of a single vision:

[14] His first efforts at writing are described in 'Mr. John Davidson', *Bookman*, and in a letter to Richards, 13 Apr. 1902, Princeton.
[15] Davidson to William Symington McCormick, 12 Apr. 1895, Glasgow.
[16] Davidson to Richards, 14 Oct. 1906, Princeton.

> . . . this grey town
> That pipes the morning up before the lark
> With shrieking steam, and from a hundred stalks
> Lacquers the sooty sky; where hammers clang
> On iron hulls, and cranes in harbours creak
> Rattle and swing, whole cargoes on their necks;
> Where men sweat gold that others hoard or spend,
> And lurk like vermin in their narrow streets:
> This old grey town, this firth, the further strand
> Spangled with hamlets, and the wooded steeps,
> Whose rocky tops behind each other press,
> Fantastically carved like antique helms
> High-hung in heaven's cloudy armoury,
> Is world enough for me.[17]

Greenock provided John with a network of conflicting, imaginative allegiances that were to remain with him all his life. Although attached to Scotland's romantic past—a monument, for example, had been erected by public subscription in 1842 to Burns's Highland Mary, who was buried in the Old West Kirk—the town was also conscious of its contribution to the progress of the British Empire. It was a matter of civic pride, for instance, that Greenock had been the birthplace of James Watt, the pioneer of the Steam Age. Municipal buildings were named after him, including the science library which he founded. Watt himself was buried near Handsworth in Staffordshire, but the grave of his forebears in the Old West Kirk served the city fathers on public occasions as an example of the town's contribution to the progress of the nation. Huge tonnages of coal, iron and steel left the port in coal-driven steamships for different parts of the Empire, along with traditional cargoes of textiles and bullion. Merchant sailing vessels were still in service, like survivors of another age, and John was to admire their 'carven antique poops' as he walked along by the harbour as a boy.[18]

The family spent their summer holidays at one or other of the two islands of Bute or Great Cumbrae, which were reached by passenger steamer from Greenock. John had ambivalent memories of a holiday at Rothesay on Bute in the summer of 1867,

---

[17] 'A Ballad in Blank Verse', ll. 23–36.
[18] 'A Ballad in Blank Verse', l. 198.

when he was 10.[19] For him that year meant the haunting tune of the 'Old Hundredth' on the barrel-organ, sounding eerily along the sea front as he fished among the rocks, or went for walks on Castle Hill. This seems not to have happened that summer, although he may have experienced similar feelings of guilty pleasure. That July the family stayed at the health resort of Millport on Great Cumbrae, where Alexander Davidson was recovering from a serious lung infection. He wrote from Millport on the 26th to tell his congregation that they would be returning to Greenock that week, and that his health was improving in spite of the cold weather.[20] But he was not able to return to his duties until September, after convalescing at the Hydropathic Institute at Skermorlie, which specialized in the treatment of tuberculosis. He had been absent for nearly four months.

This seems to have been a time of financial hardship for the family. Alexander Davidson refused to borrow money on principle, but his self-reliance meant that the family had to move house from Orangefield to a tenement house at 12 Brisbane Street in the crowded north end of town. This may account for the bitter memories recorded in several of Davidson's poems about boyhood. In 'A Woman and her Son', the son reminds his mother of the poverty and bleakness of their family life:

> We had no room, no sport; nothing but fear
> Of our evangelist, whose little purse
> Opened to all save us; who squandered smiles
> On wily proselytes, and gloomed at home.[21]

Children are resentful even of small changes in their circumstances; fear and a sense of powerlessness sometimes breed exaggerated and even lifetime grudges. The family were four years at Brisbane Street before moving in 1871 to a villa at 48 Eldon Street, in the desirable northern reaches of the town overlooking the promenade. Davidson celebrates the place in

---

[19] His memories of Rothesay are in *A Random Itinerary* (London, 1894), 108–10.

[20] Alexander Davidson's health is the subject of correspondence in the Session Records of the Nelson Street Evangelical Union Church, quoted in Alexander Monteith Currie, 'A Biographical and Critical Study of John Davidson', B.Litt. thesis (University of Oxford, 1953).

[21] 'A Woman and Her Son', ll. 94–7.

his first novel, *The North Wall* (1885, later retitled *A Practical Novelist*) when the hero Maxwell Lee walks along it 'at a good spanking pace, feeling its costly breadth, its substantiality, its triumph over nature' and 'conscious of that solid nineteenth-century comfort and luxury that lie on one side of it, ascending the hill to larger villas and more spacious grounds'.[22] But it was in the cramped conditions of Brisbane Street that he first read Shakespeare and Carlyle's *Sartor Resartus*, and began to write poetry.

On 1 November 1870 he was registered as a pupil teacher at the Highlanders' Academy.[23] The choice of pupil teachers was usually made on moral rather than academic grounds,[24] and it may have come as no surprise to anyone when exactly a year later, he left to work in the chemical department of Walker's Sugarhouse. Education was highly valued in Scotland, but there was also a strongly practical strain in the people's attitude to life. He was 14. Though a gifted child, he had never excelled at school. He had difficulty learning mathematics and Latin, the two most important subjects in those days. Davidson seems to picture his own early self in the character of Islay Inglis, the lovable schoolboy of the novel *Baptist Lake*, who has read Scott, Shakespeare, and Kingsley's *Hereward the Wake*, but confesses to being 'sick of schools': 'I've never learnt anything in them. I could read before I went, and everything I know worth knowing was not learnt in books.'[25]

Davidson did not stay long at Walker's Sugarhouse. He left after a few months to work at the Public Analyst's Laboratory in Cathcart Street, which had been established to check the levels of adulteration by sugar manufacturers such as Walker's. His main job at the laboratory was to weigh portions of 16.6 grammes of beet for precipitation with acetate of lead.[26] Chemistry was to leave a mark on his poetry, but he was not cut out to be a chemist. After just over a year, he returned to his old school as a pupil teacher.

[22] *A Practical Novelist* (London, 1891), 192.
[23] Davidson's career as a pupil teacher is recorded in the school log-books of the Highlanders' Academy, in Northey, 'The Poetry of John Davidson', Appendix B.
[24] Marjorie Cruickshank, *A History of the Training of Teachers in Scotland* (London, 1970), 60.
[25] *Baptist Lake* (London, 1894), 314.
[26] 'Mr. John Davidson', *Bookman*.

The system of pupil teachers had been introduced about fifteen years earlier with the aim of replacing the old system of child monitors with teenage assistants who would eventually join the profession.[27] There were eight pupil teachers at the Highlanders' Academy in addition to the five qualified members of staff. Pupil teachers earned between 4 and 10 shillings a week. Davidson would have been hard worked, with classes at the school averaging between fifty and seventy pupils. There were only two breaks in the school year at that time, at New Year and summer. But this appears to have been a happy period in his life. He had time to read again, particularly during the summer holidays, part of which he liked to spend each year rambling in the Ochil Hills. He devoured 'everything in the way of translation', including, it would seem, books that were banned at home. He also wrote two plays, which he 'scrupulously burned', but some of his poems from this period have survived, including his quaint, boyish love-song to a prosaically named, 'Annie Smith'.[28]

But the age of scepticism that produced the Public Analyst's Laboratory had also left its mark on him. He began to quarrel openly with his father. The immediate cause of their disagreement was the strict Presbyterian ban at that time against the theatre. He defied his parents' wishes when he went to the Theatre Royal in town to see Ellen Wallis in Shakespeare and the German-born actor Daniel Edward Bandmann in his famous role as Narcisse. 'They were practically the whole stage for me in Greenock for a year or two', he later told William Archer.[29] But the aftermaths of such outings were scenes of tearful recrimination and depressing estrangement between himself and his parents. He felt particularly bitter towards his mother who gave him no support and seemed to live only in his father's shadow.

The powerful autobiographical ballads which Davidson wrote in the 1890s, when he was in his late thirties, are heightened and dramatized rather than literal versions of these events. Certainly, Alexander Davidson was not the crude Calvinist of the poems. Nor was John as wayward as the rebellious son

---

[27] Cruickshank, *Training of Teachers in Scotland,* 55.
[28] 'Mr. John Davidson', *Bookman.*
[29] Davidson to William Archer, 27 Jan. 1901, BL.

of 'A Ballad in Blank Verse' who goes for sex to the town prostitutes: 'He sought the outcast Aphrodite, dull, | Tawdry, unbeautiful, but still divine | Even in the dark streets of a noisome port.'[30]

One witness who remembered Davidson at this time was a young student for the ministry who was a close friend of the family. John M. Sloan's impressions, which contain the first description of Davidson, are of a manly lad:

I first met John Davidson when he was in his 'teens and living at home in his father's manse in Greenock as an assistant teacher in the local Academy. We had walks and talks together. He was small in stature, with a large head, black hair tending to curl, a clear eye, a genial smile, and he was powerful in conversation beyond his years. He had then read the whole of Carlyle, been in at the death of the 'Fairie Queene', and was familiar with all the master poets. Dogmatic in tone, he was a young rebel at home in revolt against the orthodox Scottish ban of that period against the theatre and reverently critical of his father's evangelical creed.[31]

The word 'reverently' tells us much about the relations between father and son. Significantly too, Sloan identifies Davidson with Ninian in *Fleet Street Eclogues*, for whom the break with childhood pieties threatens his life and sanity. Filial piety was one of the great crisis themes of Victorian poetry. In Tennyson's 'Supposed Confessions of a Sensitive Second-Rate Mind', filial love conquers the force of reason, but in a way that confronts the precariousness of such knowledge of the heart. Writing later in the century, Davidson gives reason the upper hand. But the price paid by his mutinous heroes is misery and even madness.

Davidson's quarrel with Christianity may have seemed intensely personal to him at the time, but it was also part of a generational crisis that was transforming the whole society. Of course, the conflict of generations is a factor of every age. But the experience seems to have been particularly painful for the younger generation in the latter half of the nineteenth century. Writers like Thomas Hardy, George Gissing, Samuel Butler, and George Moore were to face hostility in trying to

[30] 'A Ballad in Blank Verse', ll. 145–7.
[31] John M. Sloan, 'A Rebel in Poetry', *John O'London's Weekly*, 15 (26 Sept. 1926), 766.

change Victorian attitudes. Many of the men whom Davidson would later meet in London were struggling in their different ways to escape from the subjugation of their Victorian fathers, and in some cases, from the inhibitions of their provincial, Nonconformist upbringing. One thinks of Edmund Gosse, for whom the new science destroyed his belief in his father's faith and authority. Or of C. K. Shorter, one of the founders of the 'new journalism', who had to keep many of his activities, including theatre-going, secret from his widowed mother.[32]

Davidson's reaction against Christianity seems to have been most acute in the early months of 1875 when he applied for membership of his father's church. There would have been strong pressure on him to do this. The responsibility for local schools had been transferred from the churches to the new local authorities three years before, but pupil teachers were still expected to attend church on Sundays. Davidson was examined by two of the church elders—Thomas Highet, a ship's carpenter, and William Hutchison, a clerk. On Sunday, 18 April, a week after his eighteenth birthday, they reported that they 'had found him satisfactory in all ways' and recommended that he be granted admission to the church.[33] Davidson seems to re-create that moment when he joined his father's congregation in the chilling scene in his poem 'A Ballad in Blank Verse', where the hero drags himself to the altar with feelings of loathing and guilt:

> In solemn tones the grey-haired presbyter—
> 'This is My body which is given for you,
> This do in memory of Me.'
> > The boy,
> Whose blood within him clamoured like a storm,
> Uttered a smothered cry and rose, but lo!
> The happy triumph on his father's face![34]

His taking of the communion is the great crisis point in the poem, the moment in which filial submission becomes self-betrayal:

[32] C. K. Shorter's experiences are in J. M. Bulloch, *Forty Years in London* (Aberdeen, 1933), 7.

[33] Session Records, Nelson Street E. U. Church.

[34] 'A Ballad in Blank Verse', ll. 173–9.

The stealthy elders creaked about the floor,
Guiding the cup and platter; looking down,
The children in the gallery smirked and watched
Who took the deepest draught; and ancient dames
Crumpled their folded handkerchiefs, and pressed
With knuckly fingers sprays of southernwood.[35]

It may be no coincidence that Davidson's health broke down completely at this time. On Thursday, 20 May, following the Whit Monday Bank Holiday, he was reported 'unwell absent for two days' in the school log-books. It was to be a lengthy illness. He was still unfit for work when the school reopened at the beginning of August. That month, his place was filled by an old pupil of the school, James Denny, then on his summer vacation from Glasgow University. Denny, who was to become a pro- fessor of theology and Principal of the Glasgow Free Church College, impressed his contemporaries at the school as a man with a future.[36] Davidson, by contrast, was a shy, awkward youth with an unremarkable school record. But during that last year as a pupil teacher—after starting back on 1 September—he quietly laid the foundations of his own success later on as a poet, committing to memory Milton's *Comus*, and writing the early drafts of his 'Elizabethan' play, *An Unhistorical Pastoral* (1889). He also read John Lyly's Elizabethan prose romance, *Euphues*. His interest in things Elizabethan may have been encouraged by his friendship with Alan Park Paton, a local poet and celebrity who charged an entrance fee of 1*s*. 6*d*. for his enthusiastic readings and lectures on Shakespeare and other authors.[37] When he was writing in the *Speaker* years later, Davidson re- ferred to Paton's pet theory that 'the capitals scattered through- out the text of the folios' had been 'marked in Shakespeare's manuscript by himself in order to teach the actors the emphatic words'.[38]

But Davidson's life in Greenock and his father's house was coming to an end. There would be visits home over the next few years, but the town which had once seemed a sufficient world to

---

[35] 'A Ballad in Blank Verse', ll. 183–8.
[36] T. H. Walker, *Principal James Denny, D. D.: A Memoir and a Tribute* (London [1918]), 19–20.
[37] Northey, 'The Poetry of John Davidson', 32.
[38] *Speaker*, 3 (16 May 1891), 584.

him now began to feel imprisoning. Two years later he would complain to Swinburne about the 'Philistinism' and 'murky atmosphere of Greenock' in which he had been brought up.[39] He was gloomy and took to walking along the shore at night: 'But in the evening by the purple firth | He walked, and saw brown locks upon the brine, | And pale hands beckon him to come away.'[40] His mood was changing: '. . . men to know, | Women to love are waiting everywhere.'[41]

On 3 November 1876, he officially completed his apprenticeship as a pupil teacher. The school log-books record that he was now qualified under Article 79 of the 1873 Education Act. There were several options open to him. Some pupil teachers in his position stayed on as assistants at their old schools. The more ambitious sought entrance to training college or university in order to qualify to teach beyond elementary level. Sometime around late October and early November, John Davidson left his father's house and took the train from Greenock Station, along the Caledonian Railway Line. He had decided to enrol at Edinburgh University.

II

Edinburgh in Victorian times presented a dramatic appearance to the thousands of hopeful students who came each winter to enrol at the university. It has not lost its charm today, the serried mass of buildings that forms the Old Town reaching steeply hundreds of feet up to the castle which overlooks the city. In 1876, the winter session at the university opened on the 31 October; there was an address by the Principal at two o'clock. Davidson enrolled in the Faculty of Arts to study Latin and Greek. His matriculation fee for the year was £1; his class fees £6 6s.[42] Classes began the following day. There were no entrance tests in those days, and many would-be teachers attended

---

[39] Davidson to A. C. Swinburne, 28 Mar. 1878, in Cecil Y. Lang (ed.) *The Swinburne Letters*, iv (New Haven, Conn., 1960), 47–8.

[40] 'A Ballad in Blank Verse', ll. 94–6.

[41] 'A Ballad in Blank Verse', ll. 457–8.

[42] Details are taken from the University Calendar and Matriculation Books of Edinburgh University.

university, sometimes just for three months before entrance to one of the four training colleges in Edinburgh and Glasgow. There is no evidence to suggest that this was Davidson's plan. The Junior Latin and First Greek classes were the usual starting-point for those beginning a four-year degree course. News of James Denny's success at Glasgow would have reached the High-landers' Academy before he left. According to Davidson, his feeling at that time was still that he was 'equal to anything another could do.'[43]

Davidson's university day began at 9 o'clock with attendance at Professor John Stuart Blackie's First Greek class, where there were daily readings of Xenophon and parts of Homer. Blackie was notorious in Edinburgh for his eccentricity and boyish rowdyism. His well-known party piece, which was always in de-mand at public dinners, was to sing his own composition on Jenny Geddes and her cutty-stool: a ballad about opposition to King Charles's interference in Scottish forms of worship, at the conclusion of which Blackie would fling a stool across the room to loud cheers and applause. Davidson was to remember this in a review of Blackie's poetry in which, with tart humour, he dismissed the 'Scotch platform' as 'an elevation from which it is difficult to obtain a very extended prospect, and where the view is liable to be intercepted by fogs of prejudice, of kettle-drummle patriotism and religious intolerance, with this, among other effects, that Jenny Geddes's stool looms through the mist like a new constellation.'[44] But that was later. At Edinburgh he appears to have regarded Blackie with the kind of scorn min-gled with admiration that is the reaction of the clever student who feels he has the human measure of his tutor. 'No one who ever saw him will forget his tall lithe lean figure, his silvery hair and comely face', he wrote affectionately, recalling 'pleasant memories of his transparent nature, his high mindedness, his genial humour, and his sweet temper'. But in the same breath he was derisive of Blackie as 'that quaintest and most incorri-gible of optimists', remembering how he paraded through the streets in a 'shepherd-tartan plaid', and 'conducted his classes as Yorick might have done, or Feste, out of "Twelfth Night"'.[45]

[43] 'About Myself', *Candid Friend*, 177.
[44] 'A Song of Heroes', *Academy*, 37 (15 Mar. 1890), 182–3.
[45] 'Stress of Weather', *Glasgow Herald* (16 Feb. 1907), 9.

Between ten and midday students prepared their exercises for the afternoon classes and had lunch in one of the many pubs close to the university. From twelve until one, Professor William Young Sellar, a former Balliol scholar and Fellow of Oriel, took them through parts of Virgil, Horace, Livy, Cicero, and Tacitus, either the *Agricola* or the *Germania*. His two sons were in Davidson's year. Sellar's lazy dignity and refined Oxford voice were a source of awe to many of his Scottish students. Davidson was always to have an admiration for Oxford men. After another hour of Greek prose composition with Blackie, who was reputedly just as likely to lecture on crocodiles, students returned to Sellar for the last hour of the day to do Latin prose exercises or to listen to a lecture on Roman history and antiquities.

There were others in Edinburgh at that time whom Davidson would meet later in London. The drama critic, William Archer, then in his final year, was already working on the *Edinburgh Evening News* and going nightly to the grimy Princess's Theatre in Nicolson Street, where the major plays had been transferred after the Theatre Royal burned down earlier that year. Davidson missed J. M. Barrie, who arrived the following year, but Arthur Conan Doyle, to become famous as the creator of Sherlock Holmes, enrolled at the same time to study medicine. One classmate, Evan Maclean, remembered meeting Davidson at a house where he also sometimes met Robert Louis Stevenson, himself a former student of the university. This may have been at 21 Albion Street, close to the university, on the second floor, where several of Stevenson's friends lodged in the 1870s. Maclean recalled friendly discussions and differences of opinion.[46] There is no hint here of anything abnormal. Yet there is evidence that it was during these months in Edinburgh that Davidson underwent one of the most decisive emotional crises of his life. When the winter session resumed on Wednesday, 3 January after the Christmas holiday, he stopped attending classes and, like Stevenson before him, took to wandering about the city. He climbed Arthur's Seat twice a day, in the morning and afternoon. The reason he gave for turning

---

[46] Letter from Evan Maclean to Grant Richards, 29 Apr. 1909, Princeton.

student drop-out was the old one: he could not study; to him the dead languages remained dead.[47]

At this time, both Blackie and Sellar were unhappy about some aspects of the junior classes.[48] Blackie felt that classes were too large and that teaching remained a school-drill. With characteristic honesty, Davidson blamed neither his teachers, nor their teaching methods for his failure. He blamed himself. He believed he was temperamentally lazy and that his mental inertia was a form of intellectual inferiority. 'It was during my one University term that I learnt this finally', he wrote.[49] It was a painful admission for him. Many of the attitudes and actions of John Davidson's life seem to follow from that moment.

Disturbing memories of this time came back to him in London years later when he was drinking absinthe.[50] He included them in the poem 'Lammas', where the gloomy and loquacious Ninian tells his fellow journalists about his boyhood and youth. Ninian first describes Edinburgh as it looked from Arthur's Seat, with the 'chill and brindled fog' curling over 'the humming Canongate' and 'the wasted towers of Holyrood'. This is the focus of a sequence of memories that vacillate backwards and forwards in time, taking us from his infancy in his father's house—'Each morn and eve, I Year after year, I heard the prophets read, I Heard strong believing prayer'[51]—to his adoption of an anti-intellectual philosophy of life based on the belief that the body itself, and not reading, was the source of real knowledge. This new sense of freedom comes to Ninian intuitively—'No well-thumbed page appeared I In the hard book of memory as I woke: I Amazed I trembled newly into life: I I seemed to be created every morn'[52]—but his visionary ecstasy is clouded by darker moments of misery and despair.

The importance of the connection between the life and philosophy of the nineteenth-century forerunners of existen-

[47] 'About Myself', *Candid Friend.*
[48] For their views on classes, see John Stuart Blackie, 'A Letter to the People of Scotland on the Reform of their Academical Institutions' (Edinburgh, 1888), and William Young Sellar, 'The Arts Faculties in Scottish Universities' (Edinburgh, 1875).
[49] 'About Myself', *Candid Friend*, 177.
[50] 'Absinthe', *Glasgow Herald* (4 Mar. 1893), 9.
[51] 'Lammas', ll. 229–31.   [52] Ibid., ll. 252–5.

tialist thought has often been noticed. Nietzsche, with whom Davidson's work has often been associated, was also the rebellious son of a minister; and Kierkegaard, often regarded as the father of modern existentialism, had a similarly strict religious upbringing. Like them, Davidson responded to the breakdown of religious belief in early manhood with a defensive faith in the exceptional man and in intense subjectivity as the new basis of truth. It may have been his way of re-establishing his identity and consolidating his personality. 'No creed for me! I am a man apart,' declares the youthful rebel of 'A Ballad in Blank Verse of the Making of a Poet' as he leaves his father's house. For Davidson the making of the visionary poet and the existentialist rebel appear to have been one.

One cannot help wondering what might have happened to him if he had left for London then. Other young men with literary ambitions were flocking south to the capital. In fact he was anxious at that time to write for the newspapers and approached several editors. But they felt that he was too poetical and undisciplined for journalism.[53] The truth is that without a university background or important connections he is unlikely to have gone to the top in Fleet Street, although some like Arnold Bennett became successful editors early on in their careers. But even had he succeeded in journalism, it may have meant the sacrifice of his poetic ambitions which developed independently during the years of struggle and obscurity that lay ahead. He himself was to consider this question during his early days in London. His attitude is perplexed. On the one hand, he recognizes the disadvantages of his late start; on the other he wants to justify his lack of method as 'a kind of faculty, and not the absence of one'.[54] This combination of insecurity and defensive self-assertion underlies much of his life and work and goes back to the circumstances of his choice of poetry and freedom.

Free spirit or not, Davidson had to work to earn a living. His first job on leaving Edinburgh in April was as assistant teacher at Alexander's Endowed School in Glasgow. He stayed in lodgings in Whitevale Street in the area of the slaughterhouse and meat

---

[53] 'The Rejected Leader', *Glasgow Herald* (4 Apr. 1907), 10.
[54] *Sentences and Paragraphs* (London, 1893), 85.

market. To the north were Denniston and Alexandra Park where he sometimes played golf, striking his golf ball great distances over the rolling hills.[55] Alexander's was a charity school where poorer children were taught the Shorter Catechism and 'the three Rs'. He found the work 'hellish drudgery', but this was not an unhappy time for him.[56] He went to the theatres in the city and was deeply moved by Henry Irving's performance in *Hamlet* at the Theatre Royal.[57] He wrote poetry and completed his verse play *An Unhistorical Pastoral* after several attempts.[58] He lifted parts of the plot from Allan Ramsay's *The Gentle Shepherd* (1728), but the atmosphere of the play is that of Shakespeare's romantic comedies, and Milton's *Comus*. He had got to know John Nichol, the Professor of Literature at the university, possibly from attending his extra-mural classes, and showed him his play. By winter that year Nichol had taken him up as his most promising student.

Nichol had been appointed Professor of English Literature in 1862. He was 44 when Davidson met him and had already written a historical drama, *Hannibal*, as well as a literary biography of Sydney Dobell, the so-called 'Spasmodic' poet. The Spasmodics were a group of mid-nineteenth-century Scottish poets whose work was characterized by heroic themes matched with extravagant language.[59] The name was coined by William Edmonstoune Aytoun to describe the group which included Sidney Dobell, P. J. Bailey, J. W. Marston, and Alexander Smith. The Spasmodics had deeply influenced Nichol's own life and work. He was an ardent Scotsman—frank, generous, and with a Carlylean hatred of shams. His passionate admiration for J. S. Mill and foreign revolutionaries such as Mazzini and Kussoth, both of whom he had met, struck a chord with the younger generation of students. He was a champion of naturalness and spontaneity and disliked the unhealthy straining after academic success that he found among a large proportion of his students. One of his favourite quotations was from Sidney Smith: 'Be what nature intended you for and you will succeed; be anything else

[55] 'The Southern Isles', *Glasgow Herald* (13 Apr. 1907), 9.
[56] Davidson to Swinburne, 28 Mar. 1878, *Swinburne Letters*, 47.
[57] 'Here Awa', There Awa'', *Outlook* (13 May 1905), 680–1.
[58] Davidson to the Editor, *Saturday Review*, 86 (5 Nov. 1898), 609.
[59] William A. Knight, *A Memoir of John Nichol* (Glasgow, 1896).

and you will be ten thousand times worse than nothing.'[60] As a great berator of 'unveracities', Nichol gave support to the Carlylean impulses which had helped the young Davidson to define his own nature. Davidson read Thoreau and the Spasmodics and was encouraged by Nichol in his poetic ambitions. It is an indication of Nichol's high regard for his new prodigy that he showed Swinburne some of Davidson's verses when the poet visited Glasgow in January 1878.

Nichol and Swinburne had been close friends since their undergraduate days at Balliol College, Oxford. Nichol was older than Swinburne and at Balliol had coached him and deeply influenced his political outlook. They had continued to write to each other and had shared occasional holidays together. In the disorder that followed his father's death, Swinburne accepted Nichol's invitation to spend a month in Glasgow. The expected visit caused a great stir among Nichol's circle. Some of the students adopted Swinburne enthusiastically as the university laureate and printed four of his sonnets on the Russian question in the *Glasgow University Magazine.*

Davidson probably met Swinburne on 31 January when Nichol invited 'some ingenuous souls, named students' to his house at 14 Montgomerie Crescent in the fashionable district of Kelvinside.[61] According to Edmund Gosse, Swinburne welcomed Davidson in Nichol's study by laying his hand on his head and calling him 'Poet'. The little, silver-faced poet with the great mop of red hair then began spontaneously to chant some of Davidson's verses aloud.[62] In the conversation that followed, Swinburne spoke to him about Jacobean drama which he thought had influenced his play, but it turned out that Davidson had never read it. Swinburne's talk also turned to various literary topics including Carlyle and Sappho.[63]

Perhaps in the tensions of their own reunion Nichol and Swinburne were more enthusiastic than is wise. Davidson was

[60] John Nichol, *Scotch University Reform* (Glasgow, 1888), 23.

[61] Knight, *Memoir,* 204.

[62] Edmund Gosse, *The Life of Algernon Swinburne* (London, 1917), 243–4. For Swinburne's visit to Nichol, see also Georges Lafourcade, *Swinburne: A Literary Biography* (London, 1932), 221.

[63] Davidson to Swinburne, not dated, incomplete [Mar. 1878], Berg.

quite carried away. During February and March he was in a state of irrepressible excitement. Perhaps encouraged by Swinburne's response, Nichol agreed that he should send his play to the university publisher, James MacLehose. Davidson waited for the verdict with daily torment while hopefully counting on Swinburne's help in finding a London publisher for his poems. One wonders if his hopes would have been as high if he had known that in Glasgow Swinburne had fallen back into habitual drunkenness, or if he had witnessed the squalid scene in Nichol's house after a night of drinking when Nichol locked Swinburne in his bedroom and the household had to listen to him rattling the handle of the door and pleading against his imprisonment by 'a petulant provincial pedagogue', he 'a poet of European reputation'.[64]

On 21 February Swinburne went back to London. Two weeks later, on 8 or 9 March, Davidson left his teaching job at Alexander's—'to gain possession of my soul' as he was to write in a draft of the excitable letter he sent to Swinburne on 28 March.[65] Alexander Davidson was dismayed when he heard about this, but John was not to be discouraged and quoted to his father the phrase, 'Wist ye not that *I* must be about *my* father's business?' Within two-and-a-half weeks he had written a lengthy piece in stanzas of fourteen lines, 'Misannthie', which he claimed had flowed from him like 'wanton, loosened blood'. He planned to send this to Swinburne with a selection of his work, including a revised version of a boyish composition entitled 'Corydon'. His conversation with Swinburne had also inspired him to read Cyril Tourneur's *The Revenger's Tragedy* (1607) and the fourth volume of Carlyle's *Frederick the Great* (1858–65). In the surviving fragment of the draft, he begs: 'Please read my poems to please me: but do nothing with them or about them save to please yourself. "May you stead me? *will* you pleasure me?" Pity my impatience and answer as suddenly as can be.' The draft then runs impetuously to four postscripts and ends with the childlike plea: 'Will you help me? Will you be my friend?'[66]

[64] Edmund Gosse, 'Essay on Swinburne', in Lang, *Swinburne Letters*, vi (1962), 233–48.
[65] Davidson to Swinburne, not dated, incomplete [Mar. 1878], Berg.
[66] Ibid.

The letter he eventually sent 'To the nightingale of poets . . . with every good wish from a singing bird of some description, and probable quality', is actually more restrained:

The drama which you looked at in Professor Nichol's and which I left with McLehose, that Barabas has not yet made any sign concerning. Meanwhile I have left my hellish drudgery in Alexander's charity, and applied myself to the rubbing up of some short pieces and the writing of a number of sonnets which were ready to flow. These, with the concurrence of Professor Nichol I send to you with the plain and outspoken request that if you think them worthy you will endeavour to find them a publisher.

I think them deserving, otherwise I would not trouble you with them. If I am what I take myself to be, my opinion carries great weight.

If I can make no money in two months by my verses, then I shall become an actor. If the theatre door remains closed, the gate of heaven is open; and by means of a pistol or laudanum I will regain that inheritance which you and I and all poets have lost, and which our writings are a vain attempt to realize.

I suppose a volume of short pieces will find a readier market than a drama, though I believe my comedy to be a more artistic production.

These pieces range from my fourteenth year.

I send them to you because I have seen you, because you did not patronize me, because I can trust you, because I take you to be not only the greatest poet since Shakespeare, but also the greatest writer as he was likewise before you. Your writings overpower and overawe me.

You will probably wonder that there is next to no echo—at least I think so—of your style in any verses of mine that may deserve the name of poetry. The reason is on account of the Philistinism in which I have been brought up, and which is both the nitrogen and oxygen of the murky atmosphere of Greenock—within the veil of which I thank God I did not live, but by the shore—such a volume of ozone as your poetry is regarded as the sublest poison, and I possessed no golden lightning-rod to attract me to it, so that it is just a year since I began to revel in that divine ether.[67]

Davidson's expectation of Swinburne's help turned out to be a sad miscalculation. Swinburne did nothing. On 10 May, possibly after another indiscreet outburst of emotion, Davidson wrote to him with a remorse as unrestrained as his previous enthusiasm:

[67] Davidson to Swinburne, 28 Mar. 1878, *Swinburne Letters*, iv. 46–8.

I am miserable about the letter I sent you—it was the child of misery itself, a wretched weakling. I do not wish to unsay a word of admiration. I am ready, and have been any day since I began to read your works, to lay my neck beneath your feet and call you King. It is that unveracious confession of realities that torments me; though perfectly safe with you it never should have been written. If it is not burned, please burn it; for supposing you were to die—may you live as long as you desire!—and some Bozzy were to lay hands on it![68]

The sad truth is that Swinburne's health had broken down completely on his return to London, and he would not have been capable of doing anything even if he had wanted to. He was unable to eat or sleep properly, and was too weak even to write letters. The visit to Glasgow, far from providing the calm he needed, had turned out to be a month of excess that finally ruined his health.

Davidson did not try to commit suicide as he had histrionically threatened to do if his poetry did not make money within two months. Nor did he become an actor, although he may have tried. That summer he stayed in Edinburgh where he completed his second play, a self-consciously theatrical piece, *A Romantic Farce* based on James Hogg's short story, 'Mary Montgomery'. But as in *An Unhistorical Pastoral*, the setting of the original is dehistoricized and romanticized. Actual and imaginary worlds are played against each other through the device of the masque, or fancy-dress ball. The hero, Earl Edmund, appeals to the other players to protest 'like noble heretics'

> Against all dogmas false and fashionable . . .
> Yea, set apart and consecrate each day
> To traversing with all your might and main
> In order, Moses' ten 'commandements'.[69]

He is the first of many of Davidson's heroes to invent and act out his own fiction, so turning desire into reality. In Edmund's final defiance of circumstance, which is reminiscent of Helena's speech in Shakespeare's *All's Well That Ends Well*, Davidson may well have sought the answer to the recent disappointment of his own hopes:

---

[68] Davidson to Swinburne, 10 May 1878, *Swinburne Letters*, iv. 52.
[69] *Plays* (London and Chicago, 1894), 88.

> ... for brooding souls that talk of fate,
> And of their helpless, brute plasticity
> In mighty, thoughtless hands, bring down the woes
> They dread and should defy ...
>
> .   .   .   .
>
> Why, this is fate,
> This only: other slave we cannot have
> Than these same hands and feet of circumstance.[70]

It has been supposed that the meeting with Davidson meant little to Swinburne, and that Davidson and Swinburne never met again. The former is cynical; the latter, untrue. It seems to be Davidson that Swinburne was recalling when he wrote to Nichol in 1882 to thank him for sending an article on his *Tristram of Lyonesse, and Other Poems*—probably the review in the *Glasgow Herald* of 17 October 1882 which quotes Swinburne's verses 'To John Nichol' approvingly. Swinburne wrote: 'I knew (through you) the author, and I was struck (you may remember) by the power and freshness of some pages of his writing which you gave me to read when I was in Glasgow.'[71] Some years later, when Davidson was attempting to establish himself in London, he and Swinburne met at The Pines, Putney Hill, the house Swinburne shared with Watts-Dunton. On that occasion Davidson had tea with the older poet sitting in the twilight, and when he got up to go, Swinburne asked charmingly: 'Now is there anything I could do for you, you most Elizabethan creature since Shakespeare?' Davidson had not come this time to beg favours. As it was almost dark and no lights were lit, he answered with a simplicity of character which he often showed: 'Mr Swinburne, won't you let me see your face?' Swinburne obliged by coming outside with him where they shook hands and parted for the last time.[72]

III

From the age of 21 Davidson taught for ten years in a variety of schools and towns in Scotland. He moved restlessly from job to

---

[70] *Plays*, 119.
[71] Swinburne to John Nichol, 8 Dec. 1882, *Swinburne Letters*, iv. 322.
[72] Rudolf von Liebich, unpublished reminiscences, Clark.

job, never spending more than two or three years in any one place. He recalled later that he had taught 'little boys, big boys, little girls, big girls, boys and girls together', as well as 'young women for University Extension Examinations'. He was often out of work, and 'each appointment that he lost made the next more difficult to obtain'.[73]

John Hammerton, the newspaper chief, who met Davidson in London, concluded that his inability to keep any of his teaching jobs for long meant that he must have been a difficult character.[74] But some of the schools where Davidson taught were in a state of administrative upheaval following state intervention in education in the early 1870s. He was poorly qualified and had little chance of promotion, particularly as English was still considered a poor second to Latin. He himself sometimes reflected on his lack of direction and errors of judgement at this time. But he satisfied himself with the thought that poetry was his vocation, teaching merely his job; and that his life of straying was healthy and helpful. Perhaps hidden behind all this was the belief that he did not have long to live. When he was in his midtwenties and applying for life insurance, the doctor who examined him diagnosed a weak heart, and he was forced to pay a higher premium.[75] He carried this shadow with him all through his life. He came to identify its symptoms in the extraordinary elation and sequel of despair which he experienced when writing poetry. He believed half-jokingly that Shakespeare too had suffered heart disease and found evidence for it in the emotional overthrows of his tragic heroes.[76] The prospect of dying young may have reinforced his temperamental indifference to the future.

His first long-term teaching post was at Perth Academy. Before his arrival, one assistant had served both the English and the Classical departments, but on his appointment the post was divided between himself for English and a classics assistant, J. K. Duff, who was succeeded after a year by a Charles Ritchie. Ritchie was to prove Davidson's undoing. The staff at that time were in a state of internecine war following the donation of a

[73] 'Mr John Davidson', *Pall Mall Budget*.
[74] Sir John Hammerton to Grant Richards, 22 June 1945, Princeton.
[75] Davidson to George Bernard Shaw, 14 Apr. 1906, BL.
[76] 'St. Leonard's Forest', *Glasgow Herald* (19 Jan. 1907), 6.

large private bequest to the school in aid of salaries. The masters could not agree among themselves about a scheme for reorganization while Thomas Miller, the Rector for forty-four years, was still in charge. On 2 February 1881, Miller resigned, and R. McCree Chambers, the Head of the Classics Department was appointed Rector of the whole school. Ritchie had Chambers's ear. In the new scheme of re-organization drawn up before the end of the session, the masters voted themselves large increases in salary, and invited the assistants in the English and Classical Departments to apply for re-appointment under new contracts. Davidson had been out-manœuvred. Ritchie was given the new joint post of assistant in both the Classical and English departments, and another part-time assistant who helped out Mr Greig in the Writing and English departments 'was now definitely recognised as a member of staff with a salary of £45 per annum'. Davidson had not re-applied. He left Perth, asking for a certificate stating why his appointment had been terminated.[77]

School photographs from Kelvinside Academy in Glasgow where he next taught show a bearded, thin-faced young man in cap and gown, standing beside his young charges.[78] There were over 200 boys at the school. One of his pupils remembered him as a badly shaped, untidily dressed little man with a brown beard who never looked happy or comfortable.[79] According to J. J. Bell, who was a pupil at two of the schools where Davidson taught, Davidson was a figure of irreverence and amusement to the boys, his 'brisk movements and quickness of manner and speech' as he went 'tripping along the airy corridor with his black gown filling and flapping' suggesting to them a bird. Their nickname for him was 'Jenny Wren' or 'Cockabendy'.[80] Davidson was at that time 24.

Among staff and school directors political intrigue was as treacherous as it had been at Perth, although it appears not to have touched Davidson directly. The school was new. It had

---

[77] Edward Smart, *History of Perth Academy* (Perth, 1932), 163–8.

[78] Colin H. MacKay, *Kelvinside Academy: 1878–1978* (Glasgow, 1978), photographs facing pp. 17 and 32.

[79] Quoted in R. D. Macleod, *John Davidson: A Study in Personality* (Glasgow, 1957), 7.

[80] J. J. Bell, *Do You Remember?* (London, 1934), 24–6.

opened only two years earlier under the headmastership of Revd William Barrack. But Barrack had died suddenly at the beginning of 1881, and from then until the appointment of the distinguished grammarian, Edward Sonnenschein, as the second headmaster in November, the school was run by James Barrie Low, who was famous among the boys for his venom and irascibility. Sonnenschein left disillusioned before the year was out to take up an academic post in Birmingham, and Low ruled the roost again until February 1883 when he was passed over for headmaster for a second time. By then Davidson himself had resigned. On 20 April he took over as teacher at Hutcheson's Charity School in the neighbouring mill-town of Paisley at a salary of £65 a year. He had some independence there, being answerable only to the Directors of the Charity, but it was grim bread-and-butter stuff for a young man with literary ambitions, and he left after one year.

However unhappy Davidson may have looked to his pupils, he had a full private life. In Glasgow, he remained a member of Nichol's inner circle at the university. Among his close friends were John Dow, a young Burns scholar; William McCormick, who had graduated in mathematics in 1880; and John Cramb, a divinity student with literary ambitions. The fashion of young men at the time was for openness and spontaneity. Cramb sketches the mood of the university of those days in his autobiographical novel, *Cuthbert Learmont*:

The stir of intellectual life among the better minds, the inter-change of ideas, rebellious or acquiescing, temperate or reckless, the harvest of new knowledge and new impressions, the range of discussion, leaving untouched no aspect of human enquiry, philosophy, art, history, poetry, the foundations of religion and the foundations of society, examining all, criticising all, could not but exercise an extreme influence upon his own and upon other susceptible minds.[81]

Davidson continued to lead a nomadic life. In 1884 he was back in Glasgow, working by day at the office of Clark's thread firm and writing poetry and plays at night. His 'In a Music-Hall' verses date from this time, as well as his novel *The North Wall*, and his verse plays, *Bruce* and *Diabolus Amans*. The last is a drama about a man who is terrified of marriage. Angelus, a rakish,

---

[81] John Adam Cramb ('J. A. Revermort'), *Cuthbert Learmont* (London, 1910), 13.

God-denying poet, falls in love with the chaste and pious
Donna. His dilemma is how to reconcile the conventional and
unconventional sides of his nature, for 'He could not love and
be Diabolus | The more a being loves the less he sins.'[82] Fearing
the strain of marriage, he exiles himself to France. In a scene set
in an Evangelical church, he interrupts the service to quarrel
with the pastor, whose prayer 'to Milton's God' and sermon on
The Last Judgement he dismisses mockingly as the invention
used to terrify him as a child. In spite of the foreign setting, the
scene would seem to recreate Davidson's own conflicts with his
father. Following this exile, there is an encounter in a London
hospital with a nun who denies that anything is impure. Encouraged by this thought, Angelus returns unrepentant to Donna.
The play ends with them reading Virgil together on their wedding night, their differences set aside in Angelus's declarations
of love's unifying power.

Davidson himself had been in love since his Perth days with
Margaret McArthur. She was the daughter of John McArthur, a
local factory owner and a dean of guild of the town. The factory
had been opened by Margaret's grandfather in 1835 to make
wooden bobbins for jute and linen manufacturers. In the 1880s
the business was carried on by her father and uncle at the
original premises, 120 High Street, where the family lived.
There is evidence from one of Davidson's letters that Margaret
had trained as an English teacher.[83] The usual impression of her
is of a shy and reserved, even long-suffering wife who submitted
quietly to her capricious and strongly opinionated husband.
She said of their relationship, 'We had no two ideas in common—that's how we got on so well—I simply let him do what he
liked.'[84] But she herself could be strong-willed and moody in
private and found it difficult to stay for long with friends or
relatives in later life, including her own sons, without becoming
involved in conflict and misunderstanding.

Davidson's approach to women was usually to strike up a
whimsical and light-hearted conversation. He makes fun of
these tactics in the novel *Laura Ruthven's Widowhood* in the

[82] *Diabolus Amans* (Glasgow, 1885), Scence iv.
[83] Davidson to Menzies McArthur ('Meem'), 'Monday' [Jan. or Feb. 1886],
Princeton.
[84] Margaret McArthur to Richards, 'Saturday 10 p.m.' [3 Apr. 1909], Princeton.

character of the clever raconteur, Aveland, of whom we are told that,

Of the two recognised methods of entertaining the female mind, Aveland preferred paradox to fun, and he was in the habit of launching out into such a discussion . . . without really knowing what he was going to say, in the full confidence that some *bizarre* presentation of the matter would suggest itself.[85]

A similar exercise in self-parody is to be found in the poem 'The Male Coquette' which he wrote when he was courting Maggie:

> My tongue drops honey like a hive;
> My hands are soft and small.
> What! I am only five feet five!
> Well, some are not so tall.[86]

In the early 1880s Davidson and Maggie went on holiday together to the island of Arran, reaching it by steamer from Greenock. They stayed in the north-west corner of the island at 'Pirnmill House', possibly one of a number of houses that were becoming popular with summer visitors. 'Isn't it the case,' he wrote later, 'that the marriage ceremony is a minor detail when a man and a woman elect to spend their lives together, and that the promise made to each other between the kisses is the true promise of which the form of marriage is a mere notification.'[87]

On Arran the weather was wet, and there were no return conveyances to take them to see other parts of the island. But they fished and walked and enjoyed the scenery within a three-mile radius, particularly the cliffs beneath the tiny village of Imachar which they visited at night on 28 July. He described them in a letter to Margaret's sister, Menzies:

These cliffs are the finest things about this quarter of Arran. One of them in particular over the brow of which a waterfall topples could only be described, and that very imperfectly by a picture, either poetical or in colours. Imagine everything fairy like and romantic in all the counterfeits of waterfalls that you have seen or read, and you will have some idea of this one.[88]

---

[85] *Laura Ruthven's Widowhood* (London, 1892), 163.
[86] 'The Male Coquette', ll. 9–12.
[87] Davidson to Meem, 'Monday' [1890], Princeton.
[88] Davidson to Menzies McArthur, 29 July [year unknown], Princeton.

Financially Davidson was in no position to marry. His poem
'In A Music-Hall' refers to his conviviality in 1884:

> I did as my desk-fellows did;
> With a pipe and a tankard of beer,
> In a music-hall, rancid and hot;
> I lost my soul night after night.[89]

But his time at the Glasgow office of Clark's thread firm seems
to have been far from happy. He was especially downcast when
William McCormick failed to get a number of his poems published, including his 'In A Music-Hall' verses. McCormick, who
was lecturing at Glasgow University, had just gone into partnership with Frederick W. Wilson to form the Glasgow publishing
firm of Wilson and McCormick. But after accepting Davidson's
verses, the publishers decided to set them aside because of 'a
certain breadth' in some of the passages.[90] Several of Davidson's
poems from this period—poems such as 'The Rev. Habakkuk
McGruther of Cape Wrath, in 1879' and 'The Rev. E. Kirk,
B. D.'—are satires of Scots religion in the manner of Robert
Burns, but his publishers are much more likely to have been
worried by the Swinburnean intoxication of 'For Lovers', where
the lovers spring naked hand in hand into the sea, or by the
daring monologue of Lily Dale, a former girl of the streets who
saucily advertises her music hall turn:

> So I give it them hot, with a glance
> Like the crack of a whip—oh, it stings!
> And a still, fiery smile, and a dance
> That indicates naughtiest things.[91]

On his twenty-eighth birthday the following year he was
cheered by a card from Maggie's sister, Menzies, but his de-
spondency is obvious in the letter of thanks he wrote from his
digs at 50 Victoria Street in Queen's Park in Glasgow. 'The
accumulation of clouds which have overtaken me make your
remembrance a little bit of sunshine brighter and more cheer-
ing than you can possibly imagine', he wrote.[92] But the clouds
were quickly to pass. That year he obtained a teaching post at

---

[89] 'Prologue' to 'In a Music-Hall', ll. 14–17.
[90] Davidson to John Lane, not dated [1891], Princeton.
[91] 'Lily Dale', from 'In a Music-Hall', ll. 21–4.
[92] Davidson to Meem, 11 Apr. 1885, Princeton.

Morrison's Academy in Crieff, a tourist town in the Earn valley, about 17 miles from Perth where Maggie lived. He also published his first book, a short farcical novel, *The North Wall.* The central character, Maxwell Lee, is, like himself 'an unsuccessful literary man . . . who had composed dramas and philosophical romances which no publisher, nor editor, could be got to read.' In a comic subversion of the kind of escapist sentimental novel he himself is writing, Davidson has Lee abandon novel-writing for novel-creation. Lee announces:

'We shall cause a novel to take place in the world. We shall construct a plot; we shall select a hero; we shall enter into his life, and produce the series of events before determined on. Consider for a minute. We can do nothing else now. The last development, the naturalist school, is mere copying, a bare photographing of life—at least that is what it professes to be. This is not art. There can never again be an art of novel-writing. But there can be, there shall be, you will aid me to begin, the art of novel-creation.'[93]

Davidson's editorial self-mockery and obtruded oddities of style owe something to Carlyle. They have a serious side, questioning in a knowingly modern way the connection between literary convention and reality, language and truth. At times, the comic adventure and mad humour scarcely disguise the real frustrations and insecurities that lie behind its composition and theme. He had evidently decided that he had to write a novel in order to be published. The book was issued by Wilson and McCormick at a shilling and dedicated to Margaret McArthur. By then the two had decided to get married before the end of the year.

He was in high spirits in the months before the wedding. Maggie and her mother visited him at Crieff for three weeks. But after they had gone he invited some of his Glasgow friends for a visit, among them the Burns expert John Dow, who was an assistant to Nichol at Glasgow University. Though he was himself a lover of Burns, Davidson considered the use of low Burnsian Scots dialect in poetry affected and hackneyed. In his ironic monologue 'Ayrshire Jock', written while part of Nichol's circle, his semi-intoxicated and humourously self-revealing speaker mocks the 'mongrel Scots' of Burns's imitators,

[93] *A Practical Novelist,* 166.

choosing instead to write his poems 'in English, catching tones
| From Shelley and his great successors.'[94] Cramb, who was to be
his best man at the wedding, was also invited to Crieff. Cramb
had just obtained a first-class honours at Glasgow University and
was about to continue his academic career with a visit to Bonn.
'I took the liberty of inviting Cramb through here at his own
expense, intending to live off him when he came; he turns out
to be as impecunious as myself', Davidson wrote to McCormick
to whom they planned to extend the same 'munificent offer'.
Among the main events of the last three months he listed the
distractions of

Jennie Watt and her legs. This is a young lady of 17 in my class who
excels in many things, but chiefly in wearing short dresses, and in
flinging one leg over the other when she sits down in such a way as to
reveal the whole of a beautifully swelling calf, and half a foot of
exquisite thigh.[95]

That autumn he and Maggie stayed at the small village of
Methven on their way from Perth to Crieff. Maggie slept at the
house of Mr and Mrs Caw, who seem to have been friends or
relatives of the family, while Davidson lodged with Mr McLaren,
the village butcher. He had two bedrooms although a kitten
slept in one of them at night. He wrote a charming letter from
here in two parts, marked 'Public' and 'Private', to Maggie's
young sister. In the first, to be read by the rest of the family, he
wrote that 'Mrs. Caw and Maggie were to have pulled the blackberries today, but the rain prevented them. They will have to
wait till Tuesday.' The 'Private' letter tells a different story,
aiming to be no less delicious to his young female correspondent in its very innocence:

Here we are in defiance of *les convenances*—if that's right. We had a
fine forenoon, and went to Cloag wood for blackberries, which we ate
to satiety. Then we sat and read books, leaning against the hay-rick. We
got to the fringe of the thunderstorm, but escaped the plumb.[96]

The wedding took place on Friday, 23 October at Maggie's
house. Davidson had borrowed £60 from McCormick's uncle,

[94] 'Ayrshire Jock', ll. 85–6.
[95] Davidson to William McCormick, not dated [1885], Glasgow.
[96] Davidson to Menzies McArthur ('Mimi'), 'Thursday' [1885], Princeton.

William Smart, to get married.[97] Robert Lyons, the minister of the local United Presbyterian church, performed the ceremony. Maggie's sister, Menzies, was her bridesmaid. There was no honeymoon. Davidson had been given the day off for the wedding but had to be back at the school on Monday morning.[98] He moved out of his lodgings at 48 East High Street to their new house at Grove Mount.

That first winter together was to be the happiest they were to have for many years, even though they both caught colds. They were not alone. The local newspaper reported that the 'medicals' were 'having a high old time of it' that winter, one of the severest for many years.[99] Davidson spent one Sunday confined to the house, breaking up stale bread with a hatchet and feeding the birds, a memory preserved in his poem 'Winter in Strathearn'.[100]

Things did not go smoothly for long. Before the winter was over they had fallen badly into debt. They began looking for another house, although they had hopes of leaving Crieff altogether. There was a vacancy for an English teacher at Stirling High School at a handsome salary of £250, and Maggie considered having 'a shot at it'. Davidson asked Meem, as he now affectionately called his sister-in-law: 'Does the Good Dean know anybody in Stirling the hair of whose ear he might just twitch apropos of the Mastership?'[101] But the hope for the English post fell through—it would have been beyond Maggie to try for a post with such a high salary, and people in those days would have been very unwilling to appoint a married woman. They found new lodgings at Victoria Buildings in Crieff and arranged for the grocer's van to move their boxes on Saturday, 18 April, the day after the end of term and the annual school sports. Davidson had been gloomy on the 11th, his birthday.

[97] The details of his loans from William Smart are in a letter from Davidson to McCormick, 22 Mar. 1901, Glasgow. Smart was Lecturer in Political Economy at Dundee and Glasgow and organized the first University Extension Scheme in 1884. His staff included John G. Dow, William McCormick, and R. M. Wenley. He was married to William McCormick's maternal aunt, Katherine Stewart, eldest daughter of Revd William Symington.

[98] Davidson to Lane, 28 May 1895, Lane.

[99] *Crieff Journal* (12 Mar. 1886).

[100] Davidson to Meem, 'Monday' [Jan. or Feb. 1886], Princeton.

[101] Ibid.

Even the announcement of the publication of his Scottish chronicle play *Bruce* in the *Academy* the day before had not cheered him up. '29 is a terrible age to arrive at', he wrote to Meem:

Some benevolent genius would bestow a genuine boon on mankind by the invention of a pill or a powder to obliterate the memory of one's age, to prevent the thought that one is growing old, to blot birthdays from the calendar. It might be done by act of parliament, all dates of birth becoming state secrets.[102]

On the afternoon after the flitting they left for a visit to Greenock, followed by a week at Davidson's old digs in Glasgow. Maggie had already sent for dress patterns to Copeland Lane, a department store in Sauchiehall Street, Glasgow, that specialized in ladies' clothes, but she did not like them and decided to select a dress on the spot. Though she did not know it at the time, she was already pregnant.

The next two years spent at Crieff were to be creative ones for Davidson. There he wrote his spasmodic verse drama, *Smith: A Tragedy*, dedicated to Nichol, and in a different vein, his two boy's stories, 'Perfervid' and 'The Pilgrimage of Strongsoul', as well as his pantomime, *Scaramouch in Naxos*. *Scaramouch* is a light-hearted burlesque which dovetails the classical legend of Ariadne's abandonment of mortal love on the island of Naxos with the characters and antics of the harlequinade. Although the play is evidently indebted to the fairy dramas, pantomimes, and 'Extravaganzas' popular in Victorian times, its heightened poetry and subtle interplay of disparate literary elements produce an original effect, anticipating by over twenty years the formal ironies of Hugo von Hofmannsthal's experimental libretto 'Ariadne auf Naxos' (1912), and the avant-garde montage techniques of literary Modernism.

The years at Crieff also brought him into his first public battle against authority. The Rector of Morrison's Academy, George Strathairn, though a kindly man, was a strict disciplinarian. In the year Davidson arrived, Morrison's Academy was described in the Inspectors' Report as a 'model school . . . thoroughness parades the whole school, the constant aim of the Rector and the masters being that everything that is done should be done

---

[102] Davidson to Meem, not dated [11 Apr. 1886], Princeton.

well'.[103] There was inevitably a price to be paid for such recti-
tude. The school itself had been established along the lines of
an English public school. The fee for boarders was 15 guineas a
quarter with extra for laundry, music, and extra-curricular activities. Under Strathairn, there was a vigorous attempt to attract
pupils from a wide area; advertisements for the school emphasized its academic range as well as its attractive location and
provision for outdoor activities, including cricket. Himself a
distinguished Hebrew scholar—his previous post had been
as assistant to Professor Sellar at Edinburgh University—
Strathairn clearly sought high academic standards and solid
respectability for his school. This together with the fear of any
scandal that normally pervades a small country town, seems to
have fostered the atmosphere of tense discipline that led
Strathairn into constant quarrels and frequent all-out battles
with his staff.

One of the biggest scandals to touch the school during
Davidson's time there arose in 1886 over the question of corporal punishment. The tawse or strap was used fairly frequently
in those days, and generally children preferred it to detention
or to a pointless form of punishment at Morrison's known as
'cubes', where the boy was given the impossible task of trying to
cube six to twenty-four figure numbers. But the main cause for
concern among the staff was the zeal with which the tutor to the
boarders, 'Paddy' White, exercised his right to punish the boys.
Paddy White was not a member of the teaching staff, but was
employed to look after the boarders during out of school hours.
The fifteen to twenty boarders slept in two dormitories—'Big
Doss' and 'Wee Doss'. Between six and nine in the evening in
winter and spring terms, and seven to nine in summer, Paddy
White used the Rector's study in the east wing of the building
to supervise school prep. His reputation among the boys was
formidable: he was believed to be able to hit the second joint
of the thumb at least once out of every two whacks. Davidson
may well have had Paddy White in mind when he created
the character of Mr Haggle, the sadistic schoolmaster in 'The
Schoolboy's Tragedy'. Reportedly a genial but rather choleric

---

[103] For this and other details of Morrison's Academy in the following pages, I am
indebted to John Williamson, *A History of Morrison's Academy, Crieff* (Auchterarder,
1978).

character, Paddy had an army upbringing and was in charge of games, where his gymnastics were described by one of his young victims as the 'monkey on a stick type'. But his enthusiasm for corporal punishment went beyond this when he began enjoying what he called 'making you a sergeant-major', that is applying four strokes of the cane on the bare backsides of the boys. The teachers and others in the community got to hear of this, and a letter soon appeared in a daily paper stating the rumour in the villages of Strathearn that,

The boys attending a public school are asserting that the teacher has introduced the ancient brutal practice of compelling unfortunates, who fall under his displeasure, to untruss their unmentionables and submit to dishonourable birching.[104]

As a result of this and other quarrels that were brewing between Strathairn and his staff, the provost of Crieff called a meeting in December at the request of the rate-payers to discuss the management of the school, where some expressed the opinion that 'there is at the present a tendency to a rather exaggerated exercise of the right of free speech in the direction of criticising the "powers that be"'. But criticism did not end there. The growing tension between Strathairn and his staff reached breaking point when he tried to force the teachers to rent rooms in houses designated by him, and insisted that they attend the church he prescribed. The subsequent rebellion resulted in the mass sacking of a number of French and German teachers for 'insubordination and disobedience', with one teacher complaining bitterly that she had been dismissed 'on the grounds of my being a Romanist'.

Davidson and Strathairn did not get on. When Davidson announced his intention to get married during his first months in the school, Strathairn had advised him against it, considering it unwise to marry on an assistant English master's salary:[105] it could not have helped relations between them when Strathairn's advice proved justified. Their relations were further strained when Davidson did not attend church and scandalously refused to have his child baptized. Nor did his comical

[104] Quoted in Williamson, *Morrison's Academy*, 16.
[105] This story is told by Currie who interviewed the Strathairn family, 'Biographical and Critical Study', 45.

performances at local concerts endear him to the Rector. The littérateur, James Cuthbert Hadden, who was at that time the organist at the local church, remembered Davidson as a talented elocutionist.[106] Hadden organized the musical events in the town, including the annual Burns' Night Concert. In 1886 he had Vilbert, a professional elocutionist for the recitations, but the following year, Davidson took over with a reading of 'Tam O'Shanter' which the local reporter found 'unusually clever'.[107]

Davidson was soon the centre of a remarkably cultured, and even cosmopolitan circle in that out of the way provincial town. This included E. T. Peberdy, the assistant classics master, and John Barlas, who was a close friend of Oscar Wilde. Barlas had relatives in Crieff. A magnetic, restless character, devoted to ideal beauty and revolutionary socialism, he claimed the distinction of having been batoned and floored during the Trafalgar Square Riots of 1886 and of falling with a bleeding head at the feet of Eleanor Marx.[108] While an undergraduate at New College, Oxford, where he met Wilde, he had addressed a sequence of sonnets to the great grand-niece of Admiral Nelson and had run away with her when he was 21 after knocking down her father and breaking through several doors of her house. At Crieff he and Davidson were both outspoken defenders of freedom and shared an interest in Elizabethan literature and drama. Barlas had already published a verse tragedy and three volumes of poetry. At Crieff he completed another, *Bird Notes*, which he dedicated, 'To my friends E. T. Peberdy and J. Davidson, in memory of Happy Days in the Highlands, gladdened by the two best things in life, Music and Literature'.

The last to join the circle was Rudolf von Liebich who arrived from London in September 1886 to teach music and languages. He was three years younger than Davidson. He describes the impression Davidson made at that time:

---

[106] James Cuthbert Hadden, 'Readers and Writers', *Wolverhampton Chronicle* (10 Apr. 1907), 2. Richards mistakenly attributed the version of this that appeared in the *European Mail* in 1945 to Sir John Hammerton, who denied authorship. J. Benjamin Townsend in *John Davidson: Poet of Armageddon* (New Haven, Conn., 1961) mistakes 'a Pethshire Academy' referred to in the article for Perth Academy.

[107] *Crieff Journal* (25 Jan. 1887).

[108] Some of the details of Barlas's life are in John Lowe, *John Barlas: Sweet Singer and Socialist* (Cupar, 1915).

I found Davidson a well knit man of medium height who wore a short clipped black beard. His beautifully chiselled nose and a pair of dark (nearly black) and most eloquently sparkling eyes, besides a nobly vaulted brow, made him look conspicuously different from the rest of the faculty and from the rather sleepy inhabitants of the tiny town. Enthusiastic he was at that time and the most tenderhearted man I had met. This (his gentleness) he disguised occasionally by a rough manner and uncouth, not to say rude speech. I had arrived in Crieff in September and in November there were great snow-storms, so severe that standing still on the street was considered dangerous. The college building was situated on a bleak hill, surrounded by extensive grounds over which the wind swept ferociously. Arriving at the main entrance one morning a few moments before him, I saw him struggling against the wind at a distance of perhaps a hundred yards. So I stood and held the heavy school door open for him so that he should not be delayed even a moment in coming in out of the cruel cold. I was already very fond of him and felt a chilling disappointment when his only remark to me was: 'Hello Liebich, that's more than I would do for you.' A few days later, I had a severe attack of tonsilitis. A high temperature kept me in bed for three days and on each one of those days Davidson called on me on his way to and from the school, arranged my pillow, straightened out the bed, mixed cooling drinks, sprayed my throat— generally nursed me as tenderly as any woman could. He told me later that any promising new comer was tested or tried out by rough joking or a feigned lack of appreciation of his efforts at friendliness. If he lost his temper or showed any signs of resentment he was voted an inferior person . . . I had kept my temper cool and so, was admitted to their inner circle. This circle included a teacher E. Peberdy . . . and the unique Prince Charming (I cannot call him less) John Barlas. All the exterior graces in looks and in manner that Davidson and I lacked, Barlas had.[109]

Maggie acted as a sort of honorary member of the circle, providing them with tea and scones. For the annual concert and exhibition in July 1887, which was a flannels and blazer day at the school, Peberdy set to music Davidson's holiday song, 'Piper, Play!' to be sung by the pupils, who, according to a local journalist sent to cover the event, unfortunately did little justice to 'the spirit of the words and the swing of the air'.[110] Davidson and Liebich also collaborated on an entertainment they called 'Dramatic and Musical Recitals' which they took on a short self-

---

[109] Von Liebich, unpublished reminiscences, Clark.
[110] *Crieff Journal* (29 July 1887).

managed tour of Perth, Stirling, Glasgow, and a few other smaller places in 1888. Davidson read from Shakespeare, Keats, Tennyson, Edgar Allan Poe, and Burns; Liebich played piano solos from Bach, Beethoven, Chopin, Liszt, and Wagner, occasionally accompanying Davidson's recitations in what they believed was a revival of the forgotten art of Mendelssohn's 'Melodrame'. Liebich thought Davidson better than the professional elocutionist, Samuel Brandram whom he had heard in concert. He particularly liked Davidson's performance of Poe's 'The Bells' which went from one line F down to great D flat on the piano. They closed their concerts with a piano-accompanied recitation of Keats's 'La Belle Dame Sans Merci' or Tennyson's 'Rizpah', a monologue of a mother whom collects her son's bones at night from the foot of the gallows and buries them secretly in the churchyard. This usually brought out the handkerchiefs among the audience. But Davidson also had his audiences laughing uproariously at a comedy sketch about a refractory mule given to running away, where he increased the comic effect by his use of broad Scots.[111] He had already tried out these comic effects on the audiences at the school concerts. Unfortunately, Strathairn disapproved of these perfomances which he considered undignified in an English master.

During 1887 Davidson became locked in a battle with Strathairn that would finally end his days as a schoolmaster. Later in London he told Yeats and the members of the Rhymers' Club that he had left school teaching because his demand for a rise in salary had been turned down. In Hadden's version of events, Strathairn made life so uncomfortable for Davidson on account of his 'undignified' recitals that he resigned his post. But the real reason for Davidson's departure was a bitter showdown with Strathairn on the subject of examinations. Relations between Strathairn and his staff had been poisoned that year by the mass sacking of the French and German teachers, when the governors had supported the Rector against his staff. They put down much of the friction and resentment in the school to the variation in salary scale between different departments and between men and women. But when they suggested

111 Von Liebich, unpublished reminiscences, Clark.

a reduction of salaries for some teachers, Strathairn used the opportunity to protest pointedly that: 'The present tone of the school is not as satisfactory as I would like it. I attribute it to the introduction of a lower class of English Masters since the reducing of salaries.'[112] This was clearly directed against Davidson. Strathairn had taught at Edinburgh University as Professor Sellar's assistant during Davidson's time there, and had first-hand knowledge of Davidson's academic weakness. His approach to teaching came from his classical training; he demanded exactitude and disciplined learning. Davidson, a failure at classics, took a more creative, child-centred approach to the study of literature. Liebich, for instance, remembered that Davidson was by far and away the most popular of all the teachers because of his enthusiasm and ardour. This is supported by J. J. Bell who was a pupil at both Kelvinside and Morrison's academies. Bell goes beyond the schoolboys' caricature of Davidson to remember him 'rolling out passages from "The Merchant of Venice" . . . wrapt in his own enjoyment, yet eager to transmit the charm to his unworthy audience'.[113]

Davidson knew he lacked formal education compared to most of his colleagues and friends, and appears to have suffered a recurrence of the inner crisis of his Edinburgh days, possibly as a direct result of Strathairn's remark. His feelings are reflected in *Smith* which he wrote at this time, where the friends of the hero mock his talk of 'philosophy, religion, books' because 'Uncultured, too; he lacks the college stamp.'[114] Defensively Smith makes this the very basis of his superiority: 'Think my thought, be impatient as I am | Obey your nature, not authority.'[115] In a later interview in the *Candid Friend*, Davidson points to Smith's 'revolutionary idea' as the undersong or keynote of all his later work. He had 'erected a finger-post' should anyone care to follow it.[116] Smith is certainly the assertive, insecure part of John Davidson.

At Crieff, his idea took actual form when Strathairn insisted on stringent examination of certain classes from time to time. Davidson felt this was tyrannous. He set about organizing the

---

[112] Williamson, *Morrison's Academy*, 18.

[113] J. J. Bell, 'The Poet as Pedagogue. Further Recollections of John Davidson', *John O'London's Weekly*, 16 (16 Oct. 1926), 14–15.

[114] *Plays*, 220.   [115] Ibid. 235.   [116] 'About Myself', *Candid Friend*.

other teachers so they could present a united front to the Trustees. Only one refused. The rest signed a statement threatening to resign in a body unless the Rector removed the unjust regulations. Davidson went personally to Edinburgh on Wednesday, 21 December to read the statement to the Trustees. Unknown to him, the Trustees had a letter before them from Strathairn which read:

His [Mr Peberdy's] character is not what it ought to be, and it will not do to have on our staff one who regularly frequents Public Houses and is spoken of as having been turned out of one of the Hotels for riotous conduct. Mr Davidson's name, I am sorry to say, has also been spoken of by several in connection with this same circumstance.[117]

In Crieff the teachers waited for the outcome of the meeting, confident in the justice of their demands.

It would be too easy perhaps to view Strathairn, as many of his staff did, as an arrogant, narrow-minded man who misused his authority to impose his will on other people, just as it would be equally simplistic to see Davidson, as he was seen by his enemies, as an assertive opinionated rebel against authority. Davidson could be rough, not to say rude on occasions, but his friends remembered him more for his kindness and good nature. Even Strathairn seems to have retained a respect for him. The quarrel between them to some extent was a quarrel between Classics and English at a time of great educational changes to the curriculum. More generally, the problem for Davidson, and like men of his generation, was that the society they had grown up in had become intellectually more open and individualistic, but organizationally more bureaucratic. Certificates and qualifications were needed everywhere. A man's merit and worth was judged on whether or not he possessed them, irrespective of his talents and abilities. This was particularly true of schools since the introduction of compulsory education. Teachers then, as now, often found their practices at odds with the theories and codes of the state and the school boards. Like D. H. Lawrence after him, Davidson grew to dislike teaching as 'mental bootblacking'. 'I for food | Have made myself a grindstone, edging

[117] Extract from a Minute of Meeting of the Trustees of the late Thomas Morrison held at 43 Castle Street, Edinburgh, on Wednesday, 21 Dec. 1887. Printed with permission of the present Governors.

souls | Meant most for flying,'[118] Hallowes, the poet-teacher, announces resentfully in *Smith*. Hallowes resigns from his post at Holofernes's School with words that seem to express Davidson's own bitterness and dissatisfaction with the system:

> 'Intolerance in religion never dreamt
> Such fell machinery of Acts and Codes
> As now we use for nipping thought in bud,
> And turning children out like nine-pins, each
> As doleful and as wooden.'[119]

These words, in a play circulating in the school by one of his teachers, could not have pleased the Rector.

Davidson received his answer from the Trustees the day after the meeting in Edinburgh. His heart must have beat heavily as he read:

Edinburgh
December 1887

Dear Sir,

Your statement and letters regarding your position in Morrison's Academy were fully considered by the Trustees and I am directed by them to inform you that the system of Examinations by the Rector from time to time of the various classes taught in the Academy and for the efficiency of which he is answerable to the Trustees has the fullest approval of the Trustees. They consider your appeal irrelevant and savouring of what would tend to insubordination if entertained for a moment. I have therefore to inform you that you will meet the Rector's views in this matter so long as you are a Teacher in the School. I may add that the Trustees do not consider that their decision in any respect lowers your position as a Teacher of English in their Academy. I am further instructed to give you notice that the Trustees will dispense with your services at the end of the ensuing quarter. Have the goodness to acknowledge that you have received this intimation.[120]

It was all over. Liebich resigned. They would meet up again later in London. But for the present, Davidson's destination was Greenock. His father had left Greenock two years earlier because of his mother's delicate health, and had taken over the Evangelical church at Leith in Edinburgh. But a flat at the family's old close in Brisbane Street was available for rent.

---

[118] *Plays*, 224.   [119] Ibid.

[120] Minute of Meeting of the Trustees, Morrison's Academy, 21 Dec. 1887.

Davidson borrowed another £25 from McCormick's uncle to leave Crieff. He is believed to have done some teaching at Greenock Academy in the year that followed, but his days as a schoolmaster were effectively over. His aim now was to make literature a career. In the summer or early autumn of 1888, the removal van was called to Crieff, and he, Maggie with their son, Alexander, who was not yet 2, started for their new home on the Clyde coast. Maggie was then pregnant with their second child.

2

London 1889–1893

I

Davidson arrived in London, alone, during the summer of 1889.[1] He was 32 and impatient for literary fame. His manuscripts and plays were in his luggage. Nothing could have prepared him for the great press and muffled roar of King's Cross. He seems to recreate that moment in his short story 'Alison Hepburn's Exploit' when the heroine, a literary aspirant, arrives in London for the first time and looks out with sinking heart on 'one of the most dismal parts of London . . . the junction of Euston Road, Gray's Inn Road, Pentonville Road, and York Road'.[2] To his middle-class Scottish ears, the Cockney accents sounded like a foreign language. He was never to like 'the horrible twang that makes day and night hideous in and about London', as he wrote later,[3] and preferred the voices of Kent and the south coast. Riding in cabs was to become one of the joys and luxuries of his life in London, but that day he took no pleasure in it. Five years later, in writing to his friend and publisher, John Lane, he was to recall that moment when, with little money and knowing no one, he arrived 'forlorn at Burton Crescent'.[4] Burton Crescent, now Burton Gardens, was only a few minutes drive from the station. He lodged with Mrs Hutchison at number 15. His single room cost 6 shillings a week.

Davidson was on the outer fringes of Bloomsbury and within comfortable walking distance of Fleet Street. His first object was to promote the volume of *Plays* he had published privately at the offices of the *Greenock Telegraph* in a run of 300 copies in the

---

[1] See my 'John Davidson's Arrival in London', *Notes and Queries*, new series, 38: 3 (Sept. 1991), 331–3.

[2] 'Alison Hepburn's Exploit', in *Miss Armstrong's and Other Circumstances* (London, 1896), 106.

[3] 'Romney Marsh', *Glasgow Herald* (3 Mar. 1894), 4.

[4] Davidson to John Lane, 8 Feb. 1895, NLS.

early part of that year. He had borrowed another £100 that year from Smart to go to London with and may have used some of the money to pay for the printing. The book consisted of his early romantic plays, *An Unhistorical Pastoral* and *A Romantic Farce*, and the pantomime, *Scaramouch in Naxos*, written while he was serving out his notice of dismissal at Crieff. The play was turned down by several publishers in 1888. Despairing of ever seeing his comedies in print, Davidson decided to publish them on his own. His authorship is indicated only in the publisher's imprint which read, 'John Davidson, 12 Brisbane Street', his address at the time. He sent copies to the libraries, as well as to leading journals and individuals. But he delayed sending a copy to Maggie's family in Perth, hoping 'to have if possible a decent notice to accompany it on its entrance into such a difficult place as 120.'[5] Disappointingly, the press took no immediate notice of his *Plays*, and on 7 May he sent a copy to Meem 'for yourself from me', putting stress on the fact that 'nobody is to pay for it', and adding darkly that she would probably guess why no inscription appeared on the book.[6] It seems that the loss of his steady job as a schoolmaster had caused a falling out between himself and Maggie's family.

Of the copies he sent out, inscribed 'With the publisher's compliments', one had gone to George Meredith, at that time one of England's grand men of letters. It was three months before a busy Meredith wrote to the unknown author acknowledging the gift. By then Davidson had left for London. When he read Meredith's kindly encouraging words, he was overcome with emotion. 'I wish I had written you, after reading your volume of Plays', Meredith wrote, and continued:

I did better perhaps in speaking of them to friends, but that does not warm the author; unless the friends grow laudatory, and a public is found for him. In truth I have to shun the duty of writing letters; I can hardly get on with my work. Your volume of plays appeared to me full of promise. Mark the word. But full: remarkable for literary skill, ease in the run of lines, and a fantastical humour good in youth. I trust that you may succeed.[7]

[5] Davidson to Meem, 7 May 1889, Princeton.   [6] Ibid.
[7] George Meredith to Davidson, 21 Aug. 1889, in C. L. Cline (ed.), *Letters of George Meredith* (Oxford, 1970), 977–8.

Here was something to raise his standing among his Perth in-laws.

Meredith had in truth done better in speaking of the book to friends. A chance remark of his obtained Davidson some reviewing for the *Academy*.[8] His first review—of a selection of Hazlitt's writings—appeared on 7 September, just a fortnight after he received Meredith's letter. He met the editor of the *Academy*, J. S. Cotton, who invited him to ask for the books he would like to review—although when Cotton refused to send them, Davidson suspected this was his way of finding out who an author's friends were.[9] But he was sent further books for review, including Swinburne's *A Study of Ben Jonson* which he praised highly.[10] It was the breakthrough he had been looking for. He left a copy of his *Plays* with George Cotterell, the drama critic for the *Academy*, and began to make some useful contacts among London's literary men. Frank Harris, who was then working for Frederic Chapman on the *Fortnightly Review*, has described the impression he made in London in 1889:

He was a little man below middle height, but strongly built with square shoulders and remarkable fine face and head: the features were almost classically regular, the eyes dark brown and large, the forehead high, the hair and moustache black. His manners were perfectly frank and natural: he met every one in the same unaffected friendly way: I never saw a trace of snobbishness or incivility. Possibly a great man, I said to myself, certainly a man of genius, for simplicity of manner alone in England is almost a proof of extraordinary endowment. I soon noticed one little peculiarity in Davidson, his enunciation was exceptionally distinct: every word had its value for him, each syllable its weight.[11]

But in spite of making some inroads into Fleet Street, Davidson found it far from easy to establish himself as a literary man. Six years later he tried to dissuade a young hopeful from trying London:

There are thousands of men in London, well-recommended, hundreds of them with English university degrees, scores of them authors of repute, battering at the doors of every newspaper, review and maga-

---

8 'Mr John Davidson', *Pall Mall Budget* (27 Dec. 1894).
9 Davidson to William McCormick, not dated [1890], Glasgow.
10 'A study of Ben Jonson', *Academy*, 36 (23 Nov. 1889), 331–2.
11 Frank Harris, *Contemporary Portraits*, first series (London, 1915), 120.

zine, and shoving each other away from the keyhole to shout through it, 'Needless to say, I don't care what I do, if I make money honestly or dishonestly.' There is no use in the world joining in the crowd, especially if you insist on being honest. I was in the crowd, I am tough, and my wounds and bruises are not whole yet.[12]

From the middle to the end of the nineteenth century, literacy had increased in England by over 30 per cent. The newspaper and magazine industry had expanded accordingly. By 1890 there were almost eighteen hundred periodicals in circulation, and this figure was to go on rising for several years.[13] Some benefited from the growth. The editors of the big illustrated weeklies could command high salaries: W. T. Stead earned £1,200 a year editing the *Pall Mall Gazette*, and C. K. Shorter around £650 as editor of the *Illustrated London News* in 1890. So could a writer with a name: Kipling was paid a huge sum—reportedly £100—for each of his ballads in the *Pall Mall Magazine*. But there were also thousands of free-lance scribblers and hacks at the lower end of Grub Street, labouring for an average rate of 10 shillings per thousand words, while those on 'staff', though regularly paid, were little better off. It was a situation that had led to the formation of the Institute for Journalists in March 1889, only months before Davidson's arrival in London.[14]

Mass literacy also created another problem for the aspiring literary man: there was now a clear separation of literature from journalism. The press had become big business. Journalism was a specialized trade that was becoming less available as a means of livelihood to the general man of letters. The 'New Journalism' of the *Star*, the *Sketch*, the *Illustrated London News*, and the *Pall Mall Gazette*, emphasized the lighter side of life, substituting sensational story for straightforward report and displacing politics from its former pre-eminence. A dislike of politics had become the mark of the younger generation. Edwin Arnold's instructions at the *Telegraph* seemed to define the commercial

---

[12] Davidson to McCormick, 11 Apr. 1895, Glasgow.

[13] James Reginald Tye, 'Literary Periodicals in the Eighteen Nineties: A Survey of Monthly and Quarterly Magazines and Reviews', D.Phil. thesis (University of Oxford, 1970).

[14] Cyril Bainbridge (ed.), *One Hundred Years of Journalism* (London, 1984), 37.

spirit that had invaded literature as it had other areas of
national life: 'Aim at the Margate bathing-woman, my boy,
don't waste time trying to be literary.'[15]

To young men with high ideals, who shared Carlyle's view of
journalism as 'ditch-water' these developments were repulsive.
George Gissing, whom Davidson later befriended, had given up
journalism in 1880, at the age of 22, because he found it
degrading. Davidson, at the age of 32, was forced to turn to it.
The articles and reviews that came from his pen during his first
year as a journalist constantly question the value of his new
trade. He compared the reviewer to 'the biologist of Gotham,
who put a body through a sausage-machine, dimly hoping to
detect the vital principle';[16] and in conversation was heard to
complain about the intolerable and humiliating necessity of
having to review new books of verse as they came out.[17] The
'New Journalism' he dismissed contemptuously as 'the defiant
reply of the "thirty villains, mostly fools" to Carlyle's doctrine of
silence'.[18] He was no literary reactionary. Commenting on contemporary poetry during his first months in London, he accepted that it would become more and more democratic, and
from this time he often found the subject-matter of his own
poetry in the popular press reports of the day.[19] But he was
always to regard journalism as something he did to make money
in order to write poetry. He made no attempt to conceal his
literary ambitions or his belief that he was a poet first and
foremost. This was hardly an attitude likely to appeal to the
hard-nosed editors of Fleet Street. Some of them resented it.

Another difficulty he faced was one that lies in wait for most
writers: loneliness. The existence of numerous literary clubs in
London at this time reflects the need for sympathetic companions among the increasing numbers of young men who flocked
to the capital each year in search of literary success. Of these,
the Rhymers' Club is perhaps the best known, but there were
many others, some of them short-lived. At first Davidson had

[15] Quoted in [Seer Green], *The Making of An Editor: W. L. Courtney 1850–1928*
(London, 1930), 45.

[16] 'The Week', *Speaker*, 3 (18 Apr. 1891), 463.

[17] James Robertson Nicholl, 'The Late Mr John Davidson', *British Weekly*, 46 (22
Apr. 1909), 61.

[18] *Sentences and Paragraphs* (London, 1893), 97.

[19] 'Popular Poets of the Period', *Academy*, 36 (5 Oct. 1889), 213.

only his old companions, Barlas and Von Liebich, from his Crieff days. Barlas was then in London preparing a lecture tour to convert the country to socialism; Liebich was trying to establish a reputation as a popular concert pianist. Davidson made Liebich an English verse translation of Goethe's well-known 'Wanderer's Night Song' to be set to music. Liebich in return provided him with some rough translations of the Hungarian poet Nicholas Lenau's verses which he turned into English verse for inclusion in an article he was writing on 'Heather in Literature'.[20] Barlas arranged for all three of them to have supper with Oscar Wilde. They met in a private room in a Soho restaurant where the meal was accompanied by claret and champagne. Wilde came with John Gray. In a brief memoir, Liebich recalls that Barlas and Wilde exchanged witty trivialities, in which Davidson joined in occasionally. But the evening appears not to have been entirely successful, with Gray bored and tired, and Wilde condescending to his old friend, perhaps influenced by Gray's mood.[21] Davidson was to see Wilde several times during the next few years, and came to love him for 'his charming gift of speech'.[22]

On first coming to London he had gone on the usual sight-seeing tour of the capital. One of the first things he did was to dine at Crosby Hall—on steak and a pint of stout and bitter.[23] But London's famous historical landmarks left him cold. His article on 'Heather in Literature' possibly indicates a homesickness for more familiar native landscapes. His mood at this time emerges clearly in a prose sketch entitled 'A Rare Character' which appeared in the *Spectator* on 5 October. In this piece, the lonely walker of his later writings emerges for the first time, combining Thoreau's natural man with the restless vagabondage and love of the open air celebrated by earlier writers like William Hazlitt, Thomas de Quincey, Walt Whitman, and Robert Louis Stevenson. To this composite figure, Davidson adds a dramatic ingredient of metropolitan rootlessness and self-doubt that foreshadows the divided consciousness of the modernists, who were to document their sense of lost connec-

[20] 'Heather in Literature', *Glasgow Herald* (11 Jan. 1890), 9.
[21] Frank (Rudolf von) Liebich, 'Oscar Wilde', unpublished memoir, Clark.
[22] 'Oakley', *Glasgow Herald* (29 Dec. 1906), 8.
[23] 'Through the Sieve', *Westminster Gazette* (29 Aug. 1908), 7.

tion, while attempting to reconstruct an imaginative order. His rare character is an ignorant man who is painfully conscious of his ignorance. There is some sharp-edged satire against schooling and unsystematic reading. But the article is more interesting for what it reveals of the loneliness and insecurities of Davidson's own life in the capital where 'throngs of men talking of business and pleasure, and looking at him as he passed—few of them doubtless noticing him—made him feel as if his soul had been torn from his body like a letter from an envelope, glanced at, and then crumpled up and thrust into a pocket among keys and cash'. The description of his visit to the British Museum to obtain his reader's ticket and so cure his ignorance, is a scarcely veiled account of Davidson's own anxieties about his new profession:

Intuitively he perceived that he had entered one of the most melancholy portions of enclosed space in these islands. The sun was shining, and the windows dim, like cataract-covered eyes, seemed ready to fall out, ashamed of their dinginess. The jaded sunbeams reached the melancholy gilding on the rows of presses, and it seemed to him as if a lance from heaven had pierced the gloom of Tophet, and touched with a more ethereal light the flames that girdle the home of the lost. Then he saw men and women, young and old, and all with a purpose, busy studying books in order to make books, or to help others to make books. He thought, 'Are there not millions of books here already?' and he sighed. The great dome appeared to him like the great skull of a super-encyclopaedic head. The musty odour infected his fancy, and he thought again, 'This mass of heterogeneous knowledge festers, and these are the maggots, the book-worms that are born of it, and live upon it.' But he turned faint, and went outside for some pure air 'to sweeten his imagination'.[24]

The sketch ends with the unhappy man leaving the city to loiter about the countryside.

After three months Davidson himself was short of money and took to living on oatmeal.[25] His thoughts were of Maggie whom he had left behind in Greenock with the two boys—Sandy, not yet 3, and Menzies, only 6 months old. The melancholy verses he sent her at this time reflect his anxiety, but he was still determined to succeed:

[24] 'A Rare Character', *Spectator*, 63 (5 Oct. 1889), 433–4.
[25] 'A Lover of Solitude', *Courier* (23 Sept. 1909) (newspaper clipping), Princeton.

I'm daunted, dear; but blow on blow
With ebbing force I strike, and so
I am not felled and trodden down
My love, my wife![26]

He returned home in October. George Cotterell reviewed his *Plays* in the *Academy* on the 19th. 'The reader almost feels he has been breathing an air to which these later centuries have given no taint', he wrote, and described *Scaramouch in Naxos* as 'a fine piece of fooling, through which runs a genuine vein of poetry'.[27] This, and reunion with Maggie, appeared to have restored his spirits, and he was soon busy again promoting his *Plays*. He sent two copies to the critic H. T. Mackenzie Bell, in the hope of securing further reviews. While in London he had reviewed a book of essays on *Popular Poets of the Period* and had found Bell's contributions—on Theodore Watts and on the democratic tendency of contemporary poetry—especially interesting.[28] The tone of the accompanying letter is that of candour tempered with tact:

It is important to me—apart from the egotistical desire to see one's book attended to—to have some authoritative reviews. I sent a copy to the *Athenaeum* in May, but it has not been noticed. May I ask you to forward the second copy of my *Plays* to Mr. Theodore Watts with the enclosed note which is open for your perusal? Perhaps if he should glance at them, he may think it worth while giving a small space in the *Athenaeum*.[29]

His persistence paid off. Bell sent the book to Watts, and although no review ever appeared in the *Athenaeum*, his letter brought a further request through Bell for a copy to be sent to A. H. Japp, another contributor to the volume of *Popular Poets of the Period*. Japp liked it. 'I am very glad you have found some pleasure in reading my plays,' Davidson wrote to him on 14 November, 'and I thank you heartily for the good intentions you entertain with regard to them.' He had given Japp's contribution scant attention in his review of *Popular Poets of the Period*, and now, in answering Japp's complaint, he dismissed

---

[26] 'From Grub Street' (Rondeau), ll. 6–9.
[27] '*Plays*. By John Davidson', *Academy*, 36 (19 Oct. 1889), 246–7.
[28] '*Popular Poets of the Period*, Edited by F. A. H. Eyles', *Academy*, 36 (5 Oct. 1889), 213.
[29] Davidson to Henry Thomas MacKenzie Bell, 28 Oct. 1889, Huntington.

the whole business of reviewing with the assertion, 'at the bottom of all my reviews I write—on the rough copy I mean—"What the deuce does it matter?"' which might seem somewhat disingenuous given his strenuous efforts to have his own work reviewed.[30]

One detects a greater assurance in his tone as he began to understand better London's literary networks. In his letter to Cotterell, he had accepted that the press took little notice of a book which did not have a proper publisher's imprint. Backed by the *Academy* review and the comments of his influential correspondents, he offered the remainder of the stock—about 150 copies—to the London publishing house of T. Fisher Unwin. The firm agreed to bring out a second issue of his *Plays* under its own imprint at the beginning of the year, but the terms were unfavourable. Unwin insisted that the author pay the cost of the new title page, plus a guinea for its announcement in his catalogue. Davidson became impatient and refused to be further out of pocket: he told Unwin to take the copies as they were and do what he liked with them, a phrase that he would later come to regret. At the time their acceptance made him happy, and he imagined himself at last on the high road to fame and fortune.[31]

He seems to have been tempted to use Meredith's letter in his negotiations with Unwin, for on 27 November he entrusted it to the keeping of the local Greenock poet, Allan Park Paton, with the words, 'I am glad on the whole to get it out of my hands, as I am tempted to show it to people who shouldn't see it.'[32] T. Fisher Unwin issued his *Plays* as a second edition in January with the new title *Scaramouch in Naxos*, and a note from the author explaining the change of title. Davidson was indignant, as he had not been consulted.[33] But the new title was certainly more appealing, and he himself had already admitted that 'Of my three *Plays* I have most faith in *Scaramouch in Naxos*.'[34] Unfortunately, the change of title did not win the book further notices, and only fifty copies were sold.

[30] Davidson to Alexander Hay Japp, 14 Nov. 1889, Huntington.
[31] Davidson to T. Fisher Unwin, 22 Sept. 1893, Berg.
[32] Davidson to Allan Park Paton, 27 Nov. 1889, quoted in J. Benjamin Townsend, *John Davidson: Poet of Armageddon* (New Haven, Conn., 1961), 57.
[33] Davidson to Bertram Dobell, 7 Oct. 1890, Bodleian Library, Oxford.
[34] Davidson to H. T. Mackenzie Bell, 5 Nov. 1889, Huntington.

On 13 December he was surprised by an invitation from the *Glasgow Herald* to write a leading article on Robert Browning who had died in Venice the previous day. Ominously, given his decision to support himself by journalism, he took a full five hours locked away in a remote part of the *Glasgow Herald* office to eke out the number of words required for a column.[35] Charles Russell, the recently appointed editor with strong literary preferences, was to accept Davidson's articles from that time on. With McCormick's help Davidson had already received a promise of work on T. Wemyss Reid's new weekly, the *Speaker*, due to be launched in January. Supported by this hope, he returned to London at the beginning of the year. The first issue of the *Speaker* appeared on 4 January. It was a Saturday paper, modelled on similar lines to the *Spectator*, but devoted to Home Rule and the policies of Gladstone.

Reid, a distant kinsman of the poet Thomas Campbell on his mother's side, was an enterprising newspaper man. While editor of the *Leeds Mercury* in the 1870s, he had succeeded in making the provincial dailies independent of the London dailies by establishing a joint London office with the *Glasgow Herald* and installing a night editor in Fleet Street. At the *Speaker* he gathered around him a brilliant team of famous and soon to be famous contributors. Among the literary contributors were Oscar Wilde, W. B. Yeats, Richard Le Gallienne, J. M. Barrie, Henry James, A. B. Walkley, the drama critic, and 'Q'—Arthur T. Quiller-Couch—recently down from Oxford. Reid's personal assistant was Barry O'Brien, who kept him informed on Irish affairs. Reid took particular delight in giving a hand-up to a new writer or a young journalist. His brother, Stuart J. Reid, often grumbled that the paper was overweighted with them, and that the staff had too free a hand.[36] This was the man to whom Davidson was always to feel deep gratitude for having given him his first chance in London.

His first article for the *Speaker*, a witty piece 'On "Shop"', appeared in the issue for 8 February, which also contained an enthusiastic review of *Scaramouch in Naxos*, probably by Quiller-Couch. But it was a setback when Reid kept three other articles for four months without giving him a decision, one of them

[35] 'The Rejected Leader', *Glasgow Herald* (4 Apr. 1907), 10.
[36] Stuart J. Reid, 'Introduction', *Memoirs of Sir Wemyss Reid 1842–1885* (London, 1905), xvii.

written, at Reid's suggestion, in the style of 'A. K. H. B.'
(Andrew Kennedy Hutchinson Boyd) who contributed regularly to *Frazer's*, *Longman's*, and the *Fortnightly Review*. Davidson
decided that Reid was a kind-hearted man with some energy,
but began to think less of his general capacity.[37] He had already
found other sources of income. The London publishers Ward
and Downey agreed to publish his boys' stories, 'Perfervid' and
'The Pilgrimage of Strongsoul' in one volume, with drawings by
Harry Furniss, the illustrator for *Punch*. For Furniss it turned out
to be a labour of love as he found the book very amusing. Ward
and Downey spent £200 on it, paying Davidson £30 of this. He
also agreed to 'ghost write' for C. J. Wills, an ex-medical officer
turned writer, and a member of the Oriental Club. Wills had
already collaborated with F. C. Philips, but he was looking for
a new collaborator, complaining to Davidson that Phillips was
an idler and that he had to write the whole of the novel *The
Fatal Phryne* and most of *Sybil Ross's Marriage* himself. By early
June Davidson had completed two volumes for Wills, writing an
average of six folio pages a day. He found that if he wrote more,
either the work was inferior or he felt ill. He seems, from the
internal evidence, to have written much of *Was He Justified?*
(1891), a 5-shilling shocker about a husband's jealousy and a
woman with a past which anticipates the frank treatment of
sexual themes in the new fiction of the 1890s. His hand is also
evident in the second volume of Wills's three-volume novel,
Jardyne's Wife (1891), for which he wrote Mrs Jardyne's song,
'Give Me What I Would be Given', and some amusingly clever
parodies of Tennyson, Browning, and Swinburne in praise of
Peach's soap.[38]

He may have entered this shady side of publishing through
the polyglot Dutchman and aged Bohemian Henri von Laun
whom he saw often in his early days in London. Barlas had
dedicated his verse drama *The Queen of Hid Isle* to Von Laun in
1885 'with grateful affection', and it was probably he who introduced the two men. Von Laun urged Davidson to help him
with a shilling dreadful, and after that a three-volume novel.

[37] Davidson to McCormick, not dated [1890], Glasgow.
[38] The details of Davidson's collaboration with Wills are in a letter to McCormick,
'Monday' [1891], Glasgow. Davidson does not give titles, which have been identified from internal evidence.

Davidson resisted, because he did not like the subjects, before going to work for Wills.[39] On the strength of Wills's 'Gargantuan order for fiction' he sent for Maggie and the boys and took a small terraced house in the developing suburb of Hornsey, North London.[40] He decided it was cheaper to bring his family to London, even though he was unable to let the flat in Greenock which he had taken on a long lease. They moved in at the beginning of June. On the 16th he wrote to Harry Furniss from his new address—2 Alfred Terrace, Park Ridings. He had just seen a copy of *Perfervid* and was charmed by the illustrations:

My ignorance . . . gives me no confidence in expressing a preference, but I am particularly grateful for your wonderful Cosmo, your gallant Ninian, your pretty Pansy, the Frontispiece, and the Meeting of the Great Men. The giant dismayed me at first as I had call to see him only in the dress of an ordinary tramp, but I soon perceived that your picture of him was right, because you represent him boldly as he must have appeared to Strongsoul's imagination. The free simplicity and suggestiveness of the Finis I think I can appreciate in some degree—above all the leg of the Highlander and Strongsoul's empty pillowslip.[41]

Perfervid was reviewed in the *Speaker* on 5 July along with Wilde's *The Picture of Dorian Gray*. The anonymous reviewer appeared not to know who 'this John Davidson might be', an indication of the complex staffing arrangements at the paper. It must have pleased Davidson to learn that he had 'every advantage over Mr. Wilde'. To modern eyes, the judgement might appear ludicrous, but it is based, interestingly, on an uneasiness about the generic uncertainty of both fictions, with their stylistic idiosyncrasies and mingling of realism with other elements. The reviewer found Wilde too profuse and paradoxical: 'Only the cook who has yet to learn will run riot in truffle.' He preferred Davidson because he had 'the art of speaking home with few words, the art so seldom learnt'.[42]

Davidson's star was rising again at the offices of the *Speaker*, and he was given steady work editing 'The Week', a column of

---

[39] Davidson to McCormick, 'Thursday' [June 1890], Glasgow.
[40] 'Mr John Davidson', *Pall Mall Budget.*
[41] Davidson to Harry Furniss, 16 June 1890, Princeton.
[42] 'Profuse and Perfervid', *Speaker*, 2 (5 July 1890), 25–6.

literary and artistic gossip introduced on 5 July. The emotional
strain of the previous months, relief at their deliverance, and
continuing anxieties about the future are all evident in a letter
he sent to his sister-in-law at this time. Written to comfort her
in a time of emotional and financial worry—her fiancé Jack
Stewart had squandered all his money at sea—the letter is
charged with the raw sensitivity of a man who has endured a
similar crisis:

I haven't the least right to advise you, or anybody, especially about
marriage, at least from the economical point of view, having failed and
failed again, although now I think we shall get on slowly, but without
another collapse.

The letter continues on a level of emotional intensity and candour that one rarely encounters in his correspondence:

It is not him and his love for you that will satisfy you—you remember
I don't believe in happiness but in satisfaction—but your own love for
him: over that no circumstances of disaster or poverty can have any
power. Your love for him, if you have it truly, is a thing that even your
own will has no control over. It is a gift from heaven, that will increase
with the demands made on it . . .
    I could cry for you myself. Why should this happen to you? So many
others have easy pleasant lives, and never have had any need to hang
their head—what have you done that you should be tortured in this
way? What does it mean at all? No; but say rather—'Here is a labour of
love given, to my hands, which I am thought worthy to undertake—in
misery, in darkness, not seeing one step before another. My bed is not
to be one of roses—to me also it is given to be a heroine—to do and
to suffer something—nobody understanding, many mocking; all by
myself I must go into the night and be strong for two.'[43]

II

At the end of the eighteenth century, the villages that lay
behind Stoke Newington to the north-west—Crouch End,
Hornsey, Wood Green, and Muswell Hill—had been small ham-
lets separated by woods and pastures. Ninety years had produced great changes. Woods, waste, meadows, and pasture were

---

[43] Davidson to Meem, 'Monday' [1890], Princeton.

things of the past; drains and roadways had been hacked across the whole area, and houses had been turned out, to quote Davidson's own words, 'in strings like sausages'.[44] The area would have been unrecognizable to Samuel Rogers, the poet of the place who, before his death in 1855, had smiled and laid his hand on the red hair of the 15-year-old Swinburne, saying: 'I prophesy that you will be a poet too', a gesture Swinburne repeated when he met Davidson.[45]

2 Alfred Terrace was a small mid-terrace house in Park Ridings, a narrow suburban street connecting Hornsey and Wood Green. The house is still there, the street narrowed further by cars lining each pavement. The cost of renting a house at that time would have been about £30 or £40 a year. The narrow strip of clayey ground at the back of the house depressed Maggie who liked gardening. Davidson tried gamely to sow some annuals amongst the bottles and broken crockery.[46] He described the house as 'that horrible brick kennel of the colour of old blood-stains'.[47] He hated the district and he hated the inhabitants. But he was in no position to move again. Maggie made friends with some of the neighbours, while Davidson commuted to Fleet Street, a journey which involved taking two trains. 'We lead a semi-patriarchal life here', he wrote to McCormick in Scotland. 'Adam delves and Eve spins.' But he was anxious to dispel any illusion his friend might have about his new life as a writer:

You needn't envy me; I'm only a 'devil', writing work for other men; it's better than teaching, it's better than reviewing and I'm satisfied in the meantime. I might be earning more money and getting some kind of reputation if I were working independently, but the other way is certain and so I hold on to it for a while.[48]

In the novel *The Whirlpool*, which was partly inspired by Davidson's life and talk, George Gissing adopted Carlyle's metaphor to suggest the lure of London and its bewildering seductions. In reality, metropolitan London, then as today, had no real centre, but was the sum of the diverse circles moving

[44] 'A Suburban Philosopher', *Glasgow Herald* (22 Apr. 1893), 9.
[45] Georges Lafourcade, *Swinburne: A Literary Biography* (London, 1932), 42.
[46] Davidson to McCormick, 'Thursday' [June 1890], Glasgow.
[47] 'A Suburban Philosopher', *Glasgow Herald*, 9.
[48] Davidson to McCormick, 'Thursday' [June 1890], Glasgow.

within its boundaries. Of these, literary London, both in and out of Fleet Street, was made up of shifting groups of individuals who came together for business or other interests in a variety of temporary and less temporary relationships. Davidson's first connections were made through his Scottish friends and associates—in those early days he met Robert Buchanan, who had taught Nichol philosophy, William Sharp, another of Nichol's correspondents, and Mathilde Blind, the poetess and friend of Mazzini—but these soon led to further contacts that drew him into London's literary and Bohemian circles.

His introduction to the Rhymers' Club seems to have come about through Ernest Rhys, a Welshman who had given up his job as a mining engineer in order to write. Davidson met Rhys at one of William Sharp's crowded Sunday gatherings at his house in Hampstead in June 1890. 'He is a good-natured man,' he wrote of Sharp to McCormick, 'but his wife has learnt her lesson, and "got 'em on"—I mean the breeches as well as the bluestockings and the spectacles.'[49] Sharp, described by Rhys as 'tall, yellow-haired, blue-eyed like a Norseman' with 'manners as frank and impulsive as a boy's',[50] had attended Glasgow University and still corresponded with John Nichol. This would account for Davidson's presence there. Among the other guests that day were the two daughters of Bennet Little of Roscommon. Davidson, in his characteristic way, struck up a 'whimsical acquaintanceship' with the younger of the two girls, probably unaware that Rhys was deeply in love with her. But the two men were soon on friendly terms.[51]

The Rhymers' Club was originally a gathering of Irishmen living in London who met to read and discuss each other's work. Yeats has described its formation in this way:

In England the writers do not form groups but each man works by himself and for himself, for England is the land of literary Ishmaels. It is only among the sociable Celtic nations that men draw nearer to each other when they want to think and dream and work.[52]

[49] Davidson to McCormick, 'Thursday' [June 1890], Glasgow.
[50] Ernest Rhys, 'William Sharp and Fiona MacLeod', *Century Magazine*, 74 (May 1907), 111.
[51] Ernest Rhys, *Everyman Remembers* (London, 1931), 107.
[52] W. B. Yeats, 'The Rhymers' Club' (*Boston Pilot*, 23 Apr. 1892), in *Letters to the New Island*, ed. Horace Reynolds (1934; repr. Cambridge, Mass., 1970), 142–8.

The Rhymers' or Rhymesters' Club met informally each Friday evening in an ill-lit, panelled upstairs room in the old Cheshire Cheese pub in Fleet Street. The Club was without rules or officers, although George Greene, who translated Italian and worked as an Examiner to the Board of Intermediate Education, acted as honorary secretary. The Celtic domination of the group ended in January 1891 when Yeats accepted an invitation from Herbert Horne for the group to meet Oscar Wilde at the headquarters of the Century Guild of Artists at 20 Fitzroy Street. Horne was the leader of the Guild and the editor of its organ, the *Hobby Horse*. The select assembly which met on 29 January included Ernest Dowson and Lionel Johnson who had rooms on the third floor of the Fitzroy Street house which Horne also shared with Selwyn Image and Arthur Mackmurdo. Dowson described the meeting as 'very entertaining; a most queer assembly of "Rhymers"; and a quaint collection of rhymes . . . Oscar arrived late looking more like his Whistlerian name, in his voluminous dress clothes than I have ever seen him.'[53]

Davidson's first known attendance was on 4 July 1890 when the Rhymers' Club was still essentially a gathering of Celts. 'We had a very jolly meeting last Friday,' Rhys wrote to an American friend,

—a sort of Marlowe night, as that afternoon a benefit performance for the Marlowe Memorial had been given at the 'Shaftsbury'. John Davidson—author of 'Scaramouch in Naxos' and other most original Plays, lately much discussed; Willie Yeats, a young Irish poet; T. W. Rolleston, another Irish poet, or rhymester, to use the club term; Nettleship the painter; O'Leary, the old Irish rebel; and two or three others less notable were there. Not a large gathering, you see, but a right jovial and friendly one.[54]

The members read their verses that night 'to the Baccanalian accompaniment of whisky', with the night ending in an uproarious scene in which Rhys ran for his life into the rain.

Future meetings were to be less jovial. When Davidson invited Morley Roberts to the Rhymers' Club, he warned him that he would have to bring a poem to read but that anything light and

[53] Ernest Dowson to Arthur Moore, 2 Feb. 1891, in Desmond Fowler and Henry Maas (eds.), *Letters of Ernest Dowson* (London, 1967), 182–3.

[54] Ernest Rhys to Edmund Clarence Stedman, 9 July 1890, quoted in James G. Nelson, *The Early Nineties: A View from the Bodley Head* (Cambridge, Mass., 1971), 158.

cheerful would be out of place. Yeats himself remembered that the talk had 'little vitality',[55] one of the reasons that Arthur Symons, a seasoned frequenter of Bohemian Paris, stopped attending. Edgar Jepson, who went to the Rhymers' with Dowson, described their smiles as 'constrained'. His descriptions of his contemporaries are generally frank, if often unflattering, and there is clearly something to be learned from his contrasting portraits of Davidson 'looking . . . like a commercial traveller at loggerheads with the world' and Yeats 'wearing in those days the air of a Byronic hero, long-haired and gaunt, and delivering his poems in a harsh and high and chanting voice'.[56]

Davidson was soon out of sympathy with the affectation and youthful narcissism that prevailed among his young friends at the Rhymers'. His irreverence is evident in his account of a special Rhymers' meeting he attended in November 1891 at Lionel Johnson's place. 'Low-ceiled room in the third floor in Fitzroy Street,' he told McCormick,

but plenty of space, walled with books and overpowering pictures by Simeon Solomon. Lionel [moving] about among them like a minnow, or an anatomical preparation—the Absin[the] you remember. George-a-Greene, the Pindar of Wakefield who translates Carducci was there; also Ernest Radford, forked radish that would fain be an eagle, and who begins his books: 'As my friend Walter Pater said to me on Saturday—no it was Sunday afternoon'; W. B. Yeats the wild Irishman, who lives on watercress and pemmican and gets drunk on the smell of whiskey, and can distinguish and separate out as subtly as death each individual cell in any literary organism; Rolleston, once an Irish Adonis—now the consumptive father of four children; Dowson and Clough, two rosebud poets.[57]

Davidson's bemusement at the Rhymers was shared by Roberts, a muscular, red-bearded man, who on one occasion arrived to find four of them sitting hand in hand before the fire.[58] This was not the sort of thing to appeal to Davidson who urged them to have more 'blood and guts'. He seems to have looked on them with a kind of exasperated indulgence. His situation was a difficult one. He was older than the others—

[55] W. B. Yeats, *Memoirs* (London, 1972), 37.
[56] Edgar Jepson, *Memories of a Victorian* (London, 1933), 235 and 239.
[57] Davidson to McCormick, 'Sunday' [1891], Glasgow.
[58] Morley Roberts, 'The Rhymers' Club', *John O'London's Weekly*, 29 (30 Sept. 1933), 901–2.

eight years Yeats's senior—but, like them, he was still struggling for recognition, with all the disadvantages of a late starter. According to Yeats, he almost brought the club to an end when he introduced four Scotsmen one evening. 'One read out a poem upon a Life-boat, evidently intended for recitation', Yeats recalled;

another described how, when gold-digging in Australia, he had fought and knocked down another miner for doubting the rotundity of the earth; while of the remainder I can remember nothing except that they excelled in argument. He insisted on their immediate election, and the Rhymers, through the complacency of good manners whereby educated Englishmen so often surprise me, obeyed, though secretly resolved never to meet again.[59]

Ernest Dowson seems to be referring to the same incident in a letter to Arthur Moore who had been to the meeting: 'How foolish of the Immortals to crown those impossible Scotchmen.'[60] Yeats claimed that it cost him seven hours' work 'to get another meeting, and vote the Scotsmen out'.[61]

It is possible that Davidson's invasion was intended as a high-spirited prank or April Fool. The poem about the lifeboat 'evidently intended for recitation' may well have been G. R. Sims's 'The Lifeboat' from *Brandram's Speaker* (1885) which Davidson had used for recitations at Crieff. Just such a note of gaming in earnest characterizes his description of the Rhymers' in the novel *Earl Lavender*, where a similar incident is introduced. In the course of the story, his absurd heroes, Earl Lavender and Lord Brumm, find their way to the old Cap and Bells, a thinly disguised Cheshire Cheese, where the Earl addresses the Guild of Prosemen, otherwise the Rhymers, with his mad-cap theories of the survival of the fittest. He is supported by one of the members, an unkempt excitable Scotsman called Rorison, 'well-known,' he says of himself, 'for the lukewarmth of my allegiance to the Guild' and 'a very irregular attendant at their meetings'. Rorison is clearly an exercise in self-ridicule, with Yeats appearing as 'the handsome Irish Proseman' who moves that no notice should be taken of either Earl Lavender's address, or of the

[59] W. B. Yeats, *Autobiographies* (London, 1955), 317.

[60] Ernest Dowson to Arthur Moore, 'Mardi' [28 Apr. 1891], in Fowler and Mass (eds.), *Letters of Ernest Dowson*, 194.

[61] Yeats, *Autobiographies*, 317.

reply of Rorison, the vain Scotsman.[62] Yeats seems not to have considered the possibility that the invasion might be a prank and was surprised when Davidson greeted him amiably at a restaurant a few days later and, on parting, shook his hand and proclaimed enthusiastically that he had 'blood and guts'.

Their temperamental differences were soon to have more serious repercussions, but initially they took each other's measure, as young men do. During the autumn of 1890, they worked together to make a success of a new literary magazine, the *Weekly Review*. Davidson was sub-editor. The office was at 68 Fleet Street on the corner of Whitefriars Street. The first issue, priced 1*d*., appeared on 11 October. No copy of the magazine has yet been discovered, but we know that one issue contained the first part of Davidson's story 'Miss Armstrong's Circumstances',[63] and that there were contributions from Yeats and several of the Rhymers, including Rhys, who was then sharing rooms in Hampstead with Arthur Symons. Davidson had high ambitions for the magazine. 'The *Weekly Review* from what I hear means to be very energetic', Yeats's father wrote to John O'Leary on the 18 November.[64] At a 'mournfully small meeting' of the Rhymers that month, Davidson plotted articles with Yeats, G. R. Green, and Charles Johnston, who had been in the services in India but wanted to take up a literary career.[65] Yeats complained to John O'Leary that the *Weekly Review* had come to take up three days of every week, and so hold up his work on Blake, but in November he received £2 for his contributions.[66] When the magazine folded in early December, the other contributors may not have been so lucky. Writing to Rhys at the turn of the year, Davidson expressed uncertainty about Rhys's prospects of being paid for his contribution:

Did you know that the *Weekly Review* died a natural death three weeks ago? Mr. Fleming announced on a Saturday afternoon that he had determined to face his loss and in half an hour I left the *Weekly Review* for ever. I don't know whether Fleming means 'to face the loss' of his

---

[62] *A Full and True Account of the Wonderful Mission of Earl Lavender* (London, 1895), 49–50 and 53.

[63] 'Note' to *Miss Armstrong's*.

[64] J. B. Yeats to John O'Leary, 18 Nov. 1890, in *The Collected Letters of W. B. Yeats Vol. 1 1865–1895*, ed. John Kelly and Eric Domville (Oxford, 1986), 236.

[65] W. B. Yeats to Ernest Rhys, [19 Nov. 1890], in *Collected Letters of Yeats*, 236.

[66] W. B. Yeats to John O'Leary, [*c*.8] Nov. [1890], *Collected Letters of Yeats*, 233.

contributors. You should write him. I shall infallibly turn up on Friday to wish you God speed.[67]

On the Friday referred to, the Rhymers had a send-off supper for Rhys before his Monday wedding to Grace Little. Davidson was to see less of Rhys after his marriage, and relations between the two cooled, possibly because of Rhys's continuing friendship with Yeats. The 'memorable evening' at Rhys's house recalled by Rhys in *Everyman Remembers* (1931), when Davidson came 'unexpectedly' to a gathering that included D. H. Lawrence, Yeats, and Ezra Pound, could not have happened, as Lawrence did not meet Rhys and his wife Grace until after Davidson's death.

Rhys believed that Davidson had been hurt and mortified by the collapse of the *Weekly Review*. 'He had not the temperament or the faculty for taking things light-heartedly', he wrote. 'Humour he had in plenty, but it was a grim humour when it came to matters of bread and butter.'[68] Davidson himself was later to refer to the magazine with regret and some pride as 'a gallant short-lived periodical'.[69] His feelings at the time can be seen in the character of Meyrick Tunstall, the Napoleon of journalism, in the novel *Laura Ruthven's Widowhood*. Tunstall founds a review based on an ideal of 'absolute veracity' only to meet with indifference and disappointment. He is forced to recognize that, compared with the other weeklies, 'its distinction was not so marked as he had expected':

Alas for Tunstall! he was only a dreamer. Journalism was developing on far other lines. The spirit of journalism can be described negatively, as the reverse of *dilettante*; and with all his earnestness and great capacity, Meyrick Tunstall was but an amateur. He himself had likened journalism to a sea. Why did he attempt to put a bridge across it, to dam it, to bottle it? While he sat complacently doling out his weekly dose of veracity, journalism roared past him, if not like a sea, like a raging flood—with a Stead for its Shakespeare![70]

Here as elsewhere, Davidson fails to give credit to his achievement as a journalist, perhaps because of his prejudice against

[67] Davidson to Ernest Rhys, 'Friday' [Jan. 1891], quoted in Ernest Rhys, *Letters from Limbo* (London, 1936), 90.
[68] Rhys, *Letters from Limbo*, 90.
[69] 'Note' to *Miss Armstrong's*.
[70] *Laura Ruthven's Widowhood*, iii. 27.

journalism as a profession. Initially, his journalistic style tended to be over-literary, shifting between Carlylean idiom and Johnsonian sententiousness. During his first year only ten of the twenty papers he had submitted had been accepted by the magazines, and he felt certain he would never succeed as a journalist. But he had soon cooked up a distinctively colourful and pungent style of the kind that gives distinction, now as then, to a press whose main fare is news, bone-dry comment, and gossip. He recognized grudgingly that there was a 'perfection of workmanship' in journalism which lay in being able 'to hit the nail on the head each time'.[71]

The collapse of the *Weekly Review* forced him back to pot-boiling. He wrote the second volume of a three-volume novel for Wills for £15, unaware that Wills had sold it for £200—probably *His Sister's Hand* (1892)—and expanded one of Wills's *St James's Gazette* stories, 'Mrs Redmayne's Complexion' into a full-length novel in the belief that they already had a publisher for it, and that they would share the profits. In the one-volume novel, which he titled *An Easy-Going Fellow* (1896), some of his own fears and preoccupations emerge in the two central characters—'lucky Jack Norris', the 'easy-going fellow' of the novel's title whose apparent wealth and luck are more appearance than reality, and Harry Brandon, the literary man who gradually slips down the social ladder. Wills also asked him to write two-thirds of another three-volume novel for a £25 advance. He agreed, because his journalism was not succeeding, but he began to suspect that Wills was fleecing him. Wills had delayed placing some of the manuscripts with publishers, including *An Easy-Going Fellow* in which they had half profits. This put pressure on Davidson to sell his rights for some urgently needed cash. Of course it might have raised some awkward questions among the members of the Oriental Club with whom Wills enjoyed a reputation as a clever novelist if too many of his books had appeared at the same time. Of all the novels on which they collaborated, only *Laura Ruthven's Widowhood* carried Davidson's name as joint author, probably at Lawrence and Bullen's suggestion, although Wills's 'Preface' to *Jardyne's Wife* did thank 'an ingenious friend' for the song and the verse

---

[71] 'The Week', *Speaker*, 1 (20 June 1890), 734.

parodies. But Davidson seems to have felt no real bitterness. He wrote at the time:

I'm sometimes inclined to grumble at my novelist's ways, but then he has given me what no publisher or editor has, bread, if not much butter. He is the only man who has said write and I'll pay you. To be sure it's inferior writing he wants, and the credit of it such as it is he would like also to secure, but what am I to do? I could starve, but I can't ask my wife and bairns to do so.[72]

Some of Davidson's work for Wills has arguably a greater appeal than *The Great Men* and *A Practical Novelist* which he submitted to Ward and Downey for publication in his own name. *A Practical Novelist* was *The North Wall* with a new title; *The Great Men* a collection of short stories and sketches written in the early 1880s to which he had added 'A Schoolboy's Tragedy'. Pleased with the success of *Perfervid*, Ward and Downey agreed to publish them in one volume. Davidson's fellow Rhymer, E. J. Ellis, was commissioned to provide the illustrations. At that time, as Davidson later recalled, 'an author might as well offer a horse unbuttered stones as a publisher a volume of short stories'.[73] Suddenly collections of short stories were becoming popular, a boom caused no doubt by Kipling's success. Davidson had been trying to find a publisher for his *Great Men* stories since his days at Victoria Buildings, Crieff. In May 1886, he had sent the manuscript, then titled 'The Salvation of Nature', to William Blackwood and Sons with copies of *The North Wall* and *Bruce* and a letter stating; 'I believe them to be the best work in prose I have done.'[74] One wonders how much belief he had in the stories four years later. He was immodestly proud of 'A Schoolboy's Tragedy', believing it to be the best short story written in English, but the other sketches are the zestful creations of the young schoolmaster and elocutionist, more suitable for recitation than reading, and including the long-winded yarn about the mule that had displeased his old Rector. The London critics were no more receptive. While Quiller-Couch praised 'A Schoolboy's Tragedy' as 'by far the truest piece of work that Mr. Davidson has yet done', he pointed

[72] Davidson to McCormick, 'Monday' [1891], Glasgow.
[73] 'The Week', *Speaker*, 3 (11 Apr. 1891), 431.
[74] Davidson to Messrs William Blackwood and Sons, 26 May 1886, NLS.

out that its success 'seems to prove that he does wrongly to follow so frequently after the fantastic'.[75]

A more substantial piece of work was his translation of Montesquieu's *Persian Letters* for the Edinburgh publisher, John C. Nimmo. It included eight etchings by the celebrated painter and engraver Edouard de Beaumont. Aestheticism and *fin de siècle* taste for the erotic and forbidden created a lucrative market for private printings and fine editions, which Leonard Smithers and other entrepreneurs were quick to exploit. The market for translations also reflected the increasingly cosmopolitan interests of the 1890s. Davidson's translation went to press in July 1891, with the introduction added in September. One does not have to look far to see the attractions of Montesquieu's work for Davidson's contemporaries, with its ironic refutations of western morality, and its erotic images of the harem, which De Beaumont's etchings 'The Pretty Woman's Dressing Room' and 'Punishment of Zachi' delicately exploit. Davidson himself had become increasingly responsive to the power of the visual and decorative arts. He visited J. T. Nettleship, his fellow Rhymer, that year and was extraordinarily impressed by Nettleship's black and white drawings 'God Creating Evil' and 'God in Glory'.[76] The job of translating had probably come to him through Von Laun, who was confidential literary adviser to John C. Nimmo. Laun was already well known for his translations of Taine, Molière, and Le Sage's *Gil Blas*. He was a useful contact for Davidson in his job as editor of 'The Week' column at the *Speaker* which regularly carried news of literary events from across the Channel.

Things French were the talk of the Rhymers and of the 'friends' he met at Robert Sherard's Charles Street rooms, where Barlas and Wilde were frequent visitors in the early months of 1891. The weather was wolfish that winter, and there was a general dread of influenza. Sherard remembered that the first time Davidson called he was wearing a pair of galoshes which prompted Sherard to say jokingly that he hoped they were the Galoshes of Fortune that might lead him to prosperity.

[75] 'A Literary Causerie', *Speaker*, 4 (26 Dec. 1891), 784.
[76] J. T. Nettleship to Davidson, 9 June 1891, Reading. Davidson's impressions are recorded in 'The Week', *Speaker*, 3 (13 June 1891), 703.

He also remembered that Davidson boasted that he was living in 'the smallest house in London'.[77] McCormick, who had recently been appointed to the Chair of English Literature at University College, Dundee, came to London shortly after this, and Davidson introduced him to Wilde and Gray, and his other London friends and acquaintances. There was a visit to the theatre with Von Laun, Maggie, and her sister who was staying with them, and convivial Wednesday evenings over old ale at the Cheshire Cheese after the *Speaker* had been put to bed. Davidson invited 'Mac' to tea and supper in Hornsey one Saturday, along with John Gray, Morley Roberts, and John Nichol, who had settled in London the previous August after resigning his professorship in Glasgow.[78] For Davidson it was the renewal of old habits in Scotland when there was never a week without an escape of some kind. He led a quieter life after Mac's departure, although he attended the Rhymers' meeting at Lionel Johnson's in November. There were strange reports circulating at the time about a robbery at Wilde's house in which money had been stolen. On one of his nights out in London, Davidson was made uneasy when 'a malicious youth pointed out . . . that there was no money to steal', and decided he 'must turn in to the Café Royal some night, and hear all about it from himself'.[79]

But when scandal did occur at this time, it concerned Barlas. Both Wilde and Barlas were involved with anarchists. At a small dinner party to which Davidson was invited at Wilde's house, one of the guests was Sergius Stepniak, the Russian nobleman and revolutionary, who was believed to have assassinated General Mezenter, chief of the Russian secret police.[80] Wilde may have imagined that Davidson's sympathies were with the anarchists, as he had been introduced to Davidson through Barlas. Davidson had attended an anarchist meeting, but merely as a bemused spectator—it had struck him as innocuous, like a 'Mission-hall'.[81] He admired Barlas's *Love Sonnets* and noticed the strange disparity between Barlas's political passions and the

[77] Robert Harborough Sherard, *My Friends the French* (London, 1909), 98.
[78] Davidson to McCormick, 'Monday' [1891], Glasgow.
[79] Davidson to McCormick, 'Sunday' [1891], Glasgow.
[80] 'Oakley', *Glasgow Herald* (29 Dec. 1906), 8.
[81] 'Among the Anarchists', *Good Words* (Feb. 1894), 125–9.

general absence of social views from his poetry. Like many in the circle he viewed Barlas's intense socialist convictions with concern.

That concern was justified. On the morning of New Year's Eve, Barlas left the rooms were he was living in Lambeth Road, and walking to Westminster Bridge, fired a revolver three times—some witnesses said five—in rapid succession at the House of Commons—'to mark', as he was to explain later at the police station, 'my contempt for the House of Commons'.[82] Sherard, who was in Paris at the time, was indignant when he saw a sensational report of the incident in the *Pall Mall Gazette* and wrote immediately to the newspaper explaining that his friend's action was 'the result of nervous irritation' brought on by the philistine public's indifference to his poetry.[83] Davidson came to a different conclusion. He had seen the signs of coming madness and was convinced that it was the result of a blow Barlas had received from a policeman's baton during the Trafalgar Square Riots of 1886. 'He has no back to his head', he told everyone at the time '—it goes right down to his neck in a straight line.'[84]

Neither diagnosis was correct. When he was later admitted to Gartnavel Mental Asylum, a cicatricine mark was found on his penis, although he denied having had syphilis. At the time of the incident, he was living with a prostitute, having abandoned his wife after frequently beating her and threatening her with a razor. On 7 January, Barlas was brought before the court. He made a sad figure in the dock. Davidson and Maggie were there with Oscar Wilde, John Gray, and Mrs Barlas and her mother. They were allowed to speak to him beforehand in a back room, and decided that he should be remanded again. They wanted to avoid the awkward situation of having him declared insane and hoped that he would recover and then get off with a fine. The court accepted their decision and they were able to celebrate with breakfast at half-past one.[85] When he was brought up from Holloway Prison eight days later, the court heard that he had no connection with alleged anarchist plots, but that, in the opinion

[82] John Lowe, 'John Barlas: Sweet Singer and Socialist' (Cupar, 1915), 8
[83] Robert Harborough Sherard to the Editor, *Pall Mall Gazette* (7 Jan. 1892), 3.
[84] Quoted in Sherard, *My Friends the French*, 98–9.
[85] Davidson to McCormick, 7 Jan. 1892, Glasgow.

of the medical officer at Holloway, he was not in his right mind and should be sent to an asylum. He was spared this when Wilde and H. H. Champion, the secretary of the Social Democratic Federation, arrived at the court and offered themselves as surety. He was bound over to keep the peace for two months on bail set at £200.[86]

The incident seemed droll to many in literary London at the time, but it also brought a sense of foreboding. It was like a warning to them all of the possible consequences of restless, overwrought emotions. 'We poets and dreamers are all brothers', Wilde wrote to Barlas three days after his release.[87] Barlas impressed the Rhymers when he attended one of their meetings after his release, probably in Davidson's company. But he left London soon after for Crieff, where he was again arrested—this time for unprovoked assault—and sent to Gartnavel Asylum near Glasgow.

Davidson's other old friend from his Crieff days also left London about this time. Liebich arrived at Hornsey one evening 'very desperate'.[88] His attempt to support himself as a concert pianist had been a failure, and he decided to try his luck in the United States. Davidson went with him to the station to see him off to Liverpool. It was a silent and sad farewell, and for fifteen minutes as they waited for the train to leave, Davidson could not stay still.[89] The two friends were never to meet again, although Maggie was to spend some months with Liebich and his wife in Chicago after John's death.

In the closing months of 1891 Davidson was excited about the turn his own life was taking. Earlier that year he had declined to contribute to an anthology of verse compiled by Yeats and other members of the Rhymers' Club. He felt lukewarm towards the group, and was in any case about to have a collection published in his own name. After Downey's departure, the firm which had published his stories finally agreed to take a chance on his collection of poems, *In A Music-Hall*. It was the realization of his youthful dream.

[86] 'The Strange Case of Mr. John Barlas, Poet', *Pall Mall Gazette* (16 Jan. 1892), 5.
[87] Oscar Wilde to John Barlas, postmarked 19 Jan. 1892, in Rupert Hart-Davis (ed.), *More Letters of Oscar Wilde* (London, 1985), 108.
[88] Davidson to McCormick, 'Sunday' [1891], Glasgow.
[89] Liebich, 'Oscar Wilde'.

His thoughts turned again to poetry. In December he read 'The Coming of Summer' by Richard Jefferies in *Longman's Magazine*, and was inspired by its fitful, sensuous prose to compose the lyric 'In the Hollow at Long Ditton' which appeared in the *Speaker* in December. The poem hymns his own pent-up emotions, 'self-caged . . . to make his singing strong'. The reviews of *The Great Men and a Practical Novelist* were disappointing, but this was neither the catastrophe nor the gloomy reversal that generally descended on him at Christmas time. His poems were to be issued in January, and he looked forward to a happy Christmas season for once. But it was not to be. On 28 December he received bad news from Edinburgh. His father had dropped dead that morning in an Edinburgh Street.

Alexander Davidson had been feeling ill for some time, but this was known only to the family. He had never been the same since the death of John's sister Lizzie after an agonizing illness three years earlier. But he worked to the end. He preached twice on the Sunday before his death, warning against drunkenness in the New Year. On Tuesday morning he left after breakfast to catch the 9-o'clock train to Glasgow to attend a meeting. He collapsed ten minutes later in Leith Walk and died almost at once in a nearby shop. He was 67. The doctor gave the cause of death as heart failure. Davidson's sister Effie, who had hurried to the shop, returned to Rosslyn Crescent with the words, 'Papa's with Lizzie'.[90]

Alexander Davidson was buried beside Lizzie in the family grave in Glasgow. Davidson went home for the funeral. 'My mother and sister are poorly left; but we shall manage', he told McCormick.[91] His father's estate was settled at the beginning of March. In the last years of his life, his salary had risen to £20 16s. 5d. a month, almost £250 a year, and since the mid-1880s he had been able to invest some of his money, mainly in the Vienna Ice Company and the Tramway Companies of Central Birmingham and Staffordshire. At the time of his death, his total estate was worth £719 12s. By the terms of his will,

[90] Ferguson, 'Biographical Sketch', p. xxvii.
[91] Davidson to McCormick, 7 Jan. 1892, Glasgow.

made twenty-five years earlier, this passed to Helen Davidson.[92]
It provided a precarious margin of security for an ageing widow
and her spinster daughter, and on moving from the manse in
Rosslyn Crescent to 40 Marchmont Crescent, Davidson's
mother and sister were obliged to take in lodgers.

A week after the settlement of his father's estate, his mother
made a new will leaving everything to Effie. The reason is clearly
stated in her will: while she entertained equal affection for
all her children, her unmarried daughter would 'be less able
to provide for herself'.[93] The will contained the proviso that
should Effie ever marry, she was obliged to pay over to each of
her brothers or their children a third, or if one of the brothers
died, half of the estate. Neither John nor his brother Thomas
were ever to benefit. Effie Davidson was to remain unmarried
until her death forty-four years later at the age of 80.

Davidson inherited his father's watch and some of his books
and papers. Bereavement compelled an emotional stock-taking,
acutely so in view of the conflict and estrangement over the
years between father and son. Something of Davidson's feelings
can be guessed from the poem 'St Valentine's Eve' in which the
Grub Street poet, Menzies, curses his fate in being the heir to a
poor father and 'a thrifty race, | Using all means of grace | To
save their souls and purses.'[94] The pun on 'saving' is heartlessly
reinvoked in his poem 'A Woman and her Son' written some
years later, in which the son rails bitterly against his late evangelist father for having spent his life 'saving souls' with the result
that his family is penniless. Davidson must have seen the bene-
fits of income among many of his London acquaintances. Yet
his response to privation and disappointment displays the same
pertinacious idealism that so frustrated him in his father. There
is little to distinguish Alexander Davidson's dedication to the
new religious causes of his youth, to his immediate financial
disadvantage, from those moments when John turned to poetry,
without any certainty that it would ever bring him money or
success. Just such a moment occurred in the early months of

[92] Scottish Records Office, Reference RP 2747; Eric Northey, 'The Poetry of
John Davidson in its Social, Political and Philosophical Contexts', Ph.D. thesis
(Newcastle, 1976), appendix B.
[93] Ibid.   [94] 'Lammas', ll. 63–5.

1892, as he leafed through his father's papers, and began to write his *Fleet Street Eclogues*.

In his interview with Jane Stoddart in 1894, he spoke in detail of how the *Eclogues* originated:

When I was a teacher in Scotland, I had the idea of writing a kind of teacher's calendar on the plan of the old Shepherd's Calendar, but this idea was never carried out. When my father died, however, among the books that came into my possession was a copy of Gibbon's 'Decline and Fall'. As I read it the old idea revived, but I was in London now, and the journalists of Fleet-street seemed closer friends than the teachers of my younger days. So I wrote a journalist's calendar, under the title of 'Fleet-street Eclogues', and every morning, before sitting down to my desk, I read a chapter of Gibbon.[95]

It is tempting to try and identify Davidson himself and his friends at the Rhymers' Club and elsewhere in the dramatic voices of the *Eclogues*, but the final impression is that of an interplay and fusion of moods, as the Grub Street hacks sing of their exilic loneliness and seasonal consolations in Fleet Street in the heart of the great metropolis. The speakers have homely English names—Basil, Brian, Herbert—or the names of members of Davidson's own family—Sandy, called after his eldest son, and Menzies, the unusual Christian name of both his favourite sister-in-law and his youngest son. The cycle consists of seven poems, each centred on an important English feast day. The cycle begins with the celebrations of 'New Year's Day', the season significantly when his father died, and continues with the Lenten atmosphere of 'St Valentine's Eve' and 'Good Friday'. 'St Swithin's Day' includes the verses 'In the Hollow at Long Ditton', gaining in dramatic force in the context of the holiday memories of the returning Londoners. The year advances with 'Michaelmas' and 'Queen Elizabeth's Day' where escape from London can only be achieved in imagination, and closes at 'Christmas Eve' with wassailing and a winter's tale from Menzies.

Davidson's acknowleged debt to Spenser's *Shepherd's Calendar* (1579) has to be reconciled with his frequently vigorous denials that any of his poetry was modelled on the works of other poets.

[95] Jane Stoddart ('Lorna'), 'An Interview with John Davidson', *British Weekly*, 17 (13 Dec. 1894), 121.

The link between *Fleet Street Eclogues* and the *Shepherd's Calendar* may not be direct, but may have come through Chambers's *Book of Days* which Davidson loved as a child. Encyclopedias, dictionaries, and factual books of all kinds were always the main inspiration for his poetry. One has only to compare the language and themes of 'New Year's Day' with Chambers's entry for January to recognize the close parallels between the two. In *Book of Days* the epigraph for each month and some of the descriptive material is taken from Spenser, thus providing the link between the poets. Davidson's eclecticism was to become a feature of the modernist poets who came after him. Literature, religious festivals, folk customs, personal memories: all are invoked by his speakers in a search for meaning and connection absent in reality from the modern metropolis.

Davidson wrote the poems in one of his father's old notebooks after removing some pages containing theological notes. The significance of this seems obvious. Through the mock pastoral, which he substituted for his Evangelist father's theological writings, he affirmed the value of poetry over a Puritan tradition discomforted by expressions of beauty and the polite pretences of art and literature. According to William Empson, the trick of the old pastoral was for the writer to keep up a firm pretence that he was unconscious of the clash in making 'simple people express strong feelings . . . in learned and fashionable language'.[96] This pretence connects Davidson's journalists with the Arcadian shepherds and rustic lovers of Theocritus, Virgil, and Spenser—with this added irony, that Davidson's columnists are in fact men of literary education compelled to submit to the snobbery and commercial imperatives of a society inimical to art. Hence they must sometimes mock themselves, in 'Ercles vein'. It was a symptom of lower-middle-class unease that was to be treated with various degrees of irony by his younger contemporaries—Wells and Bennett in particular—and became and remained a source of snobbish ridicule of their artistic pretensions.

In the pastoral, he found a way of reconciling his poetic allegiance to the modern world, which he felt should be the subject-matter of poetry, and the world of the imagination. It

[96] William Empson, *Some Versions of Pastoral* (London, 1935), 11.

thus answered the technical problems raised by his other writings. *An Unhistorical Pastoral,* as the title suggests, denies the existence of history, but the attempt at pure poetry veers towards pastiche. The introduction of the masque in *A Romantic Farce* allows for the interplay of past and present, real and imaginary worlds, but the conscious ironies of the author, here as in *Scaramouch in Naxos,* tend to twist into a sardonic ridicule of deep feeling. In his boys' stories, it is this sense of absurdity that drives the pastoral to its characteristic Victorian refuge: the child cult. By setting his pastoral in the modern city Davidson intensifies the ironies implicit in the pastoral form. What has to be recognized is that the appeal to nature and the simplicity of country life in the genuine pastoral is always the product of urban experience. The image of the countryside in pastoral mingles plain facts and hallucination. Like the related realms of fairy and legend, it is a world imagined but unrealized in the life of the poet. It may not be an exaggeration to say that pastoral is poetry in its purest form. We can see the relevance of pastoral irony to Davidson's own situation. For the toil and traffic of Fleet Street which so repel him—his private prison house of language and the world in microcosm—are what provide the occasion for the poetry by which he will be remembered. London, and not Long Ditton, has become 'a place for singing in!' To put this another way, it is perhaps too rarely admitted that the best literature is often the product of strange and desperate longings. Would Davidson, as a man, have found comfort in the thought that his legacy of disappointment and struggle was of more value to him, as a poet, than financial security? It is a question that he was to explore the following year in his 'A Ballad of a Musician'.

The influence of Gibbon on the *Eclogues* is also significant. One of the essential functions of pastoral, in the post-Hellenic age at least, has been to point to the degeneration of standards between the pastoral world and the contemporary scene. Gibbon's *The Decline and Fall of the Roman Empire,* which was attacked in the eighteenth century for its criticisms of Christianity, had by the end of the Victorian period become an exemplary history of the decline of great nations and empires that was in accord with the pessimistic mood that gripped some quarters as the century headed to its close. For the 'age-end journalists' of the

Eclogues: 'Beauty and truth are dead, | And the end of the world begun.'[97]

The apocalyptic note of the *Eclogues* is in sharp contrast to Davidson's jocular dismissal of *fin de siècle* predictions the previous year in the pages of the *Speaker*, when he concluded that 'this chronological method of marking off the ages of the world's history is not more arbitrary than it is absurd'.[98] The change cannot be put down to dramatic expediency as the *fin de siècle* mood becomes one of the keynotes of his writings. The introductory 'Note' to his novel *Earl Lavender* retracts his earlier view of the factitiousness of the 'Decadence'. Its satire is directed against contemporary Darwinian ideas of progress which are parodied in mad-cap form by the hero who takes his name from the French *l'avenir*, 'the future'. Ridicule of Darwinian evolution can be found earlier in *Scaramouch in Naxos* where the rascally Scaramouch, a freak-show impresario in the style of the American showman P. T. Barnum, proposes to discover and exhibit the missing link. But in *Earl Lavender* farce and high jinks combine with a sardonic acceptance of the 'Decadence' that brings the book to rest somewhere between earnest and jest. Davidson had come to share the mood of some of his fellow Rhymers. Yeats, for instance, wrote at this time that 'England is old and her poets must scrape up the crumbs from an almost finished banquet.'[99] Arthur Symons was to write a fantasy round a talk he had with Davidson and Barlas at the Café Royal, probably in the early weeks of 1892, in which he presents Davidson in full *fin de siècle* mood, puffing his pipe, sipping absinthe, and prophesying the state of the world a million years hence, 'burnt out, a mere moon, without inhabitants, without memory of Shakespeare, without memory of Oscar Wilde, of you and me'.[100]

---

[97] 'New Year's Day', ll. 25–6.

[98] 'Would We Live Our Lives Over Again?', *Speaker*, 3 (28 Feb. 1891), 247.

[99] Yeats, 'The Rhymers' Club' in *Letters to the New Island*, 148.

[100] Arthur Symons, *The Café Royal and Other Essays* (London, 1923), 5–7. Symons gives the date of the meeting as 1895, but in a letter to Rhys, 17 Feb. 1892, he writes: 'If a conversation at the Café Royal goes into *Black and White* I should rather like you to see it. It is just a little fantasy round a talk with Scaramouch (John Davidson) and St. Just (a John Barlas, the shooter of the House of Commons)', in Karl Backson and John M. Munro (eds.), *Selected Letters 1880–1935* (Basingstoke, 1989), 95.

A simple explanation might be that Davidson had caught the *fin de siècle* contagion—it was his habit, for instance, to apply at once new scientific theories to his own life—but ideas generally became part of his repertoire of beliefs only after they had connected with some deeply felt experience. His father's death, coming after the death of his sister, seems to have brought him to a sudden acceptance of prevailing theories of hereditary decline. Such sudden reversals are often the experience of the man of conviction, but of limited worldly experience. To a man of Davidson's openness and sensitivity, they were swift and traumatic, and occurred with increasing frequency as he exposed himself to the experiences of London.

As he worked on his *Eclogues,* in those early months of the year, perhaps as yet unaware of their true merit and significance, his life seemed far from successful. His collection of stories had been dismissed by the critics as vulgar clowning, and the collection of poems, on which he believed his reputation depended, was virtually ignored. 'It seems about to die alike unchristened and undamned', he wrote to Edmund Gosse in sending him a copy.[101] Although dated 1891, the volume had not been issued until January, so missing the publicity of the pre-Christmas period. To add to his troubles he opened the first January number of the *Speaker* to find that none of his notes had been used, and that the review of the magazines had been done by someone else. Nobody had written to him or told him—he believed out of shame—that a needy Irish MP had been appointed to the staff of the *Speaker,* and that his salary was being met by a reduction of rates of pay all round. The Irishman had taken over the magazines, the quarterlies, and the library notes. This meant the loss of two-thirds of Davidson's income. It was a severe blow, made bitter by the thought that Yeats and the other Rhymers would triumph in his misfortune. He wrote to McCormick to tell him of the fierceness he felt 'deep down' in his heart:

Wemyss Reid powerless, although retaining the title of editor, as powerless in the hands of the Irish party as the G.O.M. himself. The whole of the Rhymers' Club will now rush in—being mostly Irish—and

[101] Davidson to Edmund Gosse, 25 Feb. 1892, quoted in Townsend, *John Davidson*, 58.

review each other's poetry, and dance in triumph: for two years I have been reviewing them, to their disgust with some impartiality.[102]

Davidson's own collection of poems remained largely ignored. 'It is impossible in the case of an unknown or almost unknown man to have the neglect of editors amended', he wrote to an unknown correspondent in March.[103] One of the few notices came from Yeats to whom he had sent a copy on 13 January inscribed: 'W. B. Yeats from J. D.' Describing the Rhymers' Club to the readers of the *Boston Pilot* on 23 April, Yeats singled out John Davidson and Arthur Symons as examples of the 'search for new subject matter, new emotions'. On the face of it, he was being extremely generous in giving them extended coverage, as neither of them had shown himself to be particularly loyal to the Rhymers. His comments on their orginality are astute:

Both writers are, whether they succeed or fail, interesting signs of the times. Not merely are they examples of that desire for new subject matter ... but of the reaction from the super-refinement of much recent life and poetry. The cultivated man has begun a somewhat hectic search for the common pleasures of common men and for the rough accidents of life. The typical young poet of our day is an aesthete with a surfeit, searching sadly for his lost Philistinism, his heart full of an unsatisfied hunger for the commonplace. He is an Alastor tired of his woods and longing for beer and skittles.[104]

What Yeats fails to recognize fully is the fundamental difference between Symons's Baudelairean quest for sensations and the dramatic impersonations of Davidson's 'In a Music-Hall' sequence. Davidson clearly owes something to Browning and the nineteenth-century tradition of the dramatic monologue, but he is also following the characteristic impulse in Scottish poetry to dramatic utterance in the living speech of ordinary people. What Yeats's criticisms of Davidson reveal in the end is Yeats's own taste at the time. He admired the 'haunting and wonderful "Selene Eden"'—a monologue of an erotic dance artiste—but claimed that his enjoyment had been checked continually by 'some crudity of phrase', no doubt the frankness of

---

[102] Davidson to McCormick, 10 Jan. 1892, Glasgow.
[103] Davidson to 'Dear Sir', 2 Mar. 1892, BL.
[104] Yeats, 'The Rhymers' Club' in *Letters to the New Island*, 143.

lines like: 'My girls were nude as they dared be.' Davidson, he concluded, had more 'fire and enthusiasm' than Symons but was too near to the 'din and glitter' of his experiences: 'He has not been able to cast them back in imaginative dimness and distance.' That word 'dim' or 'dimness' was to be a favourite of Yeats in the 1890s and typifies the vagueness of his own youthful poetry. On the contents page of his copy of *In A Music-Hall*, he put a cross beside the titles of the poems he preferred.[105] These were the more romantic poems, 'The Gleeman', 'The Triumph of Love', 'Is Love Worth Learning?', and 'For Lovers'. One wonders whether some of the others influenced Yeats more deeply than he cared to admit. There are close linguistic and thematic parallels, for instance, between Davidson's 'Cheops'— in which the builder of the great Pyramid of Gizah reflects on death and immortality—and Yeats's famous poem 'Sailing to Byzantium' written over thirty years later. Cheops also rejects the mortal momentary life of the dying generations: 'Each generation passes, living, dying, | And thinks itself somewhat— yea, so much worth,'[106] and imagines himself as 'some splendid, noble bird', gleaming spectrally in the night, in defiant transcendence of time and mortality:

> . . . I'd sooner be a beast or bird
>   Than enter once again a human frame;
> For spirits are in human flesh interred
>   Not wedded unto strength, or winged with flame.[107]

Yeats's criticisms were the first public expression of a temperamental difference between the two men that was to have such damaging consequences on Davidson's posthumous literary reputation. It is a characteristic of the literary world at that time that personal antagonisms often found expression in aesthetic disagreements. It was a source of annoyance to Yeats that Davidson dismissed the delicacy of the Rhymers as 'effeminate pedantry' and delighted in the popular and robust. He was particularly offended when Davidson responded impatiently to a reference by Rhys to a connoisseur, with the comment, 'If a man must be a connoisseur, then let him be a connoisseur of woman.'[108] Davidson could undoubtedly be brusque and even

---

[105] Edward O'Shea, *Descriptive Catalogue of W. B. Yeats's Library* (New York and London, 1985).

[106] 'Cheops', ll. 49–50.   [107] 'Cheops', ll. 27–30.

[108] Yeats, *Autobiographies*, 317.

rude. He himself recognized this, and caricatured himself in *Laura Ruthven's Widowhood* in the character of Mr Banderole, 'the most impudent man in London' who is 'rather undersized, with a small dark beard and moustache, and a scalp wig which nobody could have detected',[109] and in Rorison in *Earl Lavender* whose vanity is redeemed by his sense of humour and recognition of merit in others. Yeats recognized that Davidson was able to laugh at himself, but he felt unable to get behind the air of 'Scottish roughness and exasperation'. That exasperation was to a large extent the impatience of an older man, who had experienced more of life. Yet undoubtedly, it also sprang from a sense of frustration at his unacknowledged superiority. Yeats, with poetic ambitions no less strong, seems to have guessed this.

The real conflict came with the publication of an anonymous review of Yeats's *The Countess Kathleen* in the *Daily Chronicle*. The review, which appeared on 1 September, judged the play an artistic failure and concluded that there were 'no lines which go straight home and linger in the memory'.[110] Yeats's father, Jack B. Yeats sent him the notice along with Richard Le Gallienne's enthusiastic review which appeared in the *Star* on the same day—'the poison and the antidote', he called them. He suspected that the unfavourable review might have been written by Davidson, in revenge for his son's attack on *In A Music-Hall*. 'Was it Davidson—as a *tit* for your *tat*?' he asked. 'The tats were provoking and rather unnecessary and since probably totally unexpected therefore the more bewildering and enraging to the fiery Scot.'[111] Yeats was resentful. A month later, seeing another unfavourable review in the same newspaper, this time of Le Gallienne's *English Poems*, he was still sore enough to write to his fellow Rhymer, 'Who is this entirely absurd being who wrote that review. I think it the same man who noticed my book in an even more offensive manner.'[112] His father took a more sanguine view of the whole incident and spoke with a certain respect of Davidson who, he felt, had shown himself unable to be truly malicious.

[109] *Laura Ruthven's Widowhood*, iii. 48.
[110] *Daily Chronicle* (1 Sept. 1892), 3.
[111] J. B. Yeats to W. B. Yeats, 2 Sept. 1892, in *Letters to His Son W. B. Yeats and Others*, ed. Joseph Hone (London, 1944), 53.
[112] W. B. Yeats to Richard Le Gallienne, [*c.*15 Oct. 1892], *Collected Letters of Yeats*, 32.

In fact, there is no evidence, internal or external, to support Davidson's authorship of the *Daily Chronicle* review—quite the contrary. His reviewing at this time was done mainly for the *Speaker*, where he gave generous praise to Le Gallienne's *English Poems* in October. He also wrote a short notice of *The Countess Kathleen* and E. J. Ellis's *Fate in Arcadia* for the *Speaker* the following month. The review tries to be positive, without being enthusiastic, describing Yeats's blank verse as 'often very attractive' and concluding that several of the lyrics 'have a quaint other-world note in them seldom heard nowadays'.[113]

Could Davidson have written two conflicting reports on both Yeats's and Le Gallienne's poetry? It is certainly possible. It might be significant that a week after reviewing Le Gallienne's poems in the *Speaker*, he considered the problem of the critic's changing opinion and concluded that 'first thoughts are best'.[114] Sadly, it was not to matter whether he wrote the offending review or not. Yeats believed he had and harboured feelings of hostility towards him for the rest of his life. He omitted Davidson from his selection for the *Oxford Book of Modern Verse* (1936), and in his memoirs, which had an immense influence on Davidson's reputation, portrayed him as a failure, both as a man and as a poet. His portrait concludes with a cruel echo of the words in the *Daily Chronicle* review which had so rankled him: 'And now no verse of his clings to my memory.'[115] At the time, it must have felt like a conclusive revenge.

III

In those early days in London, Davidson attributed the malice of reviewers to the conditions under which they had to work. 'The ever-increasing numbers, ambitious of literary distinction, who flock to London yearly, to become hacks and journalists, regard the work by which they gain a livelihood as a mere industry, a stepping-stone to higher things', he wrote. 'What wonder if they sometimes take to laying about them with scor-

---

[113] 'Dramatic and Other Verses', *Speaker*, 6 (12 Nov. 1892), 598.
[114] 'The Week', *Speaker*, 6 (29 Oct. 1892), 529.
[115] Yeats, *Autobiographies*, 318.

pions!'[116] He himself tried to avoid malice or michievousness in his reviews, but he began to bear grudges against those who criticized him, and became touchy and scornful. 'Why do you mention the *Athenaeum*?' he asked the publisher and bookseller, Elkin Mathews, in December 1892.[117] 'I have never written for that supercilious paper.' This was four months after a reviewer at the *Athenaeum* had decided that his *In A Music-Hall* poems showed 'minimum ability'.[118]

Davidson was identified at that time with the Liberal faction, because of his association with the *Speaker*. He himself was extremely lukewarm about politics although he shared his editor's admiration for the 84-year-old Gladstone. That summer he felt he had seen one of the most wonderful sights in London when he saw Gladstone walking towards him in an almost deserted Bond Street. It was a Saturday evening about 6 o'clock: the shops were closed and there was nobody within 300 yards of them. 'There was no sound in the street but Gladstone's light tread,' he wrote afterwards, 'for I stood aside till he should pass. . . . Black broadcloth, ordinary silk hat—it was yet to me as if a vision had passed.'[119]

By autumn he had completed another novel, *Baptist Lake*, which he sent to Ward and Downey after it had been turned down by Lawrence and Bullen and by Heinemann.[120] It is a formally eccentric work, cobbling together lifelike realism of the most ordinary kind with elements of satire and improbable romance. The story is set mainly in the north London suburbs where Davidson lived, and develops as an encounter between the Inglises, a straightforward Scottish family recently arrived in London, and Baptist Lake, a decadent socialite and wit. Davidson was strenuously to deny that the character of Baptist Lake was modelled on a well-known personage in the artistic world when the novel appeared eighteen months later, but at the very least, the novel dramatizes the inner conflicts of his own involvement with the Bohemian set into which he was drawn in the company of Barlas, Sherard, and the other fre-

---

[116] 'The Week', *Speaker*, 3 (16 May 1891), 583.
[117] Davidson to Elkin Mathews, 10 Dec. 1892, Reading.
[118] 'Recent Verse', *Athenaeum* (6 Aug. 1892), 190.
[119] *A Random Itinerary* (London, 1894), 156.
[120] Davidson to McCormick, 30 Dec. 1892, Glasgow.

quenters of Charles Street and the Café Royal. The awkwardness of the plot, with its layered and unresolved incongruities, serves to betray rather than conceal this fact. Initially it is the 16-year-old Islay Inglis, an innocent and lovable Scots schoolboy, who befriends Baptist Lake, but then, rather implausibly, the youthful hero gets involved in a fantastic smuggler's plot while his father, John, is shown the bachelor pleasures of the theatre and the middle-class club by Baptist Lake. Here he is introduced to a young attractive widow, Alice Meldrum, who thinks him unmarried. The setting for the novel's denouement is a dinner party at the Inglises' home where Alice Meldrum and Baptist Lake are both guests. Baptist Lake is outshone and finally routed by a rising star in the world of wits, Hector Almond, formerly his *ami damné*, whom Inglis has also invited. Baptist Lake repeats his best stories and *bons mots*—which have provided some of the liveliest moments in the novel—only to have them ring hollow within the homely intimacy of the Inglises' dinner party. Technically it is one of the cleverest moments in Davidson's fiction, structural irony precluding the need for moral comment. The abrupt departure of the *farceur* from John Inglis's life is followed by that of the would-be mistress, Alice Meldrum. Inglis returns remorsefully to the marriage bed and a wife who has tearfully suffered the anguish of jealousy and self-contempt in scenes that have an authentic ring in an otherwise exaggerated plot. Inglis chooses fidelity over promiscuity, duty over the desire to experience life. He explains poignantly the temptation:

'They flattered me these people: how original I was; and the women made love to me; and the man kept telling me—he kept telling me that a man ought to love more than one woman, else his mind grew dull; that all great men had mistresses—.'[121]

The battle between obligation and sexual passion is a dominant theme in Davidson's work. There were certainly plenty of opportunities for infidelity in the circles in which he now moved. Barlas went with other women, some of them prostitutes, and in the saloon bar of the Crown in Charing Cross Road, where Davidson sometimes stopped for a drink, Lionel Johnson, Arthur Symons, and other acquaintances from the

[121] *Baptist Lake*, 298.

Rhymers' Club and the Century Guild of Artists could be found in the company of ladies from the music hall and the Alhambra Ballet. Liebich, who knew Davidson as a family man, noticed that he 'took his obligations to wife and children with the extreme seriousness of the Presbyterian Scotsman—a religious quirk implanted in him by his clergyman father and one that intellectually, he fought, during most of his adult life'.[122] It is significant perhaps, as a clue to Davidson's own sexual conduct, that John Inglis should repent to having been 'unfaithful in my heart'.

Davidson's relationship with his wife's family had improved. Her parents were now affectionately 'Grandpapa and Grand-mama' to the boys. He continued to correspond with Meem. Meem had followed his advice in marrying Jack Stewart, but her troubles had not ended. Davidson's letters to her after her marriage reveal a tact and sensitivity that contrasts sharply with the impression he sometimes gave out in public:

A man is always afraid of a woman, however well he may have known her, after she becomes his wife until he gets to know her again in that new relation. Tell Jack when you write him that you know this, but don't ask him to trust you with all his secrets; say simply, 'when you get to know me better, dear, you'll keep nothing from me.' Many a weak man has been made heroic by being treated always, as if he were already a hero. . . . You have a great career with this man's life and character in your hands: but you must never let him know that either.[123]

Good fortune came to Davidson in November when the reader of the publishing house of the Bodley Head, Richard Le Gallienne, warmly recommended *Fleet Street Eclogues* for publication to the firm's partners, John Lane and Elkin Mathews, whom Davidson referred to jokingly as 'Welkin'. Mathews and Lane were well known to the Rhymers. Mathews, a neighbour of Yeats in Bedford Park, had taken over the stock of *Scaramouch in Naxos* from T. Fisher Unwin at the beginning of 1891, and later that year, the sociable 37-year-old Lane had invited the Rhymers to hold a meeting at his house in Hyde Park. The result of this association was the publication of *The Book of the Rhymers' Club* in February 1892, to which Davidson refused to

122 Liebich, 'John Davidson'.
123 Davidson to Meem, not dated [1892], Princeton.

contribute. Now he approached Mathews and Lane on his own account with his *Fleet Street Eclogues*. He had a personal reason for doing so. He had been accused, no doubt by some of his fellow Rhymers, of being unable to get another publisher than Ward and Downey. What better way to refute this than by having the publishers of *The Book of the Rhymers' Club* bring out a volume of his own verse?[124]

Elkin Mathews, a mild gentlemanly Devon man, had been running a bookshop in Exeter for four years when he and Lane went into partnership. Adopting the name of the famous Devonian, Sir Thomas Bodley, they set up their firm of the Bodley Head at 6B Vigo Street, a narrow thoroughfare connecting Savile Row and Regent Street, in the summer of 1887. J. Lewis May has described it as a 'little box of a place' with a wide window and books tiered from floor to ceiling.[125] There was a trap door leading to the cellar, and a screen to give privacy to the cashier, Roland Clarke. The new firm's first title, Richard Le Gallienne's *My Lady's Sonnets*, set the high standard in production and design that was to make the firm famous. Initially Mathews ran the shop and the business, but in February 1892, the name changed from 'Elkin Mathews of the Bodley Head' to 'Elkin Mathews and John Lane'.

Lane's career at the Bodley Head suggests the extent to which so much of what we identify as the mood of the 1890s—its gaiety, aestheticism, and erotic freedom—was in part the creation of new markets to reflect the dreamed refinements of an emergent generation of aspiring lower-class Englishmen. Lane had begun life as a junior clerk at the Railway Clearing House in Devon before moving to London where he quickly refined away his Devonshire burr. J. Lewis May remembered him as 'a little dapper man' with scrupulously brushed hair, beard turned to a point', and 'big, bluish, and decidedly expressive' eyes, who for all 'his fine clothes and spruce appearance' still 'looked like a farmer'.[126] Lane was the go-getter in the acquisition of new authors, although he relied heavily on the advice of Le Gallienne, who read for him, and on the aesthetic judgement of his assistant, Frederic Chapman, whom he had discovered managing a circulating library in a Leicester bookshop.

---

[124] Davidson to Elkin Mathews and John Lane, 'Tuesday' [1892], Lane.
[125] J. Lewis May, The *Path Through the Wood* (London, 1930), 149.
[126] May, *Path Through the Wood*, 152.

Davidson was anxious that his *Eclogues* should come out before the end of the year. He believed that Ward and Downey were about to publish *Baptist Lake*. 'It is my intention to publish shortly before or shortly after every prose book of mine a book of verse,' he wrote to the Bodley Head: 'you see I am ambitious of a double reputation.'[127] His anxiety was sharpened by the imminent publication of George Douglas's *Living Scotch Poets* which contained a selection of his verses, alongside verses by more famous poets like William Sharp and Robert Louis Stevenson. He believed that the anthology might win more readers to his *Eclogues* if the two books were published simultaneously. Neither *Baptist Lake* nor the Scottish anthology appeared that year, but he had another reason for wishing the immediate publication of his *Eclogues* when *Laura Ruthven's Widowhood* was unexpectedly released before Christmas, only to be dismissed contemptuously by the reviewer at the *Speaker* as 'an absurdly inconsequent tale'.[128] He wrote an emotional letter to Mathews on 18 January:

I wish more than I can say that it had been out by Christmas: it would have served as an antidote against the disastrous effect on my reputation of the recent publication of a novel I devilled for another man three years ago when I first came to London without a penny and knowing nobody.

Although I talk of reputation and desire for a reputation, don't imagine that I estimate it at more than its worth. Reputation means the wherewithal to support my family and myself, and leisure to do good work.[129]

There was an unnecessary panic in all this. Not everyone was to be as dismissive as the reviewer at the *Speaker*, and some even ignored Davidson's substantial contribution—he wrote volumes two and three of the three-decker novel—referring to the book as Dr Wills's novel. But Davidson's fears were real enough to himself. He was approaching his thirty-sixth birthday and felt that his whole future rested on the success or failure of his *Eclogues*. He pleaded desperately that they be issued before Easter. Forgetting his earlier conclusion that *In A Music-Hall* had failed because it had been issued after the Christmas season the previous year, he pressed Mathews with his new theory that

---

[127] Davidson to Mathews and Lane, 'Tuesday' [1892], Lane.
[128] *Speaker*, 6 (3 Dec. 1892), 688.
[129] Davidson to Mathews, 18 Jan. 1893, Reading.

'a striking book published out of season has really a greater chance than if it appears with the crowd':

It is like this: whenever I am delivered of a book, and a publisher has taken it, until it is published I feel like a man whose child is born, indeed, but from whom it has not been detached. Here have I been going about since November with *Fleet-Street Eclogues* hanging to my mind by the still uncut umbilical cord as it were—five months it will be before April. Do relieve me of this burden.[130]

This must have caused the mild, business-like Mathews to raise an eyebrow.

In the event, the book did not appear until April. In February Meem came to stay at Hornsey for a year while her captain husband was at sea. He had succeeded in getting a ship. 'I hope he has been unsuccessful in other directions, and not sent his wife here with a little stow-away on board', he told McCormick.[131] He was melancholy, particularly as the story he was working on refused to get written. He had seen nobody for weeks—

Not Oscar at all, and I am so melancholy I have no desire to, although he is the greatest man, to be without brains, who ever lived. Barlas is in Crieff, did I tell you, writing a novel for a wager. Roberts is—I don't know where . . . and the whole tribe of rhymers and Irish bog trotters among whom I fell when I came to London, more or less dead and done with.[132]

He was like an anxious father awaiting the birth of his first child. At the beginning of March, he travelled to Edinburgh where the book was to be printed. He had a personal reason for the journey which he concealed even from his closest friends. His brother Thomas had been suffering from a depressive illness for some time. Both he and his brother were rebels against their father's fierce temperance convictions, but in Thomas's case the rebellion now proved disastrous. Thomas had been unable to carry on in his mercantile position at Greenock and was at Marchmont Crescent being supported by his mother and sister. Part of the house was let to students and the two women were worried about his presence in the lodgings. He sometimes showed homicidal tendencies, and Helen and Effie Davidson

---

[130] Davidson to Mathews, 18 Jan. 1893, Reading.
[131] Davidson to McCormick, 'Saturday' [1893], Glasgow.   [132] Ibid.

were careful to keep sharp instruments from him.[133] But the situation reached a crisis when he tried to kill his mother with a carving knife hidden under the bed, and the students left the lodgings for a while. Davidson visited Edinburgh several times during this crisis and arranged for his brother to be admitted to Morningside Asylum on 8 April. Thomas was a patient there for six months until 27 September when he was discharged cured.[134]

During that first visit, Davidson visited the offices of the printer each day. On arriving at the printers on 3 March, he was alarmed to discover that the manuscript and first proofs had failed to arrive. There were urgent telegrams and exchanges of letters between Davidson and Vigo Street. He stayed in Edinburgh for a week, promising Mathews that he should 'in that time see all the proofs and have the paging rearranged'.[135] On his return to London, the problems were not over. He complained that the final proofs kept coming back to him with 'all the old mistakes' and disagreed with Mathews over the advertisement for the book. 'A sore point with me', he wrote.[136] He confessed to finding it difficult to write about himself and produced notes that were overmodest. Mathews put forward his own suggestions when Davidson called at Vigo Street on 31 March. Davidson disliked them, but said nothing until he received a copy of the advertisement, when he wrote to Mathews asking him to postpone publication in favour of a paragraph about him by William Wallace in the 'London Letter' of the *Glasgow Herald*. He had been consolidating his links with Wallace, the paper's literary editor, since the beginning of the year, and was at this time trying to interest Mathews in a collection of humorous Scottish sketches by the Glasgow journalist. 'I have not seen it,' he wrote to Mathews of the paragraph in the *Herald*, 'but I imagine it would do as an introduction to *Fleet Street Eclogues*.'[137] Whatever the difficulties between author and publisher these were finally dispelled when Mathews agreed to

---

[133] This story is told in a letter from William McCormick to Edmund Gosse, 6 Dec. 1898, BL.

[134] Medical records. For this information I am indebted to the Lothian Health Board.

[135] Davidson to Mathews, 3 Mar. 1893, Reading.

[136] Davidson to Mathews, letter card 27 Mar. 1893, Reading.

[137] Davidson to Mathews, 'Friday' [Apr. 1893], Reading.

a buckram binding. Davidson's nervousness gave way to happiness. 'I would have fought a whole hour by Shrewsbury clock over that buckram suit', he wrote to thank Mathews on 12 April.[138]

The book appeared at last in an edition of 300 copies. It appealed immediately to London bookmen. Its author was praised in the *Daily Chronicle* as 'Pan in Fleet Street'; the reviewer at the *Speaker* chose a more accurate classical analogy in headlining his article 'Theocritus in Fleet Street'. It was Davidson's first real taste of success, and he was genuinely surprised by some of the reviews. 'I am certain Balaam intended to curse', he wrote to Mathews after reading a favourable notice in the *St James's Gazette*: 'his ass must have spoken'.[139] Another surprise came from George Cotterell, the influential critic at the *Academy*. Davidson remembered his review of *Scaramouch* and concluded: 'He will be civil and good-natured, but is rather weak-kneed, and praises and finds fault with the wrong things.'[140] In fact, Cotterell wrote a glowing review of the book, praising it 'in its kind' as 'perhaps the most memorable volume of the year'.[141]

A second edition was planned almost at once. When it appeared in July, Mathews and Lane were able to include an impressive list of favourable press notices. To Davidson, the most gratifying reviews had been those in the *Star* and the *Daily Chronicle*. His satisfaction was not diminished when he learned that the author of both was Richard Le Gallienne who, as the firm's reader, had a vested interest in the book's success. 'I have just learned that you are the gracious critic in the *Daily Chronicle* as well as in the *Star*', he wrote to Le Gallienne on 11 May.

I thank you again and again. Your reviews have given me more pleasure than anything that has been written about book of mine (*sic*); but I discriminate, as I am certain you would wish me to, and recognise the magnanimous speaking-trumpet of a generous man wishing to make people hear.[142]

Le Gallienne had secured the influential post of literary critic for the *Star* with the help of John Lane who was adept at set-

---

138 Davidson to Mathews, 12 Apr. 1893, Reading.
139 Davidson to Mathews, 11 May 1893, Reading.
140 Davidson to Mathews, 8 May 1893, Reading.
141 '*Fleet Street Eclogues*. By John Davidson', *Academy*, 44 (8 July 1893), 24–5.
142 Davidson to Le Gallienne, 11 May 1893, Texas.

ting up these networks of influence. Less than a month after accepting Davidson's *Fleet Street Eclogues* for publication, the Bodley Head drew Davidson's attention to a recently published collection of short stories by Frederick Wedmore, *Renunciations*, which they wanted reviewed in the *Speaker*. 'If you send it to the *Speaker* in time to be delivered on Wednesday morning,' Davidson had written to Mathews at the time, 'I am certain to be able to ask for it.'[143] In the months ahead he publicized several Bodley Head publications through his column in the *Speaker*— notably Addington Symond's *In the Key of Blue*, Le Gallienne's *Religion of a Literary Man*, as well as his own *Fleet Street Eclogues*.

With the success of *Fleet Street Eclogues*, Davidson felt he had made his mark in the capital. Until then, much of the work he had published in London had been written during his years as a schoolmaster in Scotland. This is not to say that he was more provincial than the other men who flocked to London at this time to try literature as a career. As Yeats was to recall, they were all of them provincials when they started out: he, Symons, Davidson, Le Gallienne.[144] But from *Fleet Street Eclogues* on, Davidson wholeheartedly adopted metropolitan life as the subject of his writing. It was the reality from which he was to survey the alternative worlds of nature, as in the *Eclogues*, or his own past.

That April he began a series of walks and outings that would make the city and the suburbs his own. It was common near the end of the Victorian period for rank-and-file workers, journalists among them, to take a train on holidays and weekends to such centres as Chorleywood, Dorking, Richmond, or Epping, to explore the countryside in a walk of ten or more miles before returning to London by the evening train. Davidson's journeys were of this sort. They were less exotic than the vagabondage which took Wilde, Symons, and other acquaintances to France and Italy, but it was what he could afford. He followed his old principle of serendipity, taking no guidebooks. But there was a will and pattern to his wandering. In acknowledging this paradox, he dubbed himself 'a random itinerant'.

J. Lewis May, then the stock boy at the Bodley Head, accompanied him on some of these tramps and remembered his

---

[143] Davidson to Mathews, 10 Dec. 1892, Reading.
[144] Yeats, *Autobiographies*, 166.

high spirits and attic talk.[145] He set out on the first of his outings—to Epping Forest—at the beginning of April, dressed in a fore-and-aft cap, and a faded light tweed suit, with a shoulder satchel containing a piece of pie, some bread and butter, and three books—Shakespeare's *Sonnets*, George Wither's *Mistress of Philarete*, and Carlyle's *Past and Present*. He followed this up on the 22nd with a trip to the Chiltern Hills in Buckinghamshire. He spoke of enjoying 'this going about catching nature in the act.'[146] He had never been on a chalk escarpment before and was intrigued by the ploughed land on the hillsides. The papers that morning were full of news of the second reading of Gladstone's Home Rule Bill in the House of Commons, and he was amused to meet an irate farmer who believed that Gladstone hypnotized people to make them think as he thought. He wrote accounts of these outings for publication in the *Glasgow Herald* and the *Speaker*, possibly influenced by a series of similar articles which had been appearing in the *Speaker* under the title 'A Rambler in London', although he also had literary models in De Quincey, Richard Jefferies, and Robert Louis Stevenson.

He was in high spirits, and clearly enjoying his new role as celebrity and sophisticated cosmopolite. McCormick was in London and he invited him to a Rhymers' meeting at the Cheshire Cheese, even though he had been refusing their invitation cards for almost a year.[147] On 30 April he wrote to William Canton to arrange a meeting at the Grosvenor Club the following afternoon. Canton was an old acquaintance from his Glasgow days, who had given up his job as sub-editor and leader writer with the *Glasgow Herald* two years earlier to take over as general manager of the London publishing house of William Isbister and Co. which owned the *Contemporary Review*, the *Sunday Magazine*, and *Good Words*. Davidson admired his poetry, particularly his *Legend of a Stone Age*, with its infusion of science into poetry, and his winning *Poems of Childhood*. He found Canton's company irritating, but had decided, 'There is no getting rid of or resisting him. With all his turkey-cockishness he is good-hearted, and insists on being on intimate terms.'[148] 'We

---

[145] J. Lewis May, *John Lane and the Nineties* (London, 1936), 102–3.
[146] Davidson to McCormick, 'Thursday' [1893], Glasgow.   [147] Ibid.
[148] Davidson to McCormick, 'Saturday' [1891], Glasgow.

shall take a little cup of tea somewhere,' he wrote in anticipation of their meeting, 'dine in the St James's Restaurant to the
"music of the band", and then drink whiskey in the Café Royal,
every man jack of us courageously and quietly at his own expense. I forgot the absinthe: you must take tea earlier than five.
At that hour we shall take the absinthe—the proper time as a
whet for dinner.'[149]

His 'itineraries' continued through the summer, with visits to
Blackheath and Greenwich Park at the beginning of May, and
further trips to Epping Forest and Amersham in Buckinghamshire. Everywhere the earth was baking and cracked because of
the fantastic heat. He spent Whit Monday at Hampton Court
Park where he watched the whirling, murmuring crowds of
visitors in and around the palace with the amused fascination of
a journalist in search of copy. He was still enjoying the 'booming reviews' of his *Fleet Street Eclogues*—'more than I should', he
confessed to Canton the following day, when he wrote to thank
him for placing so many of his 'things' with the Isbister magazines.[150] Evidently their day out together had been for reasons
other than simply pleasure.

Canton took six pieces—three poems and three prose
sketches—all of which appeared pseudonymously in the Isbister
magazines at intervals over the next twelve months. 'Chrysanthemums', a slight and charming piece of magazine verse about
a child's pleading for a bedtime story, appears to have been
inspired by Canton, who had lost his first child, a daughter, in
1877, and who was already at work on the idea that became *The
Invisible Playmate*. The immense popularity of this work lay in its
appeal to the Victorian cult of the child. Davidson's poem
touches the same emotions. It must have delighted him to see
his verses in the June issue of *Good Words* which he himself had
pored over as a boy.[151]

The success of his *Eclogues*, the spendid weather, and the
invigorating effects of his walking tours had restored to him the

---

[149] Davidson to William Canton, 30 Apr. 1893, Princeton.
[150] Davidson to Canton, 23 May 1893, Princeton.
[151] His contributions were 'Chrysanthemums' and 'An Ideal Shoeblack', *Good
Words* (June 1893); 'A Forgotten Italian Worthy', *Good Words* (Sept. 1893); 'The
Birds of Summer', *Sunday Magazine* (June 1893); 'April', *Sunday Magazine* (Apr.
1894); and 'Among the Anarchists', *Good Words* (Feb. 1894).

feelings of his youth. It was an age he looked back on with special tenderness. He found an echo of that mood in Richard Le Gallienne's *The Book Bills of Narcissus* which he read that summer. He wrote to Le Gallienne to congratulate him:

Narcissus is a very absolute book; the finest youthful book I have read, and the only extant record of a stage, of a mood, that many men have falsified in the attempt to catch and fix; it is a species of miracle to have written a contemporary, or almost contemporary account of such a frame of mind and fashion of feeling. I am thinking of Thackeray's mutilation and massacre of his youth in Pendennis, and the dull prig which Goethe makes of himself in *Whilhelm Meister* and the autobiography.[152]

He and Maggie made friends with the Le Galliennes that year. In November, when Le Gallienne's wife, Mildred, was nearing the end of her pregnancy, Davidson sent them a poem, 'What Little Boat Comes o'er the Sea', written in a copy of his book of aphorisms, *Sentences and Paragraphs,* which Lawrence and Bullen published that month. Le Gallienne showed the poem to Lane, and wrote: 'Davidson has written one of the sweetest baby-poems for us that I have ever read. It touches us no little. Isn't it beautiful? Still, as in Samson's day, out of the strong comes forth sweetness.'[153]

In June, Davidson undertook a systematic tour of outer London at a radius of eight miles from Charing Cross, beginning at Turnpike Lane and ending in Green Lanes at the Great Eastern Station. A month later he returned to the Chilterns, travelling as far as High Wycombe, where he waited on a wet, ghostly evening for the train back to London. It was the last of his summer wanderings. On the 28th he sent a collected version of his travel sketches under the title *A Random Itinerary* to the Bodley Head with some sketch maps of his journeys, including a map of the 'Suburban Tour' which he thought 'ought to be found piquant'.[154] He wanted an advance of £20 on an edition of 600 copies and asked for an early decision, perhaps less

---

[152] Davidson to Le Gallienne, 7 July 1893, Texas.

[153] Richard Le Gallienne to John Lane, Nov. 1893, quoted in J. Lewis May, *John Lane* (London, 1936), 90–1.

[154] Davidson to Mathews and Lane, 28 July 1893, Lane.

anxious about the topical subject-matter of the book than by the 'payment in full' he had received that morning for his first 300 *Eclogues*—a dispiriting £6 3s.

Immediate relief came in the form of a job working nights on a paper, to replace a man on holiday. He referred to it as 'a bitter pill'.[155] He was unable to get away when Mathews tried to arrange a meeting on 4 August. In the six days since the submission of his manuscript, Le Gallienne had completed his reader's report. He recommended publication, but objected that Davidson was sometimes repetitive and had not worked up his material sufficiently. Davidson received a copy of this report from Mathews, who evidently hoped he would agree to some revision. He refused. 'The itinerant has made as much out of his ideas as he intended to, i.e. as he possibly could', he wrote, 'all the highest literature consists of jottings, e.g. the opening of the first chapter of Genesis; Lycidas, and the best dialogues in Shakespeare'.[156] It was left to Le Gallienne to admit that perhaps he had been a little severe on the 'itinerary', although sticking to his view that the book as a whole could have been made more interesting by more careful editing and heightening.

The modern reader who looks for design and directed impressionism in travel literature may well share Le Gallienne's opinion. But the refusal to strain after mood or effect, or to impose afterthoughts upon experience, had, since his Edinburgh days, been the whole basis of Davidson's artistic search for true knowledge: spontaneity was the guarantee of veracity. In playful defence, he wrote an 'Epilogue' in the form of a dialogue between the Itinerant, really himself, and the Disputant, Le Gallienne. The poem 'A Ballad of a Musician' formed a coda to this. It was added at the last moment, in belated response to the Bodley Head's wish that the book should contain some verse,[157] and tells the story of a musician whose dedication to his art brings starvation and death to himself and his family. The tale ends in heaven where the musician hears his own music and learns from God that his labours have conquered 'Time's obscure distress':

[155] Davidson to Mathews, 4 Aug. 1893, Texas.
[156] Quoted in Nelson, *Early Nineties*, 255.
[157] Davidson to Mathews and Lane, 'Sunday' [1893], Lane.

He doubted; but God said, 'Even so,
Nothing is lost that's wrought with tears:
The music that you made below
Is now the music of the spheres.'[158]

It was evidently written to console himself in the face of his own mounting financial difficulties.

As on previous occasions, the final stages of publication were a time of worry and frustration. He fretted over the proofs and the carelessness of the printers, and began to fear a repeat of the circumstances which had led to the failure of *In A Music-Hall*. In October he wrote to the Bodley Head assistant, Frederic Chapman, pleading for the book to be got out at once and asking for the date to be altered to 1894.[159] The publishers responded to their anxious author, and the book appeared in the last week in November, in time to catch the Christmas trade. It was beautifully designed with interrelated yellow coils by Laurence Houseman, who also provided a frontispiece illustrating Davidson's ballad when one by William Rothenstein failed to materialize.

Houseman had also been dissatisfied with the printers, J. Miller & Son of Edinburgh,[160] but Davidson's mood of exasperation and vexation was undoubtedly fuelled by another fierce quarrel that he was involved in at this time. Hoping to cash in on the success of the *Eclogues*, Mathews and Lane had decided to re-issue *Scaramouch in Naxos* under their own imprint, but with the original title restored. Lane had also unearthed copies of *Bruce* and *Smith* which he thought would be attractive to collectors of first editions. Hearing of their plans, Davidson came forward with another proposal—that instead of trying to sell copies of first editions, they should publish a new, one-volume edition of all his plays. 'I really think it would be good business', he wrote. 'Although my judgment is doubtless warped by my belief that these plays are much better than anyone imagines.'[161] Suddenly, there were practical difficulties. His old friend William McCormick's partnership with Frederick

---

[158] 'A Ballad of Heaven' (formerly 'A Ballad of a Musician'), ll. 101–4.
[159] Davidson to Frederic Chapman, 19 Oct. 1893, Lane.
[160] Nelson, *Early Nineties*, 340.
[161] Davidson to Lane, 'Wednesday' [1893], Harlin O'Connell Collection, Princeton.

Wilson had long since dissolved, and the firm had gone into receivership in 1890. The remainder of his *Bruce*, about fifty copies, had gone to the binder, Gardner of Paisley, along with some copies of his novel, *The North Wall*. Davidson offered Gardner £2 for the complete stock, only to receive a demand for £5 5*s*. 8*d*. plus 3*s*. 6*d*. carriage. He thought this outrageous, particularly as *Bruce* had cost him £2 to start with. Some haggling followed, with Gardner settling for £3 for *Bruce* and 5*s*. for *The North Wall*, on the understanding that the copies of the play were to be destroyed.[162] The way ahead seemed clear. Mathews and Lane generously agreed to pay him 1*s*. for each copy sold. On 2 September he announced the forthcoming volume in his column in the *Speaker*, with the news that 'a frontispiece by Mr. Aubrey Beardsley, representing the scene from *Scaramouch in Naxos*, will contain portraits of a number of living celebrities'.

Unfortunately, this prominent advertisement brought his plans to the attention of his first publishers, who came noisily forward to declare their rights. Frederick Wilson, whom Davidson described venomously as 'one of the worst types of Scotchman to deal with . . . very small, squints abominally, legs misshapen',[163] sent a threatening letter to the Bodley Head, claiming that *Smith* was the property of his new firm of Frederick W. Wilson and Co. Davidson wrote to him, offering him 9*d*. per copy, which he altered to 6*d*. per copy and 3*d*. for the sheets when his first letter went unanswered. When he wrote a third time withdrawing all offers, Wilson suddenly broke silence to announce that he wanted 1*s*. 6*d*. per copy and intended to protect his interest.[164] At this point Lane decided he had better act for Davidson and travelled to Scotland armed with a four-page account of Davidson's dealings with the Glasgow publisher, entitled 'After-Piece to *Smith*'.[165]

But Wilson was not the only villain in the piece. On 14 September, Unwin also demanded angrily to know why Davidson had not consulted him before arranging for a collected edition of his *Plays*. Davidson pointed out that 'technically' his early plays had been published 'not by you, but by me',

---

[162] Davidson to Mathews and Lane, 'Tuesday' [1893], O'Connell, Princeton.
[163] Davidson to Lane, 'Thursday' [Oct. 1893], O'Connell, Princeton.
[164] Nelson, *Early Nineties*, 231.
[165] 'Afterpiece to *Smith*' [Oct. 1893], O'Connell, Princeton.

and in apparent response to some comment Unwin had made, reminded him that 'personalities cannot help us in the matter'. This high-handed reproach served only to aggravate the situation. In the exchange of letters that followed, Davidson dismissed scornfully the idea that Unwin had helped to promote his first book—*Scaramouch* was in fact his fourth—and expressed surprise that he should still have copies when the entire remainder had been sold to Elkin Mathews.[166] He accused Unwin of professional negligence, claiming that the publisher had exploited his ignorance and destroyed the commercial value of his book by agreeing to his naïve proposal in 1890 that his *Plays* be issued as a 'second edition'. Tempers were hot, and when Davidson threatened to take legal action if Unwin should attempt to re-issue his *Scaramouch*, the publisher issued counter-threats of litigation. The laws of literary property were confused at that time, and some publishers did act unscrupulously, but Davidson found it irksome to accept that his books were not his own property, even after they had been published. This made him blind to his own part in the quarrel. 'Spleen can drive an effeminate man to extraordinary depths of stupidity', he told his publishers, and proposed that they print his correspondence with Unwin in the form of a pamphlet entitled 'Scaramouch in Paternoster Row: A Fable for Publishers'. The quarrel had excited his imagination, and he saw them being 'hailed as the champion of the author' for throwing down 'the gauntlet against all the old traditions—the colleague, not the adversary, of the author'.[167] An alarmed Mathews and Lane got him to recognize the absurdity of the pamphlet, and suggested that he send the correspondence instead to the Society of Authors. The society's secretary, G. Herbert Thring, took up the case, but he was prevented from publishing the letters in the society's organ, the *Author*, when Unwin withheld his consent.[168] Davidson was disgruntled. 'What good are these people—what good will they ever do if they don't take an opportunity when they get one?' he asked his publishers. 'It's just those letters that one wouldn't consent to publish, that ought to be!'[169] But the

[166] Davidson to Unwin, 21, 22, 23 Sept. 1893, Berg.
[167] Davidson to Mathews and Lane, 'Thursday' [c.23 Oct. 1893], O'Connell, Princeton.
[168] Davidson to G. Herbert Thring, 27 Sept., 23 Oct., and 3 Nov. 1893, Berg.
[169] Davidson to Mathews and Lane, 'Thursday' [c.23 Oct. 1893], O'Connell, Princeton.

intervention of the Society of Authors had its effect, and Unwin withdrew from the field.

Davidson was in Birmingham in November to see the proofs of his *Plays* through the final perilous stages of printing. By December he was back in London and in desperate need of money. In spite of his efforts that year, in spite of the critical acclaim of his *Fleet Street Eclogues*, he was still a penniless author. He took the manuscript of a completed novel to Lane, in the hope of obtaining an advance. He called at Vigo Street on the 19th—his son Sandy's birthday—only to learn that Le Gallienne had advised against publication. In despair, he decided to try Ward and Downey the next day, but they were unable to advance him anything until January, and in any case wanted a week to consider it. He tried to be courageous. He wrote with some emotion to Le Gallienne, telling him not to be upset at having found the manuscript unsatisfactory 'because it is first of all necessary to do one's duty', but denying the idea that the book had been got up hastily: 'If you saw the original draft—scored and rescored, holding your opinion you would wonder. I began it in February and wrote it in such genial hours as occurred or as I could compel, and if it will not do, then it is time for the pistol.'[170] He clung to the fading hope that Ward and Downey would take it, like 'racing' men who 'sometimes back their fancies through thick and thin', but he requested Le Gallienne, as his friend, that if Ward and Downey or anybody else published it, he was to decline to review it 'on any account'.

The same raw candour is to be found in the letter he wrote to Lane that same day, begging for £15 out of the £20 of royalties he believed he might be owed. His situation was desperate:

The state of Denmark is unsound to the degree that we have only £1.10.0 in the world, and nothing due till away in January sometime when a cheque for perhaps £6 at the outside may come in. . . . If you could do this but this once more, I think I shall never be in such straits again for I find your prompt good word for me has already borne fruit at the *Chronicle*.[171]

He ended by congratulating Yeats who had just been commissioned by Lawrence and Bullen for a popular edition of Blake's poems for the Muses Library. It was guaranteed the kind of

---

[170] Davidson to Le Gallienne, 20 Dec. 1893, Texas.
[171] Davidson to Lane, 20 Dec. 1893, NLS.

success that his own modest volume of *obiter dicta* for the same publisher could never hope to achieve. 'Lucky for Yeats: I shall signalize the event by praising his edition of Blake if I possibly can', he wrote generously. The eccentric spring-like weather he had so enjoyed on visits to Surrey and Epping Forest in November had now given way to rain and icy winds. He had a cold before Christmas and did not see Quiller-Couch's review of *A Random Itinerary* in the *Speaker*, giving the warmest praise of him yet written. But if he had, he could not have responded with anything other than grim irony to Quiller-Couch's expressed satisfaction that, 'Mr. Davidson writes with a thankful heart, and it is so rare just now to find an author who is thankful, even though he get many guineas per thousand words.'[172]

[172] A Literary Causerie', 8 (23 Dec. 1893), 700–1.

3
Success 1894–1896

I

The year 1894 began inauspiciously for Davidson. Everyone in the house was ill, except Maggie. Sandy had a prodigious and persistent cough.[1] He himself was laid up for a fortnight with the cold he had caught before Christmas. In a letter to Lane, he identified it as 'a Scotch cold and the first I have had since I left Scotland. This disease consists of a mangle, a steam-hammer, and a reaping machine all operating upon you at once.'[2] When he eventually saw Quiller-Couch's review, he was not in the mood to be thankful, as that morning the pipes had burst in the back kitchen, and the thaw had come.

His irascibility over minor misfortunes masked a deeper despair. He was desperately short of money. In a letter that dates from this time, he wrote to Lane begging forgiveness for having quarrelled at their last meeting; apparently, he had gone to Vigo Street to ask for money and had ended by accusing Lane of cheating him: 'When I saw that I had made a mistake I expressed regret at once, and here I say again I am very sorry I yielded to an inferior word and spoke so inconsiderately and petulantly.' The letter ends by humbly requesting a loan: 'My landlord presses me for rent and I need £5 to make it up. If I could have the sum to account—of anything, I should be deeply grateful.'[3]

He and Lane had become friends during the difficult negotiations to regain the copyright of his plays. He attended an afternoon tea party at Lane's house at 37 Southwick Street at the end of January, having recovered from his cold. Lane's entertainments brought him into contact with London's coming men in the world of literature and art. Women were not

---

[1] Davidson to William McCormick, 29 Dec. 1893, Glasgow.
[2] Davidson to John Lane, 'Tuesday' [1894], NLS.
[3] Davidson to Lane, not dated [1894], NLS.

absent either, among them the boyish Edith Nesbit, with whom
he was soon on friendly terms. He got to know Edmund Gosse
who that year was still 'Mr Gosse', but who was soon to be a
friend, with Gosse sending tickets to the unveiling of the Keats
Memorial in Hampstead Parish Church that July. He also met
the young Grant Richards and Max Beerbohm, who were to
become close friends in later years. Max had been introduced
to the Lane circle the previous autumn by the artist William
Rothenstein, the two having met while Rothenstein was in
Oxford preparing *Oxford Characters* for the Bodley Head. In
his memoirs, Rothenstein remembers how at first he coupled
Davidson with Lane's other star poet, William Watson, as he
often met them together at the Hogarth Club when Lane was
entertaining his authors. He wanted to draw them together.
Davidson was willing, but Watson preferred to sit alone.[4] His
pastel drawing of Davidson shows him lounging nonchalantly
in dandyish waistcoat and bow tie, with a monocle dangling
from his neck. Rothenstein was astonished when he learned
from Beerbohm that Davidson wore a toupée. According to
Beerbohm, he wore it not from vanity, but because he was afraid
a bald head would prejudice his chances of getting work as a
journalist. Davidson's wig was a source of amusement and some
ridicule among his acquaintances. He himself suspected this
and sometimes lifted it off his head when in boisterous mood.
Yeats found this distasteful, but Edith Nesbit took a less corseted
view, and used to describe how, when playing cricket on the
South Downs, Davidson would carefully hang his wig on the
stumps.[5] Rothenstein himself came to recognize 'a serious-
minded, straight hitting Scot' behind the dandy of his portrait.
He developed a great respect for him and wondered how a man
like Lane managed to keep authors like Davidson and William
Watson.

The truth was that Lane made his authors feel important. He
was also a go-getter. That year he launched his famous quarterly
the *Yellow Book*. Some who were in London during the 1890s
were surprised at the later glamorization of the period, and at
the importance attached to the magazine. To a young Maurice

[4] William Rothenstein, *Men and Memories* (London, 1931), 181.
[5] Doris Langley Moore, *E. Nesbit: A Biography* (London, 1933), 128.

Baring, London did not appear particularly erotic or exciting; nor did he remember the *Yellow Book* as being so very different from other literary reviews of that time, apart from Aubrey Beardsley's drawings in the early numbers.[6] William Watson, a reluctant contributor to the magazine, was to write rather caustically in later years of being 'quite unaware' whilst the 1890s were running 'that the world was being suffused with the hue of jaundice'.[7] But while London for some was as it had always been, others felt that times were changing and that they were part of the new modernity.

There are conflicting accounts of the origins of the *Yellow Book*, but all have one thing in common: the excitement of the participants. It used to be thought that the magazine was first conceived by Aubrey Beardsley during a champagne dinner party thrown by Lane at the Devonshire Club in February 1894, with Davidson seconding the idea and Henry Harland appointed on the spot as editor.[8] This incident may have happened, but the idea for a new kind of periodical in which the artwork would be independent of the literature had been forming in the mind of the excitable Henry Harland since the previous summer, which he and his wife Alice had spent in the company of Charles Conder, Alfred Thornton, D. S. MacColl and other young artists and writers at a holiday cottage, that they playfully named 'The Grob', at Saint-Marguerite in Brittany.[9] In a skit written many years later, Max Beerbohm remembers hearing of the *Yellow Book* in the late autumn of 1893:

Scene: Cambridge Street, Pimlico
Time: An afternoon in late autumn of 1893
Persons: Aubrey Beardsley and myself
AB: 'How are you? Sit down! Most Exciting! John Lane wants to bring out a Quarterly—Writings and Drawings—Henry Harland to be Literary Editor—Me to be Art Editor. Great fun. Not a thing like the *Edinburgh* or the *Quarterly*. Not just a *paper* thing. A *bound* thing: a real

---

[6] Paul Horgan, *Maurice Baring Restored* (London, 1970), 125.

[7] Quoted in James G. Nelson, *The Early Nineties: A View From the Bodley Head* (Cambridge, Mass., 1971), 301.

[8] Patrick R. Chalmers, *Kenneth Grahame: Life, Letters, and Unpublished Work* (London, 1933), 66.

[9] Katherine Lyon Mix, *A Study in Yellow: The Yellow Book and Its Contributors* (London, 1960), 64–7.

book, bound in good thick boards. *Yellow* ones. Bright yellow, and it's going to be called *The Yellow Book*.'[10]

The date may be correct, although it conflicts with another version of events in which Harland and Beardsley approached Lane with the idea after a convivial lunch at Harland's house in Cromwell Road on New Year's Day.[11] Certainly by early January rumours of the new magazine were already circulating in London literary circles. It seems likely that Lane was behind events such as the Devonshire Club dinner in February at which the magazine was spontaneously announced to enthusiastic gatherings. He was to stage-manage the launch until the end, arranging a surprise interview with the *Pall Mall Gazette* a week before the release, in which he was reported to be 'quietly walking down Charing Cross Road, when a *Pall Mall Gazette* interviewer suddenly darted from his place of concealment, and held a note-book and pencil to the head of the publisher before he had time to realise'.[12] According to Lane, the original intention had been to bind the quarterly in yellow wrappers, like the French novels, and hence the title.

Elkin Mathews was less enthusiastic about the new magazine which Harland's advertisement promised would have 'the courage of its modernity, and not tremble at the frown of Mrs. Grundy'. Beardsley's illustration depicted Mathews as Pierrot looking disapprovingly on as a 'new woman' browses for books outside the Vigo Street shop. Davidson's name appears among the list of contributors along with Max Beerbohm, George Egerton, Edmund Gosse, and Richard Le Gallienne, as well as several of his former companions at the Rhymers—Rhys, Yeats, Dowson, Symons, and Lionel Johnson. Davidson contributed 'Two Songs' to the first issue, which appeared on 15 April—'London', which echoes the feeling of Wordsworth's sonnet 'Composed upon Westminster Bridge', and 'Down-a-Down', which celebrates spring in the countryside. The songs neatly complement each other and were appropriate

[10] Max Beerbohm to Katherine Lyon Mix, 24 June 1930, in *Letters of Max Beerbohm*, ed. Rupert Hart-Davis (London, 1988), 176.

[11] Mix, *Study in Yellow*, 69–70.

[12] 'The Yellow Book: An Interview with Its Publisher', *Pall Mall Gazette* (11 Apr. 1894), 4.

to the season when the new periodical with its yellow cover suddenly appeared in the bookstores and news-stands around London.

The first edition of 5,000 copies sold quickly, and within days the press delivered its verdict. A few, like Grant Richards, were disappointed that there was nothing in it that might not have appeared in a family magazine.[13] Articles by Dr Richard Garnett, George Saintsbury, and Arthur Waugh, and drawings by Sir Frederic Leighton were hardly likely to satisfy those who had expected something new. But in general the response was one of almost unanimous contempt and derision. Criticism was directed mainly at its tasteless cover and at the eccentricities of Beardsley's drawings, particularly his elongated portrait of the actress, Mrs Patrick Campbell. But there were also expressions of outrage at the contribution of the aesthetes, particularly Symons's daring verses on boulevard love, 'Stella Maris', and Max Beerbohm's 'In Defence of Cosmetics', which many failed to detect as burlesque. The *Speaker* expressed surprise that Davidson, Dr Garnett, Henry James, and Sir Frederick Leighton 'should have joined these strolling players and donned the yellow suit!'[14] The moral pomposity of conventional literary circles only served to increase the delight of Lane and his editors. It was the *succès de scandale* they had hoped for.

As subscribers pored over the contents of the magazine on the day of its issue, those who had produced it were gathering with their spouses and friends for a celebratory dinner at the Hôtel d'Italie at 52 Old Compton Street in Soho. In the early part of that year, Davidson had resisted Lane's attempts to persuade him to attend the Booksellers' Dinner:

Your kindness about this dinner will be I am sorry to say wasted on me in so far as you have my thanks. I have no means of appearing in the ordinary garb of civilization, and am not likely to be able to do so ever apparently. My attempt to go among men must end; firstly I am unsuited for it naturally except in circumstances which can never arrive; secondly I can't afford it; thirdly I have undertaken a piece of

[13] 'The Book World: A Literary Causerie', *Great Thoughts*, 3rd series, 3 (26 May 1894), 123–4.
[14] 'A Yellow Melancholy', *Speaker*, 9 (28 Apr. 1894), 468–9.

frightful drudgery which will last me a month or six weeks, and which if I interrupt it for anything in the shape of entertainment might not be completed in time. It can't be helped.[15]

Behind all his excuses lay the misery and resentment of being poor. His attempt to be manly, and to thank Lane for all he had done, reveals a depressed man:

It is something, it is great, and high even, in a certain measure and kind, as Cromwell—who was the greatest man that ever lived—would have said, to know that one's work, such as it is, is not altogether despised. You have made men know of me: that is a great part of my ambition, and for that I shall always be greatly beholden to you. Knowing that when I die I cease for ever, I should like the memory of me to last a little.[16]

The early months of the year had been difficult, and he had become more touchy and withdrawn as a result. His friends and acquaintances noticed the change. Both Rothenstein and Lewis May recognized that he did not really belong among the aesthetes and decadents with whom they had associated him initially. Even Yeats, who already knew this, was disconcerted by his roughness when he met him in the British Museum Reading Room. Davidson claimed to be 'loafing' and writing poetry. Although Yeats failed to grasp the special significance the word had for Davidson, he rightly sensed the note of wounded pride. Davidson told Yeats that he had been writing prose for a long time and had decided he might just as well write what he liked as he would starve in any case.[17] It amazed him that people 'whose bread and butter is found' should look for work reviewing.[18]

In February, out of necessity, he had begun a series of articles about the Cinque Ports and the surrounding country for the *Glasgow Herald*. He asked Canton about getting a two-month pass for the South-Eastern Railway, as he found that as he went further afield he made less money from the expedition.[19] He had already visited Halstead in January and been down to Romney Marsh in early February. His newspaper account of his visit to Romney Marsh was to provide him with the imagery and

---

[15] Davidson to Lane, 'Monday' [April 1894], NLS.   [16] Ibid.
[17] W. B. Yeats, *Autobiographies* (London, 1955), 315–16.
[18] Davidson to William Canton, 'Friday' [1893], Princeton.   [19] Ibid.

movement of his famous short lyric, 'In Romney Marsh' in which we follow the poet on his journey to Dymchurch Wall and back again. In fact, during this visit, Davidson did not actually see Dymchurch Wall, but only heard about it from a barmaid as he waited in Dymchurch for the Folkestone bus that would take him on the first leg of his journey back to London. But the other elements in the poem are as he described them in the newspaper article: the singing south-west wind; the humming telegraph wire from New Romney to Hythe; the masts wagging their tops; and the effects of sea and evening sky. 'Nature hypnotised me, as it will anyone who submits', he wrote of that memorable day.[20]

This method of writing a prose account of his experience before turning it into poetry was to become a lifelong habit. The practice has a long tradition. Ben Jonson, for instance, wrote all his verses first in prose. It might surprise us, as it would seem to offend against normal conceptions of how poetry is written. In spite of his preference for poetry over prose, Davidson believed that a poet's work was strengthened and enriched by writing prose. He found evidence for this in the later poetry of William Morris. 'A firmer grasp of reality is required in prose to make up for the more intimate union of music, colour, and form which characterises verse', he wrote in the *Speaker* in March that year.[21] More practically, the newspaper articles served as an initial record of the random excursions which were to inspire many of his poems, and at the same time brought him in some money.

By March he had written 'In Romney Marsh', and 'Song of a Cinque Port'. According to Edgar Jepson, 'decadence', to the young poets and artists who frequented the Crown in Charing Cross Road in the 1890s, meant not an unconventional lifestyle, but a French school of poets in whose verse one found a rhythmical and emotional fall, a decadence.[22] Its chief poet was the French Symbolist, Paul Verlaine, who visited London in 1893, on that occasion being entertained by Lane and Symons. Of English poets at the time, Symons and possibly Dowson were considered most capable of achieving this effect. From this

---

[20] 'Romney Marsh', *Glasgow Herald* (3 Mar. 1894), 4.
[21] 'The Week', *Speaker*, 5 (19 Mar. 1892), 348.
[22] Edgar Jepson, *Memories of a Victorian* (London, 1933), 215.

point of view, Davidson's lyrics run counter to the 'decadence'. They may share with Symons's verse an impressionism that was fashionable at the time—the experience or mood being generally rendered without comment or any straining after effect— but in Davidson's lyrics the feeling rings or rises rhythmically at the end.

In the early part of the year, the difficulties of Davidson's home life had also added to his exasperation. A writer, much of whose work is done at home, does not enjoy the separation between domestic life and his place of work that is the general experience of workers in a modern industrial society. One suspects that his day-long trips to Kent were a welcome escape from the tensions of his small house in Hornsey. Part of the problem was their inability to manage the servant, at that time still an obligatory feature of the respectable lower-middle-class home. They had taken her on at Christmas, but she proved to be 'as mad as a March hare'.[23] Le Gallienne tried to help by inviting them to spend a fortnight with himself and Mildred at their cottage in Brentford. Davidson, who was planning to leave Hornsey that September in any case, courteously declined. He was unable to write away from his own room, which would have meant a fortnight without income, 'A common thing with me,' he wrote, 'but also minus any attempt to make any income, an unique thing for five years.'[24] He also confessed that making visits made them uncomfortable, and in this case it meant leaving the boys in the care of the servant. They were afraid they would 'find murder done or the house burned down or some worse catastrophe' on their return. He added darkly: 'Some day I may tell you how our lives have been laid waste, and our moods and characters spoiled for society.'[25] The servant problem and the desire to get out of Hornsey were still on his mind when he wrote to Meem on his birthday to thank her for the tie she had sent:

I suppose you have heard of the Great Rebellion. In the meantime it is ended and the enemy is to leave on the 7th of May. This was an unexpected turn, and she is behaving like an angel, apparently in the hope of being kept on.

[23] Davidson to McCormick, 29 Dec. 1893, Glasgow.
[24] Davidson to Richard Le Gallienne, 'Tuesday', 1894, Texas.
[25] Davidson to Le Gallienne, 'Sunday' [1894], Texas.

We are actually going to make a resolute effort to get out of here. It is a perfect marvel that none of us have [*sic*] killed anybody during these five years, when you remember the confined space, the touchwood tempers all round, and the uninteresting depressing amenities.[26]

In spite of his decision to concentrate on poetry rather than prose, he agreed to write a new novel for Joseph Dent at a royalty of 10 per cent.[27] This was probably the 'piece of frightful drudgery' he was working on when he received Lane's invitation to the Booksellers' Dinner. His *Plays* had already come out, beautifully produced in puce-coloured cloth binding and containing Beardsley's famous illustration of *Scaramouch in Naxos* with caricatures of Oscar Wilde, Henry Harland, Mabel Beardsley, Sir Augustus Harris, the theatre manager, the dancer Adeline Genée, and Le Gallienne as Pierrot. He had read a favourable review of the book in the *Pall Mall Gazette*, but he no longer felt that good reviews mattered if the book would not sell. Though in no mood to celebrate or to socialize, he gave in to Lane's wishes to attend the Booksellers' Dinner. He procured a dress coat for the occasion, 'the claw-hammer of civilization', as he dubbed it sardonically.[28]

Having started, he decided to go to the *Yellow Book* Dinner. He even appeared cheerful and animated to those who remembered him there. More people than expected turned up, and there was much bustle and re-organization in the upper room of the restaurant before everyone was seated. Davidson sat with Mrs Harland and Mrs Rhys. He referred to them jokingly as 'The Heavenly Twins'—the title of a best-selling novel by Sarah Grand—and entertained them with anecdotes. He had been spared the formality of black tie. The men wore suits or tweeds, and the women evening gowns or less formal wear. Among the guests were George Moore, between Olivia Shakespear and Mrs Craigie, Yeats and Lionel Johnson, Walter Sickert, the artist, whom Davidson liked, and Max Beerbohm, the youngest person present. At high table, the place of honour between Harland and Beardsley was given to Elizabeth Pennell whose husband Joseph had left for the Continent. Ménie Muriel Dowie, the wife of Henry Norman, literary editor of the *Chronicle*, was also at high table between Harland and John Lane.[29]

Elkin Mathews was conspicuously absent. During the speeches, Lane explained his partner's non-appearance as 'unavoidable', and there was reportedly a momentary embarrassment when one of the dinner guests shouted out that this was a lie.[30] The truth was that Lane had deliberately kept the details of the celebrations from Mathews. He felt that the *Yellow Book* was his idea, and at the end of the party, which finished late, he took some of the guests on for more drinks at the Monico.

During the dinner, Lane had handed Davidson a letter postmarked 'Yattendon' which he recognized at once as the Berkshire home of the poet, Robert Bridges. His reply to Bridges the next morning reveals what he had really been feeling beneath his outward cheerfulness and sociability the previous night:

The surprise and pleasure of your letter came upon me last night by the hands of John Lane at the dinner of the *Yellow Book* in an old street in Soho, in an old low-ceiled room with Italian crockery and candles, and half a dozen of these new women who wear their sex on their sleeves, and a score and more of these new men who are sexless—very pleasant abominations of the time. I knew who had written the letter as soon as I saw 'Yattendon', for my acquaintance with you is of five years standing now—I have read with the keenest pleasure most of your books. Your letter was like a warning to me. For five years I have kept out of London although living and working in it, and last night at my very first step into it a high voice reminds me of 'my own endeavour'. I shall have to go on with London, because it becomes apparent to me although I have tried to get on without it, that it is impossible even to get enough reviewing to buy tobacco, unless one makes and keeps acquaintance with all kinds of bosses, strappers, and understrappers, but I shall be in it but not of it.

It was indeed a very high pleasure, with bitter in it, too—as what pleasure is without it—to have a gracious message from one who has kept his singing robes unsullied—and I about to fling mine down in

---

[29] Mix, *Study in Yellow*, 81–3.

[30] Elkin Mathews to Dr Brushfield (draft letter), 7 Feb. 1895, Reading; quoted in Nelson, *Early Nineties*, 271.

the mud of a 3/6 dinner to help some stupid woman across the intervals between the entrées.[31]

A week later he was studying how he might get to Yattendon, having received an invitation from Bridges to visit him, although he knew that this could not be before summer. He was writing 'to order and to time' and knew from experience that an interruption would be disastrous.[32] He did take up some invitations. He went to dinner at Oscar Wilde's house in Tite Street, where he met Sergius Stepniak.[33] He also kept an appointment on 20 April with George Gissing. He had been introduced to Gissing by Morley Roberts. Gissing had been out of London for over two years, living in Exeter. But on his return in the summer of 1893, Roberts arranged for all three of them to have lunch at the Café Royal. Their meeting took place on a wet Saturday afternoon of 29 July. Davidson and Gissing liked each other. They were the same age and shared similar literary taste. But it was another chance meeting at the British Museum on 18 September that furthered their friendship, as it prompted Gissing to read *In a Music-Hall* and *Fleet Street Eclogues*. He admired the *Eclogues* and wrote to Davidson at once to tell him so. It is easy to see what attracted Gissing to the *Eclogues*, which parallel his own poignant account of 'wretched authordom' in his novel *New Grub Street*.[34]

The plague of personal and business worries that ended the old year and began the new one for Davidson prevented him from answering Gissing's letter for several months. When he did write, they agreed to meet. Davidson invited him to tea at the Grosvenor Club on 20 April. He also wanted to invite Lane, but forgot to mention it during the *Yellow Book* dinner. He sent a note the next day, but Lane could not come. This was perhaps fortunate, as Davidson and Gissing became close friends after remaining together till eight o'clock. Davidson confided details of his domestic problems, which Gissing was to make use of in his novel *The Whirlpool* several years later. At the time of its

[31] Davidson to Robert Bridges, 17 Apr. 1894, Bodleian Library, Oxford.
[32] Davidson to Robert Bridges, 25 Apr. 1894, Bodleian Library, Oxford.
[33] Davidson to McCormick, 'Tuesday' [Apr. 1894], Glasgow.
[34] His meetings with George Gissing are recorded in Gissing's diary, published as *London and the Life of Literature in Late Victorian England: The Diary of George Gissing, Novelist*, ed. Pierre Coustillas (Hassocks, 1978).

publication, he wrote to Davidson to assure him that one of the characters in the novel was not intended for him, although modelled on certain matters of fact and remarks of his life and conversation.[35] Harvey Rolfe, the central character, is described as a man of 'bluff jocularity' who despite his 'convivial qualities' has traits of 'the reserved, even of the unsociable, man: a slight awkwardness in bearing, a mute shyness with strangers, a hesitancy in ordinary talk, and occasional bluntness of assertion and contradiction, suggesting a contempt which possibly he did not intend'.[36] This was the impression made by Davidson on Gissing and on others who met him at this time.

There was great sadness in London's literary circles when Le Gallienne's wife, Mildred, died on 21 May. Theirs had seemed the ideal marriage. Davidson did not write to Le Gallienne immediately. When he did, it was to send a brief, touching note on the inefficacy of words:

Sometimes one can find words to sympathise with the joy of others; with their grief, with their deepest grief, perhaps, never. Grief is so terrible, so divine, that one approaches it in silence, with uncovered head. And so I have not written. But now I send you this little note: it interprets my silence feebly—as you have already interpreted it, for we are friends are we not? Maggie, too, would press your hand.[37]

Le Gallienne's affection for Davidson was deepened by this response to his wife's death. He saw Davidson as few of Davidson's male acquaintants saw him, and later wrote that

with him, as with the lion in Holy Writ, within whose jaws the wild bees built their honeycombs, it was a case of *ex forte dulcedo*; for beneath his proud, rather pragmatic exterior, and that Highland manner which brings a suggestion of always going armed against offence, his nature was full of human kindness and repressed tenderness.[38]

Davidson's delay in writing may have been caused by work. That month he was driven off his feet 'in town and out'.[39] He did some work for the *Star* whose final payment to him of a

    [35] See my ' "Of George Gissing": John Davidson's Short Notice', *Gissing Newsletter*, 26 (Oct. 1990), 16–17.
    [36] George Gissing, *The Whirlpool* (London, 1897), 2.
    [37] Davidson to Le Gallienne, 'Sunday' [1894], Texas.
    [38] Richard Le Gallienne, *The Romantic '90s* (New York, 1925), 198.
    [39] Davidson to Richard Hovey, 15 May 1894, Princeton.

guinea a column he found insulting. He also had some contact
with Andrew Lang, who was on the staff of Frank Hill's *Daily
News* and *Evening News*. He found himself revising his opinion of
Lang and rather liking him. Lang, a Scottish Tory and former
Fellow at Oxford, was for Davidson a man of a past age, when
aloofness and *nil admirari* were form, but he began to respect
Lang's culture and polish and Scottish reticence.[40] Out of town,
he was also busy writing his novel, undertaking a piece of translation work and reading manuscripts for Lane. He had been an
occasional reader for the Bodley Head from the time of his *Fleet
Street Eclogues*, one of his first reports being on R. C. Lehmann's
Songs from Vagabondia which he warmly recommended from his
mother's home in Edinburgh in March 1893, while supervising
the printing of his *Eclogues*.[41] His arrangement now became
more regular. 'I need and want lots of money', he told Lane,
and asked him to send manuscripts.[42] Lane did. Davidson's
reports—those that have survived—are shrewd, frank, and
sometimes witty. Among the manuscripts he recommended
were Joaquin Miller's *The Building of the City Beautiful* (1894),
and Francis Thompson's *Sister Songs* (1895). Henry Newbolt's
Mordred (1895), which he described as 'the work of a man of
considerable talent . . . but not in the same street as Tennyson's
work',[43] was rejected and eventually taken by T. Fisher Unwin.
He sometimes complained about the drudgery of the work, but
he liked the money it brought him, and even the drudgery
sometimes suited him, as it kept him from moping about the
house after his mornings spent writing poetry.[44]

In July, his poem 'Thirty Bob a Week' appeared in the second
volume of the *Yellow Book* which received a more favourable
reception than the first. The poem is a piece of gritty realism
that marked a return to the vernacular monologue of his 'In a
Music-Hall' verses. It has often been compared to Kipling's
Barrack-Room Ballads and shares with them a rugged, masculine
vigour. Davidson, like Kipling, had been deeply impressed as a

[40] Davidson to Lane, 3 May 1894, NLS.
[41] Davidson to Elkin Mathews and John Lane, 'Monday' [March 1893],
Lane.
[42] Davidson to Lane, 3 May 1894, NLS.
[43] Manuscript report, Lane. The report on Francis Thompson's *Sister Songs* has
not survived.
[44] Davidson to Lane, 'Monday' [1894], Princeton.

young man by the recitations of music-hall performers, and remained alert to the possibilities of popular culture and the press story as fitting subject-matter for modern poetry. In his verses entitled 'To the Street Piano', he transformed two popular songs of the day into grim statements of the times—the sentimental 'After the Ball', and Henry J. Sayers's minstrel number 'Ta-ra-ra-boom-de-ay', which Lottie Collins had made all the rage in London in the spring of 1892.

One can see the attraction of the music hall to a generation looking for out of the way experiences and new forms of expression. According to Benny Green,

> The Music Hall by the 1890s was a kind of central stockpot bounded by the other theatrical arts within whose limits anyone might drift, from a ballerina to a matinee idol, from a balladeer to a reader of literary monologues.[45]

By then, the impersonation of Cockney life by artists such as George Gamble and Gus Elen had become more realistic, their grim comedy created out of the real world of hardship and squalor. At the same time comic singers began to poke fun at the social pretensions of the clerks and other desk-men who made up a large part of the audience. It is a small step from Nellie Power's taunting 'The City Toff': 'Though limited his screw, yet | The week he struggles through it,' to the opening of 'Thirty Bob a Week': 'I couldn't touch a stop and turn a screw, | And set the blooming world a-work for me.' The difference is that Davidson's clerk pleads his own case, adopting the argot and self-deprecatory tones that belong traditionally to the Cockney costermonger. The result, as T. S. Eliot observed of the poem's influence on his own work, was the discovery of a new idiom for the 'dingy urban images' of modern life.[46]

Many readers have felt that the poem may have grown directly out of the bitterness of his own struggles to make ends meet. This would appear to be confirmed by a letter written to Lane a week before the poem appeared. He confessed to being 'unable to work properly for want of money', and calculated that his 'average income from all sources for the last month or

---

[45] Benny Green, *The Last Empires* (London, 1986), 51.
[46] T. S. Eliot, [A Tribute to John Davidson], in Maurice Lindsay, 'John Davidson—The Man Forbid', *Saltire Review*, 4 (Summer, 1957), 57.

two had been at the rate of 35/– a week'. The money he had received for the translation had already gone towards supplementing his weekly income, and 'for another purpose'. He begged Lane for £20 on the strength of future sales of his *Fleet Street Eclogues* and *Plays*. 'Were it not for the wonderful economy of Mrs Davidson,' he wrote frankly, 'our affairs would be hopeless.'[47] Yet the theme of the poem is not simply the pains of poverty, but the problem of self-esteem for those who accept a Social Darwinian view of life. In *Earl Lavender* Davidson was to lampoon the formula of 'the survival of the fittest', but the social ethos derived from this—that a man's place in society was now a measure of his personal worth—was becoming an unconscious and accepted part of social life. Davidson's representation of this conflict is charged with irony. The frustrated clerk of 'Thirty Bob a Week' has two voices singing in his heart—one is that of the meek simpleton; the other is that of the aggressive devil who would like to 'squelch the passers flat against the wall'. He tries to console himself with the laws of nature, but is only too painfully aware of the implications of accepting a Social Darwinian view of life, where

> . . . the difficultest job a man can do
> Is to come it brave and meek with thirty bob a week,
> And feel that that's the proper thing for you.[48]

Visits to Hadley Wood during the summer put him back in touch with himself. 'Not an aesthete,' he wrote, 'but a foolish patron of Nature.'[49] He was sick of the city, of writing too much, of the latest opinions, and of the strident voices of the New Men and New Women. But he was tied to the metropolis. He arranged with Lane to be paid £20 on the delivery of a collection of *Ballads and Songs* on 15 September. At the beginning of the month he was refusing all invitations until it was finished. He dreamed of a great sale and of being able to go to some unknown place to write a great book undisturbed by reviewing and occasional poems. The desire to have a free hand had become insistent. 'My soul grows sick at 37 to think I am just where I was at 20—writing poetry in despite of every economic law', he

[47] Davidson to Lane, 25 June 1894, Princeton.
[48] 'Thirty Bob a Week', ll. 87–90.
[49] 'Hadley Wood', *Glasgow Herald* (20 Oct. 1894), 7.

lamented to Lane.[50] Two days before his deadline for the delivery of the manuscript, he was feeling ill and exhausted, and was suffering from one of his great colds—'a nice little glowing head of phosphorus at the top of your windpipe, and your voice sounding like that of a cabin boy longing to shout from the masthead in a hurricane'.[51] He was caught in a storm of his own, and blamed his illness not on overwork, but on the fact that he could not work enough. It was his way of trying to tell his publisher that he needed money urgently: he did not want to ask directly for the £20 advance before the delivery of the manuscript. At last, on 20 September, five days behind schedule, he sent his *Ballads and Songs* to Lane and asked for the money. The cheque came the following day.

He thought of dedicating the book to Le Gallienne, but in the end he decided that it would be unwise to dedicate a book to a man who had praised him, and stuck to a resolution made five years earlier, never to dedicate a book to anyone again.[52] Yet *Ballads and Songs* is a tribute to Le Gallienne. The lines of the opening dedication 'To My Friend' were addressed originally to him, and the collection closes with two other poems written for him: the first anticipating the birth of his daughter Hesper Joyce, and the second an elegy written at the time of his wife's death. Davidson arranged the collection as a whole with care, with the ballads following the dedications; his London poems coming next; and pieces 'the matter for which could have been obtained only by perilous journeys on railways' coming after his 'Song of a Train'.[53]

The book was not to be published by Mathews and Lane. In August, the partnership had been dissolved. It had never survived Lane's insult to Mathews over the *Yellow Book* dinner. The two split up in silent, mutual acrimony, in spite of Lane's claims to the contrary. Lane carried the sign of The Bodley Head from 6B Vigo Street and rehung it above his new premises at G1 The Albany across the street. He also took the *Yellow Book* and many of the Bodley Head writers with him, but some stayed with

[50] Davidson to Lane, 'Monday' [1894], NLS.
[51] Davidson to Lane, 13 Sept. 1894, NLS.
[52] Davidson to Lane, 'Sunday' [Sept. 1894], NLS.
[53] Davidson to Lane, 20 Sept. 1894, Lane.

Mathews, including Yeats, Todhunter, Herbert Horne, and Frederick Wedmore, who had condemned the first *Yellow Book* in the *Academy*. The canvassing of authors was carried out in the first weeks of August. It was an awkward decision for many of them, especially for Davidson, as Mathews proposed to offer him a 'confidential post', presumably as his reader and adviser, since Le Gallienne and Frederic Chapman were definitely Lane's men. On 13 August he wrote to Mathews with his decisions:

After the most careful consideration and consultations with those whose opinions I am bound to respect, and without having seen or approached Lane since I saw you, I have elected to allow him to have my stock, and to read for him what MSS he sends me.[54]

There was a side to Davidson which preferred Lane's bustle to the quiet, mannerly business style of Mathews. Moreover, Lane seemed more responsive to the radical element in his poetry and more likely to make him money. Lane, after all, had the *Yellow Book* in which some of the poems in his forthcoming volume had first appeared, and for the past year had effectively assumed the role of friend, paymaster, and supplier of manuscripts.

One of the many manuscripts that came into his hands late that year was Arthur Symons's *London Nights* (1895). He warmly recommended it to Lane. He thought the collection was better technically than the earlier *Silhouettes* (1892) which he had reviewed in the *Speaker* two years earlier. But while he praised Symons's skill, he was uneasy about the subject-matter with its concentration on prostitutes and carnal pleasures, 'a common mood of common men' which he found personally uninteresting. 'Ten years ago I suppose it would have been to risk a sojourn in Holloway to publish "To One in Alienation", "Leves Amores", "White Heliotrope"'. . . , he wrote.[55] The comment about Holloway Prison may have scared Lane who decided not to publish. While always quick to exploit the publicity value of a *succès de scandale*, he was essentially a cautious man. The indignation roused by Symons's 'Stella Maris' in the first volume of

---

[54] Davidson to Elkin Mathews, 13 Aug. 1894, Reading.
[55] Manuscript report on Arthur Symons's *London Nights*, not dated, Bodleian Library, Oxford.

the *Yellow Book* may have suggested to him that the forces of moral reaction were gathering strength.

This seemed to be the case when Davidson's own 'A Ballad of a Nun' appeared in October in the third volume of the *Yellow Book*. Praise for the poem's descriptive power quickly gave way to controversy and moral protest. Five years later, in a letter to Gosse, Davidson delivered some caustic comments on its brief popularity and subsequent eclipse:

In this country a writer must misrepresent the world, or be understood to have done so, in order to make money. I learned this most saliently from the false vogue of a poem of mine, 'A Ballad of a Nun', an entirely non-moral piece which was mistaken for an Anglican tract, and belauded for a month or two on that account. When the error was discovered the poem and the author were shortly dropped, and criticism generally has never forgiven me for its own mistake.[56]

Certainly, while 'Thirty Bob a Week' continues to be read and admired—T. S. Eliot called it 'one of the great poems of the end of the nineteenth century'[57]—'A Ballad of a Nun' has not withstood the test of time so well. The ballad tells the story of a young nun, a portress, who escapes from the convent in order to satisfy her sexual desires. On her return, worn out and heartbroken, she finds that the Virgin Mary has taken her place as Keeper of the Door in order to conceal her shame. From the first, dicussion about its considerable technical merits tended to take second place to controversy about its treatment of virginity. A clue to Davidson's intention is to be found in a lengthy reader's report he sent to Lane about this time on a never to be published Ibsenite play. The drama centred on a Roman Catholic Scottish colonial whose Creole wife runs away to London with a secretary. He pursues the runaway pair and invites his wife to return. Davidson advised Lane to 'have nothing to do with it', not because a controversy would rage around it, but because it could only retard the day of a 'Free Theatre'. He felt that the censorship would not be overturned by such a play, nor the situation of the marriage laws in England be helped by anything so abnormal as a Creole and a Roman Catholic Scot with an illegitimate family. He concluded:

---

[56] Davidson to Edmund Gosse, 28 Dec. 1900, Brotherton.

[57] T. S. Eliot, 'Preface' to *John Davidson: A Selection of His Poems*, ed. Maurice Lindsay (London, 1961).

It is on the right lines for a great play—sex and religion at daggers drawn—but it must be true religion as Ibsen would have it, not a foolish and impossible hypocrite; and it must be a woman who shall represent sex, not a worn-out nymphomaniac from the West Indies.[58]

His own 'Nun', in spite of the abnormalities of her situation, was clearly meant to represent normal womanhood.

There are many earlier versions of the legend. One of the oldest of these is to be found in the thirteenth-century collection of stories used by preachers, the *Gesta Romanorum*. But other versions are to be found in St Alphonsus Liguori's *Glories of Mary*, and in the nineteenth-century Spanish poet José Zorrilla's *Margarita la Tornera*. Davidson's version is often thought to be derived from the English poet Adelaide Anne Procter's 'A Legend of Provence' which appeared in *Legends and Lyrics* in 1858. A much more likely source, mentioned by the littérateur J. Cuthbert Hadden who knew Davidson when he was a schoolmaster in Crieff, is Villier de L'Isle-Adam's short story 'Sœur Natalia', one of his *Nouveaux contes cruels* which came out in 1888.[59] There are some close parallels between the French prose version and Davidson's poem. At the moment of her temptation, for instance, De l'Isle-Adam's nun hears a man singing: 'l'on entendait monter . . . les accents frais et sonores d'un chanteur de sérénade'.[60] Davidson has:

> Sometimes she heard a serenade
> Complaining sweetly far away:
> She said, 'A young man woos a maid';
> And dreamt of love till break of day.[61]

The ballad was soon the talk of London. There were to be numerous parodies of it, including a version in Scots dialect in *The Quest of the Gilt-Edged Girl*, a burlesque of Le Gallienne's *The Quest of the Golden Girl*. The most popular, according to C. Lewis Hind, then editor of the *Pall Mall Budget*, where Davidson sometimes worked, was Owen Seaman's 'A Ballad of a Bun', about a poetess who traffics in the literary market place 'for a mess of Bodley bun'.[62]

---

[58] Manuscript report on B. S. Oliver's 'A Freedom in Fetters', Lane.
[59] Hadden, *Wolverhampton Chronicle* (16 Jan. 1907), 2.
[60] Villier de L'Isle-Adam, 'Sœur Natalia' in *Nouveaux contes cruels* (Paris, 1889), 93–102.
[61] 'A Ballad of A Nun', ll. 29–32.
[62] C. Lewis Hind, *More Authors Than I* (London, 1922), 78.

On hearing about the poem, Dean Farrar, then Canon of Westminster, assumed that Davidson's version was the same as that found in the *Gesta Romanorum* or in Adelaide Anne Procter's poem. H. C. Beeching, the vicar at Yattendon and another Bodley Head author, remembered how

on a certain Monday morning late in '94 a queue of respectable middle-aged ladies thrust its way along Vigo Street into the 'Bodley Head', asking for copies of 'A Ballad of a Nun' by a Mr John Davidson. When the pressure was a little eased the publisher ventured to enquire the cause of the sudden demand . . . The answer was that the Archdeacon of W.— had charged them on their soul's health to procure it.[63]

Some of those who read the poem saw it at once as a challenge to conventional morality. The poem had been refused by several nervous editors before Harland accepted it. Netta Syrett, who contributed a short story to the second volume of the *Yellow Book*, remembered Harland reading the newly arrived manuscript aloud to several people at his flat, 'making mock and scoff of it'.[64] It was not long before Davidson found himself having to defend it against his critics. Even men like William Archer, who admired the ballad, were perplexed by the meaning and propriety of its ending in having God send down the Virgin Mary to keep the nun's place. Archer, described by Shaw as a 'physically tall and upstanding well-built Scot' was a translator of Ibsen and one of London's leading drama critics. He and Davidson had been at Edinburgh University at the same time, but they had never met when Archer wrote to say that he liked 'A Ballad of a Nun'. They were to correspond regularly after that, generally sparring over fine points in literature. On this occasion, Davidson answered Archer's query with a frank statement of his unorthodox intention in the ballad:

Accepting the idea of God the import is that God's sympathies were entirely with the nun. The Virgin on withdrawing tells her not only has she made herself one with Nature by employing her body, however blindly, for its own appropriate purpose, but she has also made herself one with God while committing what she supposed to be deadly sin:

[63] [H. C. Beeching], *Pages from a Private Diary* (London, 1899), 39.
[64] Quoted in Chalmers, *Kenneth Grahame*, 66.

'You are sister to the mountains now,
   And sister to the day and night,
Sister to God.'[65]

With the letter, he sent a comic dialogue in which an exasperated Virgin Mary voices her disapproval of 'all that Sodomy and Lesbianism and masturbation' that must result from monasticism.

Davidson's views on the unnaturalness of celibacy are hardly idiosyncratic. 'I reckon the constrained celibacy of the clergy the monstrous root of the greatest part of the mischiefs of Popery. . . . If we would truly spiritualise men, we must take care that we do not begin by unhumanising them.'[66] This was William Wordsworth, writing in 1840. Protestant Britain in Victorian times was plunged periodically into hysteria over reports of female abduction and reluctant nuns. In the summer of 1894, H. Rider Haggard entered into a long and acrimonious correspondence with the secretary of the Catholic Truth Society in the pages of the *Pall Mall Gazette* on the subject of the immuring of nuns, a row sparked off by a footnote in his novel, *Montezuma's Daughter*. This may have been the immediate inspiration for the ballad.

Davidson's position, in spite of his expressed belief in a godless materialism, is recognizably Protestant; but there are elements in the original story which obtrude themselves from a Protestant point of view: the nun's sexual fall, for instance, and the moral aspect of the part played by the Virgin Mary. The discomfort felt by William Archer was to be shared by others when the poem appeared for a second time in *Ballads and Songs* in November. W. T. Stead, editor of the *Review of Reviews*, had at first been impressed by the poem, but then came to see its impropriety. Stead, an earnest Puritan, objected to the poem's confusion of sex with love. 'After all,' he wrote 'there is some difference between the Congress of animals of different sexes and the nuptial embrace of lovers.'[67] Grant Richards, who was then acting as his secretary, took the unusual step of sending

---

[65] Davidson to William Archer, 26 Oct. 1894, BL.

[66] William Wordsworth to Walter Farquhar Hook, 5 Feb. 1840, *The Letters of William and Dorothy Wordsworth*, ed. Alan G. Hill (Oxford, 1988).

[67] W. T. Stead to Davidson, 3 Dec. 1894, Princeton. For Stead's article, see 'Our Monthly Parcel of Books', *Review of Reviews*, 10 (Dec. 1894), 598.

proofs of the review to Davidson in advance of publication, which produced disagreements by letter between the two men, particularly about nymphomania, with Davidson maintaining that it was 'an insatiable letch produced by overindulgence of the flesh',[68] and therefore not applicable to his nun, while Stead argued that it was 'a malady which sometimes affects the most innocent virgin'.[69]

Discomfort over the poem was to re-surface two years later when Quiller-Couch expressed dissatisfaction with the exhibition of 'the Mother of God abetting the vagaries' of the erring nun.[70] On this occasion, an angry chorus of Catholic voices protested in the correspondence pages of the *Speaker*. For them, all ethical considerations were swept aside by the story's strong emotional appeal to pity and joy for the sinner who repents. Had Davidson entered the debate, he would surely have pointed out the Virgin's approval of the sin which had made his nun 'sister to the mountains now, And sister to the day and night'; but clearly there is a problem in adopting a traditional Christian legend in order to challenge the Puritanism of Victorian society. From a Catholic standpoint, the nun's sin lies in her breaking her vow of chastity; but for the majority of Davidson's readers, her sin is one of sexual licence. Because of this readers tended to repond to the poem with sly amusement—the poem affirmed after all that celibacy was as unnatural for women as for men—or, in the case of Quiller-Couch and Stead, with moral disapproval. Stead's absolute distinction between 'the Congress of animals' and married love is matched by Quiller-Couch's impatient: 'Be naughty, if indeed you must: but O, do not insist on justifying it by preaching!' Protestant Britain may have disapproved of the real or imagined evils of monasticism, but the Victorian ideal of marriage imposed its own forms of sexual inhibition. Though Davidson did not intend it, the nun's betrayal of her vow in 'A Ballad of a Nun' can be read as a disguised and analogous expression of marital infidelity, a feeling which is also to be found in *Baptist Lake*.

We might notice here a paradox that lies at the heart of the new hedonism, and of the new frankness in literature generally

---

[68] Davidson to Grant Richards, 29 Nov. 1894, Princeton.
[69] Stead to Davidson, 30 Nov. 1894, Princeton.
[70] 'A Literary Causerie', *Speaker*, 14 (7 Nov. 1896), 497–8.

at this time. On the one hand, the bookstalls and theatres paraded a new and daring subject: 'fallen women', women with a past, forgiven, rather than condemned as in the earlier paradigms of Victorian fiction. Oscar Wilde's *Lady Windermere's Fan* ran to large appreciative audiences in 1892; and, at the Bodley Head, Lane brought out George Egerton's *Keynotes* in 1894, with its candid statements of women's passion, and a year later, Grant Allen's sensational *The Woman Who Did*. This may have reflected in part the rapidly changing social relations between men and women at this time. Women were needed increasingly in traditionally male work-places. This was especially true of Fleet Street. When Grant Richards went to work for W. T. Stead at the offices of the *Review of Reviews* in Mowbray House, Norfolk Street in 1890, the strangest thing to him was the constant presence of young women.[71] The change often produced a split between public and private morals. The office of *The Novel* magazine, where there was a constant stream of female visitors, was well known for its freedoms; the magazine twice printed a nakedly priapic poem by John Barlas. But when Thomas Hardy's *Tess of the d'Urbervilles* appeared in 1892, the review issued a warning word to the person the magazine most respected—the British Matron. We see here the paradox; for in spite of the changes in the social relations between the sexes, and the reflection of this in the literature of the time, social consciousness continued to insist on the sanctity of marriage. 'Fallen women' were still to be 'reclaimed'. Whenever a work appeared to question this, the moral backlash could be fierce, as in the case of Hardy's *Tess*, and indeed of the situation in 'A Ballad of a Nun'. Perhaps the best clue to Davidson's own state of mind is to be found in his early play, *Diabolus Amans*, in which the hero's scornful rejection of God and conventional morality coincides with a willing acceptance of the duty and divinity of love.

Davidson's views on marriage and sexuality can be clearly seen in his response to the scandal that threatened Le Gallienne at the end of 1894. It began when Le Gallienne gave a lecture defending free love at a Sunday evening meeting of the Playgoer's Club on 9 December. This was reported in tones

[71] Grant Richards, *Memoirs of a Misspent Youth* (London, 1933), 123.

of moral outrage by the *Speaker*.[72] Lane was alarmed and contacted Davidson. Though distressed, Davidson could not believe
Le Gallienne was being other than ironical. He suspected Le
Gallienne had imitated his own ironic manner and had applied
his idea of a Harlot's Trade Union to a general Trade Union of
Sinners.[73] His attitude to Le Gallienne was mixed. On the one
hand, he sometimes regarded him with the condescension of an
indulgent elder brother. 'He is a boy, much younger than his
years,' he told William Archer, 'walks in the world with a
wooden sword in one hand and a rose-water sprinkler in the
other, but will yet take a weapon worth handling, cut his hair,
and behave himself accordingly.'[74] But, in his review of Le
Gallienne's *Prose Fancies* earlier that year, he would appear to
contrast his own life of 'obscure groping' unfavourably with the
younger man's sense of direction:

By many devious ways, by much wrongly directed labour, some men
discover at last what they can do best, and how to do it. This obscure
groping is, as a rule, the result of a defective temperament . . . These,
having come out of Egypt and crossed the Red Sea, wander about the
desert for forty years. Their opposites, with no temperamental de-
rangement to lead them astray into parched places, step out across the
wilderness as with seventy-leagued boots, and are pressing the grapes
of Eshcol before they realise what they are about.[75]

When asked by Lane to act the wise counsellor at the time of
the threatened scandal, Davidson was reluctant to approach 'so
headstrong a man', particularly as he expected Le Gallienne
would be as 'dour' and 'thrawn as a Scotchman is fit to be', and
'would probably, as a Scotchman certainly would, listen to ad-
monition and even appear to be admonished out of friendship;
and then go straight away and harbour seven other devils worse
than the first'. He then put his finger on the real cause of the
scandal, and possibly of his own initial distress: 'The real thing
that sticks in people's throats is not so much what Le Gallienne
said, but that he said it across his wife's grave, as it were: she is
hardly six month's dead. And can one talk of that?'[76]

[72] 'The New Hedonism', *Speaker*, 10 (15 Dec. 1894), 654–5.
[73] Davidson to Lane, 'Wednesday' [Dec. 1894], Princeton.
[74] Davidson to William Archer, 16 Nov. 1894, BL.
[75] 'Narcissus with a Difference', *Speaker*, 9 (30 June 1894), 654–5.
[76] Davidson to Lane, 16 Dec. 1894, Princeton.

Mildred Lee, Le Gallienne's wife, inspired love and affection in all who knew her. At the time of her death Grant Allen wrote an elegy in which she is called 'the little white maid'.[77] Wilde, who himself had been in love with Le Gallienne, referred to her as Le Gallienne's 'poem'.[78] She appears to have embodied for all of them the ideal of the child wife, and Le Gallienne himself with his beautifully pale features and long hair, the image of youthful gallantry. Their marriage seemed perfect. Le Gallienne's advocacy of free love six months after her death seemed to desecrate an ideal. In the event, Lane need not have worried. The other journals and newspapers made little of the story. But though the scandal came to nothing, it gave warning of those forces of morality that within a few month's would come crashing down on Wilde's head.

Between receiving the £20 for the completed manuscript of *Ballads and Songs* and its publication in November, Davidson suffered his usual pre-natal depression. His old friend and mentor John Nichol died on 11 October in Brighton where he had been taken in September. Nichol had settled in London in the autumn of 1890, after resigning his professorship at Glasgow University to follow a literary career. His London days were darkened by ill health and the attack on his books by literary reviewers. He was cremated at Woking on 15 October. On that day, Davidson replied to a letter he had received from Gissing, but had 'no news but the old news—work and drudgery and more drudgery than work, and not enough of either: days wasted in moping, half-hours snatched by the hair of the head out of gulfs of ennui and hypochondria'.[79] He was in low spirits as he laboured to complete a 50,000-word story by the end of November. The money he expected for it would have to go towards paying his debts rather than on the little luxuries he felt he deserved.

Even when the first reviews of *Ballads and Songs* came out, and it was becoming clear that the book really would be the success

[77] Grant Allen, 'A Poet's Wife', *Academy*, 65 (9 June 1894), 475.
[78] Quoted in Richard Ellmann, *Oscar Wilde* (London, 1987), 345.
[79] Davidson to George Gissing, 15 Oct. 1894, in Paul F. Mattheisen, Arthur C. Young, and Pierre Coustillas (eds.), *The Collected Letters of George Gissing*, v (Athens, Oh., 1994), 244–5.

he had hoped for, his situation did not materially change. On 16 November, he turned down an invitation to visit Grant Allen and his wife, aunt and uncle to Grant Richards. His tone was querulous: 'I should be free to go anywhere for a month if I wanted to, but it is not so', he wrote to Mrs Allen. 'First of all I am not well; secondly I am writing a story to order, which should have been finished by the end of November, but which, work as hard as I can, will not see "finis" till Christmas.'[80] He sent her a copy of *Ballads and Songs*. Grant Allen gave it the highest praise a week later in the *Westminster Review*. Davidson was gratified and forgave him the unfavourable review of his *Plays* which had appeared earlier that year. The favourable review cemented their friendship. The two men had much in common, combining outspoken unconventional views about sexuality with settled family lives. Allen championed a natural theory of human action over theological and religious thinking. In an article on 'The New Hedonism' in the *Fortnightly Review* in March that year, which appealed to Davidson and the younger men, he had challenged the Victorian dread of sex in frank terms: 'In sober truth, the horridness lies all the one way—in looking upon sex, the mother of all things, as gross and degraded.'[81] This is believed to have directly influenced Davidson's thinking, but as was often the case, he appears to have anticipated those who are said to have influenced him. His Sister Sybil, the nun of *Diabolus Amans* who denies that anything is impure, prefigures his own 'A Ballad of Nun'.

In early December, Davidson was 'loaded with cold', but still working on his story. Joseph Dent had come to an arrangement with Macmillan in New York to publish it jointly as the third in a series of novels. The first was to be Walter Raymond's *Tryphemia in Love* (1895); the second, Jane Barlow's collection of short stories, *Maureen's Fairing* (1895).[82] Of more immediate concern to Davidson was his own unsettled health and state of mind and the news that Thomas was ill again in Edinburgh. He had read Dostoevsky's *Crime and Punishment*, with its murderous over-sensitive hero, and that month begged Bridges not to send

[80] Davidson to Mrs Grant Allen, 16 Nov. 1894, Yale.
[81] Grant Allen, 'The New Hedonism', *Fortnightly Review*, 61 (Mar. 1894), 377–92.
[82] Frederick Macmillan to George Brett, 26 Nov. 1894, Macmillan Archives, Chadwick-Healey Publishers Archives.

him the book back: 'Burn it, or give it to Mr Beeching; I should certainly prefer that the identical volumes that made me ill for a week should infect somebody else before their destruction.'[83] He had also read Gosse's poem 'Neurasthesia' in the recently published collection of poems, *In Russet and Silver* (1894). Like *Crime and Punishment*, the poem also describes the condition of the strained and abnormal temperament, isolated from birth from the happiness of other men: 'Curs'd from the cradle and awry they come, | Masking their torment from the world at ease.' Davidson was deeply fascinated by the poem. He seems to have found in it a kindred expression of his own 'gulfs of ennui and hypochondria'. He wrote to Gosse, evidently in the hope of arranging a *tête-à-tête*:

One can write and publish things one wouldn't say. I believe two men who have had the same experience might: they would not have to explain anything: they can talk in symbols. But it would have to be a 'twa-handed crack' as they say in Scotland—the two alone together.[84]

The meeting between the two men had to be put off, but Davidson wrote a laudatory review of *In Russet and Silver* in which he quoted the poem in full.[85]

His discovery of Gosse's poem, the discovery that his feelings were understood by another, seemed to mark a turning point. So too did the news that his *Ballads and Songs* was selling. Some of the shadows which had been over him for many months began to pass away. He continued to turn down invitations. 'I have tried once or twice staying in the houses of others, but it doesn't matter how kind or unkind people are I am always insufferably miserable', he wrote candidly to Bridges in refusing his offer of a visit to Yattendon.[86] Those who suffer from asthma will understand the miseries of sleeping in a strange bed. He also turned down Gosse's invitation to meet Austin Dobson. But he did make other appointments. On Saturday, 8 December he met Jane Stoddart, a handsomely dressed young woman from the popular *British Weekly*, for the interview that was to further his reputation as 'the poet of the day'. They met at the

---

[83] Davidson to Bridges, 14 Dec. 1894, Bodleian Library, Oxford.
[84] Davidson to Gosse, 4 Dec. 1894, BL.
[85] 'Mr. Gosse's Poems', *Illustrated London News* (19 Jan. 1895), 87.
[86] Davidson to Bridges, 14 Dec. 1894, BL.

Grosvenor Club. That same day he kept an appointment with Gissing at 6.30 p.m. at the Café Royal. They went for a 2s. 6d. dinner at Cranford's in Sackville Street, where they were joined after dinner by Lane. Although Davidson told Gissing that day of his domestic difficulties and of his son's tonsils and cold, the night ended in celebratory mood when Lane invited them back to his rooms in the Albany. Lane himself had to go to Bath, but Davidson and Gissing stayed on together until 11 p.m. drinking Lane's whisky and smoking his cigars. Davidson was in good spirits and, on parting, presented Gissing with a copy of his *Ballads and Songs*, declaring, 'The first edition of five thousand copies is sold out!'[87]

His happiness was increased when he received a cheque from Lane five days before Christmas. In writing to thank him for 'the gallant increase in royalty' and to send a Christmas present from himself and Maggie, he praised him warmly as a 'rarity', a publisher 'acting as an author's agent'.[88] He was equally fulsome in praising Lane to others. 'Lane,' he told William Wallace, 'has done what has never been done before in these islands, because we never had an exclusively commercial age before. To discover and create a buying public for minor and other poetry must always be a great feat; to have achieved it now-a-days, and in the manner in which it has been done at the Bodley Head, is to have established a record.'[89] Others were to share his admiration. In acknowledging receipt of a copy of *Ballads and Songs*, whose success pleased him, George Meredith wrote to Lane: 'Something is due to you for the earlier recognition of our young poets. In my time, we pushed up a head to be trampled by hob-nails.'[90]

Davidson also received a congratulatory letter from Wemyss Reid, who had been warmed by his mention of his early days at the *Speaker* in the *British Weekly* interview. Davidson replied with a personal thanks: 'I am certain you were most tolerant and forbearing with one who often failed to do prompt work for which he was unfitted by education and temperament, but

---

[87] Quoted in Gissing, *London and the Life of Literature*, 8 Dec. 1894, 356.
[88] Davidson to Lane, 20 Dec. 1894, NLS.
[89] Davidson to William Wallace, 'Friday' [1894], NLS.
[90] George Meredith to Lane, 23 Dec. 1894, in *Letters of George Meredith*, ed. C. L. Cline (Oxford, 1970), 1182.

without which he and his would have starved.'[91] There is a suggestion here of a farewell to journalism. He must have felt that he could now live by his poetry, that he had at last achieved 'the shining crown' which he had dreamed of when he had first arrived in London five years earlier.

Before Christmas, there was a proposed visit from George Egerton whom they had met at Lane's afternoon tea-parties. Born Mary Chevelita Dunne, she was an Australian of Irish-Welsh extraction who had eloped while young with Henry Higginson, the husband of Herman Melville's widow. At the time the Davidsons met her, she was married to George Egerton Clairmonte, a Newfoundlander returned from Africa. She was loquacious and companionable, and tried to make friends with Maggie. But Maggie deputed John to reply to her letter, 'which is very bad of her, as she is one of the best letter writers in the world', Davidson wrote. He himself was nervous about receiving guests, and felt obliged to apologize for the house when extending the invitation to her husband:

As he had come from a country house and is going shortly to one, he would be vastly entertained with our little encampment in this northern wilderness: like a sandwich of two ortolons with a little piece of stale bread between.

He arranged to meet them at Hornsey Station where he promised to 'smoke cigars and drink whiskey . . . from 3 till you come—hard labour that suits me'.[92] His nervousness was unnecessary. The afternoon passed well, with Maggie serving many cups of tea to 'George Egerton', a name she preferred to Mrs Clairemont.

They received a delicately illuminated letter from her on Christmas Eve. In writing to thank her, Davidson interpreted her 'good birds' as 'an omen of a happier Christmas than we have had since the first year of our marriage. Always some disaster has overtaken us hitherto about Yuletide. So far we are scatheless this year.'[93] They were to remain so. He was delighted to see his fairly tale 'The Interregnum in Fairyland' in the

---

[91] Davidson to Wemyss Reid, 22 Dec. 1894, NLS.
[92] Davidson to Mrs Clairemont ('George Egerton'), 'Tuesday' [Dec. 1894], Princeton.
[93] Davidson to Mrs Clairemont, 24 Dec. 1894, Princeton.

Christmas number of *Good Words*. The Bodley Head was holding high holiday with Lane taking a break in Cornwall. He sent Maggie a gift of bric-à-brac for which she had 'an immense ungratified passion'.[94] Davidson himself sent out copies of his *Ballads and Songs* as Christmas gifts, one with 'a gallant inscription' to Watson. But perhaps the most significant development over Christmas was in Davidson's negotiations with Dent. He had already approached Dent about his failure to meet the original deadline only to be told that he had been given the commission only on approval. He now gave this as the reason he had stopped writing it, and probably would not finish it. But it had been evident for some time that he had not wanted to go on with novel writing. A letter to Lane two days after Christmas reveals his real and unequivocal direction: 'I have established a kind of right to go on with poetry and must try to do so.'[95]

II

In January 1895 Davidson found himself at the centre of the first of a series of rows and scandals that swept through literary circles in the early months of that year. The first began with an attack on the new critics in a series of articles by 'A Philistine' (A. J. Spender) under the headline 'The New Log-Rolling' in the *Westminster Gazette*. Grant Allen and Arthur Waugh came in for criticism, but the writer's main target was Le Gallienne who was accused of using his newspaper columns to puff the reputations of his friends. 'A Philistine' pointed sarcastically to Le Gallienne's identification of three new 'major' poets in a period of six or seven weeks.[96] Le Gallienne's attempt to answer the charges served only to draw attention to the controversy. For days, the correspondence pages of the *Gazette* were filled with angry letters taking one or other side in the quarrel, with some unknown minor poets writing angrily to complain that their work had never been reviewed at all. It was the kind of quarrel beloved in Fleet Street, and soon other pressmen were joining in. Some contributions were good-humoured, such as Ricardo

[94] Davidson to Lane, 'Wednesday' [Dec. 1894], Princeton.
[95] Davidson to Lane, 27 Dec. 1894, Princeton.
[96] 'The New Log-Rolling', *Westminster Gazette* (14, 15, and 16 January 1895).

Stephen's satirical 'Ballade of the Newest Poets' with its rumbus-
tious refrain: 'Roll thou my log, and I will roll thine,'[97] and the
spoof extract from 'The Log-Rolliad: An Unpublished Minor
Poem' by 'Criticaster' in which a nest of minor poets sings in the
style of Davidson's *Fleet Street Eclogues*.[98] *Punch* entered the affray
with a report on a meeting of the Amalgamated British Society
for the Supply of Laureates, poking fun at Lane and the Vigo
Head poets.[99] More cruel were the verses in *Truth* condemning
Le Gallienne for his praise of the 'rebellious bardlet' who
'mouths against morality | As some exploded fable',[100] an obvi-
ous reference to Davidson following the controversy surrounding his 'A Ballad of a Nun'.

In mid-January Davidson had cut his connection with the
press-cutting agency that sent him notices about himself, and so
had no idea that the 'log-rolling logomachy' had assumed
such proportions until the end of the month when he read 'A
Philistine's' final attack in the *Westminster*. He wrote to Le
Gallienne at once to offer his support and express his feelings
of disgust for the 'scavenging dogs of depreciation'.[101] Le
Gallienne took the attacks much less seriously, and even enjoyed them, but he was to write respectfully of Davidson's 'energetic fighting spirit, as well as his chivalrous loyalty to a friend'
in standing manfully by him on this occasion.[102]

Davidson felt deeply indebted to Le Gallienne. Although
generally contemptuous of the task of reviewing, he had
learned through Le Gallienne its importance in encouraging
new talent and finding a public for it. He himself began actively
to do his best for younger poets that year. When he sat down to
review John Tabb's *Poems*, which he had recommended to Lane,
he asked for his original reader's report so that he could recap-
ture the mood in which the poems had seemed so special.[103] He
also gave detailed advice to a young student of McCormick's,
Frank Kemp, who wanted to take up journalism. 'I want to know

[97] Ricardo Stephen, 'Ballade of the Newest Poets', *Westminster Gazette* (21 Jan.
1895), 2.
[98] 'The Minor Poets' Walpurgis', *Westminster Gazette* (26 Jan. 1895), 1–2.
[99] 'The Laureate Society', *Punch* (26 Jan. 1895), 47.
[100] 'The Case of the Rebellious Bardlet', *Truth* (24 Jan. 1895), 193.
[101] Davidson to Le Gallienne, 29 Jan. 1894, Texas.
[102] Le Gallienne, *Romantic '90s*, 202.
[103] Davidson to Lane, 'Sunday' [Feb. 1895], Lane.

if, and how far, one man can help another in this matter',
he wrote.[104] In another generous gesture, he wrote to Lane
announcing his discovery of 'a new poet!', William Andrew
Mackenzie who had sent him a pamphlet of verses.[105] He
thought some of them as good as *Fleet Street Eclogues* and
recommended that 'Here Lies Oliver Goldsmith' be included
in the *Yellow Book*. It was. Mackenzie became editor of the
popular illustrated weekly, *Black and White* which, as is the way of
such things, was always to give unqualified praise to Davidson's
work.

Suggestions of puffing in this regard would seem to be wide
of the mark. It was a characteristic of the younger generation to
make a display of their enthusiasms and to wear their hearts on
their sleeve. This was true in literary criticism as in everything
else. At times Le Gallienne's praise of Davidson seemed ex-
cessive—he found *Fleet Street Eclogues* more fascinating than
Spenser's *Shepherd's Calendar*, for example—but he genuinely
loved Davidson's poetry and saw that its perceived virtues and
faults were interrelated and that these were part of the personality of the man himself. A recognition of Davidson's tenderness beneath the rough exterior informed his appreciation of
Davidson's verse as well as his liking for him as a man.

Even as Le Gallienne was being attacked by some sections of
the press, other critics were coming to share his view that the
harsh note sounded in some of Davidson's verses was part of his
originality and genius. The January and February reviews of
Ballads and Songs were almost unanimously laudatory: there
were five columns from Lionel Johnson in the *Academy*, praising
their beauty and strength,[106] and a full-length article in the
Illustrated London News from Richard Garnett. Although unsure
about Davidson's realism, Garnett, with insight, singled out
'Thirty Bob a Week' as perhaps the most masterly poem in
the volume.[107] Everyone was agreed that the collection was his
best work to date, and that it put him above the general run of
minor poet.

The 'log-rolling' row was just dying down when Davidson
found himself at the centre of a more serious controversy. It

---

[104] Davidson to McCormick, 5 June 1895, Glasgow.
[105] Davidson to Lane, 6 Feb. 1895, Princeton.
[106] '*Ballads and Songs*', *Academy*, 47 (5 Jan. 1895), 6–7.
[107] 'Mr. Davidson's Poems', *Illustrated London News*, 106 (2 Feb. 1895), 146.

began with a series of savage reviews of the January issue of the *Yellow Book*, which contained Will Rothenstein's portrait of him and his own sardonic 'Proem to the Wonderful Mission of Earl Lavender'. He was identified with the Decadents and his poem attacked. Critics took particular offence to the lines:

> Oh! our age-end style perplexes
> All our elders' time has tamed;
> On our sleeves we wear our sexes,
> Our diseases, unashamed.[108]

The novel to which the poem was a prelude came out in February. It contained scenes of flagellation and an illustration by Beardsley depicting the whippings. Arthur Symons, on seeing a copy, wrote to Edmund Gosse: 'I have just got . . . an astounding novel by John Davidson about flagellation. Shades of Lord Houghton. Is the man serious or joking?'[109] The critics were scathing. With thoughts of Murger and low French novels in mind, the *Pall Mall Gazette* described it as 'a plagiarised absurdity tempered by beastliness' and recommended Davidson for one of the 'well-earned whippings . . . that he so feelingly describes'.[110]

He was stung into a reply. It was the first of many occasions when he attempted, perhaps unwisely, to take on his critics. In this instance he managed to avoid sounding irascible. He defended his book as 'good-natured irony' and denied the charge of plagiarism:

When I sit down to write prose fiction—such as it is—one idea possesses me always—the idea of modern fiction as expounded by Rabelais in Pantagruel and Panurge, by Cervantes in Don Quixote and Sancho Panzo, by Shakespeare in Henry V and Falstaff, by Butler in Hudibras and Ralpho, by Sterne in Uncle Toby and Corporal Trim, by Dickens in Pickwick and Sam Weller. Nobody needs to tell me that my Ninian Jamieson and Cosmo Mortimer, Strongsoul and Saunders Elshander, Earl Lavender and Lord Brumm fall infinitely short of the least of these glorious pairs. Delight in the idea and indifference as to the element I admit; but that my intention was always literature, pure and simple, I hope only the unintelligent require to be told.[111]

[108] 'Proem to The Wonderful Mission of Earl Lavender', ll. 5–8.
[109] Arthur Symons to Edmund Gosse, 26 Feb. 1895, *Selected Letters 1880–1935*, ed. Karl Beckson and John M. Munro (Basingstoke, 1989), 108.
[110] 'The Earl Lavender', *Pall Mall Gazette* (19 Feb. 1895), 3.
[111] *Daily Chronicle* (22 Feb. 1895), 3.

His roll-call of masterpieces was a gift to the mockers. Harry Cust, who had succeeded Edward Cook as editor of the *Pall Mall Gazette*, returned fire:

We decline to be described as unintelligent, inhumorous, or without a sense of irony, when the ironing is the divinely flattest that Providence permits to propagate its product, and the humour and intelligence exist only in their begetter's eyes. Because you imitate masterpieces there's no reason that your imitation should be a decent one, and though your intention be the decentest your result may be the dullest in the world. And to combine dulness and indecency is the nearest touch to fame that Mr. Davidson's last effort is likely to achieve.[112]

For many readers, *Earl Lavender* certainly has its dull moments. Even Le Gallienne, who enjoyed the book, wished it a third shorter, and the scenes containing the over-talkative Mrs Scrambler cut entirely. But, as Le Gallienne recognized, it was written in the spirit of burlesque.[113] The story is prefaced with a note explaining the Decadence and the recrudescence of flagellation as 'a sign of an age of effete ideals', but the story itself does not suggest a corrective intention, and although Davidson sometimes spoke scornfully of the 'New Men' and 'New Women', moral censure on sexuality was far from his sensibilities, as a poet.

Earl Lavender is really a newcomer's high-spirited response to the seeming absurdities and extravagance of London life. It was written two years earlier, and its episodes are of Davidson's first amused impressions of the clubs, hotels, and eccentric characters of Fleet Street and Piccadilly, including an outing to the New Forest. The effect is of a comic strip. George Saintsbury, who found the motive of flagellation 'not to mince matters—an exceedingly awkward one to meddle with', nevertheless recognized this. He praised 'the climax of the book, with the sentence on Lavender, "You are a caricature!"' as 'quite excellent and of far-reaching import to-day'.[114] The book's representations might be grotesque and ludicrous, but how else, Davidson seems to ask, is one to describe the realities of the age. One is reminded perhaps of Wilde who a month after the

---

[112] 'Earl Lavender', *Pall Mall Gazette* (21 Feb. 1895), 3.
[113] Richard Le Gallienne, *Retrospective Reviews: A Literary Log*, ii (London, 1896), 225.
[114] 'New Novels', *Academy*, 47 (23 Mar. 1895), 254.

book's publication was doomed to play out in the dock the imaginative role he too had assigned himself.

Earl Lavender was listed fifth in the book sales for March. The attention it received, much of it critical, was an indication of Davidson's rising reputation in literary circles. Reputation brought invitations. The winter of 1894 and 1895 was, socially, one of the most strenuous of his life. He had become a celebrity. He recognized the advantages of this. In his interview with Jane Stoddart for the *British Weekly*, he told her good-humouredly that he planned an article on interviewing 'by way of revenge'; but, in the event, his 'Prose Eclogue: On Interviewing' turned out to be a recognition of the advantages of publicity, in which Menzies, in characteristic Davidsonian manner, defends interviews as spontaneous self-revelation against the ideal autobiography or prepared legend:

In literature we have had Creators and Spectators; now we are having Experiences. All our work is becoming more and more consciously autobiographic; and we must invite experience, we must offer ourselves to the vivisection of circumstance.[115]

But the role of celebrity could be trying. Henry James, in several short stories written at this time, notably in 'The Death of the Lion', was to explore the increasing dangers of celebrity for the artist. There were frequent invitations to attend parties and other entertainments. Davidson impressed Edward Marsh at a dinner party given by Maurice Baring in Cambridge as 'a genial and lighthearted little man, with a nice Scotch accent'.[116] The young Baring had contributed an article on 'Anatole France' to the *Yellow Book*, and was at that time under Gosse's wing. There was also an invitation for Davidson and Maggie from Mrs Gordon, another contributor to the *Yellow Book* who lived next door to Meredith at Box Hill. One of the most important invitations that year came in early March from H. C. Beeching's friend, Sidney Lee, who was then editor of the *Dictionary of National Biography*. Lee's illustrious entertainments at his house in Lexham Gardens were a great gathering point for London's artists and literary men. Later that same month, there was also a cheerful farewell supper for the staff of C. Lewis

115 'On Interviewing: Prose Eclogue', *Speaker* (12 Jan. 1895), 46–7.
116 Quoted in Christopher Hassell, *Edward Marsh* (London, 1959), 58.

Hind's *Pall Mall Budget* whose 'Good-bye Number' contained
Davidson's eclogue 'May-Day'. In addition to these distractions
for a writer, there were Lane's unremitting teas at the Albany
and suppers at the Hogarth.

In his letters to Lane at this time, he pleads constantly to be
left in peace and not sent any more invitations. He was busy
writing poetry and wanted to keep away from Piccadilly Circus
as much as possible. He found it difficult to get into the right
mood for work. After a night in London, with the hour's travelling added, he was incapable of doing anything the next day.
His letters are sometimes irascible, particularly when Lane refused to take 'No' for an answer:

I don't see how I can possibly come on Thursday. I am out tomorrow
night, on Friday afternoon, and on Saturday night. I find that it is quite
impossible to go one where without going another where: one has no
excuse. 'You went there, sir? Come now, you went there! Very well you
must come here.' And I, the most good natured of all poets, past,
present, and to come, yield. The result is that I have no income for
January. I can work like a nigger, and I can play like a kitten, but I can't
do both together.[117]

He was at pains to remind Lane that 'going about costs money'.
The royalties he had received for *Ballads and Songs* before
Christmas had done no more than pay off some of his debts. On
this occasion, Lane sent him a cheque for £50 and offered to
advance more money if he needed it. Davidson seized the
chance and promptly asked for another £50.[118] All the gloom
and irascibility of the previous weeks evaporated. He was in a
buoyant and expansive mood and full of renewed praise for his
publisher when he made out the receipt for £100, the largest
sum he had ever made from his writings. This time, there was no
feeling of indebtedness. His *Ballads and Songs* was to go to a
fourth edition, and he felt confident of large sales and further
royalties.[119]

This was in early February. The £100 relieved him of worrying
about whether or not books would come for reviewing from the
Chronicle. The money also allowed a long-delayed visit to the

[117] Davidson to Lane, 'Tuesday' [1894 or 1895], NLS.
[118] Davidson to Lane, 8 Feb. 1895, NLS.
[119] Davidson to Lane, 'Sunday' [Feb. 1895], Lane.

dentist for himself and Maggie, and the payment of a small personal debt of three years earlier which rankled him as 'a secret and diabolical triumph to the creditor'.[120] He was also able to get his father's watch back from the pawnbrokers. These were the degrading circumstances to which 'the poet of the hour' had been reduced. In the belief that he could now make money from poetry he gave up all reviewing, determined 'to do my own work, meaning to write poetry, straight on for two years, and exhaust the lyric impulse that has come to me in my old age, thereafter at the age of forty to begin writing plays for the stage'.[121]

His desire to write for the stage was probably reawakened by the commission that came to him unexpectedly at the beginning of the year. *Pour La Couronne*, a verse drama by the French poet François Coppée was having a huge success at the Odeon in Paris. This came to the attention of Johnston Forbes-Robertson through Frank Schuster, the brother of Wilde's close woman friend, Adela. Robertson, who was to take over that year as actor-manager of the Royal Lyceum Theatre during Henry Irving's fifth tour of America, was on the look-out for plays with artistic as well as popular appeal. He read *Poor La Couronne*, was impressed, and on the advice of the playwright Arthur Wing Pinero, invited Davidson to prepare an English version.[122] Davidson had always considered himself a dramatist first and foremost, but since coming to London he had not written for the theatre and had only once visited it. He had never dreamed of entering it with a foreign adaptation. But he accepted the commission gladly. 'It will be a schooling for me', he told McCormick.[123]

Now that his financial difficulties seemed to be over, he decided to do what they had been unable to do in September— leave Hornsey. They had endured another miserable winter of burst pipes and sore throats. Sandy suffered particularly severely and had inherited his father's predisposition to chronic colds. They decided to send the boys to a farm on the south

[120] Davidson to Lane, 8 Feb. 1895, Glasgow.
[121] Davidson to McCormick, 11 Apr. 1895, Glasgow.
[122] Sir Johnston Forbes-Robertson, *A Player Under Three Reigns* (London, 1925), 166–8.
[123] Davidson to McCormick, 11 Apr. 1895, Glasgow.

coast while they moved to a flat in town. They had to postpone a meeting at the Grosvenor Club with George Egerton and her husband when Davidson had to go to Brighton to make arrangements for the boys. Other close friends were also told of their plans. Grant Richards offered to put them up at his flat in central London while they looked for a place of their own, but Davidson decided to put off flat-hunting until the boys were settled. He was in no immediate hurry, as the house in Hornsey was paid for until June.[124]

Davidson's reasons for wanting to get out of Hornsey were complex. There were of course the inconveniences of the house, particularly its distance from London. But more than this, the difficulty of trying to combine writing and celebrity had badly affected his nerves in the previous months, and he longed for solitude. The choice of a flat in central London seems an odd one for a man looking for quietness, but for Davidson it meant freedom from the distraction of London booming in his ear a few miles away. He would be in London, but not of it. It also meant freedom from the boys. Family life had proved a strain. A small flat in London meant a fresh start for himself and Maggie, who was worn and tired. They had been married for nearly ten years and were still honeymoonless.[125]

Evidence of strain in the marriage is to be found in Davidson's correspondence with George Egerton at this time. In one letter he wrote:

Intelligence I begin to see is only possible in absolute solitude: even between two blood mates or two mind mates, or two mates united both in blood and mind, and in moments of the closest and most perfect intimacy, an edge is dulled, a mirror is breathed on.[126]

It was not often that Davidson divulged such confidences, but George Egerton was someone with whom he shared the problem of combining marriage and parenthood with the freedom necessary for the writer. George Egerton clearly fascinated him, as she did most men who met her. On one occasion when he and Maggie were to meet the Clairemonts, he asked for a separate tête-à-tête with her in order to find out 'if my canine-

---

[124] Davidson to Richards, 28 Feb. 1895, Princeton.
[125] Davidson to Lane, 28 May, 1895, Lane.
[126] Davidson to Mrs Clairemont, 25 May 1895, Princeton.

oracularity had any meaning by your infinite probing'.[127] There
is no evidence that Maggie was jealous of their friendship,
although she refused obdurately to answer George Egerton's
letters, perhaps, as Davidson supposed, through lack of courage. But it is unlikely to have soothed her feelings to hear
herself referred to jokingly in her husband's conversations with
the Clairemonts as 'Semiramis', the name of the tsarist dictator,
Catherine the Great.

The claim of personal freedom over family duty is the theme
of 'A Ballad of An Artist's Wife', which Davidson wrote at this
time. The wife in the poem is devout and sacrificial:

> After a time her days with sighs
>   And tears o'erflowed; for blighting need
> Bedimmed the lustre of her eyes,
>   And there were little mouths to feed.[128]

He had already dealt with the theme of hardship and suffering
in 'A Ballad of Heaven', but here the artist refuses to share their
misery. Contemptuous of 'wife, children, duty, household fires',
he abandons his family responsibilities for the sensual delights
that will enrich his experience and result in great works of art:

> He fled, and joined a motley throng
>   That held carousal day and night;
> With love and wit, with dance and song,
>   They snatched a last intense delight.
>
>   .   .   .   .
>
> Amazing beauty filled the looks
>   Of sleepless women; music bore
> New wonder on its wings; and books
>   Throbbed with a thought unknown before.[129]

As in the earlier ballads, a meeting takes place in heaven after
death. The artist sees his wife in a high place of honour. Feeling
guilty, he wishes himself in hell, only to learn from God that
his wife's faithfulness has saved him. The poem is not evidence
that Davidson himself ever seriously considered abandoning his
family, but it both expresses and resolves the guilty possibility
and suggests that his response to the Decadence may have

---

[127] Davidson to Mrs Clairemont, 'Saturday' [1895], Princeton.
[128] 'A Ballad of an Artist's Wife', ll. 13–16.
[129] 'A Ballad of an Artist's Wife', ll. 49–52 and 57–60.

reached a crisis in the early months of that year as he became a reluctant *habitué* of the circles that saw in him a spokesman for the overthrow of conventional Victorian morality.

By April 1895 Davidson had found a farm in Telscombe, about six miles from Brighton, where the boys could stay. The boys went down there at the beginning of May. After they had gone, Davidson and Maggie fell ill. Davidson blamed the anticipation of moving.[130] But getting the boys settled, and the costs of removal and living expenses had eaten into the £100 he had received the previous month, and there were again money worries. Lane was in America. Davidson waited for his return, anxious before he moved to receive the balance of royalties on his *Fleet Street Eclogues* as well as a cheque for his contribution to the April issue of the *Yellow Book*.

Lane and Le Gallienne had gone to America, hoping to forge new business links and open an American office of the Bodley Head. Some saw another reason for their departure. The Wilde scandal was about to break. On 30 March, in the Marquis of Queensbury's Plea of Justification as defendant in Wilde's libel action, the first name to appear in the list of counts against Wilde of soliciting boys to commit sodomy, was that of Lane's office employee, Edward Shelley. Scandal threatened the Bodley Head, and in particular the *Yellow Book*. The truth was that Wilde had virtually snubbed Lane and the Bodley Head circle after Beardsley excluded him from the *Yellow Book*. But in the atmosphere of confusion and moral panic that surrounded the trial, this was not to matter. William Watson led a protest group demanding that Wilde's books be dropped from Lanes's list and Beardsley's drawings be withdrawn from the April issue of the *Yellow Book*. A jittery Lane listened to the advice that reached him from England, and the *Yellow Book* was delayed while Beardsley's drawings were removed and Beardsley himself dismissed as the magazine's artistic editor.

Davidson, like many in literary London, was made doleful by the thought of Wilde in Holloway—'whom we both admired to his face and behind his back, who had in the greatest measure an unaccountable something which is genius', he wrote to McCormick on 11 April, the day of Wilde's second hearing

---

[130] Davidson to Lane, 18 May 1895, Lane.

and also his own birthday.[131] He identified Wilde with Por-
phyrogene, the monarch of wit and wisdom in Poe's poem 'The
Haunted Palace', whose fall leaves desolation and disharmony.
The words of the poem kept running in his head:

> But evil things, in robes of sorrow,
>   Assailed the monarch's high estate.
> (Ah, let us mourn!—for never morrow
>   Shall dawn upon him desolate!)

But his feelings were complex. On the final day of the Old
Bailey trial, when Wilde was sentenced to two years hard labour
for homosexuality, he expressed his feelings to Lane:

At first I was sorry at the sentence on Oscar, but I have since come back
to my original opinion, that whether he is guilty of the actual crime—
crime, so called; what the law has to do with it as long as there is no
rape I fail to see—or not, punishment is his only hope for the future:
two years hard labour! it will surely purge him even in the sight of
unintelligent England.[132]

From a man whose knowledge was born in large part out of his
own experience of suffering, one would not expect a sentimental view. Wilde himself did not have one, and made his miseries
serve his art. Davidson, who had admired and observed him,
seems to have understood him more than many. There was
nothing conventional or moralistic in his attitude.

   Three days later, the cheques arrived from the Bodley Head
for the eclogue 'St George's Day', which appeared in the April
issue of the *Yellow Book*, and the balance of royalties on his *Fleet
Street Eclogues*. He was thoroughly disgusted to learn that his
account on *Ballads and Songs* was still overdrawn. Only 2,500
copies had been sold—far less than he had expected. It did not
console him to know that he was making more money by verse
than anybody else.[133] He was already beginning to ask why he
did not receive a pension, having heard of Lord Rosebury's
award of £100 a year to William Watson. The day of the removal
was almost upon them. 'We cross the Rubicon at the end of the
week', he told George Egerton,[134] with a note of foreboding far

---

131 Davidson to McCormick, 11 Apr. 1895, Glasgow.
132 Davidson to Lane, 25 May 1895, Princeton.
133 Davidson to Lane, 28 May 1895, Lane.
134 Davidson to Mrs Clairemont, 25 May 1895, Princeton.

removed from the optimism he and Maggie had shared two months earlier when, with £100 in hand, they had dreamed of arriving at their flat in the West End like the fashionable couple in stories.[135]

For over a month, no one in London knew of Davidson's whereabouts. He and Maggie had the honeymoon they had wanted. He gave the Grosvenor Club, New Bond Street, as his address for correspondence. Honeymoon did not mean a break from work. He worked more now that he did not have letters in the morning to put him off his writing. A fortnight after leaving Hornsey, he completed 'A Ballad of An Artist's Wife' which he sent to Grant Richards. Richards had been asked to edit *Phil May's Winter Annual* for that year by the powerful advertising agent, Walter Haddon, and had turned first for contributions to Davidson and Grant Allen. When Haddon got to hear of this, he demanded to see Allen's story and Davidson's ballad before payment. He did not want them outraging the readers of *Phil May's* with anything along the lines of *The Woman Who Did* or Davidson's 'A Ballad of A Nun'. 'Writing of that character may be literature, but it is not decency', Haddon told Richards.[136] His nervousness was characteristic of London literary circles in the period following the Wilde trial. Davidson's ballad, with its decadent theme of the artist's claims to experience over duty, was daring for a family magazine, although the scene of atonement in heaven satisfied conventions. Richards did not feel it was his best ballad, although he considered it 'a great deal too good for anybody's Winter Annual'.[137]

Davidson came out of hiding in July. On the 3rd he wrote to Edmund Gosse inviting him to dinner at the Grosvenor Club to meet Professor McCormick of St Andrews, and giving his new address as 18 Warrington Crescent. He had already sent McCormick his new address on 5 June. 'Whether it will be a success or not I don't know', he wrote. 'It has plenty of disadvantages, but we were very sick of Hornsey, and are now twopence in a cab from anywhere.'[138] But a month later, they had decided they had made a dreadful mistake in leaving

[135] Davidson to Mrs Grant Allen, 22 Feb. 1895, Princeton.
[136] Quoted in Richards, *Misspent Youth*, 318.
[137] Quoted ibid.   [138] Davidson to McCormick, 5 June 1895, Glasgow.

Hornsey. They were far from happy with the new flat, which was the top floor and attic of an enormous old house. 'We took it in despair, but are so unsatisfied with the change that we tell nobody where we are, and are not supposed to have an address at all—unless it be Mahomet's coffin', he told Gosse. 'I have at least an attic to work in, and that too in the heart of the promised land for it seems that Maida Hill is also called Mount Zion.'[139]

Despite the irony, and his later habit of referring disparagingly to the flat as his 'garret', there were evident advantages in the new place. He could entertain visitors for one thing. His father-in-law visited them, possibly that first Christmas, and his son Menzies recalled that J. M. Barrie, then married and living in Gloucester Road, South Kensington, and the 'bill-topping' music hall star Harry Lauder, visited his father and were befriended by him.[140] According to one visitor, Davidson's so-called 'garret' was a 'very pleasant garret indeed, and consisted of several bright, cheerful rooms' with portraits of his father and mother occupying a place of honour in the sitting room. Davidson also had his 'poet's den' in the attic high up among the chimney pots where he smoked and wrote. It was large and quiet and plainly furnished, with rows of books and a few faded photographs on the wall, one of them—an unframed picture of Michelangelo's 'Tomb of Lorenzo de Medici'—fixed to the wall with a pin.[141]

Yet there were disadvantages in the new place, not least the steep stairs, and the occupancy of the house by Charles d'Albert, Professor of Dancing. The house in Hornsey may have been small and unattractive, but there at least Maggie had had local shops, a garden, and the coming and going of neighbours. Warrington Crescent was central and fashionable—at the end of the road was the Warrington Hotel where Sigmund Freud often stayed on his visits to London—but, since they were without the means to maintain a larger house and a metropolitan life-style, central London, for Maggie, must inevitably have

---

[139] Davidson to Gosse, 3 July 1895, Brotherton.
[140] J. Benjamin Townsend, *John Davidson: Poet of Armageddon* (New Haven, Conn., 1961), 190.
[141] 'A Lover of Solitude', *Courier* (23 Sept. 1909) (newspaper clipping), Princeton.

seemed lonely and impersonal, particularly since Sandy and Menzies had gone from them.

That summer Davidson was busy selecting passages of prose and verse for a book of engravings by Birket Foster, entitled *Pictures in a Rustic Landscape*. The book was to be published by John C. Nimmo who had commissioned his translation of Montesquieu five years earlier. Davidson's selection is much as one might have guessed, with prose passages from John Lyly, Richard Jefferies, Izaac Walton, and Robert Louis Stevenson, and verses from Herrick, Cowper, Wordsworth, Arnold, and Tennyson. One interesting inclusion is the sixteenth-century scholar poet, Thomas Randolph's 'An Eclogue to Master Johnson' to accompany Foster's 'The Reapers'. The verses are appropriate, in their way, but the references to struggling authorship suggest a more personal reason for their inclusion:

> The Reapers that with whetted sickles stand,
> Gathering the falling ears i'th'other hand;
> Though they endure the scorching summer's heat,
> Have yet some wages to allay their sweat:
> The Lopper that does fell the sturdy oak
> Labours, yet has good pay for every stroke.
> The ploughman is rewarded: only we
> That sing, are paid with our own melody.[142]

Davidson did receive rewards for his poetry, but he had not yet been able to free himself from the depressing situation of having to borrow living expenses on the strength of what he had still to earn.

The meanness of his own circumstances must have been brought home to him when he and Maggie finally visited the Allens that summer at their cottage, 'Hilltop', in Hindhead, overlooking the Devil's Punch Bowl. Grant Allen was at the height of his fame as a best-selling author, drawing £25 a week from *The Woman Who Did*. He was a colourful character. Though white-haired and all but white-bearded, he was only 47. He claimed to be a pure-blooded Celt—Irish on his father's side; Scottish and French on his mother's, a descendant of the Jacobite Grants of Blairfindie who had fought in the Stuart cause. Richards remembered that when he first introduced the two

---

[142] Birket Foster, *Pictures of Rustic Landscape* (London, 1896), 173.

men, Allen looked at Davidson and said, 'You're a Galloway
Pict, Mr Davidson?', to which Davidson replied, 'But who told
you so? You have friends in the North who know me?' He
concluded that Davidson was uncomfortable lest Allen might
know too much about his origins.[143] In fact, Grant Allen had a
habit of disconcerting most people he met for the first time by
saying, 'You are a Pict', or 'You are from Devonshire', or 'Your
father was French and your mother English.'[144]

Davidson had responded with friendly goodwill rather than
enthusiasm to the success of *The Woman Who Did* earlier that
year. He admired it for its sincerity rather than its accomplish-
ment. In April his advice for McCormick's young, would-be
writer, Frank Kemp, had been to follow the example of Allen
and the other writers of Lane's Keynotes series, and look into
his heart and write:

However far astray the public may be, the reason why it reads raven-
ously 'Woman Who Did' etc. is because it finds sincerity in these books:
the incapacity may be huge and want of culture criminal in the writers
of 'Keynotes', but the cultured people seem to have nothing to say,
they seem not to have lived, while these other writers, small-brained,
small-hearted, badly-equipped even in the matter of the experience in
which they deal, yet, saying what they know of their own knowledge,
come straight home to businesses and bosoms.[145]

He had a great respect for Grant Allen and had not forgotten
his laudatory review of *Ballads and Songs*. When asked by Jane
Stoddart if anyone could claim to have discovered him, he
answered,

Well, no, I discovered myself; but I may say that I have never met a
more sympathetic and appreciative man than Mr. Grant Allen. He has
an open mind for anything new, and does not, like some critics keep
back his kind words till the author no longer requires them.[146]

The visit to Hindhead was a success. Le Gallienne, in his green
velvet jacket, joined them for the day. They made a cheerful

---

[143] Grant Richards, *Author Hunting* (London, 1934), 220.

[144] Alice L. Bird to Edward Clodd, quoted in Edward Clodd, *Grant Allen: A Memoir*
(London, 1900), 110.

[145] Davidson to McCormick, 12 Apr. 1895, Glasgow.

[146] Jane Stoddart ('Lorna'), 'An Interview with John Davidson', *British Weekly*, 17
(13 Dec. 1894), 121.

walking party with Grant Allen in his grey stalker and Davidson wearing a pair of trousers belonging to his tall host because his own were wet.[147]

Back in London, Davidson concentrated on completing a second series of *Fleet Street Eclogues*. He polished and whittled away at them through late summer and early autumn, and by 8 October they were ready to go to press.[148] His reputation was by then already reaching beyond England. There was a request from Berlin about the possibility of a German translation of *Ballads and Songs*. But his main ambition was to break into the American market. He had been unhappy about the note in the April issue of the *Yellow Book* stating that his poem 'St George's Day' was 'Copyright in America by John Lane', and told Lane in no uncertain terms that he considered himself free to negotiate with American publishers about a copyright edition of his work if he wanted.[149] As he was to discover several times that year, playing the role of both author and agent could be awkward. In January he had tried to fix 4 guineas as the lowest price for the serial use of a signed poem, only to be taken aside gravely by several editors and warned not to put up his prices.[150] He had a particularly difficult time with C. K. Shorter, the editor of the *Illustrated London News*, whom he described as having 'extraordinary and quite incomprehensible formulas and ceremonies and tape and sealing wax wrapped round the cash-box'.[151] This drove him to try agents—he eventually handed over all his business that year to Gissing's agent A. P. Watt who had offices in the Strand—although this too caused him trouble with editors. But in spite of warnings that employing Watt might sour his relationship with Lane, a deal for the *Eclogues* was struck. Lane was to publish them jointly with his new American partners, Dodd and Mead. Davidson was excited. 'It is time it was getting across the Atlantic, isn't it?' He was to receive £50 on receipt of the manuscript and £50 on 1 December on royalties of 25 per cent for the new eclogues, and 20 per cent for the

---

[147] See manuscript verses, 'Oh When, And Where, And How Sirs?', not dated [summer 1895], Yale.
[148] Davidson to Lane, 8 Oct. 1895, Lane.
[149] Davidson to Lane, 28 May 1895, Lane.
[150] Davidson to C. K. Shorter, 9 Jan. 1895, BL.
[151] Davidson to McCormick, 11 Apr. 1895, Glasgow.

John Davidson

Davidson, back row, right, at Kelvinside Academy, 1881.

Alexander Davidson, the poet's father.

A drawing by Walter Sickert, 1894.

Drawing by William Rothenstein. (British Museum)

Aubrey Beardsley's frontispiece to Davidson's *Plays* (1894)

Davidson, about 1896

THE BODY OF MR. JOHN DAVIDSON, THE POET, BURIED TEN MILES OUT AT SEA OFF PENZANCE.

Ten miles out from Penzance, and in twenty fathoms of water, the body of Mr. John Davidson was committed to the deep, this act being in accordance with the wishes expressed by the poet when alive. (3) Committing the body to the deep. Masked (x) is the Rev. J. S. Fagan, vicar of Newlyn, who read the Burial Service. (2) The late Mr. Davidson. (3) Mr. Davidson's sons, waiting in the stern, setting out to the burial. (4) Mrs. Davidson, wife of the late poet.—(Vaughan F. Foy, and Elliott and Fry.)

Davidson in 1899, age 42, by Bassano

revised third edition of the old eclogues which Lane planned to bring out in December to coincide with the second series. These were handsome terms. Dodd and Mead were also to issue a collected American edition of both sets of eclogues. In order to settle the problem of Lane's ownership of the American copyright of 'St George's Day', Davidson sent a copy of the Birket Foster volume in return for which he hoped Lane would write off the cost of copyrighting. It was a shrewd move, which took a leaf out of his publisher's book. He wrote disarmingly: 'Now, restrain those eloquent eyelids!'[152]

The contrast between the dungeon city and the countries of the mind seems, if anything, even greater in the second series of *Fleet Street Eclogues* which begins with 'All Hallow's Eve' and move backwards in time through 'Lammas'—traditionally, the August quarter-day—to 'Midsummer Day', 'May Day', and finally 'St George's Day'. For the hard-pressed journalists, the imaginative journey into the past seems more difficult than formerly. The beauties of nature keep breaking through, as in Ninian's vision of the Medway in flood in 'Lammas' and in Sandy's 'dewy memories' of the country and his first kiss in 'Midsummer Day', but the disease of the present is more evidently a pervasive infection of the mind, as in T. S. Eliot's early poetry, although in Davidson's 'St George's Day', which concludes the sequence, England itself is offered as 'the world's forlorn hope'. Though identified in some quarters as a distinctively *Yellow Book* poet— W. L. Courtney, for instance, was considered to have shown great courage in printing an appreciative study of Davidson and Watson in the March issue of the respectable *Fortnightly Review*—Davidson, more than any poet of the time, bridged the camps of the so-called Decadents and Counter-decadents. 'St George's Day', his final contribution to the *Yellow Book*, indicates that his own thoughts were moving towards Empire and the cult of manly strength.

'St George's Day' was widely admired. The reviewer in *Black and White* saw in it the quality of a national anthem and suggested that 'to know it should henceforth be part of the education of every child'.[153] In the twentieth century, the expression

---

[152] Davidson to Lane, 8 Oct. 1895, Lane.
[153] 'John Davidson, Poet', *Black and White*, 10 (21 Dec. 1895), 808.

of patriotic or imperialist sentiment in poetry has gone out of fashion, and criticism has tended to disparage such work, often irrespective of its poetic merits. Encountering a strain of jingoism in some of the best poetry of the Victorian era, readers today are tempted to dismiss it as a regrettable and embarrassing feature of the age. One could argue that Davidson's vision of Empire is essentially spiritual, an abstract ideal of a 'splendid past' through which the dark present can be seen and the future imagined; but this would be to devalue his patriotic convictions. In 'St George's Day', the imperialist Basil gives voice to the late-Victorian ideal of England as 'the foster mother of nations'. War paves the way for civilizing, humanitarian influences:

> Because, although red blood may flow,
> And ocean shake with shot,
> Not England's sword but England's Word
> Undoes the Gordian Knot.
> Bold tongue, stout heart, strong hand, brave brow
> The world's four quarters win;
> And patiently with axe and plough
> We bring the deserts in.[154]

There is little doubt that Davidson himself believed this. To imagine otherwise is to miss a characteristic allegiance on the part of the enlightened Scotsman of Davidson's background to the wider claims of progress and Britain's 'greatness'. There has always been a strong sense of investment and pride in the achievements of empire among some sections of the Scottish people. As a boy, Davidson had watched the steamships leave the quays of Greenock for the far corners of the world, driven by engines that had been invented by James Watt, the town's most famous son. 'The Scotch are just northern English, and the best of the breed', asserts the youthful hero in Davidson's novel *Baptist Lake*.[155] It is a proud self-evaluation that Davidson himself, at some level at least, would seem to have shared.

It is not unlikely that there was an element of opportunism in all this. The office of Poet Laureate had been unfilled since the death of Tennyson in October 1892. Watson had been suggested for the laureateship by Gladstone quite early on, a move

---

[154] 'St George's Day', ll. 219–26.   [155] *Baptist Lake*, 66.

blocked by James Bryce, whom Gladstone had brought into the
Cabinet in August 1892. It would have been unlike Davidson
not to harbour secret ambitions about this, even though he
knew it to be an impossibility. When the *Idler* sought the views
of some of the leading writers of the day on 'Who Should
be Laureate?', there was little variety of opinion. Davidson, like
most of those canvassed, placed Swinburne first, though it was
generally acknowledged that Swinburne's republican sentiments and amorality ruled him out. Davidson himself was mentioned only once, by the novelist Barry Pain, as a possible third
choice after Swinburne or William Morris. Watson was named
several times, and placed first by Grant Allen.[156] But that was in
April. With the critical success of *Ballads and Songs*, Davidson
had begun to outstrip him in reputation.

He was unexpectedly busy over Christmas, filling in at the
Speaker in the job he used to do at that time of year reviewing
Christmas books. The appeal had been to 'auld lang syne'.[157]
Sandy and Menzies were home for Christmas. There were
family outings to the Crystal Palace, the Tower of London, and
the Westminster Aquarium. On their return from the Crystal
Palace on New Year's Eve about 8 o'clock, they found a strange
package on the stairhead at Warrington Crescent—a gift from
Lane. 'Clearly gold nuggets, we said—a fortune at last, all at
once, and in a hamper', he wrote in his letter of thanks the
next day.

We turned them out on the floor, and they looked like nuggets: they
were wet also as if they had just been washed out of the sand. We
counted them, and calculated the value of the gold chickens. Our
estimates did not agree; but we didn't quarrel about that. We smashed
one with a hammer, but the gold in that one had gone soft. And we
determined to wait till next day.[158]

He was in cheerful mood and kept up the mystery of the oysters
with the boys until the following afternoon. According to
Maggie, he treated them 'more like chums, than sons'.[159]

The Poet Laureate was announced in January 1896. The
appointment went to Alfred Austin. Davidson spoke of it with

---

[156] 'Who Should be Laureate?', *Idler*, 7 (Apr. 1895), 400–19.
[157] Davidson to Lane, 'Saturday Night' [Dec. 1895], Princeton.
[158] Davidson to Lane, 1 Jan. 1896, NLS.
[159] Quoted in *Daily Mail* (29 Mar. 1909), 5.

disgust when he met Gissing for lunch at the Grosvenor Club on the 11th. It was widely considered a blatant triumph of establishment taste over poetic merit. But in other respects he was in good spirits. Apart from some grumbling on the part of critics about his tendency to philosophize in blank verse, the new series of *Fleet Street Eclogues* had been well received on both sides of the Atlantic. He had also another reason to celebrate. His adaptation of *For the Crown* was to go into production in February. Mrs Campbell had been persuaded to play the part of the slave girl, Militza. She had already played Juliet to Robertson's Romeo at the Lyceum earlier that season, and the London audiences were eagerly awaiting her return to the stage.

Davidson was optimistic that the play would be a popular success. But at the beginning of February he was ill with nervous strain. His correspondence suggests some deep personal crisis. The previous April there had been a recurrence of his brother's insanity and his mother and sister's financial difficulties in Edinburgh, although he comforted himself with the thought that the situation there was not as bad as he was apt to imagine. But things may have worsened, and feeling desperate 'with this that and the other' he went down to Taplow and walked along the Thames. This restored his spirits and by Wednesday, the 19th, he felt much better. That day he put together as much money as he could lay his hands on and asked Lane to send him his account and every penny he could 'by hook or by crook'.[160] He attended rehearsals. He appeared to everyone to be in a cheerful mood. He made friends with Mrs Campbell, the two giggling together over the delivery of one of the actors.[161] Davidson had replaced Coppée's solemn alexandrines—the corseted six-feet or twelve-syllable line of French heroic verse— with the more forceful and spontaneous blank verse of Shakespeare and the English dramatists. He preferred a natural delivery in the speaking of blank verse, one of the reasons he had so enjoyed Henry Irving's Hamlet. But Victorian actors generally were often pompous and exaggerated when called upon to speak in verse. He continued making changes to the text until the afternoon of the 26th.

---

[160] Davidson to Lane, 19 Feb. 1896, Lane.
[161] Mrs Patrick Campbell, *My Life and Some Letters* (London, [1922]), 110.

For the Crown opened on the 27th. At 8.15 p.m. the orchestra struck up the first notes of Mendelssohn's 'Ruy Blas' overture. London's leading drama critics were in the audience: Bernard Shaw for the *Saturday Review*; A. B. Walkley for the *Speaker*, and Arthur Waugh who wrote for the New York *Critic*. Visually the set was spectacular, with Forbes-Robertson in Balkan caftan and martial helmet. Shaw was particularly impressed by the first set, Walter Hann's 'Citadel in the Balkans', and by the life-sized equestrian statue modelled by Andrea Carlo Lucchesi in the style of Verrocchio. Set in a mythical kingdom of the Balkans in the fourteenth century, the play tells the story of Constantine Brancomir who implores his father not to betray their country to the Turks in return 'for the crown'. The two struggle, and the father is killed. Wishing to conceal his father's treachery, Constantine reports that he has died defending the country's borders, and an equestrian statue is erected in the dead hero's honour. The play ends in scenes of intense melodrama. The stepmother Brazilide discovers the truth and tricks the people into believing that Constantine is a traitor. He, to preserve his father's good name, accepts the terrible punishment of being chained to the base of the statue and left to die. He is saved from a slow and miserable death when Militza, the slave girl who loves him, stabs him through the heart before turning the knife on herself. One of the most moving moments for the audience was Mrs Campbell's rendering of the song 'Butterflies' which Davidson let her recite instead of sing.

Davidson himself had decided not to be there, but Maggie was smuggled into the gallery.[162] He appears to have hung nervously about the theatre, drinking whisky at the theatre bar and joining Maggie at the end of the performance when it was clear that the play was a success. When the enthusiastic audience called for Davidson at the final curtain, Forbes-Robertson came forward to explain that he was not present, but he was seen looking 'modest and elated' by Arthur Waugh who believed he had been in the gallery.

Congratulations began to pour in the next day. There was a letter from Gissing. There were also requests for the verses recited by Mrs Campbell. In Paris, Robert Sherard reported that

---

[162] Davidson to Lane, 'Wednesday' [Jan. 1896], Lane.

everyone was delighted to hear of the success of Davidson's adaptation. The critics were enthusiastic. Waugh told his American readers that the play had 'held the audience spellbound', and that Davidson was 'the one man needful to the English drama'.[163] Shaw, alone, was sceptical. He rejoiced at the return of 'Mrs. Pat', but he ridiculed the play itself and Davidson's blank verse. At this time, Shaw was battling for a new, more realistic type of drama dealing with contemporary life. He had already placed the Balkan mountains on the English stage in *Arms and the Man*, an anti-romantic comedy which satirizes the conventions of heroic melodrama to which *For the Crown* so unashamedly appeals. He claimed with tongue in cheek to be 'a little sore' that the adaptation had not gone to him for this reason, and considered that Davidson had succeeded in outdoing Coppée in 'rhetorical folly'. For Shaw, in short, everything except the play was worth seeing.[164]

Shaw's ridicule was not immediately damaging. On 24 April Davidson was able to report to his father-in-law that the play had safely weathered fifty performances—fifty presumably ensuring some financial return—and that he expected his first cheque at the end of that week. John McArthur had begun to follow his son-in-law's career with interest. He had a copy of *For the Crown* which Davidson asked to borrow. A publisher was keen to issue it and had approached Davidson with terms. Carelessly, he had not bothered to keep a copy, imagining that Coppée owned the rights and would veto any attempt to publish the play while it was still taking in money at the box office. He was optimistic that the play would run until at least the end of July.[165]

It was not to be. *For the Crown* was given its last performance on Saturday, 30 May, bringing the total number to just over a hundred. It was a respectable but not a spectacular showing by the standards of the time. Those involved were satisfied. Mrs Campbell remembered it with affection as 'a fine play' and 'a fine success'.[166] Davidson was less happy. His share of the receipts came to £200, much less than he had hoped for even on a short run. It was his first experience of the commercial

[163] Arthur Waugh, 'London Letter', *Critic* (New York), 28 (14 Mar. 1896), 187.
[164] 'The Return of Mrs. Pat', *Saturday Review*, 81 (7 Mar. 1896), 248–50.
[165] Davidson to John McArthur, 24 Apr. 1896, Princeton.
[166] Mrs Campbell, *Life and Letters*, 110.

theatre, and he believed Robertson's manager had cheated him.[167]

As on previous occasions, Davidson followed up his successes with a pot-boiler. The critics were dismayed by *Miss Armstrong's and Other Circumstances*, a hotchpotch of stories and journalistic sketches which Methuen brought out in May. It was not the kind of book they had a right to expect. Davidson had to redeem himself, and by the middle of July he had put together a new collection of poems. He was also in 'great pain and misery conceiving a play'.[168] He was keen to follow up the success of *For the Crown* with an original play. 'I begin to have an unquenchable lust for gold, and think of giving it full swing', he told Lane.[169]

Sadly, when his nervously awaited biennial account finally arrived on 27 August, it gave him a severe shock. His books had not sold as well as he had hoped. He was particularly distressed to find the 381 copies of the third edition of *Eclogues* reckoned as sold at Christmas 1895 suddenly reduced to 131. Only 122 copies had been sold since, leaving a deficit of 128 for which he had already been paid royalties. So it seemed that he owed Lane money! He was far from satisfied and demanded to do his own audit the following Monday afternoon. That day he also took the manuscript of his *New Ballads* to the Bodley Head and haggled over the final terms for the English edition. Lane had originally proposed a cash payment on the day of publication. Davidson asked for a bill for £150 to be handed over that day, on royalties of 25 per cent.[170] His recent experiences had hardened his resolve in business matters. He was beginning to live up to Richards's later description of him as 'a cross between Khubla Khan and a bank manager'.[171] Lane finally sent the bill on 3 September, Cromwell's Day. 'A very auspicious day on which to conclude any business or begin any enterprise', Davidson wrote.[172]

He seems not to have recognized how near he had come in those months to nervous breakdown. The pressures of celebrity

[167] Davidson to McCormick, 6 Dec. 1898, Glasgow.
[168] Davidson to Lane, 18 July 1896, NLS.
[169] Davidson to Lane, 27 Aug. 1896, Lane.   [170] Ibid.
[171] Richards, *Author Hunting*, 220.
[172] Davidson to Lane, 3 Sept. 1896, Lane.

had played a part in this, not least the demands for photographs and for his time. When he dined with Lane in July to discuss the terms for his *New Ballads*, he resolutely refused to meet anyone he did not know. By autumn he had become virtually a recluse. He was working hard to complete his play. He began to notice that his work got on his nerves much more than it used to, but he convinced himself that it was none the worse for that.[173] The problems mounted in September as he fretted over the proofs of his *New Ballads*. Watt's negotiations with an American publisher for a separate American edition fell through, and he quickly settled with Lane for the American copyright for a further £50.[174]

Then on the 20 September, Davidson's mother suffered a cerebral thrombosis. He travelled to Edinburgh and was with her when she died at home three days later. She was 72. When he registered her death the next day, he gave her father's name and profession as 'Alexander Crocket, schoolmaster', but was unable to tell the registrar her mother's Christian name, merely giving the surname 'Ferguson'. His signature on the death certificate is smudged and shaky. The funeral was held on Saturday, the 26th, but he decided to stay in Edinburgh until the middle of the following week to help Effie settle their mother's affairs. The will was read to them on the Monday. It was the same will that his mother had made four years earlier when his father had died. Everything went to Effie. The meagre estate had dwindled to £541 12s. His mother had tried to increase her capital the previous year by lending £300 to a neighbour, a Mrs E. Ritchie in nearby Minto Street at an interest rate of 5 per cent.[175]

It is generally assumed that Davidson's poem 'A Woman and her Son' expresses his own feelings towards his mother at this time. We know that he worked on the proofs of the volume of *New Ballads* in which it appears on the eve of her funeral.[176] Certainly the son's account of his mother's orphaned child-

[173] Davidson to Lane, 28 Aug. 1896, Princeton.
[174] Davidson to Lane, 17 Sept. 1896, Lane.
[175] Scottish Record Office, Reference RP 2747; Eric Northey, 'The Poetry of John Davidson in its Social, Political and Philosophical Contexts', Ph.D. thesis (Newcastle, 1976), appendix B.
[176] Davidson to Frederic Chapman, 25 Sept. 1896, Lane.

hood and marriage to a 'crude evangelist' resembles Davidson's own family history, and his complaints seem to express Davidson's own resentment at having to support his mother after his father's death. The poem itself appears to range the son's aggressive atheism unequally against the mother's passive simplicity of faith, but the battle is far from one-sided, and the hardness of the son is 'softened' into morbidity and madness beside her corpse:

> Thus did he see her harden with a hiss
> As life went out in the cold bath of death;
> Thus did she soften him before she died:
> For both were bigots—fateful souls that plague
> The gentle world.[177]

That Davidson was deeply affected by his mother's death seems clear. On his return to London he was touched by the letter of sympathy he received from Max Beerbohm, but given the circumstances, he asked not to be addressed by his Christian name, 'only my Pagan one'.[178] Bereavement for him did not have the consolations of religious faith. Nor did he benefit financially. Max spent the evening at Warrington Crescent the following Tuesday (6 October). It was to seal their friendship.

Effie came south to spend some time with John and Maggie at Warrington Crescent. She and Maggie got on very well. But Davidson and Maggie were both suffering from anxiety and depression. The first reviews of Davidson's *New Ballads* were far from favourable. Everyone was prepared to recognize in him a genuine poet, but the strenuousness of his new collection was unanimously condemned. Neil Munro described it as 'a sort of "Hill-Topperism"', and the tone like that of a 'new evangelist— a Provincial one at a street corner on a Saturday night'.[179] Quiller-Couch took a similar view. His two-page literary *causerie* rekindled the old controversy about 'A Ballad of a Nun' which was argued out in the letter columns of the *Speaker* throughout November. Certainly, the 'message' is more blatant in *New Ballads* than in Davidson's earlier poetry. His version of the Tannhauser legend, for example, stresses the value of sexual

---

[177] 'A Woman and her Son', ll. 246–50.
[178] Davidson to Max Beerbohm, 1 Oct. 1896, Merton.
[179] 'Mr. John Davidson's "New Ballads"', *Bookman* (Dec. 1896), 89.

passion in the medieval hero's struggle between his love for Venus and his Christian guilt. His note to the poem states explicitly his aim to lay the ghost 'of the unwholesome idea that still haunts the world—the idea of the inherent impurity of nature'. Oddly enough, not one of his critics appeared to notice in the collection one of his most accomplished poems, 'A Northern Suburb'. Like his earlier prose sketch, 'A Suburban Philosopher', on which it was based, the poem expresses much more than an environmentalist's distaste for the destruction of the countryside and the tackiness of the new suburbs. Here, as in the prose piece, horror is redirected by a thought for

> The lowly folk who scarcely dare
> Conceive themselves perhaps misplaced,
> Whose prize for unremitting care
> Is only not to be disgraced.[180]

In this Davidson differs from Gissing who also wrote about the suburbs at this time. Whereas Gissing is generally contemptuous of his suburban characters and their way of life, in 'A Northern Suburb', Davidson affects something closer to a discovered human identification.

Davidson sent Gissing a copy of his new collection. The two men arranged to meet for a second time that year. Davidson went as Gissing's guest to an Omar Khayyam Dinner at Frascati's in Oxford Street on 20 November. The Omar Khayyam Club was a dinner club for men with literary interests. At a club dinner the previous year, when Meredith and Hardy were guests of honour, Henry Cust had closed the evening with a parody of Davidson's 'A Ballad of a Nun'. This time there were many new men among the sixty-two diners, including Conan Doyle, with whom Davidson was friendly.[181]

Some time between that Friday-night dinner on 20 November and Saturday, 12 December, Davidson left London suddenly without telling anyone and went alone to Shoreham in Sussex. He appears to have gone in the vague hope that a month or two of the sea and the downs would set him right. He had been in a state of mental exhaustion for several months, but he had forced himself on. Recalling the events a year later, he

---

[180] 'A Northern Suburb', ll. 25–8.
[181] Gissing, *London and the Life of Literature*, 427.

was to compare himself at the time of his breakdown to a London cab horse, stumbling on between the shafts long after he should have been turned out to grass.[182] Even after his departure, he continued to worry about the American rights to his *Ballads and Songs*, and Henry Massingham's failure to publish one of his poems in the *Chronicle*.[183] He had been anxious that the poem should appear on the same day as Lane's advertisement for the second edition of *New Ballads*. Apparently, the adverse reviews had not affected sales. He was even capable of a grim joke, and threatened to send the bundle of books Lane had sent him to his father-in-law in Perth unopened. 'He has a big furnace and with a strong draught on, the whole hypothec will go up in smoke in two minutes', he wrote.[184]

But he kept asking himself why he was there. The place and the house seemed quite unsuitable. Shoreham, a dismal industrial backwater six miles from Brighton, with a harbour and a few streets of holiday villas, did not provide the peace he needed. It was no help to his nerves that his house was only a few yards from the Brighton and South Western Railway line. His confusion is evident in a note he sent to Max, apologizing for not inviting him round for another evening to Warrington Crescent: 'When I made up my mind to leave London, things precipitated themselves, and I am here—why I don't very well know.'[185] His mind was darkening and he was afraid. In one of the last letters he was to send that year and for some time afterwards appears the statement: 'The demons that haunt me are more than a match for me now.'[186]

---

[182] 'On the Downs', *Speaker*, 17 (5 Feb. 1898), 179.
[183] Davidson to Lane, 19 Dec. 1896, Lane.
[184] Davidson to Lane, 12 Dec. 1896, Lane.
[185] Davidson to Beerbohm, not dated [Dec. 1896], Merton.
[186] Davidson to Lane, 19 Dec. 1896, Lane.

4

Breakdown 1897–1898

During the early weeks of 1897 Davidson shut himself away from the world in his rented house at Hove Park Villas in Shoreham. He was joined there by Maggie and his sister Effie, who had decided to stay with them for the time being. Davidson and Maggie were both in poor health, he bedridden much of the time, suffering from depressive hypochondria. Ignoring his doctor's advice, Davidson continued to read, lying on his back to ease his nervous strain. 'When a Scotsman finds himself at cross purposes with life,' he wrote later, '. . . he either sits down and drinks deeply, thoughtfully, systematically, of the amber spirit of his country, or he reads philosophy.'[1] Davidson did the second. The green curtain of his bedroom was never drawn, and the window was left open day and night. The distant sound of waves breaking on the shore reminded him of Tennyson's *Maud*, a poem significantly about breakdown and temporary madness.[2]

Overwork, money worries, public criticism, the strain of his brother's insanity, his own prolonged spells of illness and insomnia, and his mother's recent death, all seemed to have contributed to his breakdown. The doctor he consulted at Shoreham tried to dismiss his mental instability as the natural pathology of a man of 40 and recommended exercise and rest, but Davidson was familiar with contemporary accounts of nerve disorder and took a more complex view of the problem.

Neurasthenia—or 'suffering from nerves' as it was coming to be called—was discussed frequently in the newspapers at the time, where it was generally considered to be a peculiarly modern malady, the consequence of living in an age of exceptionally rapid change. In Cyril Bennett's popular study of the subject, which appeared in 1890, it is explained in terms of hereditary weakness, although the physiological explanation is linked to

---

[1] *A Rosary* (London, 1903), 25–6.
[2] *Rosary*, 112.

social factors, including the rebelliousness of the younger generation. 'Much misery and nerve deterioration has been occasioned in families by the rejection by the younger members of tenets held sacred by their parents', Bennett wrote.[3] In 1895, an English translation of Max Nordau's *Degeneration* with its hysterical theory about the physiological and mental degeneration of the educated classes had captured the public imagination. Davidson's work is peopled with figures who suffer emotional disorder as a result of their rebellion, although it is noticeable that it was only after moving to London that he makes conscious use of the scientific account. He had been especially moved by Gosse's description of the diseased mind in 'Neurasthesia'. His own representation of the nervous malady is ambiguous: on the one hand, it is seen as a symptom of a degenerate age; on the other, it is viewed as a weapon in the heroic struggle against it, reaffirming the potentially transformative consciousness of the abnormal temperament, straining after truth in a world where disease and disintegration are the natural order of things.

Davidson had always been especially prone to anxieties about ageing and death; he had worried about getting old while still in his twenties, and on coming to London had worn a wig. The move to England seems to have aggravated the peculiar conflicts of his non-conformity. In Scotland, for all his theoretical defiance of convention, his life had been rooted in traditional ties and in the friendships of his youth. In London he lived a life of exile. His occasional attempts to prove himself a sophisticated cosmopolite only served to expose his temperamental shyness, and the division between his individualistic doctrines and his stern adherence to his responsibilities as a husband and a father. His nights in town among strangers only left him feeling embarrassed and remorseful in the morning. The effect was to drive him back into himself. By the time of his retreat to Shoreham he was already a near recluse.

The 11 February brought news from McCormick, whose fortunes seemed to rise as his own fell. McCormick had begun canvassing support from distinguished figures in the literary and academic world for the chair at St Andrews. Davidson was

---

[3] Cyril Bennett, *The Modern Malady* (London, 1890), 125.

in low enough spirits to ask, 'Are you certain my name would not be an offence?'[4] But he wrote a warm testimonial, and asked to be kept informed about the tactics of the enemy, promising to write a strong letter to Gosse should he hear of Gosse supporting anyone else. That weekend the boys stayed with them— one of the reasons they had chosen Shoreham was to be near them. But life was far from normal. He and Maggie were still suffering from 'monstrous depression' and saw no possibility of a return to London until the end of autumn. He confessed to McCormick:

I have got in among the briars and am trying to get out. It is horrible, the slough is tight; it is like flaying alive; but I shall cast it. I foresaw it, postponed it again and again, but I shall be forty in April and must go through with it now. Be happy.[5]

Illness did not stop him working, but he could not write as much as before. He began a play and wrote a series of imperial poems that mark an important development in his work. In 'St George's Day' the imperial ideal had been offered as a humanitarian hope. In the new poems the emphasis is on violence and the strong man. The first of these, 'Waiting', the call for a captain to lead the 'millions of useless souls' in England to some positive action, may have been written the previous year. But the others were written in response to the international crisis then developing in the eastern Mediterranean. On 11 February, after months of reported atrocities by Turks on the Greeks in Crete, Prince George of Greece left Piraeus with a flotilla of torpedo boats to liberate the island. Davidson, perhaps lifted by McCormick's letter, celebrated the event in 'A New Song of Orpheus' which weaves contemporary event with mythological allusion. The poem's philohellenic ideal was shared by many in England at the time, irrespective of political sympathies. For several days the peace of Europe hung in the balance. Davidson followed developments in the newspapers. His 'Coming', an appeal to England to join the fight on the side of Greece, was overtaken by events when the six major powers, the Concert of Europe, united to condemn the invasion and declare the island

[4] Davidson to William McCormick, 13 Feb. 1897, Glasgow.
[5] Davidson to McCormick, not dated [Feb. 1897], Glasgow.

an international protectorate. In the Graeco-Turkish War that followed, Europe watched from the sidelines and in May opened armistice negotiations with the brutal Ottoman Sultan, Abdul Hamid II, when his victory seemed certain. Davidson's 'Hymn of Abdul Hamid' which appeared that month, seems inspired by his contempt for the political compromises of Europe. Abdul Hamid derides Europe and its God and boasts of his own God-given victory over the Christians. The word 'cumberers' which in 'Waiting' describes the 'millions of useless souls' is Abdul Hamid's epithet for the Christians he has slaughtered: 'Foul cumberers of the earth; | Now theirs is ours; and they, | Fuel for Shetan's hearth.'[6] 'The Badge of Men', the last of the poems of violence from this period, sounds a more personal note of defiance against the world and Davidson's own self-consuming frustrations. The speaker of the poem abandons the wilderness as an even greater enemy to his peace of mind than his fellow men and returns to the city in a new mood of heartless egotism that will ensure his success.

Among the books that had come into Davidson's possession were translations of some of the works of Nietzsche that had been issued the previous year as part of a proposed collected edition: the general editor, Alexander Tille's translation of *Thus Spake Zarathustra* and Thomas Common's translation of the shorter works. Davidson had already read about Nietzsche in an article by Theodor de Wynzewa in the Paris journal *Revue politique et littéraire* in 1891 and may have heard of him even earlier. Student exchanges to Germany had brought news of Nietzsche to Glasgow University in the late 1880s and early 1890s where he became the subject of fierce debate. Davidson's own version of de Wyzewa's article appeared in the *Speaker* in November 1891,[7] and again in a revised version in the *Glasgow Herald* in 1893.[8] Initially Davidson viewed Nietzsche's ideas with some scepticism, characteristically separating speculative freedom from everyday responsibility—the point of crisis, significantly, of many of his ballads in the 1890s. 'Any man who has work to do in the world, any man who has children, any man

---

[6] 'The Hymn of Abdul Hamid', ll. 26–8.
[7] 'The New Sophist', *Speaker*, 4 (28 Nov. 1891), 641–2.
[8] 'Frederick Nietsche', *Glasgow Herald* (18 Mar. 1893), 9.

who enjoys ordinary health, is furnished with an answer to Nietsche', he wrote.[9] But at Shoreham he began to commit Nietzsche's writings systematically to memory.

It is tempting but perhaps too simplistic to attribute the new tone of aggression in Davidson's poetry to his reading of Nietzsche. According to Le Gallienne, his temperament was one that was always ready to respond to the latest change in the intellectual and spiritual atmosphere.[10] After 1895, with the return of Lord Salisbury to power, popular enthusiasm for the British Empire had become more belligerent and jingoistic. In poetry the taste for the blaring trumpetry of the Counter-decadence was gathering strength. Wilde was in prison. Many of his admirers were abroad. The shift in Davidson's work is clearly part of this sea change. But his celebration of the imperial ideal is far from straightforward, having little in common with the sentimental conservatism of contemporaries like Alfred Austin, William Watson, and Henry Newbolt. He disliked Kipling's poem 'Recessional', which was written that year, describing it to Gosse as 'a paltry hymn—and not nearly so good as some of Wesley's we used to sing in my father's church—a very antique quack poultice for an uneasy conscience, a pill against an earthquake'.[11] He was impatient with the way it dressed up the ruthlessness of Empire in religiose euphemisms. His own approach, as in 'The Hymn of Abdul Hamid', is generally sardonic, amoral, intolerant of the kind of feeling to which patriotic poetry appeals. This is how his conversations about the British Empire struck at least one of his contemporaries at the time. In *The Whirlpool*, a novel about the claims of the Decadence and Counter-decadence, Gissing seems to be recalling Davidson's conversations in the character of Harvey Rolfe, who accepts sardonically the need for personal and national struggle to counteract a universal sense of decline. In Davidson's poetry the cult of strength is charged with a similar sardonic sense of redress; there is a genuine attempt to embrace violent contraries which are felt to make up the whole of existence.

[9] 'Frederick Nietsche', *Glasgow Herald* (18 Mar. 1893), 9.
[10] Richard Le Gallienne, *Retrospective Reviews: A Literary Log*, ii (London, 1896), 243.
[11] Davidson to Edmund Gosse, 31 Dec. 1900, Brotherton.

Gissing's novel came out in the spring. Davidson received a letter from him, apologizing for the novelistic licence but assuring him that a portrait was not intended.[12] By May, he had finished his play, a costume drama set in fourteenth-century Provence. He believed that Romance expressed essential reality and truth and appealed more to audiences than realism.[13] He took his play up to London where George Alexander listened to a complete reading but declined it. Immensely disappointed, Davidson then tried Forbes-Robertson. He made three trips to London in all, the third time to see Frederick Harrison at the Haymarket Theatre. But all of them refused it. 'The ice becomes thin', he told McCormick.[14] McCormick was about to be married to Mabel Emily Cook, the daughter of a second baronet. Davidson proposed a reunion with John Cramb in London 'before you also leave behind you the days that were'.[15] In the early 1890s Cramb had followed him to London to try literature. At the time Davidson had thought that 'as a lion' he was 'not a success' and had been a 'much nobler beast when he was a divinity student'.[16] Cramb had returned to academic life to become Professor of Modern History at Queen's College, London. The two had kept in touch and met occasionally.

By the beginning of July, when 'The Badge of Men' was written, his health had begun to improve, and he was optimistic about returning to London by winter.[17] His financial situation had also been helped by a commission to revise Carl Armbruster's translation of Elsa Bernstein's fairytale drama *Königskinder* for the Royal Court Theatre. The play, with a musical accompaniment by Engelbert Humperdinck, had been produced in Munich in January. Martin Harvey, who had left the Lyceum the previous year after fourteen years with Henry Irving, was to take the role of the prince who falls in love with the goose girl, played by the popular music-hall artiste, Cissie Loftus. It was Harvey's first great opportunity as a leading actor. *The Children of the King* opened on 13 October with Isabel Bateman as the witch and Dion Boucicault as the minstrel.

---

[12] 'A Railway Journey', *Glasgow Herald* (27 Apr. 1907), 9.
[13] 'Prologue' to *Godfrida* (New York, 1898), 3–4.
[14] Davidson to McCormick, 'Friday' [May] 1897, Glasgow.
[15] Davidson to McCormick, 'Wednesday' [May 1897], Glasgow.
[16] Davidson to McCormick, 'Saturday' [1893], Glasgow.
[17] Davidson to John Lane, 2 July 1897, Lane.

Davidson had planned a visit to London to take in the performance, but he was reluctant to interrupt his writing.[18] The audiences who did go, a large number of them children and their nannies, were rather overawed by the play's solemn allegory of love through suffering. The play was replaced after two weeks by Louis Napoleon Parker's romantic comedy, *The Vagabond King*. The management decided that *The Children of the King* might succeed as Christmas entertainment if more concessions were made to public taste. Davidson was invited to make the changes, and the play reopened at the beginning of December with the same cast.

This time he did go to London. He took lodgings at a private hotel at 149 Sloane Street, close to the theatre. He managed to see Cramb and got in touch with Lane, hoping the two of them might dine together, but Lane left instructions with Frederic Chapman to tell Davidson he was away.[19] In the revised version of *The Children of the King*, some parts of the original Humperdinck score were dropped in favour of interpolated songs. This displeased the critic for *The Times* who compared the effect to 'the lower grades of comic opera'.[20] The audiences on the whole remained apathetic, although many who saw it, including Mrs Campbell, were charmed by the play and Martin Harvey's graceful, boyish prince.[21]

Davidson returned to Shoreham disappointed. He would have to rely again on his journalism. Following the hostile reception of his *New Ballads* he had tried to avoid reading anything about himself and was angry when Lewis Hind, now the new editor of the *Academy*, sent him the year's restrospect of 'Some Younger Reputations' in which he was mentioned along with Yeats, Gissing, Anthony Hope, and others.[22] He thought it condescending to someone of his reputation to be sent a notice and suspected that an insult might be intended, particularly as he had not published a book that year.[23] He had been cruelly reminded of this when William Watson sent him a copy of his new book, and for the first time he had no book to send in

[18] Davidson to Lane, 7 Oct. 1897, Lane.
[19] Davidson to Lane, not dated [Dec. 1897], Lane.
[20] 'Court Theatre', *The Times* (6 Dec. 1897), 10.
[21] George Edgar, *Martin Harvey: Some Pages of his Life* (London, 1912), 213–15.
[22] 'Some Younger Reputations', *Academy*, 52 (4 Dec. 1897), 489–90.
[23] Davidson to Lane, not dated [Dec. 1897], NLS.

return. He tried to involve Lane in his quarrel with Lewis Hind and then immediately apologized for bothering him. He realized he was not yet well and was allowing his emotions to get the better of him. He agreed to meet Lane alone at the Café Royal in Brighton, but there would be no return to London just yet.[24] He and Maggie settled in for another winter at Shoreham. He was determined to get well, and on Saturday, 28 January he went out on the first of a series of walks on the Downs in the hope that the exercise would improve his health. The walks also provided him with copy for a new series of articles for the *Speaker*, which though not autobiographical in a strictly premeditated way convey through allegories and symbols his personal anguish and confusion during those months.

The first of them, 'On the Downs', takes its title from Swinburne's poem on the theme of the poet's search for meaning in a godless universe. The Itinerant watches a ploughman on the lowest slopes of the Downs and reflects: 'The lines of the old peasant's poem did not run smoothly on the sheet of earth he scored: but the sun and the rain and the seasons will make it all right.'[25] The article contains a story that Davidson was later to use in his 'Eclogue on the Downs'. It tells of a young man who builds up alone a palace of porphyry roofed with gold and writes many volumes attempting to answer the riddle of the universe. When he emerges at the point of death to stand by his grave side, his final answer to the 'What?' and 'Why?' of the universe is 'Live to Die!' At that moment another hermit emerges from a parallel palace and replies with an angry 'Die to Live!' before the two fall into the grave together. The 'Live to Die!' is clearly Davidson's own despairing state of mind at the time of his mother's death: it is the harsh message of the son in 'A Woman and her Son'. The 'Die to Live!' is more difficult to interpret but suggests a painful moment of personal, spiritual renewal. The tragic weakness of Davidson's heroes is always paradoxically their humanity, and the temptation to return to traditional pieties.

His subsequent articles for the *Speaker* return again and again to the possibilities of violent rebirth. In the second,

---

[24] Davidson to Lane, 17 Dec. 1897, Lane.
[25] 'On the Downs', *Speaker*, 17 (5 Feb. 1898), 79.

'The Triumph of the Wind', it is the cleansing wind on Thunderbarrow Hill that becomes a symbol of destructive renewal. The Itinerant identifies with the furze bush, an inverted form of the burning bush which spoke to Moses on Mount Sinai. The furze does not burn: it is a 'prickly, sceptical plant' which cannot tell whether it will flower again each spring and so chooses to 'possess its soul in patience, and look out and down upon the world, sinister and aloof'.[26] More powerfully, in an article which appeared on 5 March, he described for the first time the figure that was to give imaginative direction to much of his remaining life and thought—'The Man Forbid'. The Man Forbid, or the Hermit, whom the Itinerant meets on the Downs, 'neither hopes nor fears, nor hates nor loves'; but he is far from serene. The story he tells the Itinerant is a version of Davidson's own life. Like Davidson's early Spasmodic heroes he is a rebel with an iconoclastic message:

Break with the past. All that men have imagined, thought, and felt—art, philosophy, religion: all that is only a spiritual tail which must be got rid of if your souls are to develop.

His poetry is well received until his true meaning is understood. Feeling rejected, he turns his back on his fellow men. He knows that this is an act of spiritual suicide—'Man grows out of the past; his tap roots descend, drawing nourishment from every strata, and are warmed by the central fire'—but he is unable to recant. He appears on the Downs like Coleridge's Ancient Mariner to warn the Itinerant of the dangers of cutting himself off from the past and ordinary human feelings.[27]

The phrase itself—'The Man Forbid'—is taken from the witches' scene in *Macbeth*, Davidson's favourite play:

> Sleep shall never night nor day
> Hang about his penthouse lid.
> He shall live a man forbid.[28]

But the phrase also seems to echo the description of Eve's meeting with Satan in Milton's *Paradise Lost*. Waking in Eden, Eve relates to Adam a troublesome dream in which she finds

---

[26] 'The Triumph of the Wind', *Speaker*, 17 (12 Feb. 1898), 202–3.
[27] 'The Man Forbid', *Speaker*, 17 (5 Mar. 1898), 297–8.
[28] *Macbeth*, I. iii. 19–21.

herself beside the Tree of Knowledge. A beautiful angel tempts her to eat the forbidden fruit, claiming that it is 'able to make Gods of men'. He shows her how to sin by example: 'Forbid who will, none shall from me withold | Longer thy offered good, why else set here?'[29] The Man Forbid feels similarly forbidden—forbidden to do his best work or to achieve his true potential. He believes that his new knowledge—in this case, that there is no God—is a state of higher human awareness, but as in the first Fall, it brings no rest.

In the poem, 'Epilogue to Fleet Street Eclogues', also written that year, Davidson explored his dilemma in an extreme version of irony prefigured in his earlier ballads and eclogues. Here the Artist finds himself a prisoner in the Vale of Hinnom, a materialist vision of a visceral darkness where the mass of mankind, life's cast-offs and failures, is ground into human offal in order to sustain the beauty and harmony of the universe. The conclusion, though melancholy, indicates the beginnings of a reconciliation to suffering through poetry:

> We are the fire,
> Cut off and cooled a while: and shall return,
> The earth and all thereon that live and die,
> To be again candescent in the sun,
> Or in the sun's intenser, purer source.
> What matters Hinnom for an hour or two?
> Arise and let us sing; and, singing build
> A tabernacle even with these ghastly bones.[30]

By February Davidson had completed a revised version of the costume drama he had tried unsuccessfully to place with the London theatre managers the previous year. The central theme of *Godfrida*, as the play was called, is the contrast between the healthy and the brain-sick. The healthy are Godfrida, the heroine, and her lover Siward; the brain-sick, Duchess Emergarde, a woman ill with jealousy and chagrin, and her chancellor Isembert who helps her conspire against the lovers. The happy ending, in which the lovers make their escape, was one of Davidson's late additions to the play.[31] But the stress, as in Jacobean drama, is on irony rather than resolution.

[29] Milton, *Paradise Lost*, v. 62–3.
[30] 'Epilogue to Fleet Street Eclogues', ll. 211–18.
[31] Davidson to McCormick, 20 Feb. 1898, Glasgow.

Davidson himself located its theme in the lines spoken by the tormented, divided Isembert:

> . . . no felicity
> Can spring in men, except from barbed roots
> Of discontent and envy deeply struck
> In some sore heart that hoped to have the flower.[32]

He concluded: 'The discontent and envy of those who fall is not accidental, but the order of the universe; and if we could understand it better we should find that victory and defeat are one—the flower and the root.'[33]

Such consolatory fatalism was very much in the air at the time. It can be found in H. G. Wells's scientific romance, *The War of the Worlds*, which Davidson 'ran through' when it came out that year. He accepted its prophecy, 'that the world will proceed to be under changing forms just what it has been, or more intensely what it has been: comfort, pleasure, splendour for a few rooted in the misery, pain and degradation of the mass'.[34] The idea had its basis in popular accounts of the 'survival of the fittest' in which human society, like nature as a whole, was conceived mechanistically as a place of struggle, scarcity, and limited energy. A similar account of success and failure is also to be found in Gissing's novel *The Emancipated*. Davidson had a signed copy of this novel. Although he was never to be gloomily deterministic, such views dovetailed neatly with his own acceptance at this time of the ironic nature of the universe.

He was anxious to have *Godfrida* published in a small edition in England and America by Easter. He needed money. As his account at the Bodley Head was in a hopeless state, he considered trying another publisher.[35] In the end he decided to put the matter to Lane frankly, and invited him to dine with him in London on Wednesday, 9 February 1898.[36] He took a private room as he did not want to meet anyone else. Over dinner Lane agreed to publish *Godfrida* in April at 5 s. in an edition of 750. Davidson was to receive 1 s. for every copy sold. He returned satisfied to Shoreham the next day.

[32] *Godfrida*, 68–9.
[33] *Daily Chronicle* (20 Oct. 1898), 3.
[34] Davidson to William Archer, 9 Mar. 1902, BL.
[35] Davidson to Lane, 4 Feb. 1898, Lane.
[36] Davidson to Lane, 7 Feb. 1898, NLS.

With the contract agreed he began to worry about the format of the book. He wanted octavo rather than quarto, the format of his unsuccessful *Plays*, and begged Lane to issue *Godfrida* uniformly with his successful *Ballads and Songs* 'in blue buckram that my soul loveth and West's good birds'.[37] Lane agreed to everything. Davidson delivered the final manuscript in late February. He pinned his hopes as a dramatist on it and planned a production at Shoreham town hall before publication to secure the dramatic rights.

The background to his desperate fight-back that month was another financial collapse. He had to bring the boys home from school and taught them himself, a task he found hateful.[38] To make matters worse, the weather turned bad during March, and they were all ill.[39] He kept his spirits up with the thought that *Godfrida* was bound to succeed as a book and on the stage. 'I have stiff times again', he told McCormick. 'Still I had a rest, and a short taste of something like prosperity. I thought it was to last. It may come again—it will come again, and I shall make a different use of it.'[40] He obtained a licence from the Examiner of Plays on the 15 March to produce the play in the town hall.[41] But by the end of the month the proofs had still not come. He was bitterly disappointed. He knew now that the play could not be published by Easter as he had hoped. 'Do help me by a speedy publication . . . it dangles about me like a thing born but unsevered, and I cannot conceive or bring forth again until I am relieved', he pleaded with Lane the day after his birthday.[42]

With the publication delayed, he decided to approach some of the London managers with another play he had been working on. He had written the first act. He asked Pinero for an introduction to Henry Irving. Pinero obliged, describing Davidson in his letter to Irving as 'a shy creature' but 'a considerable man, as well as a modest one'.[43] Davidson had also begun

[37] Davidson to Lane, 18 Feb. 1898, Lane; Joseph Walter West (1860–1933) designed *Fleet Street Eclogues* for Lane.
[38] Davidson to McCormick, 21 Sept. 1898, Glasgow.
[39] Davidson to Lane, 25 Mar. 1898, Lane.
[40] Davidson to McCormick, 20 Feb. 1898, Glasgow.
[41] Davidson to Lane, 15 Mar. 1898, Princeton.
[42] Davidson to Lane, 12 Apr. 1898, Lane.
[43] Arthur Wing Pinero to Henry Irving, 13 Apr. 1898, in *The Collected Letters of Sir Arthur Wing Pinero*, ed. J. P. Wearing (Minneapolis, Minn., 1974), 180.

preparing a new collection of poems to be ready for Christmas. In the meantime he wrote again for the periodicals to keep himself in money, although he confessed to feeling 'miles beyond that now'.[44]

Among the books which had come his way for review was Georg Brandes's controversial two-volume biography of Shakespeare. He admired Brandes's attempt to derive the personality of Shakespeare from his work, although like Swinburne and most English critics of this time he favoured the idea of Shakespeare as the impersonal artist.[45] But the question continued to bother him, particularly when he began correcting the proofs of *Godfrida* and recognized with something of shock how much of himself was in the play. He brooded on the problem more than once in his 'Itinerant' articles for the *Speaker* during that spring and summer. Was it impossible, he wondered, for a dramatist to portray anyone but himself? He found an answer in Ibsen whose characters seemed to him to 'smoke' with Ibsen's personality. He had been reading Ibsen in William Archer's translations and concluded that Ibsen's characters were studied from life but were alloyed with Ibsen's personality.[46] But this did not satisfy him for long. In an imaginary dialogue with Ibsen which appeared in the *Speaker* that June, romantic self-expression is rejected in favour of an enlarged idea of the impersonal artist. Ibsen argues that the disease of conscience has brought a 'new wretchedness' to the world, but that this is the universal insight that reconciles all great artists. In a later addition to this article, Ibsen tells the haunter of the Downs: 'I found out, as Shakespeare also found out, that madness is the thing. You cannot have the essence till the shell is broken and the kernel bruised.'[47]

Davidson was to formulate these ideas more clearly in an important article on 'The Art of Poetry' the following year, where he argued that the subconscious of man is best visible in narrative or drama: here one found the voice of the species, the impersonal in 'personation'. Like T. S. Eliot over a decade later,

---

[44] Davidson to Lane, 12 Apr. 1898, Lane.
[45] 'A Portrait of Shakespeare', *Speaker*, 17 (12 Mar. 1898), 325–6.
[46] 'Chanctonbury Ring', *Speaker*, 17 (30 Apr. 1898), 553–4.
[47] Reprinted in *Rosary*, 174; originally 'Ibsen Himself', *Speaker*, 17 (25 June 1898), 790–1.

he takes his literary bearings from the Elizabethan and Jacobean age:

the freest utterance is always to be found in the narrative or the drama. Subconsciousness, which the poet singing in his own character inevitably obscures—that is to say the eternal, the voice of the species—becomes audible in personation. The Elizabethan-Jacobean age, the great period of drama, is also the great period of poetry, when every aid to free and full utterance was employed in the disdain of art. It was in 'The Spanish Tragedy' that Kyd revealed the new and excellent way of the madman. Here was liberty at last; everything could be said; and the kernel of the world appear through the rent in the heart, the crack in the mind. Hieronimo announces the woe of the awakened intelligence trembling on the verge of madness in three lines, three crude lines that are not surpassed by any piercing utterance of Hamlet, Timon, or Lear:

> This toils my body, this consumeth age,
> That only I to all men just must be,
> And neither gods nor men be just to me.[48]

Davidson's meditations on drama had brought him to the conclusion that he had already reached about life in general—that it was only in an agonizing disintegration of the self that one gained insight into the true nature of things.

In June the printing of *Godfrida* was delayed a second time. He tried to be stoical, but he was exhausted and sick at heart. He suspected that there was something seriously the matter and wrote to Frederic Chapman offering to withdraw the play if Lane had any regrets about having taken it.[49] In fact Lane was busy in the United States, where he was considering marriage to Annie King, the widow of a Boston lawyer. She was the daughter of Julius Eichberg, the director of the Boston Conservatory of Music, and at sixteen had written the words of the American national hymn 'To Thee, O Country' for music composed by her father. Davidson met her and her sister in Lane's company late that summer at Selbourne. The marriage had by then been arranged for the 13 August. Lane wanted to wait until after his American honeymoon before publishing *Godfrida*, when he promised to use his personal influence to ensure a successful launch. Davidson agreed to the delay and accepted Lane's offer

---

[48] 'The Art of Poetry', *Speaker*, 19 (4 Feb. 1899), 153–4.
[49] Davidson to Frederic Chapman, 7 June 1898, Lane.

of £75 by bill on 1 November for his new volume of poems to be called *The Last Ballad, and Other Poems.* He had still to write the title piece which he planned to complete by the end of September.[50]

By August Davidson had left Shoreham and settled with his family at St Winifred's, Fairmile Avenue, in the south London suburb of Streatham, intending to stay there only a few months, by which time he expected *Godfrida* to re-establish everything.[51] Although he appeared cheerful before the company at Selbourne that month, his private life was far from happy. The boys were still at home and studied from 9.30 a.m. to 12.30 p.m. each morning in the back room downstairs. Davidson heard their lessons before and after lunch. They had no servant. Davidson described their misery to McCormick: 'Maggie is like a ghost, and I am like the devil, but the poetry is great. Our life is like that of dogs in a kennel: for days we don't speak.' He ordered McCormick 'not to call as your friendship would perhaps dictate'.[52]

The first copies of *Godfrida* reached him on 15 September. He was irritated to find review abstracts at the end. He thought them vulgar. He wrote to Chapman to complain, indicating the high terms in which he now felt his work was to be judged: 'Tennyson and Browning never did, Meredith doesn't, Swinburne doesn't. In this small matter I can at least be on the level of the great names.'[53] They considered issuing the book at once, but decided to wait for Lane's return. It came out at last in the third week of October. Davidson sent a copy to old friends as well as to the new Mrs Lane. It had been a long and painful birth. By the end he had become less convinced that it would be favourably received, but was hurt all the same by the unsigned review in H. D. Traill's *Literature* on 29 October which concluded that the play was 'neither original enough, nor strong enough, nor dramatic enough for the stage'.[54] Max Beerbohm admired it but feared that publication seriously impaired any

[50] Dàvidson to Lane, 'Wednesday' [Aug. 1898], Lane.
[51] Davidson to McCormick, 20 Feb. 1901, Glasgow.
[52] Davidson to McCormick, 21 Sept. 1898, Glasgow.
[53] Davidson to Chapman, 15 Sept. 1898, Lane.
[54] 'Mr. Davidson's New Drama', *Literature*, 3 (29 Oct. 1898), 389.

chance of it ever being performed.[55] Gosse's laudatory review in the same issue of the *Saturday Review*, though welcome, was full of misconceptions and Davidson wrote to tell him that he had never read Jacobean playwrights like Massinger, Shirley, or Beddoes who were supposed to have influenced him, a disclaimer he repeated in an open letter to the editor of the *Saturday Review*. He objected particularly to Gosse's application of evolutionary ideas to literature:

the evolutionary idea is a misleading one in literature even more than in science and philosophy. Since the Ptolemaic system nothing more satisfactory to common-sense has been offered in any branch of knowledge than evolution; but it is now supposed that the sun does not go round the earth, and it may very well be that the apparent descent of man is a sense-illusion also.[56]

Davidson's correspondence with the *Saturday Review* brought renewed contact with Frank Harris who was to leave as editor of the magazine that year. He told Harris:

I keep searching for images of the crisis of life, the first heave and shudder of the turn of the tide, the racking agony, the distractions of the whole trend and volume of the ocean, but afterwards an atonishingly full and rich vision of the world as one swings out to sea and the sunset.[57]

Harris claimed to be in a similar state of mind. He wanted to meet, but Davidson declined:

A brief spate of letters now and again is more to my mind. There is more cement in a written word than a spoken one: certain: and you know besides how tongue-tied I am. Since the time of Moses, no man, great or small, was ever so tongue-tied as I am.[58]

He still felt in Harris's debt for a favour during his early days in London, but he was not attracted to Harris as a person, and it was clearly a strain for him to keep up the intimate tone of their correspondence.

[55] 'Godfrida', *Saturday Review*, 86 (29 Oct. 1898), 559–60.
[56] Davidson to the Editor, *Saturday Review*, 86 (5 Nov. 1898), 609; originally Davidson to Gosse, 29 Oct. 1898, BL.
[57] Davidson to Frank Harris, 24 Nov. 1898, Texas.
[58] Davidson to Harris, 'Monday' [Nov. 1898], Texas.

He was asked to write a review of George Meredith's *Odes in Contribution to the Song of French History* (1898) for the *Saturday Review*, which also bought his poem 'The Last Ballad', prior to its publication in book form. The poem was already in type for inclusion in the review on 26 November when Lane got to hear about it and, fearing the loss of the American copyright, insisted that it be withdrawn. An embarrassed Davidson had the task of approaching the magazine to ask that it be dropped.[59] His 'Epilogue to Fleet Street Eclogues', the final poem in his forthcoming collection, appeared in its place.

The Last Ballad and Other Poems was issued in December to catch the Christmas sales. Like *Godfrida*, it was printed in the United States. It was his last book to be published by Lane. In the days before publication he was confined to the house with bronchial catarrh, and had to cancel a visit to the theatre. He was also unable to answer a summons to jury service. This provoked him to his usual grim humour 'I expect I have committed contempt of court; if they behead me for it—it would help to sell my work.'[60]

The critics as usual mixed praise and blame. The most generous review came from the *Spectator* which compared his case with that of Shelley, in that 'whether we agree or disagree with his moral and political theories, there can be no two opinions as to the brilliance of his line and the fervour of his imagination'.[61] In America, William Dean Howells also had a good word for it,[62] possibly one of his reasons for believing that Britain had retained its ascendancy over America in poetry; but the book was not popular, and Davidson was never to receive more than his £75 advance.

In the title poem Davidson shifts between traditional ballad narrative and the tormented inner life of its hero, Lancelot. The title 'The Last Ballad' is ambiguous, although probably intended to suggest that the poem was the last word on the Arthurian legend. Lancelot was a popular subject of literary ballads in the Victorian age, and Davidson's poem is evidently indebted to William Morris's 'The Defence of Guenevere' (1858).

[59] Davidson to Lane, 11 Nov. 1898, Lane.
[60] Davidson to Lane, 29 Nov. 1898, NLS.
[61] 'Mr. Davidson's New Volume', *Spectator*, 82 (4 Feb. 1899), 169.
[62] Davidson to McCormick, 22 May 1900, Glasgow.

Davidson's version tells of Lancelot's year of madness as a 'wild man of the wood'; his vain attempt to commit himself to the quest for the Holy Grail; and his final return to Arthur's service, unrepentant in his love for Guinevere. Like 'A Ballad of a Nun' and 'A New Ballad of Tannhauser', 'The Last Ballad' elevates carnal love above a falsifying spirituality. But whereas the ecclesiastical complications of the earlier ballads tended to place the emphasis on heretical rebellion and pagan sensuality, the emphasis here is on an ironic acceptance of conflicting values in life. 'The meaning of the ballad is simply that there are those who follow the Holy Grail and those who do not, those who can and those who cannot, and . . . that is the last word on the matter the poet is entitled to speak, leaving the criticism of conduct to others', Davidson wrote.[63] For all its medieval trappings, the poem is clearly an account of Davidson's own breakdown and recovery. The pressures of his mid-life crisis seem to have forced him to consider the possibility of a return to his parents' religious faith, but he found this impossible to do. Like several poems in the collection, 'The Last Ballad' seems to reflect his own determination to be self-reliant. In 'The Outcast', based on an essay by Emerson, are the lines:

> Soul, disregard
>   The bad, the good;
> Be haughty, hard,
>   Misunderstood.[64]

The poem spells out the terms in which Davidson himself had decided to return to the world of action.

---

[63] Davidson to Lane, 1 Dec. 1898, Lane.
[64] 'The Outcast', ll. 17–24.

5

The Lure of the Theatre
1898–1901

London had changed during Davidson's eighteen months away from it at Shoreham. Many of his old friends and acquaintances had moved on. Wilde, the doyen of literary London in the early 1890s, now lived in poverty on the Continent. Lane had gained respectability in marrying a wealthy American widow. Le Gallienne had sailed for America. Beardsley was dead. Gissing was spending more and more time abroad. The 'other George'—George Egerton—was in South Africa. Grant Richards was soon to be married. Only his 'dear Max' remained the same, and he could look forward to occasional days of bachelor truancy in his company.

He himself had changed. His slow and painful recovery at Shoreham had been a time for assessing the past and planning the future. He returned to London determined to transform English poetry in the twentieth century. His thoughts had already turned to the possibility of a new kind of epic that might express the spirit of the times. Meredith's *Odes in Contribution to the Song of French History*, with their epic vision of Napoleon, 'humanly just, unhumanly unwarmed', had directed his imagination towards the possible form and subject matter of his Testaments.[1] In the meantime he needed money. He still hoped for a commercial success in the theatre, but he had come to accept that this would not be with *Godfrida*. The book had sold badly, and *The Last Ballad* had not sold enough copies to justify a second edition, although he persuaded Lane to force one.[2]

He might have gone under again if McCormick had not been secretly active on his behalf. On learning of Davidson's situation

---

[1] Davidson's ambitions are suggested in his description of Meredith's *Odes in Contribution to the Song of French History* as an 'epic of Democracy', in 'Another View of Mr. Meredith's Odes', *Saturday Review*, 86 (19 Nov. 1898), 664–5. See also Davidson to William McCormick, 4 Oct. 1900, Glasgow.

[2] Davidson to John Lane, 5 Jan. 1899, Lane.

in September McCormick had approached Gosse who advised an application to the Royal Literary Fund. In the 100 years of its existence, the Literary Fund had helped many distinguished writers, including James Hogg, Coleridge, Leigh Hunt, and Richard Jefferies. But McCormick had to be sure that Davidson would accept an award. He had sounded him out at the end of November. Davidson's response at the time was one of astonishment:

I could not possibly refuse the gift from the Royal Literary Fund. It will enable my boys to go to school for a time: it will be a great deliverance for my wife who had almost lost all hope; and it will enable me to do what I should be doing under less stress of worry, and perhaps to pull things out of the fire altogether.[3]

Without telling Davidson, McCormick wrote a long and moving letter to Gosse outlining Davidson's personal circumstances. It was important that Gosse should have a clear picture of Davidson's private affairs in order to make a strong case to the committee, and he included the grim details of Thomas Davidson's insanity, leaving it to Gosse's discretion to give it to the Council or not. He wrote: 'Circumstances that would have overwhelmed most men were with him an incentive to still more strenuous effort.' He estimated that Davidson had made perhaps £100 a year from his poetry when he was fashionable, and since then considerably less. But he added:

Please note that any figure I gave as to Davidson's possible sources of income are mere guesses. The absolute facts could be got only from asking Davidson himself. But one point I know for certain, which I see I have omitted. In the case of *every* volume, he had to obtain, by the kindness of his publisher, an advance of a considerable part of the probable proceeds long before its publication, and has therefore never been able to pull himself out of the miserable condition of having to live upon what he has not yet earned.[4]

This point was crucial, as Gosse had to establish that Davidson was in urgent need of some assistance. This would have been difficult without McCormick's testimony. Davidson was a successful author. His volumes of poetry and prose had appeared regularly over the previous few years and had attracted much

[3] Davidson to McCormick, 30 Nov. 1898, Glasgow.
[4] McCormick to Edmund Gosse, 6 Dec. 1898, BL.

attention. He continued to write articles and reviews. It was difficult to believe that he was facing actual want. A century later, it may still be difficult to persuade ourselves that Davidson made as little as McCormick estimated, or that his situation was not the result of extravagance.

In 1895, when his reputation was at its height, he received £100 in February for his *Ballads and Songs* and a further £100 in December for his second series of *Fleet Street Eclogues*. By 31 December his total royalties for the year amounted to £244 17s. 1d., although his account was overdrawn by £3 3s. 3d., this in contrast to William Watson whose royalties for the year were £544 14s. 2d., and Grant Allen with an staggering £1,047 15s. 9d.[5] Davidson's journalism was limited that year to a handful of newspaper articles and reviews, but he charged 4 guineas for his poems, and accepted other commissions such as the Birket Foster volume. His income that year would have averaged about £6 a week, a comfortable living in those days for someone in Davidson's position and roughly equivalent to his father's salary at the time of his death. His earnings in 1896 were similar and may even have increased with the relative success of *For the Crown* and the publication of *New Ballads* for which he received £150, his largest advance on royalties. But these figures in no way refute McCormick's claim, in a separate letter to the committee, that the Davidsons had 'always been frugal to the utmost'.[6] It was during this period that Davidson had to pay for his sons' schooling in Sussex, help support his mother and sister in Edinburgh, and provide funds for his brother who emigrated to Australia. By March 1897 his unpaid royalties were still £78 11s. 10d.,[7] but he had the additional expense of doctors' bills for himself and Maggie and was too ill to do sustained work. Since then, as McCormick stated sadly, Davidson's income had been steadily decreasing 'in spite of every effort' and he 'had to face the possibility of actual want'.[8]

Gosse filed the application on 6 December. He asked for an award of £250 and promised to explain 'the peculiarities of

[5] Ledger Balances, 31 Dec. 1895, Lane.
[6] McCormick to Royal Literary Fund, 4 Dec. 1898, BL.
[7] Ledger Balances, 31 Mar. 1897, Lane.
[8] McCormick to Royal Literary Fund, 4 Dec. 1898, BL.

the case' at the meeting on the 14th.[9] But two days before the meeting he decided that the committee ought to have some prior knowledge of the case and forwarded McCormick's original letter about Davidson's private affairs to A. Llewelyn Roberts, the committee chairman, informing him that Lord Crewe was coming to the meeting and stressing, 'I am very eager about this case'.[10] The meeting was held at the Literary Fund's offices in Adelphi Terrace on 14 December. Afterwards Gosse was jubilant. 'We had a great triumph this afternoon. The best afternoon's work done in my time', he wrote to the committee chairman.[11]

The next day Davidson received £150 as the first instalment of the grant with the committee's 'sympathy and earnest wishes for your restoration of health which will enable you to pursue your literary work freed from anxiety'.[12] The second instalment of £100 was promised in June. Not knowing who was behind the extraordinary and unexpected payment, Davidson wrote to McCormick, describing it as a 'great jail-delivery of despair and temporary installation in the seventh heaven. . . . I am unable as yet to connect it with any name. It is the entirely magical operations of a great unknown and unknowable entity, a Fund.'[13]

On 17 January he wrote an emotional letter describing the change the money had made to their situation:

For the first time in a year and a half we are able to breathe freely in this household. The boys have gone to a good school, and have ceased to beleaguer our minds. That was really the terrible thing: two creatures, of ten and twelve now, dependent on us for everything, education, amusement, and we ignorant all the time where the bread and butter was to come from. . . . Consider it: with my knowledge and experience of school, it would have been criminal in me to send them to a cheap promiscuous school: the attempt to teach them—such a hateful relation between a father and his children: and Maggie thinking it, feeling it, knowing it: hers was by far the hardest of the burden.[14]

He prepared the boys for school by taking them to see Barnum and Bailey's freak show, where he joined in the fun of the

[9] Gosse to Royal Literary Fund, 6 Dec. 1898, BL.
[10] Gosse to A. Llewelyn Roberts, 12 Dec. 1898, BL.
[11] Gosse to Llewelyn Roberts, 14 Dec. 1898, BL.
[12] Llewelyn Roberts to Davidson, 15 Dec. 1898, BL.
[13] Davidson to McCormick, 18 Dec. 1898, BL.
[14] Davidson to McCormick, 17 Jan. 1899, Glasgow.

Dwarf, the Giant, the Wild Man, and the Jointed Twins. He also took them to the pantomime at Peckham, where Marie Lloyd was appearing as Dick Whittington. He described her to McCormick as 'the genius of vulgarity, an artist in the jejune, in the phosphore and sordid, in blunt lechery'. He knew his 'little wretches' understood these things, but considered them 'as harmless as doves'. He had read Henry James's *The Turn of the Screw* when it came out that year and found his view of child-hood sexuality prudish:

To his old maidish mind what he presents seems to him very terrible, but it is the history of all children: that is how the knowledge of good and evil comes to them, only there is no foolish clairvoyante to kill them as a rule.[15]

Davidson discovered that Gosse had been the moving mind behind the Literary Fund award and wrote to thank him: 'I was going down into the gulf, the ice smooth and keen with nothing anywhere to impede or arrest. Suddenly I am hooked up and set on terra-firma.'[16] He had decided to write a new play. He wanted it to be something high, but he knew that if he was to avoid further disaster, it would also have to appeal to audiences, preferably on both sides of the Atlantic, and that it was essential to secure a commission and the certainty of production. This meant writing a scenario, something he had never done before. He worked on it in January, loafing as he often did when working on a new idea. After a fortnight smoking and drinking 'some of the Literary Fund money' he had the scheme for a new play in a shape presentable to a hearer.[17] He took it to Max's half-brother, Herbert Beerbohm Tree, proprietor manager of Her Majesty's Theatre. Tree listened, and with hardly a criti-cism, told him to write it in his own way.[18] It was to be called 'The King of the Lombards'.

He began writing at once. He was interrupted only by his usual yearly bout of influenza, which he described as 'a pariah among respectable complaints'.[19] In February the whole family

[15] Davidson to McCormick, 17 Jan. 1899, Glasgow.
[16] Davidson to Gosse, 29 Jan. 1899, Brotherton.
[17] Davidson to McCormick, 27 Jan. 1898 [for 1899], Glasgow.
[18] Davidson to Gosse, 29 Jan. 1899, Brotherton.
[19] Davidson to Max Beerbohm, not dated [Feb. 1899], Merton.

had it. He was the first to get well. He fought the temptation to socialize, telling Max:

Thus I say 'I am not getting on: the business won't march: the dialogue you write today is hapless platitude from beginning to end, little of it as there is. Carrots are clearly indicated. Very well, then, you shall have the pleasure of lunch in town with Max Beerbohm when you have broken the back of your play, but not before. So, gallop.'[20]

In fact they were able to meet for lunch at Dieudonné's on the 23 February when he found that 'consummate ignorance' necessitated a visit to the British Museum to do some research. He also kept an appointment to have photographs taken by Bassano, at Lane's request. They show a mature Davidson, bald, with goatee beard, gazing calmly at the camera. He preferred the standing one; the other he found 'too sweet and poetical'.[21]

He avoided going up to town after that. Besides getting his play ready for the stage, he also wrote signed reviews for the *Speaker*. This involved him in public controversies, but his characteristic combativeness was tempered by a new note of patient self-assurance that year following his return to London and the receiving of the grant. Gone was the old irascibility. His reviews were more than just notices; they provided him with a platform for his own ideas about the nature of poetry. 'Academic questions of rhyme, rhythm, and diction have little more to do with poetry than epaulettes and pipeclay have to do with strategy', he wrote, perhaps with those critics in mind who had ridiculed his rhyming 'ordeal' with 'cordial': 'Poetry is not always an army on parade; sometimes it is an army coming back from the wars, epaulettes and pipe-clay all gone, shoeless, ragged, wounded, starved, but with victory on its brows.'[22] But it is noticeable that many of Davidson's ideas are in advance of his own poetic practice at this stage. Although Davidson had opened up new areas of subject-matter for poetry, his poems and ballads of the 1890s still look backward to the nineteenth century, in particular to Scott's *Minstrelsy*, and to the imagery and idiom of the Romantics and Pre-Raphaelites. During

[20] Davidson to Beerbohm, 18 Feb. 1899, Merton.
[21] Davidson to Lane, 12 March 1899, Lane.
[22] 'The Criticism of Poetry', *Speaker*, 19 (4 Mar. 1899), 258–9.

1899 his call was for a new poetry beyond such conventional limitations.

He adopted the term 'Pre-Shakespearianism' in his poetic manifesto.[23] He claimed to have hit upon it by chance, but it may be no coincidence that he had dipped into Chaucer for the first time the previous year when McCormick sent him his and A. W. Pollard's new edition of Chaucer's *Works*. With D. G. Rossetti and Holman Hunt's attitude to Raphael in mind, Davidson argued that his objection was not to Shakespeare, but to 'the prismatic cloud that Shakespeare hung out between the poets and the world'. Although he dressed up his argument historically, his dissatisfaction was with the whole temper of contemporary Victorian verse which he claimed either 'hid its head like the fabled ostrich in some sand-bed of Arthurian legend, or took shelter in the paradoxical optimism of *The Ring and the Book*'.[24] His impatience is evident in a review of W. B. Yeats's *Wind Among the Reeds* that spring in which he wrote that 'it is difficult to believe that Mr. Yeats has not been dead for many years'.[25] Davidson called for poetry to be democratized, and its subject-matter found in the newspaper; but like the Modernists of the future, his credo was essentially aristocratic. In the early 1890s, his aim had been to popularize poetry for a mass audience. By 1898, he had turned his back on popularity. He was 'terror-struck' to see *The Last Ballad* listed in a Bodley Head advertisement headed 'Poetry for the People', and when a second edition was considered in January he wrote his own advertisement with the provocative heading, 'Caviare to the General'.[26] Davidson's call for democratic subject-matter was meant to challenge Matthew Arnold and the apostles of culture who believed that poetry could spiritualize the masses. His model was James Thomson who inspired the following description of his ideal 'Pre-Shakespearianism':

The city slums and the deserted villages are haunted by sorrowful figures, men of power and endurance, feeding their melancholy not with heroic fable, the beauty of the moon, and the studious cloisters, but with the actual sight of the misery in which so many millions live. To this mood the vaunted sweetness and light of the ineffective apostle

[23] 'Pre-Shakespearianism', *Speaker*, 19 (28 Jan. 1899), 107–8.
[24] Ibid. 107.
[25] 'A Spirit', *Speaker*, 19 (29 Apr. 1899), 499.
[26] Davidson to Lane, 5 Jan. 1899, Lane.

of culture are like a faded rose in a charnel-house. . . . The poet is in the street, the hospital. He intends the world to know that it is out of joint. He will not let it alone. With whatever trumpet or jew's-harp he can command he will clang and buzz at its ear, disturbing its sleep, its pleasures; discoursing of darkness and of the terror that walks by night.[27]

Later that year a young Edward Thomas, still at New College, Oxford, was to note in an article in *Literature* the 'apparent destruction of the boundaries between poetry and prose'.[28]

Davidson's views on poetry were challenged publicly by Quiller-Couch. In a series of four articles in the *Speaker*, Quiller-Couch argued that the function of the poet was to reveal eternal human truth—which was beauty itself—even in following it 'into the darkest slums', and that truth to phenomena, in particular the kind of contemporary horrors that were being shown 'in prose fiction', was the business of fact and science.[29] Quiller-Couch's argument is at least as old as Sidney, though directed by the nineteenth-century Coleridgean and Kantian belief that the superiority of the artist lies in his ability to see beneath the appearance of things, as other men experience them, to the things-in-themselves. Davidson did not argue with him, but confessed that behind phenomena he had found not beauty, but inexorable irony. He concluded:

I may ultimately find that irony includes beauty, and is greater than beauty. If poetry, aided by science, should find that truth is ugly, poetry will say so; but, as nothing is ugly to science, perhaps poetry may learn a lesson.[30]

This conflict of views about the nature of literature was to continue into the twentieth century. Quiller-Couch, like other influential educators of his time, assumed a strongly ethical function for literature. Literature provided an answer for society and the new world of science. Its appeal was moral, emotional. Davidson had come to the view, discomforting to the liberal mind, that literature need not imply a criticism of life. The role of literature might simply be to state the nature of the

[27] 'Pre-Shakespearianism', *Speaker*, 107.
[28] Edward Thomas, 'The Frontiers of English Prose', *Literature*, 5 (23 Sept. 1899), 301, quoted in R. George Thomas, *Edward Thomas: A Portrait* (Oxford, 1985), 66.
[29] A. T. Quiller-Couch, 'A Literary Causerie', *Speaker*, 19 (4, 11, 18, and 25 Feb. 1899).
[30] Davidson to the Editor, *Speaker*, 19 (4 Mar. 1899), 260.

universe and man's place in it. But he took a complex view of this and recognized that literature could be made to serve 'other functions, other aims'.[31]

The arguments did not end there. The examples he gave of 'the World as Irony'—the good fortune of the few rooted in the misery of the many, and love as 'a mere broker for posterity'— outraged many readers who wrote to the *Speaker* accusing him of pessimism and mockery. In defending himself, he explained that,

Irony is not a creed. The makers of creeds have always miscalled, denied some part of the world. Consciously, it is the deep com- placence which contemplates with unalloyed satisfaction Love and Hate, the tiger and the nightingale, the horse and the blow-fly, Messalina and Galahad, the village natural and Napoleon.[32]

The controversy raged for nine weeks in the letter columns of the *Speaker*. At that point Davidson decided that his work was suffering and that he would answer no more attacks. He found that he could write only once a day, usually for an hour or two in the morning. He continued to send reviews to the *Speaker* but from early May, these took the form of a literary *'Tête-à-Tête'* between real and imaginary speakers, some of them characters from his own fiction. He had first tried this method in the *Daily Chronicle* the previous November when it had attracted the interest of bookmen.[33] He now adopted it as his exclusive method. It followed logically from his view of 'the world as irony', but it was also a convenient safeguard against the kind of controversy that might have been caused by statements made in his own voice.

By summer his health had improved. At an afternoon enter- tainment at the sister of Lord Crewe, Mrs Henniker's in June he was introduce to the son of the Lady Charlotte Elliott who was looking for a publisher for some of his late mother's unpub- lished verses. He promised to arrange a meeting with Lane.[34] On the 15th he received a second cheque for £100 from the Royal Literary Fund, exactly six months to the day after the first. He wrote in acknowledgement to the committee: 'My health is,

[31] Davidson to the Editor, *Speaker*, 19 (18 Feb. 1899), 206.
[32] Davidson to the Editor, *Speaker*, 19 (6 May 1899), 523.
[33] *Daily Chronicle* (14 Nov. 1898), 3.
[34] Davidson to Lane, 7 June 1899, Lane.

I am glad to say, almost entirely restored. The play I am engaged in has already I think advanced satisfactorily.'[35]

He finished the play that summer. Its theme was the failure and belated recognition of the great man—a subject near to his own heart. The play opens with a competition in which Urban 'the man of action' wins the crown of Lombardy over Lucian 'the man of thought', only to forfeit it again because of his disregard for the state. He is banished, and the people of Lombardy believe him dead. But after twenty years of miserable exile, he returns incognito and in rags to discover that he has been made into a national hero and that a statue has been erected in his honour. He dies at the foot of it, and the play ends on a note of heroic wish fulfilment not unlike the ballad ending ridiculed in the second act: 'Time lapses; fancy shifts | Impressions wither; we are reconciled.'[36] But the dominant feeling of the last act is one of waste and disillusionment. Urban's return to Lombardy as a beggar destroys the heroic ideal of him held by the townspeople, while Lucian 'the man of thought' has died in the meantime, devoured 'by slow chagrin'.

After finishing the play, Davidson enjoyed a month to six weeks of good health and high spirits. Prosperity had come again after all. The boys spent five weeks 'on the top of the Downs', while he and Maggie had 'a famous fortnight' on the south coast, which seems to have included a day trip to Calais.[37] He also visited the Lanes at Alton, putting up at a local inn, the Queen's Arms, and meeting Lane's mother-in-law, Mrs Eichberg. He left a whimsical note for Lane's wife Annie on the morning he left, describing his visit as 'a very agreeable, unexpected, and actual holiday'.[38]

But by September things had started to go wrong. The *Speaker* decided it no longer wanted his reviews. Sir Wemyss Reid was about to retire, and the paper was to be revamped in October. Another casualty of the change was his adversary of that year, Quiller-Couch whose 'Literary Causerie' had been a feature of the review from its earliest days. But this setback was as nothing

---

[35] Davidson to Llewelyn Roberts, 15 June 1899, BL.
[36] *Self's the Man* (London, 1901), 62.
[37] Davidson to McCormick, 12 Oct. 1899, Glasgow. The day trip is suggested in 'Tête-à-Tête', *Speaker*, 20 (9 Sept. 1899), 266–8.
[38] Davidson to Lane, 18 Aug. 1899, Lane.

compared to another disappointment that month: Beerbohm Tree did not like his play.[39] Davidson had allowed himself to relax that summer, anticipating that his play would be a financial success. Now he had to find money elsewhere.

While working on 'The King of the Lombards' for Tree, he had also accepted a commission from the American theatrical impresario, Charles Frohman, for an English version of Catulle Mendes's comic opera *La Reine Fiamette* which had been a hit at the Odeon in Paris in 1898. The contract had been drawn up in New York on 28 June by the American agent Elizabeth Marbury who had offices at the Empire Theatre Building, 40th Street and Broadway. Davidson was to receive a $500 advance for the adaptation with the promise of another $500 on delivery of the manuscript 'on or about 20 February 1900'. His agent's fee was 8 per cent of the advance and $25 for drawing up the contract.[40]

He had already done some work on the play in August, looking on it 'as a holiday'.[41] Now that he was dependent on its success he found the writing irksome. He could not shake off the mood of depression that had gripped him following Tree's rejection of his play. In October he wrote to McCormick:

I burn my own smoke or try to; and go on with the version for the American manager. My great difficulty is that I have infinite matter of my own to write, and have to spend the whole day banishing that, and the consuming ambition and inspiration of that, in order to get a page of the adaptation that means bread and butter done at night. I have tried to write my own things along with the other; but when I do the grudge against adaptations becomes unmanageable. I am defeated; it will not help me to hide the fact. At forty two I have still to write against my will in the hope of obtaining time to do my own things. It is a sheer defeat, because I have tried to make money. There is nothing to distress me in the fact that my poetry doesn't pay; but it is the bitterest chagrin to think that I have written novels of my own and of other men, made translations, done everything indeed that was offered and lay in my power, and that, after ten years of this, when I had, in spite of the distracting and sometimes degrading drudgery, attained distinction in original work, I have only blunted my finer sense with no compensating advantage. This condition and mood you will note, as a psychologist, is that which the ancients called Hell.[42]

[39] Davidson to McCormick, 12 Oct. 1899, Glasgow.
[40] American Play Company File 1577, Berg.
[41] 'About Myself', *Candid Friend*.
[42] Davidson to McCormick, 12 Oct. 1899, Glasgow.

An unfavourable remark on his *Plays* in Archer's column in the *Daily Chronicle* did nothing to restore his peace of mind. He had still not forgiven Archer for a dismissive review of his *Plays* in the *Westminster Gazette* five years earlier. This time he responded with a spoof article celebrating the centenary of their publication and pointing to Archer's lack of perception 100 years earlier.[43] Archer, whose remark in the *Chronicle* was the result of his ideas for a book on *Poets of the Younger Generation*, favoured prose drama on contemporary themes and had lent Davidson a copy of Pinero's *Mrs Tanqueray* as a model to follow. Davidson returned it in December, unable to do anything but repeat the argument he had used in his letter to Gosse the previous year:

It seems to me that there is no such thing as dramatic art—no art at all, species or genus, that can be so discussed: every authentic person will do his own things in his own way, and no standard can be applied to authentic productions except the law of their own being.[44]

That December the Anglo-Boer War was at its height. In London, there was another epidemic of influenza, described enterprisingly in Bovril's magazine advertisements as 'the enemy at home'. Davidson had his own description for it as 'one of the ten plagues that has lingered on in emasculated form, but with the nasty nature of a eunuch well developed'.[45] It woke him in the night and caused him insomnia. He often sat up in the middle of the night trying to catch up on his correspondence. The French play was costing him infinite trouble. It was a miserable end to what had promised to be a year of renewed health and success.

The New Year brought some consolations. There was an invitation from McCormick to join 'a little crowd' at the Savile Club, Davidson's first social outing for some months. 'It is only with a revolver to my head that I can compel myself to ask a man to meet me', he wrote, putting this down 'largely to the loss of molars'.[46] Then on 13 February a grand 'Masque of War and Peace' at Her Majesty's Theatre to aid the widows and orphans of the Boer campaign concluded with a reading of a poem

[43] Davidson to William Archer, 25 Nov. 1899, BL.
[44] Davidson to Archer, 8 Dec. 1899, BL.
[45] Ibid.
[46] Davidson to McCormick, 2 Jan. 1900, Glasgow.

which, reluctantly but at Lane's insistence, he had written especially for the occasion—'They breathed no slur on her Imperial force'. A fall of snow had buried London in a dismal slush, but there was a large audience, which included the French and Russian ambassadors. The Prince and Princess of Wales and the leaders of London society were present, many of them taking part in the tableaux and pageants on stage.[47]

But this was a poor compensation for Tree's refusal of his play. He met the February delivery date for *Queen Fiametta*, only to learn that there would be no more advance until the play had passed forty performances.[48] He decided to do his own things. He began revising 'The King of the Lombards' for publication, but held back from approaching Lane until he had an exact statement of his account from the Bodley Head. He also wrote 'Eclogue on the Downs' which reproduces in verse form many of the images and allegories of his prose sketches for the *Speaker* during the time of his convalescence two years earlier. The poem follows the conversation of the pragmatic Urban, the melancholic Eustace, and the philosopher Lucian on their walk across the Downs. On their arrival at the Fox and Hounds in Steyning, Lucian recalls his encounter there the previous year with a strange, tormented solitary—another, more positive version of the humorist in Hinnom, the Man Forbid:

> ... scorned
> By fame; by fortune jilted, flayed and raw
> As to his vanity; bankrupt in love,
> But by a habit soldered into life,
> Transmuting pain to pity, grudge to grin,
> And solving all in morbid fantasy.[49]

The Poem appeared in Lady Randolph Churchill's new *Anglo-Saxon Review*, which was derided in some quarters as 'the *Yellow Book* in court dress and bedroom slippers'.[50] But there was nothing unbuttoned about 'Eclogue on the Downs' with its theme of transformation through suffering.

---

[47] See *St James's Gazette* (14 Feb. 1900), 4, and *Black and White*, 19 (17 Feb. 1900), 248.
[48] Davidson to McCormick, 22 May 1900, Glasgow.
[49] 'Eclogue on the Downs', ll. 277–81.
[50] Chapman Huston, *Sidney Low* (London, 1936), 101.

The poem was completed in February. In March Davidson learned that Lane had begun to move the powers to get him a pension: Lane had already succeeded in getting one for Watson. Lane's insistence on the poem for the 'Masque of Peace and War' at Her Majesty's may not have been without purpose. He was about to leave for America but had applied through Mrs Henniker to George Wyndham, Under-Secretary of War and a pupil of Henley, proposing a petition on his return. Davidson was grateful but felt gloomy about Lane's chances of success. He told McCormick: 'It was easy in the case of Watson. He had a great reputation and had served the party in power. I, on the other hand, am suspect, and am unknown in politics.'[51] However, he set out his career in an open letter for Lane's use.

His finances could not hold out for much longer. The first deadline—1 May—passed and no date had been fixed for the production of *Queen Fiametta*. He learned that Charles Frohman had passed the script to his brother, Daniel, for advice about possible changes. But then there was no further word.[52] He was tired of asking for a statement of his account at the Bodley Head. Lane was still in America and was not due to return until the end of May. He decided he could not wait until then and sent his play, now retitled *Self's the Man*, to Lane's manager, Frederic Chapman. Since he could not expect Chapman to accept the play without taking advice, he suggested that he send it to William Archer to read. On the face of it this seems a foolish thing to do, given Archer's recent attack on his work, and one cannot escape the impression that he was wilfully courting rejection. He received word about Archer's decision on 16 May: Archer declined to advise. He took this to indicate that Archer thought the play inferior. Lane was due back in ten days. He decided to wait for his return, but had little doubt that Lane would refuse him an advance.[53]

There was a note of querulousness in all this that belies his determination to be forthright and coldly impartial. He was haunted by the passage in Disraeli's novel, *Contarini Fleming*, in which the father warns the hero about the miseries of a poet's

[51] Davidson to McCormick, 10 Mar. 1900, Glasgow.
[52] Davidson to McCormick, 22 May 1900, Glasgow.
[53] Davidson to Frederic Chapman, 4 and 16 May 1900, Lane.

life: 'A poet! . . . The most miserable of the species.'[54] On 22
May he wrote a long, emotional letter to McCormick trying to
explain his feelings:

Self-pity is the only honour left a man on whom the world has turned
its back. Besides, a year and a half ago I was practically dead; and I
know when a man comes to die there is nothing for him to rely on, but
his own thought, and his opinion of himself.[55]

Godfrida; *The Last Ballad*; *Self's the Man*; *Queen Fiametta*: he felt he
had suffered 'four Waterloos' and was 'entitled to a pension
and St. Helena'. Yet he could not explain satisfactorily to himself why he had no money. In the nineteen months from November 1898 to the end of May 1900, he had received £250
from the Literary Fund, £75 for *The Last Ballad*, as well as £150
from Tree, £200 from Frohman, and £50 for his articles and
poems—giving a total of £750. From that he had to deduct
£160 of debt contracted while at Shoreham—£100 from the
bank, £10 from McCormick, and £50 from his father-in-law.
This gave him a net income of £565 or £360 per annum. 'It is,
I know, supposed that I ought to have money—and of course I
ought, but I haven't. I do not think it is my fault', he told
McCormick forlornly.[56] He was due to be paid £20 in June for
his 'Eclogue on the Downs', but after that there would be
nothing.

Davidson waited impatiently for Lane's return. When he
heard that Lane was delayed because of illness, he asked
Chapman to return his play.[57] He had come to the conclusion
that even if Lane did publish it, it would suffer the same fate as
Godfrida and 'be dropped like a cuckoo's egg in a deserted nest
never to be hatched or heard of'.[58] It was a stategic withdrawal
which avoided embarrassment and left him feeling that he was
still in control of his own destiny. But it was a sad end to his
career at the Bodley Head. All that was left was a final examination of his account. However bad it was, he felt he ought to
know exactly where he stood. The long-awaited statement came

[54] Benjamin Disraeli, *Contarini Fleming* (Bradenham Edition; London, 1927),
151.
[55] Davidson to McCormick, 22 May 1900, Glasgow.
[56] Ibid.
[57] Davidson to Chapman, 30 May 1900, Lane.
[58] Davidson to McCormick, 22 May 1900, Glasgow.

in June. It revealed some slack bookkeeping—a hundred copies of *Ballads and Songs* sent to America in 1897 remained unaccounted for.[59] But there was no altering the conclusion: his days as a Bodley Head poet were over.

That month, following the withdrawal of his play from the Bodley Head, he took an overdraft at the bank. He had done this twice before in order to go on writing, but this time he felt 'too collapsed' to work. He was again close to breakdown. He seems to have feared some hereditary disease. He told McCormick:

I can neither read, write, think, talk, nor sleep—and my two uncles and my brother sit in a row on the toilet-table all night and crush together to make room for me and nod their heads as much as to say 'His turn's coming'. In the morning I always know that my turn to sit on the toilet-table will never come; dreams and waking visions go by contraries, but they exhaust.[60]

His nerves were like 'frayed fiddlesticks'. He abandoned strict economy that month to take Maggie to the Handel Festival at the Crystal Palace to hear the *Messiah*. The outing brought a temporary relief from his nerves. He found the enthusiam of the 1,500 crowd 'like Derby Day', and the music 'beautiful and splendid'.[61]

In July the boys went down to Ermingham for their annual summer holiday on the South Downs. This eased the situation at home. He worked on his new play and went for bike rides to keep fit. He had taken up cycling at Shoreham on his doctor's advice, but he had never been comfortable riding a bicycle, and during one of his Sunday outings in August he swerved and fell. He had to sit for an hour before he could move. He believed he had suffered a heart attack and wrote to McCormick asking for the address of his doctor. He was convinced that the doctors he had consulted at Shoreham had not told him the whole truth.[62] His worries about his health had again become obsessive. 'The hideous anxiety, this mental degradation of heart-disease no one can imagine', he wrote. 'You sit on a sloping ice flow and rush down towards a gulf that you cannot reach; you are like

---

[59] Davidson to Chapman, 'Saturday' [June 1900], Lane.
[60] Davidson to McCormick, 28 June 1900, Glasgow.
[61] Ibid.
[62] Davidson to McCormick, 12 Aug. 1900, Glasgow.

one drowning in the Dead Sea, and who cannot get drowned, because of the specific gravity of the asphaltic water, while the Dead Sea apes pelt you with apples of Sodom.'[63]

With the return of the boys, he had to find money for their school fees. The quarter's rent was also due. There were rumours that *Queen Fiametta* would play at the Duke of York's but no date was fixed, and in spite of promises there was no word of an American production. He was at the end of his tether. He waited anxiously for news about the pension. He suspected that the truth might have been kept from him. In desperation he sent the manuscript of *Self's the Man* to Grant Richards who had gone into publishing on his own in 1897. Richards had remained one of his most faithful admirers, and the two had kept in touch despite the difference in their ages. In sending his play, Davidson was completely frank about its lack of popular appeal, and asked for an advance of only £20.[64]

By 4 October he still had not heard from Richards. There was a pleasing request from Quiller-Couch for permission to include a selection of his poems in Quiller-Couch's *Oxford Book of English Verse* for the Clarendon Press. 'It is an honour to be included in a selection of your making', he wrote. He felt less honoured when he saw the pieces Quiller-Couch finally included, his 'Song' from *Scaramouch in Naxos* and 'The Last Rose', and wrote to complain: 'Why did you include in this Oxford Anthology the best, or at any rate the best known and most admired, poems of Meredith and Watson, and two happy enough, but quite insignificant and unrepresentative pieces of mine.'[65] His inclusion in the Oxford anthology only reminded him of how much he wanted to get on with his own things, in particular the long poem he had brooded over since he left Shoreham. He confessed to McCormick: 'the matter . . . which will take me years to write, and for which I would expect no money at all, comes up every morning on my study table in the shape of my heart hot from the grill; I mumble it, but cannot swallow it; and my attempts to do what will please sicken me'.[66]

[63] Davidson to McCormick, 'Wednesday' [1900], Glasgow.
[64] Davidson to McCormick, 4 Oct. 1900, Glasgow.
[65] Davidson to Quiller-Couch, 3 Oct. and 9 Nov. 1900, in F. G. Atkinson, 'John Davidson: Some Contributions to Standard Biography', *Notes and Queries*, 220 (1975), 449–50.
[66] Davidson to McCormick, 4 Oct. 1900, Glasgow.

Then on the 26 October news came from Richards: he accepted Davidson's offer and planned to publish his play in the spring. Richards apologized that he could not offer a bigger advance but was doubtful whether the book would make even as much as £20 for several months. 'Those happy days when Lane could work off editions on unsuspecting booksellers and infatuated undergraduates have gone by; and the number of the elect who care for poetry seems to grow smaller', he wrote.[67] The play was given a copyright performance at Her Majesty's in December but no production was planned.

Before Christmas, Davidson was active around Fleet Street trying to promote John Cramb's recently published book on the *Origins and Destiny of Imperial Britain*, which had been ignored by reviewers. The book—based on a series of lectures Cramb had delivered during the summer—was a celebration of British imperialism over the *de monachia* despotism of other ancient and modern states. Davidson sent a copy to Sidney Low at the *St James's Gazette* and asked Lewis Hind if he could review if for the *Academy*. He also sent a copy to Gosse, describing it as 'the ablest, freshest, most imaginative and therefore most intelligent statement of British Imperialism'.[68] Cramb's book is often cited as an important influence on Davidson's own views about imperialism. Their ideas are certainly similar, particularly their rejection of despotism and religion, their glorification of war, and the identification of English democracy with heroic individualism. This was the result no doubt of their long friendship and many conversations. After Glasgow University Cramb had gone for a year to Bonn where he had attended the lectures of Professor Heinrich von Treitschke, the German historian. Treitschke argued that the Teutonic race's natural reverence was for valour, heroism, and the doing of great deeds and that this had been thwarted by the adoption of Christianity and the culture of the vanquished by the Teutonic people after their conquest of Rome in the fifth century. Von Treitschke's glorification of Germany's aggressive aims was matched by his contempt for Britain: he believed the greatness of England had passed in the seventeenth century with Cromwell and Milton. These arguments gave Cramb many of the ideas for his lectures

---

[67] Grant Richards to Davidson, 26 Oct. 1900, Richards.
[68] Davidson to Gosse, 24 Dec. 1900, Brotherton.

at Queen's College during the 1890s.[69] They also suggest an important link between Davidson's imperial beliefs and his attachment to Nietzsche. For in Cramb's theory of history, taken down during lectures by his students at Queen's after Davidson's death, Nietzsche's significance is that of a re-interpreter of the old religion of valour, who clears away the 'accumulated rubbish' of 1,200 years of servitude to Christianity. It is a role he shares with Napoleon whose principles of heroic action battle with the hypocritical teachings of Christian morality for control of men's minds. Davidson held both of these views, but it may well be that it was he who influenced Cramb. Interestingly, the review of Cramb's book which eventually appeared in the *Academy* in February, most likely by Davidson, praises Cramb as 'The Poet as Historian', but takes issue with his idealism and sentimentality.[70] The reviewer in *Literature* was less kind, dismissing Cramb as 'The Jingo as Philosopher'.[71]

Davidson found the lack of response to Cramb's book heart-breaking. Cramb was almost totally blind and had dictated it in the belief that he would soon no longer be able to work or write. But there was nothing further Davidson could do. His efforts to promote Cramb's book had brought about a renewal of his correspondence with Gosse who asked after his own affairs. Daniel Frohman had allowed the final deadline for the pro-duction of *Queen Fiametta* to pass—1 November—and in doing so had forfeited all their rights to the play. Davidson's adapta-tion was worthless. 'There is a terrible sentence in George Eliot,' he told Gosse, '—the only thing of hers I ever remember, and I do not remember *it* properly, but it means that there are people in whose expression you find it written—"sold, but not paid for". With wrinkles of laughter, however, I can still dislimn such an expression.'[72] But his attempt to shrug off the whole affair could not disguise his despair. Maggie was broken-hearted. Everything depended now on getting the pension.

The new year began more hopefully than the old one

---

[69] Lilian M. Rigby (Mrs Charles E. B. Russell), *John Adam Cramb: Patriot, Historian, Mystic* (London, 1950), 78–9.

[70] 'The Poet as Historian', *Academy*, 60 (16 Feb. 1901), 141–2.

[71] 'The Jingo as Philosopher', *Literature* (6 Apr. 1901), 268.

[72] Davidson to Gosse, 28 Dec. 1900, Brotherton.

had ended. He was irritated at home by Sandy who had bought a fretsaw for 1 *s*. 9*d*. and was off school with a cold; but he finished his play, the third in as many years. It was a romantic comedy, *The Knight of the Maypole*. He sent it to Charles Frohman in America, offering *Queen Fiametta* meanwhile to the actor-manager, Lewis Waller. As he waited for news, he allowed himself some relaxation. He went to see Stephen Phillips's *Herod* on 4 January. He thought it was well acted, but found the writing very tedious and undramatic, and not as fast or fluent as his own dramatic verse. He had a talk with Tree after the play and decided he still liked him in spite of his having refused 'The King of the Lombards'.[73] He also met Gilbert Keith Chesterton for the first time at a lunch organized by Lane to convince James Douglas of the *Star* that the author of *The Wild Knight and Other Poems* and John Davidson were not the same person. Davidson had been irritated by the identification, particularly after reading Chesterton's verse. He thought poems such as 'Vulgarised', with its phallic suggestions, were 'frantic rubbish'.[74] But he discovered at lunch that Chesterton shared many of his views of literature and, according to Chesterton, the two developed 'a lasting liking for each other'.[75] There was also satisfaction in the 'New Century Number' of the Edinburgh University magazine, the *Student*. He had been asked for a contribution in November and had sent an unpublished 'Villanelle', calling on the young to seize the day. But his main pleasure was in a contribution by William Archer which revived happy memories of the Edinburgh theatre of his youth and particularly of the performances of Ellen Wallis. It restored his faith in his own theatrical judgement.[76]

But by then there was more bad news. Charles Frohman did not want his play. The year before he had nursed his wounded pride with the thought that 'a writer must represent the world ... in order to make money', and that the popular literature of England and America was 'fake to the core';[77] but now he was faced with the uncomfortable truth that this latest rejection

[73] Davidson to McCormick, 5 Jan. 1901, Glasgow.
[74] Davidson to McCormick, 7 Jan. 1901, Glasgow.
[75] G. K. Chesterton, *Autobiography* (London, 1936), 95–6.
[76] Davidson to Archer, 27 Jan. 1901, BL.
[77] Davidson to Gosse, 31 Dec. 1900, Brotherton.

followed a definite effort to write for the commercial stage. He could not accept that he had fallen short artistically or technically. But where could he lay the blame?

The shifting demands of the popular theatre have destroyed many ambitions and reputations, particularly among poets. Although Davidson's plays contain popular elements and highly dramatic scenes, there is a strain in them that looks beyond the immediate demands of the commercial stage. Davidson aimed at timelessness as a dramatist—one of the effects of his literary education—and in doing so he missed the mood of contemporary theatrical impresarios and their audiences. In October that year, for instance, Charles Frohman had a huge success at the Hollis Theatre, Boston, with Justin Huntly McCarthy's *If I Were King*, a play which uses the romantic plot device of Davidson's *The Knight of the Maypole* to more popular effect. At the same time, the individualistic elements in Davidson's plays seemed strident and uncongenial, and to pose a threat to the expectations of Victorian audiences. One might say the same about Shaw, with whom Davidson was to quarrel some years after this, except that, for all his polemics, Shaw continued to work within the mould of the well-made play and often saw his intention sacrificed to the techniques of the players and the desires of the theatregoers.

On 14 January Davidson heard from McCormick that Lord Balfour, then First Lord of the Treasury, was disinclined to give him a pension on the grounds that he was not 'permanent'. The news had come in a letter from Gosse which McCormick passed on to him. Davidson wrote back angrily:

Who taught Balfour that I was not 'permanent'. But in any case what a ridiculous argument against a pension: he is a conservative; where is his precedent? Was Sharon Turner permanent? he had £200: is Herman Merivale permanent? he had £200. If I am not permanent, the thing for Balfour to say is—'I shall provide for the necessities of himself and his family, and then it will not be my fault if he does not produce what will be permanent.'[78]

Davidson believed that Balfour had heard that his poetry was bad morally and feared to offend some divisions of his party.

[78] Davidson to McCormick, 14 Jan. 1901, Glasgow.

But there was still hope; no decision had been taken. As Davidson waited, the newspapers announced the death of Queen Victoria on 23 January. The theatres had closed the previous night. On the 29th, four days before the funeral, he learned that Grant Richards had issued his play ahead of the proposed publication date in March. He was incredulous and telegraphed to try to stop it, but it was too late. He told McCormick: 'It seems to me he might as well have dropped the edition in the Sahara or down a lavatory. It is ruin to the book.'[79] In fact the reviews when they appeared were generally favourable. His discovery of his Lane days, W. A. Mackenzie, had resigned as editor of *Black and White* in August the previous year because of ill health, but the magazine remained loyal to him, describing the final act as 'a triumph of dramatic and poetic effect'.[80] The *Academy* also recognized in the last act 'an effective piece of sardonic irony',[81] while Arthur Waugh, reviewing it with Yeats's *The Shadowy Waters* in the *St James's Gazette* wrote of it that, 'the situations are exciting. With a little cutting, the piece might play well. It has practical qualities, and opportunities for the stage manager.'[82] One of those to show an interest in the play was Bernard Shaw who wrote to ask about the rights. Putting a brave face on it, Davidson answered that Beerbohm Tree was about to dispose of them to Forbes-Robertson. He also defended his use of blank verse, to which both Shaw and Archer were strongly opposed. He wrote defiantly to Shaw:

I do not expect highly commendatory or intelligent notices . . . two or three generations hence will be time enough for that. There is nobody understands blank verse except me, and nobody who can use it so variously.[83]

But whatever the qualities of his play, verse drama was no longer in vogue, in spite of the brief success of Stephen Phillips which astonished even his contemporaries. However, it was one thing to interest audiences in *Herod* or *Becket*, characters with whom

[79] Davidson to McCormick, 29 Jan. 1901, Glasgow.
[80] 'Books and their Writers', *Black and White*, 21 (6 Apr. 1901), 460.
[81] 'Mr. Davidson's Drama', *Academy*, 60 (16 Feb. 1901), 140–1.
[82] 'Two Poets', *St James's Gazette* (20 Feb. 1901), 6.
[83] Davidson to George Bernard Shaw, 5 Feb. 1901, BL.

theatregoers were familiar; it was more difficult to interest them in the history of Lombardy.

On 7 February, five days after the Queen's funeral, Gosse received word from 10 Downing Street: while Balfour had 'great sympathy for Davidson's struggles', he could not satisfy himself that 'in point both of quality and quantity' Davidson's work sufficiently merited 'the gracious consideration of the Sovereign and the gratitude of the country' within the meaning of the Civil List Act. However, he was willing to contribute £200 (giving an annuity of £10 a year) from another fund and £50 towards subscription to provide Davidson with permanent financial help.[84]

Gosse, who had made countless visits to Downing Street to plead Davidson's case, was disappointed. He wrote to McCormick, indicating that only 'a very small pension indeed' had been offered. McCormick sent Gosse's letter to Davidson. They both seem to have decided that 'a very small pension' meant £50 a year. But Davidson read between the lines and concluded that Balfour was trying to force a withdrawal. His reply was unhesitating:

So small a sum could not fail to be regarded as an intended slight upon those who had interested themselves on my behalf; and it would certainly be a mockery of my hopes. £50 a year carries no mark of honour: it would be recognised in every quarter as grudging charity extorted by importunity and pauperising the recipient: it would be less disgraceful to retire into the workhouse than to accept £50 a year; and there it would cost the ratepayers more to support my family and me.[85]

McCormick asked Gosse for more details and learned that Davidson had guessed rightly. According to Gosse, the £250 had been offered just to keep him quiet, 'for I have been as you know boring him to death to do something for Davidson'. He gave three reason for Balfour's refusal of the pension. First, Balfour could not get over the fact that Davidson was 'in early middle age, in good health, and strength', and yet unable to earn a living. 'I have argued up and argued down, but W. B. returns to this', Gosse told McCormick. 'And, you know, it is

---

[84] F. S. Parry to Gosse, 7 Feb. 1901, Brotherton.
[85] Davidson to McCormick, 12 Feb. 1901, Brotherton.

very difficult to find a conclusive answer, is it not?' Also, Balfour had already refused a pension to Francis Thompson and Stephen Phillips and did not want to appear inconsistent. Finally, as Davidson had suspected, Balfour did not care for his verses. Gosse was unsure whether they should accept or refuse it:

I hope to see Lord Crewe today (and he is very staunch) and I shall see what he suggests. In the meantime I should like you to put the whole story before Davidson, who has a manly fortitude of mind, and can know it. We should know a great deal better how to proceed if he is with us in what we are doing.[86]

Davidson had already given his answer. In the week that followed he tried energetically to place *Queen Fiametta* and his comedy. The payment of his bank loan was already overdue; he was in the miserable situation of having to borrow again if the bank called it in. But he refused to give up hope. He told McCormick: 'the stage is such a lottery that both my masterpieces may turn up trumps before I break'.[87] By 20 February he had lost heart and was no longer able even to present a confident front. At home his grumbling was a torment to Maggie. He ate and drank and smoked all day, unable to do anything else. He described his 'megalomaniacal' mood:

I am a man fighting the Universe who is beaten down into a London suburb where it is no longer the stars and space he must match himself with, but shaky health, domestic worry, cantatious managers (and disappointed too), caliginous editors, illuculent publishers—and all this in a rattling cage of trains and a menagerie of back-gardens, dogs, ducks, stock-brokers' assistants, merchants' clerks, shoppers, milkmen, turncocks, jobbing gardeners and the whole rank and press of doleful villadom.[88]

He was nostalgic for Scotland and wanted to return to the Ochil Hills to write the poem he had been planning for several years. He could no longer have serious ambitions about the theatre. That phase of his life appeared to be over.

[86] Gosse to McCormick, 13 Feb. 1901, Glasgow
[87] Davidson to McCormick, 12 Feb. 1901, Glasgow.
[88] Davidson to McCormick, 20 Feb. 1901, Glasgow.

6

Facing the New 1901–1907

I

At the beginning of March 1901 Davidson asked his new publisher, Grant Richards, to meet him for lunch.[1] They drank deeply of old brandy after the meal, so that afterwards Richards found that his notes about their agreement were indistinct, but that day the general terms for the publication of Davidson's proposed series of adult poems—his *Testaments*—were agreed. It was not a profitable venture. They were to be sold in pamphlet form at 6*d*. He was to receive no advance, no royalty on the first thousand copies, and after that a mere ½*d*. on the second thousand.[2]

In order to write them he needed money. Once again he turned to his friends in Scotland. This time he borrowed £100. £50 of it came from McCormick and the other £50 from William Smart, so taking his debt to Smart to £245 for various loans over the years. His bank account was overdrawn so he asked for the money to be paid to his wife.[3] McCormick sent the first £50 to Maggie; the second £50 arrived by telegram in £5 notes on 22 March. Davidson tried to make light of things in writing to thank him: 'When I come to my last sixpence, and cannot beg borrow or steal another anywhere at all, I shall employ it in sending a telegram curse to—Balfour, perhaps, and then, step into the Thames, if I have pawned my revolver— a three-guinea Colt.' He felt self-contempt. He calculated that a month's income from a successful play would clear all his debts, but confessed: 'I write studiously in this matter-of-fact way. If I were to attempt anything else I should break down; and I have done that so often already in this room that I cannot imagine a man sicker of himself than I am.'[4] In these black

---

[1] Davidson to Grant Richards, 5 Mar. 1901, Princeton.
[2] Richards to Davidson, 6 Mar. 1901, Richards.
[3] Davidson to William McCormick, 6 Mar. [1901], Glasgow.
[4] Davidson to McCormick, 22 Mar. 1901, Glasgow.

moods he felt he should never have married or had children.[5]

He planned to write the *Testaments* in Scotland, but bronchitis delayed his departure until 11 April when he travelled north, taking lodgings at Struan House in Blairlogie, a small village in the foothills of the Ochils, where he had spent many happy holidays as a boy.[6] Before leaving London, he had been lucky in obtaining a commission from the Lyceum—an adaptation of Victor Hugo's romantic comedy *Ruy Blas* for Lewis Waller. He was in Scotland through the early part of that summer, taking in a visit to Edinburgh and going for walks each day and climbing Dunmyat, with its unrivalled views of central Scotland, when he was not writing. He completed the first two of his *Testaments—The Testament of a Vivisector* and *The Testament of a Man Forbid*. The third, *The Testament of an Empire-Builder*, was begun in London later that year.

His aim and overall intention in his *Testaments* have often been a source of confusion. The device of having an eminent figure review his life in the form of a last will or testament is part of a long poetic tradition. Davidson's choice of title may well have been inspired by the moving complaint of Robert Henryson's 'The Testament of Cresseid' (*c.*1492), as well as by the ribald mock-testaments of the fifteenth-century French poet, François Villon, whom he admired. But of more direct, though less obvious influence on Davidson's treatment and theme were Meredith's *Odes in Contribution to the Song of French History*, which he read in 1898. Like Meredith's Napoleon, Davidson's men of strong mind defy ordinary human values in their efforts to change the course of human history—in their case to confront the theistic Old and New Testaments with a new gospel of materialism and will to power. There is an important difference. By substituting the monologue or testament form for Meredith's epic overview, Davidson dramatizes the grandeur and monomania of heroic individualism without the distancing moral irony that characterizes Meredith's concluding poem in the sequence, 'Alsace-Lorraine', with its return to tranquillity and traditional pieties. Such authorial distance is also to be found in other representations of the man of will in writings of the period, notably in H. G. Wells's *The Island of*

[5] Davidson to McCormick, 17 Jan. 1899, Glasgow.
[6] Davidson to Richards, 13 Apr. 1901, Princeton.

Doctor Moreau and in Conrad's *Heart of Darkness*, where the practical Marlow is placed between Conrad's over-reacher, Kurtz, and the reader. In Davidson's *Testaments*, there is nothing to counteract the proud inhumanity of the speakers.

In the first of the poems, *The Testament of a Vivisector*, Davidson took as his theme an emotive and controversial issue. Article after article in the press had been devoted to the subject of vivisection during the 1890s. Piecing together fragments of Nietzsche, natural science, St Paul, Heraclitus, and an atheistic revision of the Shorter Catechism, his speaker sets himself above all judgement in a new anti-religious, anti-supernatural account of man and the universe that justifies his own lust for knowledge and transgression of human inhibitions. With callous dispassion he tells of how he experimented on horses, 'to carve | a scale of feeling on the spinal cord'.[7] But he too suffers pain in his pursuit of self-knowledge—isolated, abandoned by his wife and daughters, an insomniac tempted to suicide. In his Promethean ambition, he resembles Mary Shelley's Victor Frankenstein, although scientifically he is a more credible figure. Davidson himself had in mind pioneers of nineteenth-century medical science such as François Magendie, Claude Bernard, and Paolo Mantegazza. To Archer who asked for an explanation, he wrote:

I do not concern myself with the ordinary Vivisector who cuts up a dog or two in an underground room of a college because he believes it is the thing to do. . . . but the passionate, obsessed giant, hating religion, despising the 'humanities', searching into the secrets of Nature in his bloody way with the patience, delight, and self-torture of the artist. . . . The poem is . . . not a condemnation or a criticism of him, but a dramatic account of him without any intention on the author's part to persuade the world for or against.[8]

The Testament of a Vivisector was published on 4 June. *The Testament of a Man Forbid*, which appeared in September, is a more personal poem based on the prose sketch, 'The Man Forbid', written at Shoreham three years before. There are interesting differences. In the poem as in the prose sketch the Man Forbid is tormented by a longing for 'human neighbour-hood', but here he speaks directly to the reader, and the warn-

[7] *Testament of a Vivisector*, ll. 182–3.
[8] Davidson to William Archer, 15 June 1901, BL.

ing against cutting oneself off from the past is spoken by one of
the crowd which finally drives the Man Forbid out of society:

> 'There is no harbour here for such as you.
> You know not what you say nor understand
> How you have hurt yourself . . .
>
> .   .   .   .
>
> Man springs from out the past: his tap roots pierce
> The strata of the ages, drawing strength
> From every generation, every cult.'[9]

The conflict is thus sharpened dramatically, although the effect is to make less intense the Man Forbid's inner crisis. This
may suggest Davidson's own deepening identification with the
plight of the outcast. The poem ends with the solitary at the
'ocean's shifting verge', awaiting the end of the world—'a new
time' which will be heralded by the apocalyptic marriage of the
earth and the sun.

During July and August, as he waited for the poem to come
out, Davidson stayed on in London to work and attend the
dentist rather than holiday on the south coast.[10] He sent his
adaptation of *Ruy Blas* to Waller who praised it ecstatically as
'perfectly splendid' and 'magnificent work'. He had become
cautious about these 'managerial phrases', as he called them,[11]
but Waller seemed genuinely to like it, and his financial horizon
looked less cloudy. On 7 September he went reluctantly to the
first night of Mrs Campbell's revival of Pinero's *The Second Mrs
Tanqueray* at the Royalty. His reasons for going were 'business'
as well as 'courtesy'.[12] It was the first time he had seen the play,
and he found himself enjoying it. He wrote flatteringly to Mrs
Campbell after the performance:

It was exceedingly beautiful and powerful, sometimes terrible, and of
extraordinary sweetness whenever the tender note was struck. 'Paula'
is like an opal of many lives and lustres, with stains of life and wounds
of passion through which the disastrous fires glow that shatter it in the
end. There are no words in which to thank so incomparable an artist.[13]

---

[9] *Testament of a Man Forbid*, ll. 168–78.
[10] Davidson to John Lane, 1 Aug. 1901, Lane.
[11] Davidson to McCormick, 9 Aug. 1901, Glasgow.
[12] Davidson to Archer, 'Saturday' [16 Sept. 1901], BL.
[13] Davidson to Mrs Patrick Campbell, Sept. 1901, in her *My Life and Some Letters*
(London [1922]), 78.

The 'business' turned out to be a commission for an English dramatization of Alphonse Daudet's novel *Sapho*. Réjane, the continental actress, had been thrilling English audiences that summer in a French adaptation. Davidson found Daudet's novel 'a nauseous affair of superficial realism and essential unveracity', but he accepted the contract.[14] It meant that he could go on with his *Testament*s. He was already planning a third—*The Testament of an Empire-Builder*. In researching it he read John Hobson's *The Psychology of Jingoism* (1901) and John Godard's *Patriotism and Ethics* (1901), both of which attacked the barbarism of the national character and the jingoism of the popular press.[15] But he decided to postpone work on his poem until after he had completed his adaptation of Daudet's novel. His hopes for an early production of *Ruy Blas* had been disappointed. Lewis Waller was booked to play Napoleon at the Imperial on 25 January opposite Lily Langtry in Paul Kester's romantic comedy *Mademoiselle Mars*. In November Davidson travelled again to Scotland, this time staying at Rothesay on the island of Bute. It was another place that held happy childhood memories. The change acted as a stimulant, and by the 30th he had practically finished his adaptation of *Sapho*, which he re-titled 'Fanny Legrand', needing only to make some revisions to the fourth act. He had found Daudet's French version with Adolphe Belot 'simply the novel cut into lengths' and useful only as an indication of 'what not to do'.[16]

Back in London he prepared his third *Testament* for the printer. It contained over 700 lines, making it almost double the length of the first two *Testament*s put together. The septuagarian speaker is a heroic figure in the mould of Cecil Rhodes. The opening lines recall Davidson's account in *A Rosary* of his own bedridden state at Shoreham:

> . . . recumbent nerve
> Evolves sublime designs, quintessences
> Of wit, and strokes of power, when the veins swell
> And tightened muscles twang; but in my head
> The turbid lees of blood settle and fume
> And harass me with dreams.[17]

---

[14] Davidson to McCormick, 30 Nov. 1901, Glasgow.
[15] Davidson to 'Dear Sir', 27 Aug. 1901, Glasgow.
[16] Davidson to McCormick, 30 Nov. 1901, Glasgow.
[17] *Testament of an Empire-Builder*, ll. 4–9.

The speaker then recounts his dreams of the previous night. In the first, a parliament of beasts discusses man's evolutionary place in the animal kingdom and concludes that man taints instinctual life—'the noble evil of the universe'—by his appeal to 'Soul' and conscience. Unlike Kipling's *Jungle Book* of 1894, Davidson's *Testament* emphasizes man's lack of kinship with the beasts. The targets of this ironic allegory are human hypocrisy and sentimentality. The first dream ends without anything being offered to heal man's self-division. The Empire Builder then finds himself walking between the sea and the slopes, and hears from the woods the throstles and starlings tuning their throats 'with tortured snails'—an image associated with Davidson's walks round Shoreham churchyard four years earlier. 'The music of the murderous singing-birds' turns the poem to the central irony of nature—beauty's origins in the gross and uncouth. The way is thus prepared for the Empire Builder's second dream—a new vision of Heaven and Hell in which those who triumph on earth ('Kings, statesmen, pro-consuls, popes | Dishonest brokers, robbers, millionaires') are triumphant in Heaven, and those who are damned on earth ('The merciful, the meek and mild, the poor') are damned in Hell. The vision provides the Empire Builder with the catachismal 'mandate of imperial doom' which concludes the poem:

> Do I believe in Heaven and Hell? I do;
> We have them here; the world is nothing else.
> Beauty and power and splendour and delight
> Of chosen ones, elect ere Time began,
> In loathsomeness, debility, disgrace,
> Humiliation, travail, terror, woe,
> Of multitudes, of myrmidons, of all
> The labourers, soldiers, servants, rooted deep:
> *He* is a slave: a prisoner: damned: in Hell,
> Whose daily bread depends on toil approved.
> For me, I clambered into Heaven at once
> And stayed there; joined the warfare of the times
> In corner, trust, and syndicate: upheaved
> A furrow, hissing through the angry world,
> A redhot ploughshare in a frozen glebe,
> And reaped my millions long before my prime.[18]

[18] *Testament of an Empire-Builder*, ll. 686–701.

From the first, Davidson's *Testaments* provoked controversy and outrage. He had expected it. His introductory note to the first of them had promised a 'new statement of materialism . . . likely to offend both the religious and the irreligious mind'. He had wanted as much publicity as possible, even pleading with Richards to have the first number prominently displayed on Smith's bookstalls.[19] Unlike the next generation of poets he looked for his audience in the popular market-place rather than in the intellectual coterie and the little magazine. But the majority of Smith's customers, waiting on station platforms or hurrying to and from their places of work and leisure, were unlikely to be interested in buying poetry at all, let alone the kind that promised to offend both the religious and the irreligious mind. Davidson's idealistic hope of converting the masses to his poetic ideas has much in common with the zeal with which his evangelist father had gone hunting for souls in the streets of Glasgow.

Accounts of the hostility of critics to Davidson's *Testaments* have tended to overlook the fact that the reviewers at the time recognized that their ambition and scope placed him above the range of the minor poet. Even the *Athenaeum*, never renowned for its generosity to authors, accepted that *The Testament of an Empire-Builder* was a poem that mattered.[20] The main problem was that few critics found his ideas congenial. The poet, Francis Thompson followed the publication of the *Testaments* with increasing suspicion. In his review of *The Man Forbid* he wrote: 'Really, no one stones Mr. Davidson, whose views have much in common with those here set forth.'[21] Davidson responded with a provocative prose parable which appeared as a 'Preface' to *The Empire-Builder*. It tells of a poet who is stoned to death in the market-place because he refuses to sing 'the old songs, the old lullabies, the old flatteries'. Though intended to answer those like Thompson who felt that his theme was not the proper subject-matter of poetry, his parable served only to reinforce his identification with his rebellious outcast. It left Thompson in no doubt about his intentions, and in

[19] Richards to Davidson, 5 June 1901, Richards.
[20] *Athenaeum* (30 Aug. 1902), 277–8.
[21] *Academy*, 61 (21 Sept. 1901), 240.

his review of *The Empire-Builder*, he denounced Davidson scathingly as a poetic disciple of Nietzsche.[22]

There are certainly elements of Nietzsche in the *Testaments*, most evidently in the *Man Forbid*'s prophecy in the market place, which echoes *Zarathustra*, and in the hackney's protest against captivity 'between the shafts' in *The Empire-Builder*, which quotes directly from *The Genealogy of Morals*. Davidson acknowledged the debt but rebutted Thompson's charge in a letter to the *Daily Chronicle*, claiming that it was not himself but the Hackney that spoke, and that the gist of Nietzsche could be found in his work long before he had heard the name of Nietzsche.[23] Davidson was not alone in rejecting the label 'Nietzschean'. R. M. Wenley, who had taught on the University Extension at Glasgow in the 1880s with Cramb and McCormick and later lectured on Nietzsche at the University of Michigan in 1899, was to point out that Nietzsche was seen by English readers at the time not as the bearer of a new brand of philosophical scepticism, but as an intoxicating spokesman for all the unresolved paradoxes of Romanticism with which they were already familiar.[24] Though Davidson did not mention it in his letter to the *Daily Chronicle*, the reversal of the Christian version of the saved and the damned in *The Empire-Builder* which might be identified as Nietzschean, is in fact derived from his own writings. One finds a humorous version of it in *Baptist Lake* in the 'gospel of damnation' of the Calvinist John Inglis, the first in his family to embrace the modern world. The reader is asked to consider whether 'the seas and streams dividing the Covenanters' prayers from John Inglis's topsy-turvy gospel of damnation would shrink into small bulk could thought be stripped of expression, and the real meaning behind words made plain'.[25]

The idea was one that also occurred to others at the time, among them John Sloan, one of the few people ever to visit Davidson in his modest home in Streatham. Sloan had left the ministry and moved to London in 1900 to pursue a career in journalism. Writing in the *Fortnightly Review* about the Scottish Free Church controversies that were interesting English readers

[22] 'A Poetic Disciple of Nietzsche', *Daily Chronicle* (22 May 1902), 3; also as 'A Prophet of Nietzsche', *Academy*, 61 (7 June 1902), 572.

[23] Davidson to the Editor, *Daily Chronicle* (23 May 1902), 3.

[24] R. M. Wenley, *Monist*, 31 (Jan. 1921), 133–49.   [25] *Baptist Lake*, 119.

at this time, he speculated that 'one of the features of the intellectual development of the last quarter of the nineteenth century was a return to a philosophy akin to Calvinism'. Specifically he refers to the way in which the doctrine of predestination—in particular, 'a crude adumbration of the sovereignty of law, the conservation and persistence of force', and 'the absoluteness of causation in all the knowable universe'—had installed itself in the body of truth guaranteed by science.[26] It is an argument that is unlikely to have surprised the author of the *Testaments*. For all his strongly voluntarist tendencies, his own secularized vision of Heaven and Hell has evident affinities with the severe scholastic Calvinism from which his father had rebelled.

Yet one has to be careful about identifying Davidson with the speakers of his *Testaments*. An ironic distance is maintained by the use of the monologue form and the inclusion of dream visions. During the printing of *The Empire-Builder* he had been alarmed by the omission of quotation marks at the beginning of every line of speech within speech—'a distinction necessary in writing of this kind'.[27] It was not that Davidson did not share the materialist convictions expressed in his *Testaments*, only that he saw these as poetic statements which he was anxious should be distinguished from his life. He was upset, for instance, when the *Morning Chronicle* described him as a 'perverted volumptuary':

To call me a 'perverted volumptuary'—I like to smoke and drink upon occasion and am extravagant in the matter of hansoms—but to call me a 'perverted volumptuary' who has been the husband of one wife since I married in 1885 is to be disingenuous and malicious if the writer knows me at all, and if he does not know me!—but it is a waste of time and emotion to think or feel about it at all.[28]

Yet Davidson continued to respond to attacks on him in the press. He was particularly angered by a facetious review in the *Outlook* which called for an injunction to prevent him and Grant Richards from 'befogging the issue by the publication of further testamentory documents'.[29] He wrote a second parable in which

[26] John M. Sloan, 'The Scottish Free Church Case', *Fortnightly Review*, 82 (Sept. 1904), 450–61.

[27] Davidson to Richards, 6 Apr. 1902, Princeton.

[28] Davidson to Archer, 'Thursday' [May 1902], BL.

[29] 'The Protagonist's Jungle Book', *Outlook*, 9 (31 May 1902), 561.

the people pull the protagonist down from his pedestal and use his dead body as a stepping stone. When the *Outlook* refused to publish it, Grant Richards arranged for it to appear in the *Westminster Gazette*.[30] An older publisher might have shown more caution, as Davidson's response to insults merely fed the caricature of him as a deranged prophet. Davidson himself may have realized this, because from June on he resisted all attempts to draw him into controversy. In December in spite of Richards's encouragements he declined to write for the provocatively titled *The Eagle and Serpent* 'a journal for free spirits and for spirits struggling to be free' to which Shaw had been a willing foil. He explained its sensation-mongering techniques:

Whatever you write them they publish, with comments intended to provoke a reply; that is their method for securing sales. Shaw is different from me, because he has always been a publicist which I never was. It is all right that they should publish extracts from my things and criticize, and if they like to send me their reviewing after publication; but to ask for a letter before doing so is like a naked form of bribery and corruption.[31]

He was to show a similar caution when he was attacked in the United States by the American journalist W. L. Alden the following year. Alden was a fierce opponent of Nietzsche, describing his work in the *New York Times* in February 1903 as 'bad through and through'. By December he had included Davidson in his attacks. Richards brought this to his attention, but Davidson refused to become embroiled in a verbal battle, recommending instead that Richards should 'boycott the advertising columns'.[32]

In June 1902 Davidson thought he had found a more appropriate way of answering his critics when the *Daily Chronicle* requested an ode on the Coronation of Edward VII for publication on Coronation Day. He enjoyed writing 'the indubitable thing', as he called it, and believed it would squash any idea that he was either a 'disciple' or 'prophet of Nietzsche'. He told Richards: 'My "Ode" is the reverse to the obverse of my Empire-Builder'; by which he seems to have meant that it expressed the

---

[30] Davidson to Richards, 15 June 1902, Princeton.
[31] Davidson to Richards, 18 Dec. 1902, Princeton.
[32] Davidson to Richards, Nov. 1903, Princeton.

positive side of his vision of 'the world as irony', and of man as Matter.[33] England is seen as home of the sovereign race:

> a breed of men
> Concerned alone to be what them behoves;
> Forthright regarders, looking not askance
> Through doctrine, lifeless vision turned to stone
> And lenses warped and flawed, but seers indeed;
> Perceivers deeply versed in certainty,
> Who challenge light with light of faithful looks,
> Within whose souls a lamp self-nourished burns
> As on an altar fed with sacred fire.[34]

Although its unashamed imperialism is unlikely to appeal to readers today, the 'Ode' was warmly received at the time. So much so that Richards offered to speak to W. J. Fisher at the *Chronicle* about giving him regular space in the newspaper. Davidson rejected the idea, as he had Richards's suggestion earlier that year that he should approach the *Daily News*, offering a daily poem in blank verse. His reason was the same:

I could not keep up a series of poems the matter of which would please. I am consumed with a desire to state the evil of the world as well as the good, and I should want a free hand. The *Chronicle* is not adventurous enough, its basis and appeal are entirely bourgeois, so much so that I was astonished at the welcome given my Ode, the full meaning of which is not on the surface, as you would see—but say nothing about.[35]

Davidson was already planning a fourth *Testament*. He was still bitter over Balfour's refusal to give him a pension and responded contemptuously to Balfour's appointment as Prime Minister in July on Salisbury's retirement. He decided to write a *Testament of a Prime Minister*. He went to the British Museum in November to read Balfour's recently published *Defence of Philosophic Doubt*. He decided it was 'a very meagre, miserable production' and envisaged his own 'Prime Minister' as a heroic figure.[36]

But work on the poem did not begin at once, and it was to be two years before it was finally completed. His hopes for a quick

[33] Davidson to Richards, 7 July 1902, NLS.
[34] 'Ode on the Coronation of Edward VII', ll. 101–9.
[35] Davidson to Richards, 'Thursday' [June or July 1902], Princeton.
[36] Davidson to Richards, 22 Sept. 1902, Princeton.

theatrical success that year had already been dashed. His 'Fanny Legrand' had reached rehearsal only to be cruelly forestalled when Clyde Fitch's version of *Sapho* had opened at the Adelphi in May with Olga Nethersole, the star of *The Girl from Maxine's*, in the leading role. He told Richards: 'There is no language for the intense chagrin of this.'[37] His *Ruy Blas* was also postponed indefinitely when Waller accepted the lead role in the melodrama, *Monsieur Beaucaire*, adapted from a novel by Booth Talkinghorn, whose later Pulitzer-Prize-winning novel *The Magnificent Ambersons* was to catch the attention of Orson Welles. *Monsieur Beaucaire* was tried out first in Liverpool before opening in London at the Comedy Theatre on 25 October. Davidson followed its brilliant success at the box office with resignation. He would have to look elsewhere for money.

During the next two years he undertook a variety of commissions for the London stage in order to raise enough money to support himself during the writing of his final *Testament*. In November 1902 he went to Rothesay where he stayed until 23 January working on an original Lancelot play for Alexander for which he was paid £200, enough to keep him during the six months it took to write. Then in 1903 he adapted Miguel Zamaco's one-act play *Bohémas* and undertook a version of Racine's *Phèdre* for Mrs Campbell, who was planning to play it in Paris. The first was written in rooms in London during the summer while Maggie and the boys were in Scotland.[38] To write *Phèdre* he spent September and October alone in the Ochils, where he enjoyed bumping about the hills on his cycle.[39] Of all these commissions, only *Bohémas* ever reached production—opening at the Court Theatre in January 1904.

During those two years he also published two books which enjoyed some critical success. The first was his play *The Knight of the Maypole* for which Richards paid him an advance of £25 in August 1902, with an agreement to publish that Christmas.[40] Davidson had good reason for wanting it to appear that year. On 30 August a lavish and expensively staged production of Justin Huntly McCarthy's *If I Were King* opened at the St James's

[37] Davidson to Richards, 8 June 1903, Princeton.
[38] Davidson to McCormick, 'Thursday' [summer, 1903], Glasgow.
[39] Davidson to McCormick, 15 Sept. 1903, Glasgow.
[40] Davidson to Richards, 28 Aug. 1902, Princeton.

Theatre, after a successful eight-month run by Daniel Frohman in New York. Davidson believed Frohman had followed the skeleton of his rejected scenario and went to George Alexander to complain. The resemblance between the two plays might seem superficial: the impersonation of a king by a vagabond is a stock-in-trade of romantic drama. But the correspondences must still arouse suspicion, particularly as McCarthy appears to have taken some trouble to copyright the story as a novel in the United States. Alexander was shown Davidson's play and admitted the similarity.[41] His commissioning of Davidson's Lancelot play may have been his way of offering compensation. *The Knight of the Maypole* was warmly received, although in terms that could only annoy Davidson, as critics welcomed his return to a happier manner after his sombre *Testaments*.

In October 1903 Richards also published *A Rosary*, a miscellany of Davidson's journalism and some unpublished poems. The critics again liked it. Their praise took Davidson by surprise, particularly as he had received no advance for the book, and had even threatened to withdraw it at one point. The reason was a quarrel with Richards over his proposal to use a cheap binding. He had written angrily to demand a good cloth or buckram binding or nothing at all, adding, 'everybody knows or feels unconsciously that a pasteboard cover is amateurish and insolvent'.[42] It was a cruel and insensitive remark, particularly as Richards was publishing Davidson's work at a loss and had taken on Davidson's son, Sandy, to work for him. Richards was financially stretched, and one must admire his calm appeal to Davidson in the face of insults which must have been all the more hurtful because so nearly true:

Your book is already in the printer's hands so unless you wire insisting it is to be stopped I would rather go on with it, not so much because it is with the compositor, though, as because I have so much pleasure, as you know, in having all your books on my list, even if for the moment the result may not be what we should both like. You ask me, in effect, whether I can prophesy 'an actual sale'; where literature is concerned I have given up prophesying anything, but I hope we shall do better with this.[43]

[41] Davidson to Richards, 12 Oct. 1902, Princeton.
[42] Davidson to Richards, 29 June 1903, Princeton.
[43] Richards to Davidson, 4 July 1903, Richards.

In the event the book was given a handsome cover, although it was never to make money in spite of some excellent reviews.

Davidson's health improved while he was in Scotland writing *Phèdre* for Mrs Campbell, but he suffered from nervous tension again when he got back to London at the end of October. He was busy on several fronts. He had been assured by Waller that *Ruy Blas* would go to rehearsal at the Imperial as soon as the run of *Monsieur Beaucaire* ended at the Comedy and had already negotiated with Richards for its publication in England and America the day after the first performance.[44] Richards wanted to hold back until he had found an American publisher to share the costs, but Davidson knew about American publishing from his experience at the Bodley Head and persuaded him to a single printing in America, dangling before him the prospect of a triumphant tour of the play in the United States.[45] The contract was drawn up giving Davidson 10 per-cent royalties on the first 2,000 copies.

For two uneventful years, driven by work and the need to earn money, he had been frustrated in his desire to get on with his own projects. Now all that was about to change. He had been assured that *Ruy Blas* was certain to be a success at the box office. But instead of relaxing, he became anxious that the book should be equally successful. From observing the effects of stardom in the theatre, he had become convinced that success could be achieved by advertising the man more than his books. He wrote a self-advertisement along these lines and proposed to Richards that they place it at intervals in the newspapers in the run-up to the first night.[46] It was a method of sales promotion that was to occur to others as the market for books expanded in the twentieth century. Richards refused, as it meant spending two or three times more than he could ever expect to earn.[47]

Davidson was disappointed. But he had resumed work on his fourth *Testament,* which he planned as 'an actual book'.[48] *The Testament of a Prime Minister,* which contains over 1,100 lines, is a complex work. The poem may be more strident and

[44] Davidson to Richards, 4 Oct. 1903, Princeton.
[45] Davidson to Richards, 6 Oct. 1903, Princeton.
[46] Davidson to Richards, 23 Nov. 1903, Princeton.
[47] Richards to Davidson, 26 Nov. 1903, Richards.
[48] Davidson to Richards, 1 Nov. 1903, Princeton.

millennal in its rejection of God and sin, but Davidson's speaker is also a more tormented figure, clinging to his materialist convictions in the face of doubts and fear of death:

> Undone by mystery, smitten by a thought,
> A poisoned arrow from the infinite.
> Or is it that my spirit slays itself?
> A doubter always I; and doubt is death—.[49]

The Prime Minister recalls the moment of his emotional overthrow a year earlier while delivering a materialist speech in Parliament. He stammers to an end, then leaves the House. His subsequent journey along the Thames embankment takes him to an encounter with a group of vagabonds, and a vision of the Last Judgement that reiterates the materialist version of the saved and the damned in *The Empire-Builder*. The poem ends with the Prime Minister's nightmarish wait for death, tortured by hideous involuntary dreams—'material memories'—of the past history of the world, in which his self-conscious 'masterdom' of time and space is also his martyrdom.

The blank verse is assured. The lurid tale of rape, sexual obsession, and murder told to the Prime Minister by one of the vagabonds draws on the sensational news stories of the day and is clearly meant to conform to Davidson's theory of democratic poetry. But the modernity of *The Prime Minister*, as of the three earlier *Testaments*, lies principally in its denial of the supernatural foundations of prophecy. This is what the term 'modern' suggested to some theologians at the turn of the century. The Prime Minister, for instance, insists that, 'It is my bones that speak, my skeleton, | The inmost core of me, the soul of soul; | The skeleton's the soul; it must be so.'[50] Modern, too, is the use of scientific language in the *Testaments*. This was one of Davidson's innovations in poetry, although it had been tried earlier by William Canton, Grant Allen, and Matilde Blind. However, the limitations of the *Testament* form are more evident with *The Prime Minister*. The interest of the dramatic monologue form lies in the peculiarities of the speaker's situation. In so far as Davidson's speakers become prophets of a new materialist vision of man and the universe, what they are or do in the world

---

[49] *Testament of a Prime Minister*, ll. 23–6.
[50] *Testament of a Prime Minister*, ll. 1037–9.

ceases to matter very much. Davidson intended to go on writing
*Testament*s, taking as his theme the Harlot, the Artist, the Christian, the Mendicant, the Criminal, the Millionaire, the Prolet-
arian, the Evolutionist, and finally the Deliverer. Only one
other, written as his own *The Testament of John Davidson*, was ever
completed.

During the writing of *The Prime Minister*, he seems to have
suffered mental torment similar to that described in the poem.
He was so preoccupied at a Christmas party hosted by Mrs
Campbell that he left abruptly without taking leave of his host-
ess or Grant Richards and his wife, whom he had taken as
guests. His thoughts were on the effects of certain letters he had
sent.[51] Two weeks earlier, after several months of hesitation, he
had admitted in the letter page of the *Saturday Review* the prophetic purpose of his *Testament*s. His letter announced:

I have been waging war in Gaul, and have now reached the Rubicon:
permit me to cross it in your columns. . . . I am often asked what I
mean by 'intelligence', a frequent word in my 'Rosary'. By 'intelligence' I mean a virgin understanding, sentient Matter, unsmirched by
theology, philosophy, morality, or immorality, and self-exiled from the
inheritance of imagination. Such an understanding is beginning to be:
it dates I think from the 'Origin of Species': my 'Testaments' await its
maturity. . . . these when completed will be my 'Statement of the world
as it is'.[52]

Davidson's confession that the materialist views expressed in
the *Testament*s were his own could hardly have come as a surprise to the critics. But Davidson himself had found it difficult
to make the admission. When the *Prime Minister* appeared the
following October he told Gosse he had concealed his message
for so long because he had been afraid that to deliver it might
entail starvation for himself and his family.[53] This is consistent
with his strenuous efforts to dissociate himself from the speakers of his *Testament*s. But it does not fit all the facts. It is
unlikely that he tried deliberately to mislead. His attempt to
maintain an uncommitted façade is more likely to have been
the result of his continuing attachment to his role as ironist.

---

[51] Davidson to Richards, 29 Dec. 1903, Princeton.
[52] Davidson to the Editor, *Saturday Review*, 94 (12 Dec. 1903), 733–4.
[53] Davidson to Gosse, 1 Oct. 1904, Yale.

The *Testament*s are dramatic works. Each of their speakers is torn between the spiritual and the material, the creed of the strong man and ordinary human hopes and longings, acutely so in the case of the *Prime Minister*. While at work on the poem, Davidson seems finally to have accepted wholeheartedly the vitalistic monism to which his work had been tending from very early on and which had reached its crisis at Shoreham. In its synthesis of spirit and substance, monism provided him with a way of reconciling and explaining many aspects of his life and work, from the sensory empiricism of his early Random Itinerant to the warring mind and matter of his later poetry. The step was decisive in defining his poetic mission. When the *Prime Minister* appeared the following year he told William Archer:

My purpose in these Testaments is to aid the rotten overthrow of the rotten financial investment called Christendom: I perceive that this can only be done by purging the world of everything that is meant by spirit, soul, 'other' world, though all the literature and art and religion of the past should go with it. I would start the world over again from the only mystery, Matter.[54]

His identification with his Man Forbid was now complete.

There has been much speculation about the literary and scientific origins of Davidson's materialism. Elements of it have been traced to Wordsworth's pantheism and to Goethe who believed that spirit and matter could not be separated. Other names mentioned are Charles Darwin, Herbert Spencer, T. H. Huxley, John Tyndall, and William Clifford, the Cambridge mathematician and publicist of the nebular hypothesis of Kant and Laplace. Davidson is much more likely to have received his ideas from scientific popularizers of the period such as Edward Aveling whose *Darwin Made Easy* (1887) served as a handy guide for the curious. 'The evolutionist regards all the phenomena of the universe as natural, and does not believe in the intervention of the supernatural', Aveling wrote in what might be a para-phrase of Davidson's own convictions.[55] Aveling had been influenced by the German zoologist Ernst Haeckel, whose work Davidson certainly knew in 1905—possibly Joseph McCabe's

---

[54] Davidson to Archer, 22 Oct. 1904, BL.
[55] Edward Aveling, *Darwin Made Easy* (London, 1887), 1.

translation of *The Wonders of Life* (1904), although he may have already been familiar with *The Pedigree of Man* (1883) and *The Riddle of the Universe* (1900).[56] In *The Riddle of the Universe* one finds many of the key ideas of Davidson's own version of scientific materialism: the recognition of one sole substance in the universe, Matter; the rejection both of dualism and the kind of practical materialism that denied the existence of spirit; and a highly developed account of the ether theory. Significantly Haeckel finds an illustrious pedigree for his vital monism in Goethe and Wordsworth, poets who are referred to as possible influences on Davidson's ideas.

Although Davidson's ideas seem outdated in the twentieth century, a poet has to be judged not by the scientific accuracy of his world view, but by his effectiveness in transmuting this into poetry. In this respect his conception of the universe is no less tenable than, say, the cosmologies of Blake's prophetic books or Yeats's *A Vision* (1925), which were also attempts to answer the riddle of man's conflict between the life of the body and the life of the spirit. Although Shaw considered the influence of John Tyndall and the physicists dangerous to thinkers opposed to the disorder of the human world, if only because they saw in Tyndall's crystals 'beauty and vitality without the corrupting appetites of fleshly vitality', he believed Davidson had found his highest inspiration in it.[57]

On 4 January *Beaucaire* reached its 450th performance. That same day *Ruy Blas* went into rehearsal. Mrs Campbell had been persuaded to play the Queen, and for business reasons Waller asked for the play to be re-titled *A Queen's Romance*.[58] From the middle of the month Davidson's club became his office as he read the final proofs of the play. Meanwhile on the 9th *Bohémas* had opened at the Court with Charles Lauder in the leading role. On 10 February Waller played *Beaucaire* for the last time. *A Queen's Romance* opened at the Imperial the following day. After more than two years of frustrating delays, his adaptation had finally reached the footlights.

[56] Telegrams from Davidson to Richards, 25 and 27 May 1905, and a letter of 29 Oct. 1905, Princeton, indicate that Davidson borrowed a volume of Haeckel from Richards during the writing of his 'Preface' to *The Theatrocrat*.

[57] George Bernard Shaw, *Back to Methuselah* (London, 1930), i. lxv.

[58] Davidson to A. N. Lyons, 23 Nov. 1903, Princeton.

There was a record audience at the first night. The king and queen were there, and the play was received enthusiastically. But the leading reviews in the Sunday papers the next morning were hostile. Davidson wrote to Mrs Richards: 'I am more perplexed in many ways than I have ever been in my life.'[59] In the gloomy post-mortems of that day Waller found out that *Ruy Blas* had never had a good run in any theatre in London or Paris, and that every version produced in London had failed financially.[60] The cruellest blow came from Max Beerbohm who ridiculed with heartless wit Waller's 'sonorous declaration' and Mrs Campbell's underacting. He did not spare Davidson's solemn blank verse which, in his view, only succeeded in reducing the 'jolly healthy unreality and monstrosity of Hugo's romance' to a 'silly story' performed by 'a community of idiotic frogs trying to puff themselves to the semblance of bulls'.[61]

Quizzed by Richards at the office, Davidson's son Sandy reported that his father was angry at the actors. Davidson was furious when he heard this and wrote of Sandy:

He seems to have talked thoughtlessly and misrepresented me. I am entirely satisfied with the production of *A Queen's Romance* and with the acting and above all with Waller and Mrs Campbell. I have reason to be. The play was never seriously hurt by the adverse criticism of the principal players.[62]

A few days later the play closed after only a fortnight. His percentage of the takings had not even paid off the £200 advance he had received for the play. In her memoirs years later Mrs Campbell blamed the critics for the play's failure. She wrote: 'The public did not come and judge for themselves.'[63]

Failure, as in the past, spurred him to further effort. He completed his fourth *Testament* that summer and began writing his first tragedy, *The Theatrocrat: A Tragic Play of Church and Stage*. The play takes a cynical look at the London stage. The main characters are Sir Tristram Summer, the bankrupt

[59] Davidson to Mrs Grant Richards, 14 Feb. 1904, Princeton.
[60] Davidson to McCormick, 'Sunday' [Feb. 1904], Glasgow.
[61] Max Beerbohm, '*Ruy Blas* and the O.U.D.S.', *Saturday Review*, 97 (20 Feb. 1904), 230–1.
[62] Davidson to Richards, 22 Feb. 1904, Princeton.
[63] Mrs Campbell, *Life and Letters*, 237–8.

owner of the Grosvenor Theatre; his wife Lady Summer who is to play Shakespeare's Cressida opposite her old lover, Warwick Groom, now a penniless and broken-down artist; and Lady Summer's cousin, the atheistic Bishop of St James's, who is the mouthpiece for Davidson's own materialist beliefs. There is a touch of personal venom in Davidson's portrayal of Mark Belfry, an American manager, who wants to buy the theatre and turn it into a music hall. Belfry, we learn, has bought a poet's play and had 'a commodious hack' vulgarize it for profit, a reference to Davidson's own bitter experience with Daniel Frohman.

The cynicism and sexual obsession of *The Theatrocrat* owe much to Shakespeare's *Troilus and Cressida*, although Davidson had also read Chaucer's version in McCormick's edition. *The Theatrocrat*, like its Shakespearean play within the play, is concerned with the stripping away of illusion. Much of the play is wild and flamboyant expressionism, of a kind unknown on the English stage at this time, particularly the final act in which the outraged audience tears the stage and the Bishop to pieces as he tries to introduce his new materialist drama. The linking of Church and Stage is not simply part of its expressionism, however—a way, one might imagine, of allowing Davidson a platform for his own anti-religious ideas. The alliance of Church and Stage was in fact a historical feature of Davidson's day. In 1879 the Revd Stewart Headlam, a Christian Socialist, had founded the Church and Stage Guild to reform the theatre and to bring actors and clergymen together. In the second act of *The Theatrocrat*, Warwick Groom recalls the past greatness of the theatre when it was looked on disapprovingly as 'the house of sin':

> . . . for Church and Stage are deadly foes;
> They can be strong only in enmity;
> And both were shrines of art when either shunned
> The other, or met in battle: now that they mix,
> Illicit lovers and against the lust
> Of nature, sterile hybrids mock their couch;
> And soon the lofty strain of either ends
> In mere abortion.[64]

[64] *The Theatrocrat*, 112.

Davidson's target in *The Theatrocrat* was the newly won respectability of the contemporary theatre, where actor-managers like Henry Irving were being honoured with knighthoods, and the stage was seen as a potential force for moral good. He believed that the artist had a right to be 'immoral'—that is, to challenge conventional morality—and said so frankly in a series of articles he wrote the following year, 'Wordsworth's Immorality and Mine', which he used as part of his 'Preface' to his play. Wordsworth is cast in his own image—as wayward child and original poet who thinks and imagines the world for himself.[65] Davidson wrote to Beerbohm of *The Theatrocrat*:

In this book I try to lift the lid from the world. God and Sin and Heaven and Hell which were once so great and high, are now only a rusty lid hiding the Universe from men, and stifling thought and imagination. Those who have got out from under this lid are in worst case, because if they try to cooperate anywhere with men—not eccentrically, but in the processes of the world—they have to slip in beneath it again: it is so, notoriously, in the Church; I have found it in the schools, in the theatre, in literature, and, most withering of all, in science. But the lid can be lifted; I have tried to; I believe I have done so.[66]

With the failure of *A Queen's Romance*, Davidson was again hard up. In March 1904 he approached his old publisher, Lane, and asked for £50 in return for the copyright of his unpublished plays. He was insulted when Lane refused to sink more money on him:

You could not 'sink' money to fuller account than on me and my writings. When all the others are forgotten, it will be remembered that it was you published my books—when nobody else would; and believed in them—when the world gladly believed that their day was past.[67]

Lane was not unmoved, and decided to publish a 'Selected Poems'. They quarrelled about the contents. Davidson especially wanted 'Butterflies' excluded—'a nice poem enough, but

---

[65] 'Wordsworth's Immorality and Mine', *Outlook*, 15 (10 and 17 June 1905), and 16 (8 and 22 July 1905).
[66] Davidson to Max Beerbohm, 21 Nov. 1905, Merton.
[67] Davidson to Lane, 28 Mar. 1904, NLS.

nothing like its reputation'[68]—and 'The Testament of a Man Forbid' included, though this meant approaching Richards for permission. The quarrels continued up to publication in October. His *Testament of a Prime Minister* came out on the 5th, ahead of Lane's *Selected Poems*, but received some hostile reviews. Davidson believed that Lane had the reviewers in his pocket, possibly even on *The Times*, which compared its negative vision of life unfavourably with the dark elements in Dante, Shakespeare, and Lucretius.[69] He felt this was unfair as his *Testament*s were incomplete. There were also strong objections to the sordidness of the police story at the centre of the poem. He wrote to Lane directly to protest against the reviews, insisting: 'I have made one of the ugliest things that ever happened beautiful for all eternity.'[70]

Not all the reviews were bad. Some recognized its vigour and suggestion of modernity. But *The Times* notice still stuck in his throat. He wrote defiantly to Richards: 'Did he [*The Times* reviewer] really imagine that he could interfere with my purpose? As if anything but death by starvation could stop me.'[71] One sees him driven by a new determination in the closing months of that year, as he worked to finish *The Theatrocrat* and to seek out new contacts and allies in Fleet Street.

II

Although he had always been uncomfortable about getting old, Davidson in 1905 was still a comparatively young man, not yet 48 and with his best work still to be written. The year began with a return to journalism. This was the outcome of a commission from the imperialist organ the *Outlook* for a poem 'A Song of Change' supporting Chamberlain's campaign for Tariff Reform, which challenged Victorian faith in Free Trade and *laissez faire*. He was paid 5 guineas, and the poem appeared in January. The commission for a poem had come through Lane from the

---

[68] Davidson to Lane, 14 Apr. 1904, NLS.
[69] 'Mr. John Davidson's Poems', *Times Literary Supplement* (28 Oct. 1904), 328.
[70] Davidson to Lane, 'Sunday' [Oct. 1904], NLS.
[71] Ibid.

magazine's new editor, James Louis Garvin, who was to become one of the most brilliant editors in Fleet Street.[72] Garvin's background as the son of Irish parents living in England might well have fitted him to become an anti-imperialist, but though he opposed Little Englandism, he was devoted to the wider patriotism of Empire. He had already worked on the *Fortnightly Review* and the *Daily Telegraph* when he was appointed to the *Outlook*. His brief was to counter the influence of the *Spectator* which strongly supported the conventional wisdom of Free Trade. He quickly transformed the *Outlook* into the unrivalled sixpenny review on the market.[73]

Davidson, in need of a new source of income after the failure of *A Queen's Romance*, was quick to make use of his new contact. He offered Garvin a signed weekly review of the latest poetry. He felt that poetry, unlike the other arts, was still 'at the mercy of the friends and enemies of the poets and their publishers' and wanted to put discussion on a more serious footing. He explained: 'I require a peg to hang my discussion on, and shall take stock in dailies weeklies and monthlies of the current opinions and circumversions on poetry, which require overhauling—almost in every case, keel-hauling in fact.'[74] Garvin was looking for ways to tranform the *Outlook* into a quality review and invited him to submit a sample article. Davidson's first piece, 'The Poet in the Market Place' described the fickleness of the reading public in the matter of literary reputation, using his own experience with 'The Ballad of a Nun' ten years earlier as an example. Garvin liked the article and encouraged him to continue. But he seems to have felt that Davidson's talent was wasted for he suggested that he also submit 'outdoor articles' and 'imperial poems'. He asked specifically for an article on Fleet Street. Davidson responded enthusiastically to the idea: 'I shall write about Fleet Street as if nobody has ever written about it before.'[75]

His 'Fleet Street: A Fantasy' appeared in the *Outlook* that March. It is a piece in which the impressionistic spirit of

[72] Davidson to James Louis Garvin, 11 Jan. 1905, Texas.
[73] See Alfred M. Gollin, *The Observer and J. L. Garvin 1908–1914* (Oxford, 1960), and James D. Startt, *Journalists for Empire* (New York, 1991).
[74] Davidson to Garvin, 17 Jan. 1905, Texas.
[75] Davidson to Garvin, 22 and 23 Jan. 1905, Texas.

Davidson's 'Random Itinerant' articles is aesthetically and intellectually enlarged by the defamiliarizing perspective of the
materialist philosopher. Here, liberated from normal per-
spectives of time and space, Davidson's scientific imagination
passionately celebrates the oneness of matter dispersed
throughout the universe in many diverse forms, from the spectacular rings of Saturn to the humblest bricks in Fleet Street.[76]
He was to carry the words and phrases of his article around in
his head for three years until they emerged in finished form as
his poem, 'Fleet Street'. It is a distinctly modern poem, not only
in its combination of scientific language and prosaic subject-
matter, but in its displacement of man from the centre of the
universe. One literary critic, referring to Conrad's 1907 novel
The Secret Agent, has characterized the destruction of the 'comfortable dream of a humanised world' as 'the essential movement of the modern consciousness'.[77] One finds this shattering
of the human world in Davidson's writings from early on. In his
suburban tour of the spreading brick suburbs of London in
1893, he had observed: 'How many millions of millions of
bricks there must have gone to build up London! Man is your
only true ant and coral insect.'[78] Davidson looked on life with
something of a zoologist's eye, his impressions derived not from
ordinary pre-existent human assumptions but from an ironic
receptiveness to the oddness, immediacy, and sometimes gross
materiality of life in the city. It is this aspect of modernity which
also links him to T. S. Eliot. Eliot's Prufrock, who wishes to be
turned into 'a pair of ragged claws' is evidently indebted to
Davidson's clerk in 'Thirty Bob a Week', imagining himself in
the shape 'of mollusc or of ape'.[79] Davidson's writing from 1905
shows an intensification of this use of the naturalist's language
and perspective.

A visit to the Crystal Palace early that year also provided copy
for a *Glasgow Herald* article that was to become the basis of one
of his most celebrated poems. The Crystal Palace was a huge
prefabricated building of glass and iron which had been de-

---

[76] 'Fleet Street: A Fantasy', *Outlook*, 15 (25 Mar. 1905), 409–10.

[77] J. Hillis Miller, *Poets of Reality* (Cambridge, Mass., 1965), 47.

[78] *A Random Itinerary*, 98.

[79] Robert Crawford, *The Savage and the City in the Works of T. S. Eliot* (Oxford, 1987), 59.

signed by Joseph Paxton to house the Great Exhibition of industrial and technical inventions at Hyde Park in 1851. Perma-
nently re-sited at Sydenham in 1854, its exhibits and
entertainments continued to attract huge holiday crowds during the late Victorian and Edwardian ages. Though it success-
fully captured the hidden dreams of the age, it was often
ridiculed as tasteless, particularly by the intelligentsia.
Dostoevsky included it in his derision of nineteenth-century
ideas of human perfectibility, while in Gissing's novel of work-
ing-class London, *The Nether World*, published in 1889, the
satire is directed against the 'imbecile joviality' of the crowds
swarming to the Crystal Palace for their bank-holiday
outing. Davidson's attitude combines both of these view-
points, although it is complicated in his case by an imaginative
fascination.

On a visit to the Crystal Palace with Maggie in June 1900 for
the Handel Festival he had been distracted from the music by
the restless enthusiastic mood of the crowd during the *Messiah*.
He had seen many displays of prophetic inspiration as a boy at
the prayer meetings and hymn-singing services of his father's
church. His observations on this occasion registered a sense of
incongruity between the secular mood of the event and the
religious form of its expression; during the 'Hallelujah' he
imagined that 'the crowd believed in its mind's eye some glorified Prince of Wales leading in the winner'.[80] He felt a similar
incongruity when he visited the Crystal Palace six years later,
although this time he decided there was an important difference between a concert audience and the bank-holiday crowds.
He explained the distinction to Max Beerbohm:

A theatrical audience is a mob, so is a church audience, or a concert
audience: each of these is *a* mob, but it has a mind, it is occupied with
something, has a special purpose in assembling. But a crowd in the
Crystal Palace on a bank holiday is not *a* mob; it is Mob, aimless,
featureless, enormous, like the great Boyg.[81]

Davidson's impressions of the restless, pleasure-seeking
crowds at the Crystal Palace—'Crowd; Mob; a blur of faces
featureless, | Of forms inane; a stranded shoal of folk,'—[82]

[80] Davidson to McCormick, 28 June 1900, Glasgow.
[81] Davidson to Beerbohm, 'Easter Monday' [16 Apr. 1906], Merton.
[82] 'The Crystal Palace', ll. 144–5.

marks an important step in the making of literary modernism. His technique is in some ways like that of Gissing's in the chapter 'Io Saturnalia!' in *The Nether World*. It is interesting to compare them. In each case, the speaker takes us on a guided tour, observing and commenting sarcastically on the meaningless activity of the crowd. Both use classical allusions and a form of free indirect discourse for satirical effect. But Davidson's irony seems more sharply focused. The emphasis at the time of the Great Exhibition was on the Smilesian values of industry and self-help, with frequent reference being made to 'the working bees of the world's hive'. In Davidson's 'Crystal Palace' the crowds are reduced to a noisy locust-swarm, hungry for diversion: 'They all pursue their purpose business-like— | The polo-ground, the cycle-track.'[83] The pleasure is 'business-like': irony indeed.

Davidson's language also differs significantly from Gissing's. The combination of gruff acerbity and underlying tenderness which Le Gallienne identified as characteristic of Davidson's personality is here given free rein in a satirical 'flyting' that mixes aureate and ordinary language, the serious and the grotesque. In this, Davidson's poetry owes much to the characteristics of Scottish speech and writing, and in particular to Carlyle's emphatic language and heightened emotional effects. In spite of its effort to mimic the mood of the crowd, Gissing's language remains aloof, scornful, distanced: he describes the poor, for instance, quarrelling and making love—'the latter in somewhat primitive fashion'. Davidson observes the alfresco sex of the London crowds with less derision:

> And look!—Among the laurels on the lawns
> Torn coats and ragged skirts, starved faces flushed
> With passion and with wonder!—hid away
> Avowedly; but seen—and yet not seen!
> None laugh; none point; none notice: multitude
> Remembers and forgives; unwisest love
> Is sacrosanct upon a holiday.[84]

He also looks beyond the social forms of the crowd to the horrifying vision of the animal in man. A 'voluptuary' is spotted in the grill-room:

[83] 'The Crystal Palace', ll. 44–5.
[84] 'The Crystal Palace', ll. 90–6.

> With cauteries on his cranium; dyed moustache;
> Teeth like a sea-wolf's, each a work of art
> Numbered and valued singly; copper skin;
> And nether eyelids pouched.[85]

This savagery surfacing and dissolving again within the 'blur of faces featureless'—Wordsworth's 'blank confusion'—is Davidson's modern 'nether world'.

Perhaps the most significant aspect of Davidson's ironic perspective is that it is theological rather than cultural. It arises, as on his visit to the Handel Festival, from his sense of the incongruity of seeing the sacred in degraded secular forms. Significantly, this is more fully realized in the poem than in the prose article which he sketched immediately after his visit. The opening scene of his prose sketch records his amusement at the sight of a respectable middle-aged commuter putting a penny in a fortune-telling machine at London Bridge Station. His sense of the absurdity of this then transfers itself to the Crystal Palace where he imagines the flying machine fantastically as it might appear to visiting Tibetans, as a sublime rotary prayer engine spinning the petitioners about in space. But the glass and iron building itself is ridiculed simply because it is an 'ugly thing' and 'nature's outcast'.[86] However, in a boyishly irreverent letter to Max Beerbohm the following year, we see his sense of the incongruous widening to include the building itself and what it represented:

It was glass and iron that did it: transparent brittleness and tough endurance determined to have an erection of their own, and to beget something in the clouds, Ixion-like. For fifty years it has been standing there in perpetual Priapism, but the clouds, except for a balloon on Saturdays and bank holidays, remain sterile. . . . Royalties used to build Cathedrals: this is a temple without art, without religion, without a priest, dedicated to nothing, representing nothing except transparent brittleness and tough endurance in a perpetual Priapism.[87]

This irreverence is the starting point of the poem which he finally completed after another visit to the Crystal Place with Max in June 1906. In the opening stanza, where he and Max

---

[85] 'The Crystal Palace', ll. 179–82.
[86] 'Automatic Augury and the Crystal Palace', *Glasgow Herald* (18 Mar. 1905), 9.
[87] Davidson to Beerbohm, 2 June 1906, Merton.

appear as 'Irreverent, we' before Sir Hiram Maxim's flying machine, the building is ridiculed not just for being ugly and unnatural but for its incongruity as a 'fane unique' and a 'temple of commercialism'. But the mocking tone is not sustained throughout the poem, and the voice begins to hint at emptiness and even horror. The compelling voice of literary Modernism can be located here, as in Eliot's early poetry, in a negativism in which the speaker's ironic superiority turns hollow in the absence of any alternative meaning or value. There is no humanizing centre, or human identification, as in Wordsworth, with ordinary men, to dispel the poet's chillingly impersonal vision.

It is characteristic of Davidson's uneven development that even as he was laying down the basis for a new poetry, he was still drawn to older, more traditional verse forms. 'Fleet Street' and 'The Crystal Palace' were to be three years in maturing. In the meantime he needed money and offered Garvin a new calendar of Fleet Street Eclogues at the rate of one a month, beginning with his spring poem 'The Ides of March'. This was not the kind of imperial poem Garvin wanted, but he bought it and agreed to Davidson's proposal after meeting Watt. In the months ahead Davidson came to hate this chore of turning out an Eclogue to order and came to resent Garvin's editorial interference. But initially he was enthusiatic about the idea. 'To give up a good space occasionally, say, once a month, to one favoured poet is no more than poetry, the long-suffering servant deserves', he wrote.[88]

He also became interested in rhyme and tried experiments with Poe's method of rhyming the same word. Among the poems he completed that summer was the ballad 'A Runnable Stag' which was singled out for special praise when it appeared in his collection *Holiday and Other Poems* in 1906. The poem is often interpreted autobiographically, with the stag as symbol of the heroic, sacrificial victim, hounded to his death. It is certainly charged with personal force. But the image is a common one. Referring to Parnell's death in 'The Tragic Generation', Yeats, for instance, quotes Goethe's, 'The Irish seem to me like a pack of hounds always dragging down some noble stag.'[89] And Arthur Conan Doyle's ballad 'The Old Huntsman', which is similar in

[88] Davidson to Garvin, 3 Mar. 1905, Texas.
[89] W. B. Yeats, *Autobiographies* (London, 1955), 316.

style and theme to Davidson's poem, appeared in 1898 in the
March issue of the *Speaker* that contained Davidson's prose
version of 'The Man Forbid'.[90] Davidson's immediate source
would seem to be Richard Jefferies's *The Red Deer*, published in
1894. Like many of the poems in *Holiday*, 'A Runnable Stag'
celebrates the liberating outdoor life and the spirit of holiday.
In this Davidson was in touch with the mood of the Edwardian
age with its enthusiasm for hunting, games, sports, and bicycles.

He himself was surprised by the impulse to return to more
popular verse forms—the theme of his lyric 'The Last Song'
written at this time—but he decided to look on it as an 'inter-
mezzo' among his 'Testaments and Tragedies'.[91] His *Theatrocrat*
remained unpublished. He had finished it the previous December, but only weeks before it was ready Richards had gone
bankrupt with liabilities of £50,000. Davidson had hurried
round to his house in Park Crescent on 15 December in a
state of anxiety about who was to publish his play.[92] He approached Lane and several other London publishers with
the manuscript,[93] but no one would take it. He encouraged
Richards to return to business, and by September Richards had
established his new firm in his wife's name, E. Grant Richards,
with offices at 7 Carlton Street, an old corner shop off the lower
end of Regent Street. Out of gratitude to Davidson, he chose
The Theatrocrat to launch the new firm. Richards's generosity
was not without strings. During October, Richards pressed him
to approach G. Herbert Thring, the Secretary of the Society of
Authors, to establish his right to repurchase his books from the
receiver, Alexander Moring. Davidson was anxious at the prospect of being out of pocket, but Richards reassured him: 'The
idea would be that my wife should, once you had freed your
books in principle, attempt to make arrangements with Moring
. . . to take the present stock over at a fair price.'[94] Davidson
accepted an invitation to dinner at the Richards on the 26th,
presumably to hear more about their plan. He was not to know

[90] Arthur Conan Doyle, 'The Old Huntsman', *Speaker*, 17 (5 Mar. 1898), 298.
[91] Davidson to Richards, 5 Sept. 1905, Princeton.
[92] Davidson to Richards, 16 Dec. 1904, Princeton.
[93] Davidson to Lane, 30 Dec. 1904, Lane.
[94] Richards to Davidson 24 Oct. 1905, Richards.

that he would become involved in an acrimonious dispute with Moring that would last for several years.

During October he struggled with the proofs of his play, doubly burdened with bronchitis and bad teeth. He also completed a lengthy preface setting out his monist convictions about the inseparability of body and soul. Earlier religious accounts of man's place in the universe are dismissed. God is described as a 'projection of self-consciousness as Other World', and sin as 'the exhaustion of the material forces of man'. He believed that great poetry needed a great audience and attributed Wordsworth's decline into pedantry and moralism in his later years to the lack of such an audience. His own faith was in the young. In January that year he wrote: 'The most poignant appeal of the best poetry is to the uncultured mind, the undebauched imagination of youth.'[95] He had already received confirmation that his poetry had its most receptive audience among young people. He had been invited to speak to the students at Edinburgh University, an offer he had declined.[96] And early that year he had heard from a young undergraduate admirer at Trinity College, Oxford, James Elroy Flecker, who had produced a group of anti-religious sketches under his influence, and was preparing a paper on him to be read to a college society. In March, after the paper had been read, Davidson cut it to a suitable length and helped him place it in the *Monthly Review*.[97] As his play went to press, he added some dedicatory verses 'To the Generation Knocking at the Door', urging the young to,

> Break—break it open; let the knocker rust:
> Consider no 'shalt not', and no man's 'must':
> And, being entered, promptly take the lead,
> Setting aside tradition, custom, creed.[98]

Davidson was by turns anxious and belligerent as the printing progressed, and Richards had to suppress as 'impolitic' parts of

---

[95] 'A Personal View', *Outlook*, 15 (28 Jan. 1905), 128–9.
[96] Davidson to John Purves, Hon. Sec. Edinburgh Univ. History Society, 19 Sept. 1899, NLS.
[97] John Sherwood, *No Golden Journey: Biography of James Elroy Flecker* (London, 1973), 50.
[98] 'To the Generation Knocking at the Door', ll. 1–4.

Davidson's publicity material announcing that the book had been refused by nearly every publisher in London.[99] By the end of November the book was in type, and Davidson received his cheque for advance royalties. He had already spent some of the money, but he was in a celebratory mood and invited Richards and a new young author, Filson Young, to dinner at the Trocadero.[100]

Young was to become one of the few close friends of Davidson's final years. He was 29 when they met. He was a motor-car enthusiast as well as a lover of literature and had worked as a special war correspondent for the *Manchester Guardian* during the Boer War before moving to London to edit the literary page of the *Daily Mail*. Richards had accepted his novel *The Sands of Pleasure* and had taken him on as reader for his new firm. Davidson read the novel in proof and was taken by its treatment of illicit passion which he felt had been ignored in English fiction since Fielding and Smollet.[101] But he wanted Young to end the novel in tragedy, which Young refused to do, confiding in Richards that he knew what readers wanted and that Davidson 'seems to like being out of sympathy with the public'.[102]

In his memoirs Richards remembers his evenings at the Trocadero as Davidson's guest. Usually they met at the Grosvenor Club for a glass of sherry before walking or taking a cab to the restaurant. Davidson always ordered the best meal, at that time half a guinea, and a bottle of very good claret. But he also showed thrift—making a point of choosing the most appropriate rather than the most expensive cognac and bringing his own cigars from the Grosvenor Club. Richards describes Davidson's after dinner manner on these occasions:

There in the Trocadero we would sit and talk. Davidson would mellow, would cast off all doubts as to the future, would be certain of a great success, and he would give you the feeling that he loved the world for your sake. And indeed those evenings were the occasions when the world became attractive in his eyes, rosy—and that not because his stomach lusted after rich food and good wine but because they were

[99] Richards to Davidson, 6 Nov. 1905, Richards.
[100] Davidson to Richards, 1 and 7 Nov. 1905, Princeton.
[101] *Daily Mail* (22 Nov. 1905), 6.
[102] Filson Young to Richards, 2 Nov. 1905 and 12 May 1906, Richards.

for the moment the symbols, the outward signs, of the comfort, the luxury, he knew to be his due.[103]

Davidson had a characteristically Scottish attitude to money, despising the worship of it, but accepting unconsciously that the possession of it was a sign of one's worth. On the night he entertained Richards and Young at the Trocadero, he did not know that Richards was planning to issue both *The Theatrocrat* and *The Sands of Pleasure* on the same day. Richards's reasons were purely practical: he wanted to cut down on invoicing and parcelling and to avoid delay in catching the pre-Christmas sales.[104] But Davidson objected strongly when he heard of Richards's plans. With the ways of editors and reviewers in mind, he wrote: 'One will be actively published, and the other dropped in the ditch.'[105] Richards relented. *The Sands of Pleasure* was issued on 22 November; *The Theatrocrat* appeared a week later.

Before publication Richards sent a dozen copies to people who might have influence, including one to Shaw, although of Shaw Davidson wrote: 'In sending a copy to Bernard Shaw I wish you to say to him that when you suggested that I should send him one I declined on the ground that his mind lived in a different world from mine and that he would not be interested.'[106] Davidson saw its publication as an international event and asked that copies should be sent to leading continental critics, including Georg Brandes and René Ghil.[107] He himself wrote to every editor he knew to promote his book. 'I want to make a new public, and I want great editors to help me', he told one.[108] He also tried to obtain special notices from Israel Zangwill at the *Daily Mail* and W. L. Courtney at the *Daily Telegraph*. He was driving himself into the ground with work. Richards recommended that he take a rest, and suggested that his slavish commitment to his engagements might be 'undermannish'. Davidson snapped back: 'I am not afraid of doing an "undermannish" thing: no overman ever is.'[109] But by

[103] Grant Richards, *Author Hunting* (London, 1934), 221–2.
[104] Richards to Davidson, 14 Nov. 1905, Richards.
[105] Davidson to Richards, 13 Nov. 1905, Princeton.
[106] Davidson to Richards, 17 Nov. 1905, Princeton.
[107] Davidson to Richards, 22 Nov. 1905, Princeton.
[108] Davidson to 'Dear Sir', 23 Nov. 1905, Princeton.
[109] Davidson to Richards, 21 Nov. 1905, Princeton.

the end of the month he felt beaten. His bronchitis was getting worse, and he could not breathe properly with asthma. Maggie was also ill and took to her bed on 3 December. That morning Davidson made breakfast, packed Sandy off to work, and kept Menzies at home to help him with the housekeeping.[110] By then he had already seen the first reviews of his play.

They made unpleasant reading. Later he complained that,

Out of two or three dozen columns of grudge, ineptitude, patronage, astonishment, goodwill without understanding, [whining] *literary criticism*, good-natured satire and ill-natured flippancy, one thing the reading public knows that a man has written a play in which blank verse is spoken over the telephone.[111]

The majority of the reviews had headlines such as: 'Stark Nonsense', 'A Bard Who Bewilders', 'A Stage Shocker', and 'Mid Winter Madness'. Archer dismissed it in the *Daily Chronicle* as a crude and sensational vehicle for his philosophy,[112] while the *Westminster Gazette* criticized his 'fanatical propagandism of a new religion'.[113] He asked Richards angrily: 'Who is X in the *Westminster*? How mean and paltry under the guise of good will! And what an inferior brain! He excuses himself for a most inadequate review of *The Theatrocrat* by the fact that it gave him a headache.'[114] But the review that hurt him most was in the *Times Literary Supplement* from the influential A. B. Walkley who confessed derisively to being unable to make head or tail of it.[115] Davidson asked Richards in bewilderment: 'Why did Walkley write that article? It wasn't witty; it wasn't interesting: it read like the ordinary mean attempt of a trade rival to settle someone's hash.'[116]

Davidson was so upset by the hostility to his book that he decided to take to the platform, although he knew he made a poor public speaker. The need to have three extractions that month provided him with an convenient excuse for not carrying out his threat. Instead he wrote letters to *The Times*, the *Daily Chronicle* and the *Westminster Gazette*. In protesting to the *Westminster*, he pointed out that he was bringing not a 'new religion'

---

[110] Davidson to Richards, 3 Dec. 1905, Princeton.
[111] Davidson to Eden Phillpotts, 'Sunday' [Feb. 1906], Princeton.
[112] 'Mr. Davidson's New Play', *Daily Chronicle* (27 Nov. 1905), 3.
[113] 'Mr. Davidson's *Theatrocrat*', *Westminster Gazette*, 26 (9 Dec. 1905), 7.
[114] Davidson to Richards, 'Monday' [Dec. 1905], Princeton.
[115] ' "The Theatrocrat" ', *Times Literary Supplement* (8 Dec. 1905), 431.
[116] Davidson to Richards, 12 Dec. 1905, Princeton.

but a 'new poetry': 'The real poetries of the past lived in symbols of the Universe . . . the abode of my imagination is the Universe itself, and I would have it so for all men.'[117] He wrote personally to Archer defending his blank verse: 'I use blank verse as Wagner did music. If you take a chromatic score of Wagner's and attempt to play it in common time in the key you will have a terrifying result. You cannot sing-song my blank verse.'[118]

His disgruntlement threatened to spill over into his relationship with Richards when he demanded more advertising to boost the sales of the book: 'Books are a luxury, costing money, and therefore they compete with everything for which money is paid, with cigars, dresses and soap, whisky and Cook's tours, fur-coats and kisses.'[119] But Richards would have none of it: he told Davidson that books cost more to produce than pills or soap, and in any case money spent in advertising must pay for itself.[120]

The truth was that in spite of Davidson's success in promoting *The Theatrocrat*—it was the most widely reviewed and discussed of all his works—there was no real market for plays. Mudie's Library, for instance, would not take a copy. By the end of the year only 189 copies had been sold, and only another 47 copies were to go by the end of April.[121] By contrast Filson Young's *The Sands of Pleasure* was selling well. Davidson had written a laudatory review of it in the *Daily Mail* on the day it was published. Perhaps embarrassed that Davidson had not enjoyed a similar success Young urged Richards to republish *Perfervid* which he thought had 'a chance of selling'.[122] But Davidson would not hear of it. For him *Perfervid* was a thing of the past.[123] As a cruel footnote to the reception of *The Theatrocrat* he received a 'very French letter' from René Ghil asking him to write to his publisher Grant Richards thanking him for sending *The Theatrocrat*, and offering to write a book of his own doctrines, philosophy, and poetical technique.[124]

He still had his income from the *Outlook*, but he had come to look on the writing of his monthly eclogue a gruesome chore,

[117] Davidson to the Editor, *Westminster Gazette* (11 Dec. 1905), 4.
[118] Davidson to William Archer, 29 Dec. 1905, BL.
[119] Davidson to Richards, 3 Dec. 1905, Princeton.
[120] Richards to Davidson, 4 Dec 1905, Richards.
[121] Richards to A. S. Watt, 27 Apr. 1906, Richards.
[122] Young to Richards, 13 Oct. 1906, Richards.
[123] Davidson to Richards, not dated [Jan. 1906], Princeton.
[124] Davidson to Richards, 26 Jan. 1906, Princeton.

sometimes forcing it out at a single stanza each day. He resented having to write to order when he wanted to get on with his 'Testaments and Tragedies'. While working on 'St Andrew's Day, in October, he had complained: 'It is like asking a woman about to bring forth a lusty son to stop and produce a litter of puppies first. The miracle is that I can do it: "nine farrow of that sow" already: shall I manage a tenth and an eleventh and a twelve.'[125] By then Garvin was showing more reluctance to publish them. Watt had to coerce him to accept the eighth, '*Our Day*', which celebrated the centenary of the Battle of Trafalgar on 21 October that year. Davidson's tenth and final eclogue, 'New Year's Eve', appeared on 30 December, when the series was dropped. But he did have one final contribution to make to the *Outlook*—a short poem on Tariff Reform, 'A Song of Triumph', anticipating with grim irony a Liberal victory in the coming general election in January, and with it the weakening of Empire.[126] Garvin had again extracted from him the imperial poem he wanted.

III

The first week of the new year brought Davidson what he was later to describe as 'the most extraordinary commission in the history of letters'.[127] He was down on his luck again, having lost his monthly poem at the *Outlook* and having accepted the failure of *The Theatrocrat*, when a letter arrived on 4 January from Shaw, offering to finance an original play and telling him to name his own fee. Davidson's hopes were raised. He wrote enthusiastically about the project: 'I come out of your shower-bath glowing and refreshed, and can think of nothing but your challenge which I seize with both hands.'[128]

It is difficult to determine exactly what Shaw's motives were. Davidson had agreed to Richards sending Shaw a copy of *The Theatrocrat* on condition that he passed on his—Davidson's—opinion that Shaw would not like it and that they lived on dif-

[125] Davidson to Richards, 'Saturday', and 'Sunday' [Oct. 1905], Princeton.
[126] 'A Song of Empire', *Outlook*, 17 (6 Jan. 1906), 20.
[127] Davidson to Eden Phillpotts, 'Sunday' [Feb. 1906], Princeton.
[128] Davidson to G. B. Shaw, 4 Jan. 1906, BL.

ferent planes. But some of the reviewers compared them, including Archer, and Davidson's young admirer at the *Morning
Leader* James Douglas who placed them with Ibsen and Tolstoy
among the 'great anarchists of contemporary literature'.[129]
Shaw read *The Theatrocrat* and decided it was theatrically impracticable, although he must have been sympathetic to something independent of narrowly theatrical considerations,
following his own experiment with *Man and Superman* three
years earlier. His main objection came down in the end to
Davidson's use of blank verse.

In a later recollection of their arrangement, Shaw maintained
that he had intended Davidson to write the great verse drama
that he claimed was in him.[130] Unfortunately Shaw's half of
the correspondence has not survived, but it seems reasonably
clear from Davidson's surviving letters that Shaw challenged
him to write a modern play that was actable and in prose.
The situation of one writer giving money to another was bound
to result in embarrassments and misunderstandings. The
main confusion seems to have come about because Davidson
was anxious to justify Shaw's financial investment in him
by writing a successful comedy, rather than the serious
play Shaw envisaged. Shaw did nothing to enlighten him
once the contract was accepted, possibly because he was preoccupied at the time with *Captain Brassbound's Conversion*. In a
humorous 'Memorandum of Agreement' dated 4 January,
Davidson promised:

a play of modern life, practicable on the stage . . . in ordinary col-
loquial prose, complying sufficiently with all vulgar human require-
ments, illustrating the working of certain truths considered important
by the said party of the third part, adultery and murder barred, titles
barred, only normal modern life and incident to be presented, and all
characters to be in ordinary health and reasonable spirits at the fall of
the curtain.[131]

He asked for £100 advance, non-refundable as he had 'no
money and no income', and an additional £150 on delivery in
four months' time. He received the first £100 and an agreement

[129] *Morning Leader* (24 Nov. 1905), 4.
[130] G. B. Shaw to Richards, 23 June 1927, *Author Hunting*, 224.
[131] Davidson to Shaw, 4 Jan. 1906, BL.

four days later. In writing to thank Shaw, he spoke of going 'to the sea or somewhere to get out of the tragic element in which I live'.[132] But he did not forgo the opportunity to answer Shaw's objections to his use of blank verse in *The Theatrocrat*. He refused to accept that blank verse could not be 'modern' and put Shaw's aversion to it down to temperament: 'I require it, because so far as I can judge from your writings I am a more emotional man than you, and the rhythm and pauses and the music of blank verse sustain me, and lift me, and prevent me breaking down chaotically.'[133]

Davidson's intention was clearly to write a popular prose play that would out-Shaw Shaw. He promised a *tour de force*. He was in high spirits, never his best mood when writing, as his imagination then tended to the fantastical and bizarre. Before leaving London he went to see Mrs Wynne Mathiesson and Granville Barker in the revival of *Major Barbara* at the Royal Court, and noted the enjoyment of the audience. The Salvation Army scenes in which Barbara, the high-minded Salvationist finally submits to the munition manufacturer Undershaft's new religion of power, struck a deep chord. Over the next few days he re-read *Arms and the Man*, *You Never Can Tell*, and *Man and Superman*. He had always believed that he and Shaw were poles apart, but now he became convinced that he and Shaw were saying 'in the fibre of it, the same thing' and wrote excitedly to Shaw to point out the similarity between the third act of *Man and Superman* and the 'new myth of Heaven and Hell in my *Testament of an Empire-Builder*'.[134] He was probably wrong about Shaw—*Man and Superman* seems closer in the end to Plato than to Nietzsche—but both he and Shaw get their effects from giving the Devil his due.

Davidson left London for St Ives in Cornwall on 18 January, having picked it out on the map. It was a tedious nine hours' journey away by train. He wrote to Shaw the next day from his new address, 'Corvean, St Ives', describing his strange dream on the journey—'pictures out of the past' of a man and a woman with a mammoth and a giraffe, and tigers copulating on the

---

[132] Davidson to Shaw, 8 Jan. 1906, BL.
[133] Davidson to Shaw, 19 Jan. 1906, BL.
[134] Davidson to Shaw, not dated [19 Jan. 1906], BL.

beach.[135] It is noticeable that Davidson's later writings are filled increasingly with images of male violence and sexual revulsion. It is probably mistaken to interpret this in any simple sense as an expression of Davidson's own sexual problems. In his revolt against the traditional Christian separation of body and soul, he invested physical love with spiritual significance and ultimate personal fulfilment. This is as true in the later writings as in his 1890s ballads. But with *The Theatrocrat* we see the nightmarish side of the sexual revolution, as that intense emotional dependence collapses in the face of fragile human relationships. *Troilus and Cressida* was clearly important in influencing this change. Alongside the prophecy of sexual joy in Davidson's later writings emerges a language of jealousy, anger, and violence against women. In *The Theatrocrat*, Sir Tristram Summers gruesomely describes a 'woman's soul' as,

> A sooty cobweb diapered with limbs
> And empty hulls of captives long undone.
> I shook it, but the spider made no sign:
> It too was dead. I brushed the film away
> And where it hung a mortal crevice yawned—
> Obscene and dark and barren as the grave.[136]

Richards was put out when he learned that Davidson had gone to Cornwall without telling him. His wife had a cottage in Ruan Minor which he felt would have been more congenial for Davidson than St Ives.[137] The Richards and the Shaws had already spent some time there together. In fact St Ives turned out to be not quite what Davidson wanted, but he decided it would do.[138] His stay was brightened by a surprise letter from the bestselling writer, Eden Phillpotts, praising *The Theatrocrat* and suggesting that Swinburne might like it. Davidson wrote to thank him, but stressed that he was 'indifferent to all opinion except as a commercial asset', a claim belied by the depth of feeling in his reply:

No one has magnified my book as you have done; your letter stirs me deeply. A volume has been written about *The Theatrocrat*, but with the

135 Davidson to Shaw, 8 Jan. 1906, BL.
136 *Theatrocrat*, 128.
137 Richards to Davidson, 22 Jan. 1906, Richards.
138 Davidson to Richards, not dated [Jan. 1906], Princeton.

exception of the facile writer in *The Star* and *The Morning Leader*, James Douglas, no one has noted any great quality in it . . .

About that of there being nothing higher than man . . . We are as it were the brain of the Universe; now the brain of us is an ugly loathsome thing; nevertheless it is the highest life has done. You must consider it thus: it is not a matter of good or bad: in man the Universe has become self-conscious, able to grasp and understand itself: there is nothing more to do: I feel also an infinite satisfaction in the idea that the Universe having been self-conscious once need never be so again. When life ceases on the earth, then the whole Universe will be for ever unconscious: I contemplate that with transcendent delight.[139]

Meanwhile his friends in London were planning to apply again for a pension for him. The Liberals, under the leadership of Henry Campbell-Bannerman, had been returned to power in a landslide victory in the January elections. Lord Crewe, who had supported Davidson's petition in 1901, was now in the Cabinet. Circumstances looked favourable. Davidson returned to London at the beginning of March with the play practically finished. On the 16th he learned from Arthur Legge that Mrs Crackanthorpe had been active on his behalf in compiling a list of petitioners, and that Lord Haldane had agreed to present it. The list included some distinguished names—Meredith, Hardy, Augustine Birrell, Alfred Spender, the editor of the *Westminster Gazette*, who had attacked Le Gallienne's log-rolling in 1895, and Herbert Paul, the historian and literary journalist who had just been returned for Northampton in the general election. But first they had to win over the permanent secretary to the Treasury, Henry Higgs, who had been involved in the negotiations with Balfour the first time round. Davidson decribed him venomously to McCormick as 'the man with the stop-cock of the shower bath always ready'.[140] Legge had interviewed Higgs who objected to any change to Balfour's original offer of £200 of Treasury money at 5 per cent—£10 a year—on the grounds that Davidson 'wasn't an old man' and had two sons who should shortly be able to support him. The suggestion that his sons should support him weighed on him like 'a ton of ill-will'. He thought it 'mean and hateful.' He protested: 'It is not a

---

[139]   Davidson to Phillpotts, 'Sunday' [Feb. 1906], Princeton.
[140]   Davidson to McCormick, 17 Mar. 1906, Glasgow.

question of a bricklayer's sons.'[141] And in another distressed letter:

Besides a distinguished man's sons expect always to be supported by him. My two boys also owing to certain peculiarities of temperament and mind are likely to be dependent on me as long as I live. This official standpoint is partially a survival of Balfour's grafting: he wished to regard me as a pauper, instead of an important man with notable things to do which are not marketable.[142]

He wrote to Higgs directly, and then to Haldane, warning him of Higgs's objections.

By 16 March he had sent his play, now called 'The Game of Life', to the typist and approached Shaw anxiously for the remainder of the money. He had already spent the first £100. Shaw did not want to be troubled until after the revival of *Captain Brassbound's Conversion* which was then in rehearsal with Ellen Terry at the Royal Court Theatre, but he posted the final payment of £150 that day. Davidson was relieved and thanked him again for all he had done: 'It was thus that wealthy men created in feeble minds the idea of Providence.'[143] But on the 30th, when he received Shaw's verdict on his play, his opinion of his benefactor immediately turned sour. Shaw's manner of writing as a debater rather than personally did nothing to soften the blow.

Later, when the quarrel was over, Davidson asked Richards for a copy of the letter he had sent to Shaw with *The Theatrocrat*, presumably to satisfy himself as to Shaw's motives. He found the letter 'as it ought to be'.[144] But Shaw's report was devastating. Shaw disliked everything about the play: the stagecraft was out of the question; and scenes of violence ridiculous, and the lasciviousness of the play's heroine objectionable on the grounds that 'plays are written largely for women'. He advised Davidson to be 'satisfied with being a poet and genius'. Davidson tried to answer the specific charges, particularly against his heroine, whom he saw as 'a *maitresse femme*, like Napoleon's mother', but his defence quickly turned into an attack on Shaw and the contemporary stage generally:

[141] Davidson to McCormick, 20 Mar. 1906, Glasgow.
[142] Davidson to McCormick, 17 Mar. 1906, Glasgow.
[143] Davidson to Shaw, 16 and 17 Mar. 1906, BL.
[144] Davidson to Richards, 2 May 1906, Princeton.

One of the remarkable things in your plays—I note it as a feature without condemning it—is that you perpetuate unconsciously the old-world male conception of women, especially in the stupendous humour of 'Man and Superman' where John Tanner is a woman—a reluctant old maid, indeed; you can hear him menstruate—and Ann is the male creature. Since Chaucer I am the only English writer who has really understood women.

In the end he put Shaw's criticisms down to jealousy:

The truth is, 'The Game of Life' is so much better than anything you thought I could possibly do in prose that you resent it bitterly; you are most unhappy because you are pleased. Subconsciously you feel that 'The Game of Life', if produced, would be the most successful comedy of the day; and so you have become spiteful, as you warned me you might do.[145]

The quarrel and Davidson's insults went on for another week. Shaw's suggestion as to ways the play's ending might be improved was answered with a letter addressed derisively to the 'Man of the Wood': 'You could cut six Shaws out of me and there would still be a splendid Davidson left. . . . But the best thing you can do now is to send me another £250 and buy the play outright, delete my name, call the author David Bernardson, rewrite it and do whatever you like with it.'[146] Shaw only made matters worse by telling him not to be a fool. Davidson replied with wounded dignity: 'Not a fool. Only a great man. You have entered my mansion by the back door, and have not yet found the way to my apartments.'[147] His dented pride was not helped by Shaw's unwillingness to accept his full rights of 10 per cent in the event of the play ever reaching performance.

It is impossible to judge whether Shaw or Davidson was right about the play, which was destroyed on Davidson's intructions at the time of his death. What is certain is that, within a fortnight of Shaw's criticisms, Davidson went to work on revising the play very much along the lines that Shaw had suggested, although he continued to quarrel with Shaw's view that plays had to be 'projected—into the womb of the theatre'. He pre-

---

[145] Davidson to Shaw, 30 Mar. 1906, BL.
[146] Davidson to Shaw, 6 Apr. 1906, BL.
[147] Davidson to Shaw, 7 Apr. 1906, BL.

ferred to see it as 'a male product, from the head of Jupiter, like Minerva'. But he reduced the elements of crudity in the heroine, including her passion for snuff, and recast the third act. Clinging to his dignity he reported to Shaw: 'I shall place it in the hands of my agent and trouble you no more about it until I have an account to render.'[148] The matter was left at that, and in spite of some interest from Waller, who read the revised version that May and promised to talk about it after his run as Othello, the play was never performed.[149]

Shaw believed that this failure was responsible for Davidson's death.[150] This seems unlikely—an instance of the inevitable egotism within which we view our influence on other men's lives. By the end of their correspondence Davidson seems neither bitter nor broken. On 14 April, hearing that Shaw was ill, he wrote encouragingly:

Get well: life and letters in England want you a while yet. I know about ill-health: twenty-three years ago when my life was insured they put 5% on my premium on account of the condition of my heart: to have survived at all is itself a kind of success for me, as it was for Caesar.[151]

Admittedly, the tone is gloomy, but he usually fought against such sentimentality, and the next day we find him writing to Beerbohm to invite him to an 'ineluctible adventure' at the Crystal Palace on Easter Monday. A day out with Beerbohm was generally his antidote to self-pity and depression. In phrases that were still in his mind from the previous year, he promised to show Max a place,

without comeliness or colour, without life, without growth, without decay, and the gigantic featureless thing called mob, wandering aimlessly in masses and eddies, and if it rains for an hour or two, as I hope it may, you will find the place like a beach in Hades where souls are ground up together by an unseen sea, and Voltaire (Houdon's statue) sitting grinning admidst [sic] it, and Cellini's Perseus and Angelo's Moses like lost gods in Nifelheim. I shall show you this as Virgil showed Dante terrible things; and our Paradiso shall be a seat at a window overlooking Surrey and a bottle of claret.[152]

[148] Davidson to Shaw, 14 Apr. 1906, BL.
[149] Davidson to Shaw, 17 Apr. 1906, BL.
[150] Shaw to Richards, 23 June 1927, *Author Hunting*, 224.
[151] Davidson to Shaw, 14 Apr. 1906, BL.
[152] Davidson to Beerbohm, 'Sunday' [Apr. 1906], Merton.

Max Beerbohm was booked to spend the holiday at Canter-
bury, and the tryst had to be postponed until Whit Monday.
Davidson again contacted Max—his 'Beloved' as he playfully
called him—a few days before the bank holiday and arranged to
meet him from the 11 o'clock train from Victoria: 'Whether we
shall have soul-curdling experiences of mob or not, we shall
have a spacious place in which to expiate and confer.'[153] Their
adventure was a success. The day after, Davidson wrote to thank
Beerbohm for 'the crystalline and palatial hours of yesterday'.[154]
His poem, 'The Crystal Palace' was to incorporate the spirit of
their visit, in particular Davidson's comic anticipation of their
Inferno and final Paradiso at the window of the grill-room.
The 'you' addressed in Davidson's famous poem is surely
Beerbohm: 'Reserved seat at the window?—Surely; you | And I
must have the best place everywhere.'[155]

The weeks before and after the outing on 4 June were taken
up with the publication of *Holiday and Other Poems*. As always in
the run-up to publication Davidson found himself at cross purposes with his publisher. This time it was the result of his
increasing reliance on Watt. Richards had refused the £25 advance he wanted for *Holiday*, and had offered only £10.[156]
Davidson turned to Watt and on 4 May reported that his agent
was 'drawing up the agreement with the imperturbable solidity
and stolidity of a Government Office'.[157] Although Richards did
not object to dealing with Watt, like most publishers, he dis-
trusted agents and preferred the traditional-style author–
publisher relationship. With Davidson, he found himself having
to operate both systems at the same time. Davidson would frequently come to an agreement only to disclaim it afterwards
with such expressions as, 'Watt does the business, not I', or
'Anything I have written to you is a friendly intimation of no
value unless Watt endorses it. . . . He is a commercial man; I am
not.'[158] The agreement was finally signed on 26 May, although
not before Richards had lost his temper when Davidson fussed
over the loss of some specimen pages. 'For a man of vigour

[153] Davidson to Beerbohm, 28 May 1906, Merton.
[154] Davidson to Beerbohm, 5 June 1906, Merton.
[155] 'The Crystal Palace', ll. 163–4.
[156] Richards to Davidson, 27 Apr. 1906, Richards.
[157] Davidson to Richards, 4 May 1906, Princeton.
[158] Davidson to Richards, 3 May and 12 June 1906, Princeton.

with work to do in the world you waste an inordinate amount of time dealing at length and repeatedly with the absolutely inessential!' he wrote.[159]

Richards's distrust of Watt had increased during the negotiations with the receiver to secure the release of Davidson's *Testaments*. He believed that Watt was jeopardizing the whole transaction by sending on his letters to Moring—the knowledge that he was involved in the negotiation to get back his old stock would encourage Moring to put obstacles in the way or raise his prices. Richards was a business man; he knew that the battle was between himself and Moring as rival publishers. Davidson, by contrast, naïvely believed that the *Testaments* were his, and that the whole business could be settled amicably and in the open. He answered Richards's complaint about Watt's interference with a rather pointed sermon on his agent's honesty and straightforwardness in business:

I am very much pleased with Watt and wish him to manage all my business. In all likelihood Moring is one of those publishers who object to Watt and will make all kinds of delays and excuses and waste endless work and paper in correspondence whereas if he could ask Watt to be prepared to come to an understanding, the matter could be arranged satisfactorily in 10 minutes. . . . Watt's methods, as far as I have found, are always aboveboard. It's not a question of him getting the better of anybody but of making a fair bargain; hence the extent and security of his business, and his great value in the condition of things to the author and the publisher.[160]

These were noble sentiments, but Richards's fears proved right. Moring put up his prices, and Davidson was left cursing him as 'a dog in a manger'.

In spite of their business differences, Davidson and Richards remained good friends. Richards was grateful for Davidson's immediate offer of support when E. V. Lucas accused him of plagiarizing the distinctive format of *The Open Road* in W. G. Water's *Traveller's Joy*. Lucas, who had been Richards's first bestselling author and reader, claimed he was still owed money by the bankrupt firm of 'Grant Richards'. For three weeks Richards's name was dragged through the mud, and the legal-

[159] Richards to Davidson, 8 May 1906, Richards.
[160] Davidson to Richards, 6 June 1906, Princeton.

ities of the situation heatedly argued over in the pages of the *Athenaeum*.[161] 'Lucas seems to be a very small mind, even for a bookmaker', Davidson wrote at the beginning of June. 'If it were a question of having written the "Iliad" or the "Bible"; but to try to get in a kick at a man whom he supposes to be down . . .'.[162]

Then it was Davidson who was embarrassed. On the morning of 21 June, he looked for his name among the long list of Civil List pensioners. At the beginning of April he had thought the 'outlook dismal', but since then he had been assured that the pension was certain, probably by Gosse who was a frequent visitor to Haldane's rooms at the War Office at this time. But his name was not on the Civil List. He felt humiliated, particularly as the whole question of his pension had been aired in the newspapers. He learned unofficially that nothing else could be done until the following year. He tried to put a brave face on things, but to Richards he admitted his true feelings: 'I had built myself up on it—ah, as wildly as Anasher!—and the bubble bursts—and makes a bad smell.' He wanted to buy 'a powerful air gun that can be carried up the sleeve and shoot off the members of the government one by one.'[163] He believed his books, and especially his *Testaments* had been his 'enemies' in the ultimate decision. He did have the publication of *Holiday* to take his mind off things, but he had no immediate prospect of making money. Waller wanted 'The Game of Life' but was pledged to two other plays in advance of his next production. Davidson described his gloom: 'So I stagnate and rot like "the fat weed on Lethe wharf"'.[164]

Holiday appeared at the beginning of July. As it contained a number of eclogues, Richards had wanted to issue it with the same binding and design used by the Bodley Head for *Fleet Street Eclogues*, but Davidson declined to approach Lane for permission on the grounds that 'the effusive benificence of the reply, as if he were conferring the Victoria Cross, would be nauseous'.[165] On 3 July he had dinner with Legge to hear the inside

---

[161] See, *Athenaeum* (2, 9, 16, 23 June 1906).
[162] Davidson to Richards, 9 June 1906, Princeton.
[163] Davidson to Richards, 21 June 1906, Princeton.
[164] Davidson to McCormick, 23 June 1906, Glasgow.
[165] Davidson to Richards, 14 June 1906, Princeton.

story of the whole 'prutrescent business' of the pension.[166] The news turned out to be less gloomy than he had supposed. There had been moves behind the scenes, and in spite of the official line that nothing could be done until the next financial year, he was finally granted an annual Civil List Pension of £100 in August.

Unquestionably the most significant change in Davidson's state of mind in his last years was caused by the pension, more than by any other single factor. He had wanted it for so many years; during that time it had come to represent in his mind not only his financial deliverance but the public respect he deserved as a poet. The £100 he was awarded satisfied neither of his ambitions. It was not enough for him to live on; nor did it confer much esteem. Watson had been receiving £100 for more than a decade. His mood can be seen in his identification with the pavement-hawkers between Liverpool Street Station and Bishopsgate on his way through London that October. 'These people were like me; they were outside the world, outside of Christendom', he wrote.

I saw that these people had made it up with fate—for the evening. Late at night or next morning, they will again do battle. Suicide is the diurnal temptation: the river is always there; some of them carry poison. But every day towards the afternoon they win the fight; they think 'It is better to be than not to be.' And they are so right; and have such prodigious courage: to stand in the gutter, in the gaslight, shuddered at, flamed on, 'moved' on, gathering the coppers that shall enable them to continue in the hell of their own making. . . . I thought these gutter-merchants were awful, were magnificent; and I thought further, 'There stand I, the most unpopular writer in England, were it not for his Majesty, King Edward, who has honoured me with £100 a year for literary merit.[167]

He was wrong about being 'the most unpopular writer in England'. *Holiday* was well received, helped by a favourable review in the *Westminster Gazette*,[168] and its preface 'On Poetry' was widely discussed and admired. The *Times Literary Supplement*, for instance, quarrelled with his distinction between the artificiality of rhyme and the freedom of blank verse, but acknow-

---

[166] Davidson to Richards, 30 June 1906, Princeton.
[167] 'Epping Forest Again', *Westminster Gazette* (2 Nov. 1906), 1–2.
[168] 'Mr. John Davidson and his Poems', *Westminster Gazette* (21 July 1906), 11.

ledged that 'it would be hard to find elsewhere as many fine sayings about poetry got together in so small a space'.[169] But his sententiousness towards the press and the public during the publication of the *Testaments* and *The Theatrocrat* had made it difficult for many readers to read his poetry without feeling that it was a threat to conventional values that might corrupt or implicate them.

Periods in the arts are often decided by public events such as the death of monarchs or the outbreak of war. But though no climactic event occurred in the years between 1905 and 1909, there was a definite feeling among literary people that the nineteenth century was behind them and that literature was about to change. They had absorbed the strained anti-Victorianism of Samuel Butler's *The Way of All Flesh* in 1903. Gosse's obituary to the Victorian age, *Father and Son*, appeared four years later, the same that saw the publication of Conrad's *The Secret Agent*. Whereas the mood of the *fin de siècle* writers had been a determination not to live in the past, the temper of the moderns was to face and re-make the present.

Davidson was to respond to the new with a group of poems written towards the end of his life that were neither strained nor strident in style. The poems were based on a new series of Itinerant articles which he undertook for Wallace at the *Glasgow Herald* and Alfred Spender, one of his Civil List petitioners, at the *Westminster Gazette* between October 1906 and June 1907. London and the South had undergone dramatic changes in the twenty years since his arrival. The separation of town life and country life which he had celebrated in his *Fleet Street Eclogues* began to seem less convincing as distances and local differences were annihilated by the train and the motor car. Davidson observed these changes with a sense that a tremendous revolution in the way people lived was imminent. As in 'Fleet Street' and 'The Crystal Palace', which have their place in this group, the voice of Davidson's last poems is that of the Itinerant experiencing and responding, sometimes ironically, to the contemporary world. His method is the subject of 'The Aristocrat of the Road', a poem about writing poetry in which we see how the pedestrian's plod 'Through gross suburban miles | And over

---

[169] 'Blank Verse and Rhyme', *Times Literary Supplement* (17 Aug. 1906), 281.

leagues of undistinguished ground' leads him to 'the stretch of pleasure ground'—poetry itself—where experience and desire are finally reconciled.

In several of the *Holiday* poems he had already overturned the town–country divide in images of London as the garden-city. But here he goes much further in representing town and country, the natural landscapes and the man-made world as a continuum, notably in 'Liverpool Street Station', where the 'metal foliage' of Epping Forest in autumn is linked to the rusty, iron vaults of the railway station, or in the impressionist piece 'The Thames Embankment' where the industrial debris and urban setting of the Thames at low tide merges with the natural scenery in a Turneresque vision of light. The animate and inanimate are interchangeable, as again in 'Snow', which was probably inspired initially by a passage in Chambers's *Book of Days*. Chambers informs us:

In the view of modern science, under favour of the microscope, snow is one of the most beautiful things in the museum of nature; each particle, when duly magnified, shewing a surprising regularity of figure, but various according to the degree of frost by which the snow has been produced. . . . It is in obedience to a law governing the crystallisation of water, that this angle of 60 degrees everywhere prevails in the figures of snow particles.[170]

Davidson has:

> Water-crystals need for flower and root
>   Sixty clear degrees, no less, no more;
> Snow so fickle, still in this acute
>   Angle thinks, and learns no other lore:
>
>   .   .   .   .
>
> Every flake with all its prongs and dints
>   Burns ecstatic as a new-lit star:
> Men are not more diverse, finger-prints
>   More dissimilar than snow-flakes are.[171]

In these poems of Davidson's final phase the doctrine of matter is subtly subsumed within the imagery, rather than the subject of prophecy.

[170] Robert Chambers, *The Book of Days: A Miscellany of Popular Antiquities* (London, 1878), 21–2.
[171] 'Snow', ll. 9–16 and 21–4.

Davidson's persona as the irreverent, free-spirited individual-
ist—the 'Aristocrat' for whom the universe is his home—was his
response to the levelling that he observed on his journeys in and
beyond the capital. He believed that a new spirit of individualism would emerge with the democratization of everything. He
saw evidence of this in the motor car, which he made the subject of a satiric 'Testament of Sir Simon Simplex Concerning
Automobilism', after travelling by car to Liverpool with Filson
Young in September 1906. He also saw it in publishing. The
main talking point in the book trade that year was the 'Book
War' between The Times Book Club and the Publishers' Association. It involved the attempt by two Americans, Horace
Hooper and William Jackson, and the managing director of
The Times, Charles Bell, to break the monopoly of the book-
selling establishment by selling new books directly to the newspaper's subscribers at reduced prices. There was a widespread
fear that fiction and other forms of popular literature were
about to pass into the hands of the newspaper syndicates,
so bringing about the death of traditional book-publishing
methods. Publishers threatened to withdraw their advertisements. Davidson saw these developments as another sign of the
democratization of things and urged Richards to issue a new
expensive library edition of the World's Classics, including a
section of blasphemous and erotic 'Books for Men and
Women', beginning with John Payne's translation of Villon's
poems (1881), Rabelais, Voltaire's *Philosophical Dictionary*,
Lucian, and Ovid's *Art of Love*.[172] He promised a triumph in 'the
coming *débâcle*':

You see, a double event is in progress, and I am the first to detect it.
The democratization of everything has pushed out with such a fanfare
that the inevitable and tremendously more important complement of
that has not been noticed, partly because it is not yet much in evidence: in twin births sometimes the womb opens twice with a
day between: the Aristocratization of everything by everybody whose
senses are fine enough to note the unresolvable discoveries of
Democracy . . . is the second birth, and it comes forth with teeth and
armed, intolerant, militant, hating and hated.[173]

---

[172] Davidson to Richards, 29 Sept. 1906, Princeton.
[173] Davidson to Richards, 14 Oct. 1906, Princeton.

While urging a whole series of publishing schemes on his publisher, Davidson continued to resist Richards's wish to re-issue some of his early works. At the beginning of October, a bookbinder, Madgewick, had called on Richards. When Downey and Co. had gone into liquidation, the stock had gone to Russell, a printer, who in turn had sold it to Madgewick. Madgewick held the copyright of *Perfervid* and *Baptist Lake* and some stock of *In a Music-Hall* and *Earl Lavender*. He wanted £40 but eventually settled for 10 guineas on condition that Richards would not reprint for five years. But apart from one or two poems from *In a Music-Hall*, and the short stories 'The School-boy's Tragedy' and 'The Interregnum in Fairyland', Davidson did not want to see his early work reprinted:

I do not wish any one to know of them. They will be all very well when I am dead in a collected edition: in the meantime their reissue would only distract attention from my actual work if they were a success, and if as is more probable they dropped soon into the category of undesir-able remainders, they would only revive the memory of old failures and depreciate what name I have.[174]

By 'actual work' he meant a new tragedy that he was then busily preparing for Richards. Davidson's path in literature was never straight. Even as he was gathering the material for his last and most accomplished poems, he turned to the verse drama as a vehicle for his prophecies about the coming revolution. He had outlined his idea to Richards at the beginning of May on a walk west of Marble Arch. By October he was hard at work, driven 'like a 40 hp motor'.[175] In *The Triumph of Mammon*, the first part of his proposed trilogy, *God and Mammon*, Davidson's hero, like the allegorical Mammon of Bunyan's *The Holy War* (1682), starts a revolution whose aim is to overthrow Christian con-sciousness and morality. The action takes place in Chris-tianstadt, the capital of the kingdom of Thule. Though ruled with the appearance of traditional authority by King Chris-tian, the country is rotting from within with competing factions of reactionaries and reformers. Mammon, his son, has been disinherited and banished for renouncing God. He returns impenitent at the beginning of the play just as Guendolen, who

[174] Davidson to Richards, 9 Oct. 1906, Princeton.
[175] Ibid.

would have been his bride, is about to marry his younger brother Magnus. King Christian has Mammon bound to a pillar in the royal chapel and attempts to castrate him for his blasphemies, but Mammon frees himself and turns the knife on his father.

The theme of parricide is a recurrent one in Davidson's work, from the death of the evangelist father in 'A Ballad in Blank Verse' to the gory murder of King Christian. It is a subconscious fantasy that runs deeply through the literature of this period, though generally it finds less lurid expression, and would seem to express not only the refusal to live in the past but the desire for a new identity. We find it in Joyce's work and in J. M. Synge's *Playboy of the Western World*, which provoked riots on its first production in January 1907 when Davidson was still at work on his play. *The Triumph of Mammon* ends in a blood-bath as Mammon assumes the throne and announces the overthrow of Christianity in the name of a new doctrine of ecstatic natural love and glorified will to power.

As winter set in, he went down again with 'wretched bronchitis'. He prophesied to Max Beerbohm that it would go on all winter at intervals, making it impossible for him to arrange anything. He went out to the public library on 10 December and read Max's parody of him in the *Saturday Review*, laughing so much that the janitor warned him to be quiet. He had hoped that the outing would acclimatize him for dinner with Max at the Cavour Restaurant in Soho the day after, but the next day he had a severe relapse and had to cancel the arrangement. He congratulated Max on his parody, describing the clown's suicide as 'the high water mark of tragic art'.[176] Max had written:

> CLOWN (TO PANTALOON):
> These sausages are I, and I am they:
> Mark them again. (*Eats several of them.*)
>   They are not thus transmuted
> Into my substance. I, digesting them,
> Do but digest myself, none other,
> In anthropic anthropophagy
> Most high-magnifical. Or have it they
> Are digirent of me. What Matter? Equally

[176] Davidson to Beerbohm, 11 Dec. 1906, Merton.

We spring from ether—are but calcium,
Phosphorus, iron, lead, magnesium,
Fluorine, copper, sulphur, natrium,
Silicon, manganese, et cetera,
Et cetera. (*Stabs himself with red-hot poker.*)
        This is the freedom of
The Universe. (*Dies.*)[177]

Davidson told him half-seriously:

All great men kill themselves with their own red-hot poker: Gladstone ends himself with Home Rule; Chamberlain with Tariff-Reform, Irving with playing 'Becket' (What a tough one Irving was: the first night of 'Becket' would have killed a very robust actor); and 'The Times' dies by prolonged torture of its own advertisements.

At some time before he left London—it may have been late that year—he took a bedroom and a sitting room for a week at 39 St James's Place, in the most fashionable district of London, aiming to satisfy at least once his desire for the good life he felt he deserved. He wrote in high spirits to Beerbohm revelling in his new address and inviting him out for lunch at the Café Royal. St James's Place itself had turned out to be a disappointment 'full of noises—motors, cabs, hawkers, and the weather has been impossible to saunter in'. He had hoped to loaf and write but had only managed 'some gnarled lines on chagrin'.[178]

Such truancy had become rarer in his later years, and normally he lived at Fairmile Avenue in almost total seclusion with his family. The houses had been re-numbered, but he still retained the original address, the gentrified St Winifred's, in *Who's Who* in order to confuse strangers from Scotland and other places who sometimes came uninvited to see him. One young admirer, a fellow Scot who did call on him that year as ambassador of the Greenock Burns' Club, has recorded the savage reception he received:

the door was only half opened. Davidson blocked the passage, and, with an arm stretched out to the wall, he let me see, without a word being spoken, that I was as far as I should get, and a little further than he wanted.

[177] 'Matter and I', *Saturday Review*, 86 (8 Dec. 1906), 703–4.
[178] Davidson to Beerbohm, 'Thursday' [1906], Merton. Another likely date for Davidson's stay at St James's Place is summer 1903.

I knew him at once from his portraits. He looked exactly as he appears in them. He was quite well-groomed and shaven, and looked as if he ate well and slept o' nights. What struck me most was the clear white of his eyes. He has large and quickly moving eyes that make me think of some abnormal bird's, and he swung them about—anywhere but in my direction—the white of them almost mesmerized me. I felt myself listening in a half-dwalm [half asleep].

'What do you want?' he shot at me, as if I were a cadger. 'My name is —.' I stammered. 'I come from Greenock, and I have been asked by the Greenock Burns' Club —' But I got no further.

'Ah! I never go to Burns Clubs,' he interjected hurriedly. 'I never go anywhere. I never see anyone. I am not like other men. People ought to think of these things.'

I tried to stammer out that I was sorry to have troubled him, and that I did not think—'There it is, you did not think!' he broke in. 'You should have thought. You *should* have said' (this with finger tapping forehead and eyes fixed on some far horizon), 'here is a man different from other men! I must not treat him like other men! I must think, think, think! I must not go knocking at his door and expect to be received. I must write to ask him if he will receive me.'

There was just one more shot in my locker—the message to him from Dr Wallace about the 'Random Itinerary' articles, and I delivered it by this time reduced to so mean and abject a frame of mind I would have let a blind cripple kick me.

'What made him ask *you* to call?' he exclaimed passionately. 'He has written to me already. Doesn't he understand that I'm very busy? Perhaps in three months I may send him something.'

All this time he hardly once glanced at me, but darted his eyes here and there over my head, and ever kept his arm across the entrance. When he had finished the above confession of faith—in himself, he let his eyes drop on me for a second, shoved out a perfunctory hand to shake mine, and then slammed the door shut.[179]

The misleading address prevented some of these invasions of his privacy. But the drawback was that some of his letters also went astray; there was another St Winifred's at Norbury, a mile further on the Brighton Road. He was upset at the beginning of January when an invitation from Beerbohm went to the wrong address. He was also worried that his pension might have suffered the same fate when it failed to arrive on 1 January, and he threatened jokingly to blow up both the paymaster and the

[179] Neil Munro, *The Brave Days* (London, 1931), 175–8.

postmaster general.[180] On the 15th he began the last act of his play, which he expected to finish by the middle of February.[181] He had already arranged with Richards for its publication on 11 April, his fiftieth birthday, which he thought 'a very significant date for any man'.[182] He wrote the last lines on 19 February and sent it off at once to the typist. He visited Windsor Forest the next day, but as in his walks about London at the end of the year, he found himself preoccupied with the past and the value of his life's work.[183] His fiftieth birthday had turned his thoughts to death, one of the reasons he gave for wanting to spend as much time as possible with Max, with whom he could recover the feelings of his youth. 'These things are too fine not to be done as long as we can', he wrote. 'I am thinking of me who am half a centurian, and of you who are not long past the silver wedding of life.'[184] He decided to celebrate the completion of his play. But the results of an outing to the Cavour Restaurant with Max were laryngitis and loss of voice. He also met McCormick, who was in London, for lunch at the Grosvenor Club at the beginning of March. It was the last time the two would meet.[185]

Ill health as much as the need to write more travel articles for Wallace finally drove him out of London in early March. His first stop was Lyndhurst in the middle of the New Forest. He felt immediately better, although he still had no voice. He spent the next fortnight sightseeing and learning about the place. He decided that William Rufus was 'a very great man', maligned by the chronicles.[186] At Lyndhurst church he was impressed by Lord Leighton's huge fresco illustrating the parable of the virgins, but decided that Christ as 'a simpering Jove' in the midst of the women was 'very stupid'.[187]

By 20 March, only three weeks before the publication of his play, he had received only sixteen pages of proofs. He began to panic that the book would not be ready for his birthday as

---

180 Davidson to Beerbohm, 4 Jan. 1907, Merton.
181 Davidson to Richards, 15 Jan., 1 and 19 Feb. 1907, Princeton.
182 'Windsor Great Park', *Glasgow Herald* (2 Mar. 1907), 11.
183 Davidson to Richards, 'Friday' [28 Dec. 1906], Princeton.
184 Davidson to Beerbohm, 4 Jan. 1907, Merton.
185 Davidson to McCormick, 28 Feb. 1907, Glasgow.
186 Davidson to Richards, 8 and 17 Mar. 1907, Princeton.
187 Davidson to Beerbohm, 'Some day in March' [17 Mar. 1907], Merton.

announced. It did nothing to calm his peace of mind when Richards decided to go to Portugal for ten days on a complimentary ticket from the Booth Line. Richards arranged for the proofs to be sent to him directly from the printers in West Hoe, W. Brendon and Son, to save time.[188]

Davidson left Lyndhurst and travelled west. He kept the printer informed about his changes of address. He took lodgings at 19 Stow Street in Christchurch, Hampshire. The weather was hot for the time of year, and he spent two pleasant weeks exploring the coast and the surrounding district. He visited the Isle of Wight on Easter Monday. On 4 April he wired Richards anxiously to ask if his book would be out by his birthday, and became irritable when Richards told him not to fuss: 'I am not fussing. I never fuss. A very hateful and unnecessary word.' He also asked that advance copies should not go to Shaw or to the *Academy,* as Shaw 'hates all poetry', and the *Academy* would 'come out immediately with some stale impertinence'.[189]

He left for Devon the next day, stopping first at Fortnes as the place nearest to Dartmoor and the shore. He described the house where he lodged at 69 Fore Street as old and one-sided 'with no front or back; only a gable at either end'.[190] He resisted the suggestion that Richards join him there for the weekend to celebrate the publication of his book: 'Of course I should like very much to see you at the week end: but you couldn't possibly stay with me. I have to do this in the cheapest way possible and even then I don't make ends meet.'[191] He suggested instead that they meet up later somewhere in Cornwall, which he planned to visit.

He had the first press notices of his play sent to him. Few of the critics liked it. Some like Edward Thomas at the *Daily Chronicle* were reluctant to say so. Thomas described his review to Gordon Bottomley as 'one of my saddest jobs lately' and thought that Davidson's brain 'must be giving way': 'Of course I couldn't praise it, yet I did not like having to say anything about this sad serious very "clever egoist".'[192] Others were not so

[188] Richards to Davidson, 21 Mar. 1907, Richards.
[189] Davidson to Richards, 4 Apr. 1907, Princeton.
[190] 'Totnes and Salcombe', *Glasgow Herald* (11 May 1907), 11.
[191] Davidson to Richards, 8 Apr. 1907, Princeton.
[192] Edward Thomas to Gordon Bottomley, 22 Apr. 1907, in *Letters from Edward Thomas to Gordon Bottomley,* ed. R. George Thomas (London, 1968), 137.

restrained. The *Academy* condemned it for its 'railing' and 'violent absurdities' and compared Davidson to 'a small boy in a passion shouting bad words at his nurse'.[193] The *Times Literary Supplement* wrote it off in the same sardonic way it had reviewed *The Theatrocrat*. Even the *Outlook* which had published so many of his things dismissed it as 'a sort of blank verse edition of Bunyan' overburdened with his philosophy.[194] He had determined not to reply to attacks on him as he had done in the past, but he could not resist one 'auspicious letter' to *The Times* and the *Athenaeum*, informing his critics that he rejoiced in having them as this enemies.[195]

He had by then decided to leave London. On the train to Fortnes he had remembered Gissing who had died in the Pyrenees four years earlier, another exile from metropolitan London. His own seemingly random itinerary had seen him drift further from the capital. He consulted a house agent at Totnes, on his way to Penzance, and was shown the district. On 26 April he was lodging at 3 Lannoweth Road, Penzance, having travelled by train that week from Totnes. He travelled first class, preferring gentlemanly privacy to the crowded bustle of the third-class compartments. During his fortnight in Penzance, the weather was bad, but he chose a good day to run down to the Lizard, visiting Caerleon, Richards's country cottage in Ruan Minor on the way. By 8 May he had taken a house in Penzance at 6 Coulson's Terrace. He told Richards: 'I hope ultimately to be all spring summer and autumn in London but I must get out of it in the winter if I am to live.'[196]

He returned to London the next day. It was time to pack and move again, after nine years at Streatham. This time it meant breaking up the family. Sandy, now 20, had his job in London and would have to go into lodgings on his own. Something of the turmoil and grief of the Davidson household in those last days in London is hinted at in a cryptic note Davidson sent to Richards on Whit Monday. Richards wanted to meet him the following evening. Davidson refused on the grounds that it

---

[193] 'The Tragedy of Failure', *Academy*, 72 (27 Apr. 1907), 408.
[194] 'God and Mammon', *Outlook*, 19 (11 May 1907), 623.
[195] Davidson to the Editor, *Times Literary Supplement* (3 May 1907), and *Athenaeum* (4 May 1907).
[196] Davidson to Richards, 2 and 8 May 1907, Princeton.

would be 'impossible on several counts which I can't go into. I stop, or my pen could hurry to say what shouldn't be told.'[197] On Wednesday, Pickfords arrived at Fairmile Avenue at 6 o'clock in the morning. They had to make an early start for the long journey ahead of them.

[197] Davidson to Richards, 20 May 1907, Princeton.

7

Penzance 1907–1909

When he began to explore the district, Davidson found Cornwall to be 'a low lying land of unworked tin mines, four hundred of them, grey, ghastly scabby ruins, inhabited by a lazy, lying Wesleyan shoal of pilchards and congregation of choughs'. He concluded that the Cornish riviera was 'a delusion of the guide books and the interested railway', and that there was 'nothing great about it except the Atlantic, and that is not Cornish alone'.[1] Penzance in his view was no better. One of the first things he did after his arrival was apply for a gun licence 'to shoot the fauna of the place—cats and small boys', he told Richards sardonically: 'the latter are turned into the streets all day and the former all night. I should also expect to be allowed a shot at larger game, to pick off a military bandsman now and again.' Richards offered to show him the beauties of the coast, but he disliked having things pointed out to him and told Richards so bluntly: 'the monstrosity of it: to take a man out and watch him enjoying scenery!'[2]

He continued to look on his residence in Cornwall as temporary, forced on him by his health and the need to live cheaply. He missed London. In one sense he had not left it. When the annual circular arrived from *Who's Who* he asked Richards if he could give '7 Carlton Street' as his address, as he did not want anyone to know he had left London.[3] In London hostility towards him surfaced when his name appeared on the Civil Pension List that July. The list always caused controversy in literary circles. There were many who felt that he did not deserve a state pension. His old acquaintance from his Crieff days, J. Cuthbert Hadden, who now syndicated a weekly 'Readers and Writers' column for the regional press, was one: 'Why should he not have been an English master today, earning his salary and

[1] Davidson to Max Beerbohm, 20 Apr. 1908, Merton.
[2] Davidson to Grant Richards, 'Friday' [May 1908], Texas.
[3] Davidson to Richards, 19 June 1907, Princeton.

writing his poetry in leisure hours. He has come through "the hards" I know. But that is by his own choice.'[4]

The severest attack on him came from the *Academy* which felt that his blasphemous views disqualified him. He was misquoted as having said, 'the more masculine and less delicate among men dislike women except in their sexual relations'.[5] He had in fact written, 'the more masculine, and therefore more delicate, minds among men dislike women except in their sexual relations, as mothers, wives, lovers, sisters'.[6] He wrote angrily to demand an apology and the editor's resignation, making sure to post an additional copy of the letter to the proprietors of the magazine so that it would not be ignored.[7] Anger turned to disgust when he discovered that the editor of the *Academy* was in fact Lord Alfred Douglas, whose appointment had not been announced publicly. 'Such a thing should have been published from the housetops', he protested to Richards. 'In the name of the Universe what have we to do with such filthy fellows! And Frank Harris will be in on it also of course, a man with a low voice and a dull pen who knows and understands nothing.'[8] His resentment was left to fester when Douglas refused point blank to apologize for his 'inadvertent' error.

He found one supporter in George Foote, the atheist editor of the *Freethinker*, who had himself been imprisoned for blasphemy in the 1880s. Foote wrote two articles defending Davidson's right to a pension and quoting extensively from *The Theatrocrat*. But in spite of his admiration for the play, he took issue with Davidson's refusal in the 'Epilogue' to be called an 'Atheist'.[9] The articles reached Davidson through Carlton Street. He was interested. He had always liked Foote. 'Although his mind lives in "mob", he is a good man', he told Richards.[10] His reply to the articles appeared in the *Freethinker* in September. He argued that it was time for Freethinkers to

---

[4] J. C. Hadden, *Wolverhampton Chronicle* (31 July 1907), 2.
[5] 'The Literary Week', *Academy*, 73 (20 July 1907), 692.
[6] Davidson to Richards, 27 July 1907, Princeton.
[7] Davidson to the Editor, *Academy*, 73 (27 July 1907), 734.
[8] Davidson to Richards, 7 Aug. 1907, Princeton.
[9] George Foote, 'What Price God?', *Freethinker*, 27 (18 and 25 Aug. 1907), 513–14, 529–31.
[10] Davidson to Richards, 29 Aug. 1907, Princeton.

rise above theism and atheism: If we accept the name Atheist, we limit

ourselves, we distort our growth . . . There is a word, Man, a virgin word, a zero. Let us call ourselves Men, and begin all things over again as if the world had never dreamt of a drunken deity.[11]

He was to incorporate the idea in the second of his *God and Mammon* plays: 'Your very atheist is a Christian, since | Denial warrants that which is denied.'[12]

Initially he called the play 'The World's Failure', a title he had used for his poem in the Duchess of Sutherland's anthology of living poets, *Wayfarer's Love*, in 1904. He had already sent a revision of his 'Lancelot' play to Watt as a 'forlorn hope' and by June had compiled a lengthy 300-page collection of his recent prose pieces under the title 'Causeway and Forest'. He asked Richards initially for a £20 advance for the prose miscellany.[13] Three weeks later he raised this to £25, not, he claimed, for business reasons, but because £20 was 'less than a living wage'.[14] Richards wanted to publish even before he had read the manuscript, but he refused the advance after carefully going through his books. He wrote apologetically: '£25 is not a very large sum, it is true, but I have looked into the books this morning and I find that we are not a great deal short, up to the present, of having £100 to make up before we are even on your books.'[15] Davidson argued and cajoled, but Richards would not budge, and Davidson in the end preferred not to publish rather than take less than he had asked although he had wanted desperately to publish it in order to have the 'pleasure of gibbiting' Douglas's 'reiterated lie'. The manuscript, in accordance with his instructions, was destroyed after his death.

As in the past, their friendship survived their business transactions. Richards went down to Cornwall in the summer and invited him to spend some time at Ruan Minor. At first Davidson was reluctant, complaining about its inaccessibility and suggesting a meeting half way, but in the end he travelled

[11] 'Mr John Davidson's Position', *Freethinker*, 27 (22 Sept. 1907), 593–4.
[12] *Mammon and His Message* (London, 1908), 8.
[13] Davidson to Richards, 22 June 1907, Princeton.
[14] Davidson to Richards, 16 July 1907, Princeton.
[15] Richards to Davidson, 15 July 1907, Richards.

down on Friday, 2 August after making elaborate travel arrangements to avoid staying overnight. He claimed that an overnight
stay would put him off the thing he was writing, but he was
always anxious about staying in other people's houses. He was
particularly obsessive about going to the barber every morning
to be shaved. In Penzance his special barber was behind his
house between Smith's Library and Morrab's Public Library. He
tried to make light of his anxiety, telling Richards, 'I have no
valet in the meantime.' In the event he and Richards were able
to spend six happy hours together in the privacy of Caerleon
Cove, before he picked up the last bus from the Lizard shortly
before 7 o'clock.[16]

By Christmas Davidson had finished the second part of *God
and Mammon*. He had changed the title to *Mammon and His
Message*. The play presents scenes of genocide, torture, rape,
and mass destruction as the racked and tormented Mammon
tries to hold on to power in his mission to lead the world
out of Christendom. Mammon takes as his heroes Zenghis,
Tamerlane, and Attila:

> City to city, land to land shall speed
> The message of deliverance, nightly flung
> In brindled flame against the firmament,
> As burning belfries topple into heaps.
>
> .   .   .   .
>
> . . . the truest creed
> Dies like a mollusc when you crack the shell
> Instead of temples I bring the universe;
> Instead of creeds I offer you yourselves.[17]

One of the central themes of the second of the *Mammon* plays
is that the doctrine of total living involves a necessary escape
from the analogy of language itself, including the final meta-
phorical illusions of time and space. 'Times's a liar | And space
a trick,' Mammon announces in his rejection of a dual universe.[18] It is an attitude that repeats Davidson's own dissatisfaction with language as analogy in an article in the *Westminster
Gazette* in 1903: 'My mission is to deliver the world from analogy', the Scarecrow tells the poet whose faith lies in the rich

---

[16] Davidson to Richards, 22 and 27 June 1907, Princeton.
[17] *Mammon and His Message*, 134.   [18] *Mammon and His Message*, 55.

expressiveness of English. '. . . I point out that truth is unattainable as long as language remains by your analogy prismatic, by mine corrupt'.[19] One might see this as a characteristic shift in the mind of the modern poet, for whom the seeming god-like power of language, what Davidson in his 1899 article 'The Art of Poetry'[20] called 'the voice of the species, the impersonal in "personation"', in the end fails to heal the poet's sense of self-division. In the 'Epilogue' to *Mammon and His Message* Davidson claimed to be making a new poetry out of the 'semi-certitudes of science':

I would have all men come out of Christendom into the Universe; into a new poetry. The great poetries of the past lived in symbols of the Universe—Olympus and Hades, Asgard and Nifelheim, Heaven and Hell; but the abode of my imagination is the Universe itself.[21]

Davidson was delighted at Christmas by a present from Richards of a box of cigars and promised to smoke them in his memory 'in the purlieus of Penzance'.[22] He had been in straitened circumstances since the move from London and had often to sacrifice the luxury of tobacco and whisky to make ends meet. He had already given up his London club. The saving of his 8-guinea-a-year subscription had been his answer to Maggie's complaint that the rent at Coulston Terrace was too high.[23] In his New Year greeting to Richards he spoke of longing to be in London in the spring, if circumstances 'devils of fellows' allowed.[24]

He was cheered up when Richards told him he wanted to reissue all of his *Testaments* in one volume and had sent George Wiggins, his manager, to see Moring to try and come to a satisfactory arrangement about the transfer of his books. Davidson was contemptuous of Moring. 'I have not encountered such a dog in a manger as the stock-holder, and we should have no mercy on him now', he wrote.[25] When Moring refused to negotiate, they decided that Watt should press him for a statement of accounts and any money owing to Davidson for the

[19] 'By-Ways', *Westminster Gazette* (22 Aug. 1903), 1–2.
[20] *Speaker*, 19 (4 Feb. 1899), 153–4.
[21] 'Epilogue' to *Mammon and His Message*, 150.
[22] Davidson to Richards, 26 Dec. 1907, Princeton.
[23] Mrs Davidson to Richards, 'Wednesday 14' [Apr. 1909], Princeton.
[24] Davidson to Richards, 31 Dec. 1907, Princeton.
[25] Davidson to Richards, 16 Jan. 1908, Princeton.

sale of his books. Richards's hope was that Moring would be unable to pay and that Watt would succeed in disengaging the books.[26] Davidson was less optimistic. Nothing was due on the first three *Testaments* until after the sale of 1,000, and the advances on *Self's the Man* and *The Knight of the Maypole* had not been paid off. His only assets were *The Testament of a Prime Minister, A Rosary,* and *A Queen's Romance.* He believed the most they could hope for was £10. Even this proved wildly optimistic. Moring came up with a derisory balance in his favour of 6*s.* 6*d.* for three years' trade and asked for £50 for the stock. Davidson himself had no money, but he urged Richards to pay the £50 and be done with it and made elaborate calculations about future sales to convince himself that they would benefit.[27]

Since the beginning of winter he had enjoyed better health than he generally did in London, but with the stress of Moring's 'business swamp', as he called it, his health broke down again. By 17 February he was suffering from acute depression and believed he had had 'a very distinct notice that I have hardly a year or two to live now'.[28] When Richards wrote anxiously to ask what he meant, he described feelings of 'dismay and despondence from prolonged insomnia; and the hideous enfeeblement of asthma'. He believed he had to write poetry every day if he was not to die: 'it is physiological: one could die of a constipated brain as well as—otherwise'. There were other 'things' he refused to disclose in a letter.[29]

Richards was so alarmed that he decided not to involve Davidson any further in the Moring case. He turned to C. F. Cazenove, the London Literary Agency in Covent Garden, whom he trusted more than Watt, and explained that Davidson was 'not in very good health, and nobody is likely to help him unless I do'.[30] They decided that Davidson's *Testaments* might be got from Moring with the help of Professor Israel Gollancz, who had been co-defendant with Moring in a widely publicized copyright action brought against them by the author, Edward Abbot Parry. Davidson was not told about this until March when his

[26] Richards to Davidson, 18 Jan. 1908, Richards.
[27] Davidson to Richards, 29 Jan., and 8, 17 Feb. 1908, Princeton.
[28] Davidson to Richards, 17 Feb. 1908, Princeton.
[29] Davidson to Richards, 20 Feb. 1908, Princeton.
[30] Richards to C. F. Cazenove, 27 Feb. 1908, Richards.

health temporarily improved. He rejoiced at the news: 'The battle of the *Testaments* engages astonishing champions. I hope Moring can be brought to his senses.'[31]

For Davidson the one positive aspect of the interminable business wrangle had been Richards's suggestion that he write a fifth *Testament* to be included in the planned one-volume re-issue. He had long wanted to write his final 'Testament of a Deliverer', but he planned it to be as long as 'the other four together' and was not keen to have it 'mixed up with them at the start'. He decided to let the idea ripen and turned instead to the final part of his trilogy, called provisionally 'The Last Triumph of Mammon'.[32] He hoped to have it finished in time for publication at Christmas. He asked Richards to send the proofs of the second part quickly as this always inspired him 'as much as my first proofs did'.[33] He tried to visit Filson Young at Ruan Minor in March, but the weather made this impossible. He had some hope that an article by Young praising him as a metaphysician would be published in the *Fortnightly Review* at the same time as his *Mammon and His Message*, but suspected that its editor W. L. Courtney would delay.[34]

In London people had begun to ask after him. A caricature of him by Beerbohm had appeared in January in the *Morning Chronicle*. Davidson was delighted with it:

Doubtless, one of the cleverest—a presentation of the terrible intellectual disease, swelled head. The face and skull are entirely disfigured by the turgidity of the brain, of the thyroid gland, and the pharyngeal organs; the eye crushed out of position; the nose is extended and spread like an inverted snout; the hat has to be carried in the hand because it is much too small for the head; the body becomes stunted; the other extremities small in sympathy with the cranium; and a constant vertigo requires the assistance of a staff to maintain an erect posture.[35]

Not all the attention was pleasing. He suspected that Lane was again influencing reviewers when his name was mentioned in the *Bookman* in March in connection with Lascelles

[31] Davidson to Richards, 13 Mar. 1908, Princeton.
[32] Davidson to Richards, 17 Feb. 1908, Princeton.
[33] Davidson to Richards, 13 Mar. 1908, Princeton.
[34] Davidson to Richards, 2 Apr. 1908, Princeton.
[35] Davidson to Beerbohm, 20 Jan. 1908, Princeton.

Abercrombie's recently issued *Poems and Interludes*. He thought Abercrombie talented but still a novice, and responded churl-ishly when Lane sent him a complimentary copy as the work of a brother critic: 'I am not the brother of any critic; nor did I ever practise criticism except in the bitterest grudge.'[36] How-ever, he was amused to hear from Lane that a lady enquirer had believed him dead. A few weeks earlier he had laughed at a clipping about himself in an Australian newspaper in which the 'uninformed biographer' had announced, 'Meanwhile his wife has died.'

In March a severe dose of flu forced him to abandon work on the third part of his trilogy. He had begun to recover by the beginning of April, but he felt miserable and frustrated. He wrote to Max on the 20th: 'Should you ever require to get well don't come to Penzance. Should you ever have a pension of £100 a year don't try to live on it. This is wisdom. I have done neither and abandon both attempts.' He was missing London desperately:

It is the greatness of London which is the profound subconscious satisfaction of living in it. Here, in Penzance, the wallflower blooms on the back-kitchen walls in March, arum-lilies grow like weeds, and flowering geraniums climb the house like virginia-creepers; but all that is not novelty and one season exhausts it: only primeval, everlasting things are interesting, and these frequent the flanks of mountains and the streets of cities. Happily I know mountains and cities, and Cornwall doesn't matter. When the sun shines the sky is wonderful and so is Mount's Bay.[37]

Davidson's days now followed a regular pattern. He wrote at his desk from nine until lunch-time every morning. In the afternoons he would read and think and go for a solitary walk through the streets of Penzance. Later there might be a visit to Morrab's Library and another lonely walk before bed. He encouraged Maggie to visit the neighbours, but he disliked people calling. As it was, he was constantly disturbed during the morning by the yelling of the children in the slum in front of his terrace house. When he sat down on 24 April to begin his fifth *Testament* he was unable to continue when a discordant

---

[36] Davidson to John Lane, 13 Mar. 1908, NLS.
[37] Davidson to Beerbohm, 20 Apr. 1908, Merton College.

bellowing of horns burst out in the street outside. 'Marbles are
out; and horns are in; the week after it will be the spinning of
tops', he complained to Richards.[38] He suffered again from
insomnia and sought escape from his feelings of weakness by
imagining a fantastic race of superhuman men and women. 'I
created a people the other night in whom I take great joy', he
told Max:

The warp and woof of us is Oxygen, Hydrogen, Carbon and Nitrogen
with Calcium in the bones and Phosphorus and Srephin in the nerves
and the brain. The new race I have created have flesh evolved from
Gold, Silver, Copper and Iron, with Bismuth in the bones; and besides
Phosphorus and Sulphur, Fluorine, Chlorine, Beryllium, Rubidium,
Mercury and Radium in the brain and marrow. The blood of these
people is molten gold and silver, and their seed is the finest flower of
flame; their thoughts and fancies are of a most inwoven eternity,
unutterably ethereal, space-filling and profound.[39]

Davidson's mind was becoming disordered. News from
Richards that *Mammon and His Message* was to be published on
5 May raised his spirits, but his response was extravagant: 'The
fifth: that's Ascension Day, when Christ opened the Kingdom of
Heaven to all believers. By all means let me, in the same day,
throw wide the gates of the Universe to all unbelievers.' Illness,
insomnia, the strain of writing, and the solitariness of his life
had brought him again to the point of breakdown. He saw
enemies everywhere. He told Richards that he did not want a
copy of his play to be sent to Archer whom he suspected of
being the anonymous author of some unfavourable notices
of *The Triumph of Mammon* in the *Daily Chronicle*. After years of
seeking Archer's approval, he dismissed his fellow Scot derisively as a philistine, 'wrapt up in Ibsen, one of those belittlers of
men; and when not revising his translations of Ibsen . . . reading
"Wee Magregor" and eating "taiblets".' He decided that Archer
had no right to express an opinion on his work on the grounds
that 'a man who can write a book about thirty seven living
poets understands nothing about poetry'. Beerbohm was the
only person in London 'out of all the crowd' that he felt he
cared for.[40]

[38] Davidson to Richards, 24 Apr. 1908, Princeton.
[39] Davidson to Beerbohm, 20 Apr. 1908, Merton College.
[40] Davidson to Richards, 28 Apr. 1908, Princeton.

The reviews of *Mammon and His Message* that summer were almost unanimously hostile, further deepening Davidson's megalomania. Scottish reviewers were generally more receptive. He had already noted this the previous May when he had written: 'Whenever a Scot is not a hard-and-fast church man, if he thinks at all, he is broader than the Englishman.'[41] But there could have been little satisfaction in this for a man who sought a place among English poets. He thought that, of all the critics, only James Douglas in the *Star* had understood Mammon's point in the final act that Christ's apophthegm about God and Caesar had justified the false division of body and soul, heavenly and earthly ways throughout Christian times. He preferred Douglas's view of him as a metaphysician to that of critics who recognized his merits as a poet but recoiled from his message.[42] Walter de la Mare described the play in the *Bookman* as, 'one long orgy of sound and fury',[43] while the *Pall Mall Gazette* dismissed it as 'an impossible mixture of Clytemnestra and Nietzsche's Übermensch'.[44] But more wounding was the continuing facetiousness of the *Times Literary Supplement* towards his work. He thought the paper 'in parlous state. It is so old, so bureaucratic, so in-bred in all its management that it has become a noxious journalistic slum.'[45]

Filson Young believed 'that reviews really mattered to him' in spite of the pretence at indifference.[46] One of the main problems in the reception of Davidson's tragic cycle was the difficulty critics had in seeing its possibilities as theatre at a time when Marlowe's *Tamburlaine* and much Jacobean drama—the drama with which Davidson's work was most often compared—was generally thought unactable. His own insistence on the importance of his message did not help him. One person who did recognize the theatrical intention behind Davidson's later work was Gordon Craig. That year Craig had rented a disused opera theatre in Florence, the Arena Goldoni, which served as

[41] Davidson to Richards, 11 May 1907, Princeton.
[42] Davidson to Richards, 24 Aug. 1908, Princeton. For James Douglas's review, see *Star* (16 May 1908), 1.
[43] 'Mammon and His Message', *Bookman*, 34 (July 1908), 151.
[44] 'Man and Matter', *Pall Mall Gazette* (14 July 1908).
[45] Davidson to Richards, 8 May 1908, Princeton.
[46] Filson Young. 'The Truth About John Davidson', *Saturday Review* 102 (15 May 1909), 623–4.

the headquarters for his magazine of the new theatre, *The Mask*. He tried unsuccessfully in April to get Richards to publish it conventionally. During the summer he was in touch with Davidson, explaining his ideas. Craig was keen to re-introduce an architectural massiveness into the theatre of his day, and to create a drama of Übermarionettes who would have the theatrical dimensions of gods and demons rather than of ordinary men and women, and it is not difficult to see what might have attracted him to Davidson's work, apart from the hope of finding a publisher for *The Mask*. Davidson asked Richards to send him *The Triumph of Mammon* and *Mammon and His Message*: 'He carries a huge lateen sail in a very small and unbalasted xebec, but he has read *The Theatrocrat*, and the iron has entered into his hold.'[47]

That July Davidson again visited Richards at his cottage in Ruan Minor. This time he was persuaded to stay for three days and confessed afterwards to having enjoyed 'a remarkable holiday'.[48] He had good reasons for seeing Richards. His financial situation was worse than it had ever been, so much so that he offered to read manuscripts for Richards at £100 a year to be paid monthly. Richards seems to have been embarrassed but agreed to think over his proposal. They talked mainly about his fifth *Testament* which he had finished before coming on holiday. He promised the original manuscript to Richards as a gift. He had originally called it 'The Passionary of John Davidson' but he decided that such an unusual word as 'Passionary' might handicap the book and changed the title to *The Testament of John Davidson*.[49] He planned to dedicate it in a formal letter 'To the Peers Temporal of the United Kingdom of Great Britain and Ireland', urging more government and an end to the 'old, effete, economic world of Christendom'. Richards seems to have argued against it, and Davidson let the matter drop until he was back home, when he wrote:

I did not choose to proceed with the discussion yesterday which would have spoiled the pleasure of the day—especially as there was nothing to discuss. I enclose the proposed dedication. It might be to the village

---

[47] Davidson to Richards, 14 May 1908, Princeton.
[48] Davidson to Richards, 17 Aug. 1908, Princeton.
[49] Davidson to Richards, 20 July 1908, Princeton.

idiot, or the German emperor, or to Jenny Willocks, or to the Pope; it is my letter that matters, not the person addressed.[50]

Davidson's final *Testament* is a lengthy and intricately woven poem of over 2,000 lines of blank verse. It opens with the protagonist's defence of suicide as man's supreme act of fearlessness and self-mastery in the face of senility and waning powers. His desire is to melt back into the infinity of the primary ether from which all the matter in the universe is seen to evolve:

> 'None should outlive his power,' I said. 'Who kills
> Himself subdues the conquerer of kings:
> Exempt from death is he who takes his life:
> My time has come.'[51]

What stays his hand is the conviction that he has attained the highest consciousness of the Universe, and that when he dies 'the Universe shall cease to know itself'. The body of the poem is a materialist revision of Keats's *Endymion* (1818) in which the legendary figure of 'John Davidson' seduces the virgin goddess Diana and so delivers men from the last remnant of 'other world'. The identification of virgin worship as the controlling centre of a falsifying duality of body and soul is consistent with Davidson's lifelong celebration of sexual satisfaction over chastity. In his last *Testament,* as in early poems like 'The Ballad of A Nun', his rejection of 'other world' and Edenic innocence is free of the political trappings that have always disturbed readers of the *Mammon* plays. The *Testament* ends with 'John Davidson's' crucifixion in Hell, his punishment for the belief that he himself is God—'Pernicious slander of material truth | So terribly avenged in the last Hell'[52]—before returning to the material world in a state of achieved self-knowledge which he knows may die with him.

Typing was by now becoming almost obligatory for professional writers, but he found he had to count the pennies and copied his poem himself, changing his grip repeatedly to ease his cramped fingers. On 11 August he added a 'Prologue', a new version of his earliest celebration of the pleasures of sexual

[50] Davidson to Richards, 11 Aug. 1908, Princeton.
[51] *Testament of John Davidson*, ll. 71–4.
[52] *Testament of John Davidson*, ll. 2090–1.

love 'For Lovers', which he retitled 'Honeymoon', and an 'Epilogue—The Last Journey'. In 'The Last Journey' we find a personal and poignant negation of the analogies of time and space already expressed by Mammon's 'Time's a liar | And space a trick':

> The way is steep, but I would have it so;
>   And dusty, but I lay the dust with tears,
> Though none can see me weep: alone I climb
> The rugged path that leads me out of time—
>   Out of time and out of all,
>   Singing yet in sun and rain,
>   'Heel and toe from dawn to dusk,
>   Round the world and home again.'[53]

In sending the poems, he explained his intention: 'I place my Testament thus between the dawn and close of my life: my personal utterance on the Universe become conscious between the two most personal poems I have written as a brother man.' He asked for his book to be bound in the red buckram that had been used for *The Testament of a Prime Minister*—'for auld lang syne if nothing else.'[54]

It is clear that Davidson's thoughts had again turned to suicide. When Filson Young stayed with him for two days that July he sensed it would be the last time they would meet. He recognized 'the bitterness and misery' deep underneath Davidson's laughter as they sat for three hours on a seat overlooking Penzance and the sea:

We were silent, feeling, as we always did when we parted, that a memorable time had come to an end. He came to the station with me, and we were joking and laughing and making fun of a pompous man whose appearance offended us. When it came to say 'goodbye' he suddenly turned gravely to me and put his hand on mine. 'If we do meet again,' he said and paused; 'why, we shall smile'; then, as the train began to move, 'If not,' he went on, and finished the line in a whisper, 'if not, why then this parting is well made.'[55]

By 11 August when the last parts of his *Testament* were delivered Davidson had still received no word from Richards about

---

[53] 'The Last Journey', ll. 21–30.
[54] Davidson to Richards, 11 Aug. 1908, Princeton.
[55] Young, 'The Truth About John Davidson', 624.

his proposal to read manuscripts for him. Three days later he made two copies of his first and only will in holograph, without witnesses. He put one copy in his desk with Maggie's name on it. The other he sent to Richards the following day, asking him to 'keep it safely until my death tomorrow or next day, or twenty years hence'.[56] He hung on in agony, waiting for Richards's reply to his proposal. The answer came on 1 September. Richards had had good reasons for delaying. Besides Filson Young, he also had Scott James reading for him and had just renewed his contract for six months before Davidson had spoken to him. He had other doubts besides:

I am doubtful whether I can afford it on the one hand, and on the other I am doubtful whether either you or I will get the most out of such an arrangement when we live at so great a distance and meet, unhappily, so seldom. However, if you are willing to try, I can—on one condition: that I may without umbrage on either side—on your side, of course—stop the work at a day's notice. You must depend on my not doing this without good cause! Therefore from today onwards, and at the rate of £8.6.8 a month, I shall call upon you to read manuscripts.[57]

Davidson's reply was simply, 'Thanks, at a day's notice.'[58] But his spirits were raised. He began to talk again about the accidental circumstances that kept him in Cornwall and of his plans to return to London for the spring, summer, and autumn months of each year. When a week passed without any manuscripts being sent from Carlton Street, he asked his publisher anxiously: 'What happened to the British Author?'[59] That 'one day's notice' clearly made him insecure.

He was soon kept busy with the proofs of his *Testament* which began to arrive in September. The poem appeared at the beginning of November. Within days the *Academy* attacked him personally as a 'despairing sort of posturer', and linking his ideas to socialism and the other dangerous manifestations of free thought that threatened the establishment.[60] He wrote to protest against what he felt was a deliberate misrepresentation of his views, rejecting in advance the plea of inadvertence, but this

---

[56] Davidson to Richards, 15 Aug. 1908, Princeton.
[57] Richards to Davidson, 1 Sept. 1908, Richards.
[58] Davidson to Richards, 2 Sept. 1908, Princeton.
[59] Davidson to Richards, 15 Sept. 1908, Princeton.
[60] 'The Supergod', *Academy*, 75 (7 Nov. 1908), 439–40.

only provided the *Academy* with an opportunity to revive the controversy about his state pension:

Considering *The Testament of John Davidson* in all its ghastly and bumptious enormity, we for our part fail to comprehend how it comes to pass that in a Christian country it should be possible for a person who considers himself a poet to be writing at his leisure such dangerous and stupid twaddle on a pension which is paid to him quarterly out of the Treasury of a Nonconformist Government. . . . The King is the Defender of the Faith, and we consider that it is against public policy and decency that Mr. Davidson should be allowed to huckster offensive atheism from a booth subsidised out of the State purse.[61]

More was to follow. When the *Academy* ignored his second and third letters, the *Star* printed his version of events on its front page. Criticizing Douglas's 'Philistinism and Tartuffery' he demanded that Douglas should apologize to his readers:

Noblesse oblige is doubtlessly a dead letter to you; but if you have any spark of fire or pulse of manhood in your veins, you will make the amends honourable to your readers, and lift the *Academy* out of the slums, at least, if you cannot give it distinction.[62]

The *Academy* seized on the absurdity of Davidson airing his views in a popular evening paper which published sporting news and starting prices and answered him in a ribald article full of horse-racing puns.[63] It was not the first time that the *Academy* under Douglas had adopted the style of the yellow press in order to promote its right-wing views. Shaw too had been attacked in May that year in an abusive article on *Getting Married* (1908). The *Academy* repeated its mockery in its 'Life and Letters' column a week later, in the hope of provoking Davidson, but he refused to comment further.

The effect of this campaign of persecution on Davidson's already frayed nerves appears to have been devastating. In November he again hinted darkly to Richards that an event of importance might happen at any moment[64] and spoke at home of 'doing away with himself', although no one took him

[61] 'An Epistle of Davidson', *Academy*, 75 (14 Nov. 1908), 462–3.
[62] *Star* (1 Dec. 1908), 1.
[63] 'John Davidson's Paddock Finals', *Academy*, 75 (5 Dec. 1908), 535–6. The debate concluded in *Academy*, 75 (12 Dec. 1908), 557.
[64] Richards to Davidson, 11 Nov. 1908, Richards.

seriously.[65] He continued to work on a new collection of poems which he planned for the following spring. He sent some to the *Westminster Gazette*. He also planned two further sequences of poems to make up the new volume—the first a series of four poems on 'Railway Stations'; the second, five poems on 'Cain', 'Judas', 'Caesar Borgia', 'Calvin', and 'Cromwell' under the general title 'When God Meant God'. He wanted to conclude the volume with a second Testament in his own name.[66] He knew that the collection was unlikely to make money, but he refused Richards's offer that he write a series of books for younger readers on myths and legends using a pseudonym. The idea for the series had come from Davidson himself, but he felt it was not his kind of work.[67] Instead he proposed further ideas for publications that he thought might make money for both of them. He had already suggested a series of illustrated books, beginning with Pepys's *Diary*, and a selection of Voltaire which he volunteered to do in a week at the British Museum Reading Room for two guineas.[68] He now suggested a 'Grant Richards Monthly Magazine' modelled on *Blackwood's*, *Murray's*, and *Macmillan's*, but having 'no prizes, no fiction, no news, no poetry, no illustrations'. It was to consist of personal confessions, a critical forum for aggrieved authors, and a major article on the principal topic of the month.[69] Richards thought the idea impracticable, but he expressed a keen interest when Davidson proposed a volume made up entirely of Napoleon's sayings, to be called, 'Napoleon Speaks'. Davidson's idea had grown out of a scenario he had written for a Napoleon play years earlier. He imagined it as a new kind of biography and anticipated world-wide sales. He himself asked for 1 per cent of the published price. Richards commissioned the Harvard historian Professor R. M. Johnson to undertake the work. Davidson thought Johnson to be 'the very man', and details of the final format became the subject of intense negotiations between all three during the early months of 1909.[70]

[65] Menzies's testimony at the inquest, in *Daily Telegraph* (21 Sept. 1909), 4.

[66] Davidson to Richards, 18 Nov. 1908, and MS, not dated [Mar. 1909], Princeton.

[67] Richards to Davidson, 24 Sept. 1908, Richards.

[68] Davidson to Richards, 2 and 4 Sept. 1908, Princeton.

[69] Davidson to Richards, 15 Nov. 1908, Princeton.

[70] The reports and correspondence about 'Napoleon Speaks' are at Princeton.

By then Davidson was reading books and manuscripts regularly for Richards. These grew from a trickle in September to fourteen a month in January and February. He took great pleasure in writing out his reports on Richards's official headed paper. Among the works of all sorts that came his way was a modern version of the medieval poem, *Pearl*, which he felt had 'really no significance, except for specialists'.[71] He also read French works, including five novels by Jules Verne which he ranked out of 100:

La Chasse au météore	100
Le Pilote du Dantile	80
Le Volcan d'or	60
Le Phare du bout	40
L'Agence Thompson & Co	30.[72]

When Maggie became anxious at the rate at which the parcels were flowing in and threatened to write to Richards to complain, Davidson checked her threat by saying that he had already asked Richards to 'pile them on'.[73] A letter to Richards on 27 January seems to squash the suggestion that he read less. Of his monthly cheque, he writes: 'Let me earn it. It is half my income. I should have satisfaction in reading a Ms a day—Sundays excepted.' On Sundays he worked on his own things. He still longed to be back in London: 'I wish I could see you. I wish to the Universe we could sit down together in a club or a restaurant with a bottle of claret and a dish of meat, and eat and drink the stars!'[74]

Davidson continued to receive mail at Carlton Street. He turned down a request for an interview with Rudolf de Cordova for a series 'My First Success' on the grounds that he wanted 'people to be interested in my writings and not my affairs'.[75] He was tempted by a commission for an imperial song for a Dr Charles Herriss that came to him through Richards. It was the sort of thing he had done many times before, but he had doubts about his ability to produce something that would satisfy him. He told Richards, 'already as I scribble, I feel I am going to try;

[71] Reader's report, 14 Mar. 1909, Princeton.
[72] Reader's report, 4 Feb. 1909, Princeton.
[73] Mrs Davidson to Richards, 'Saturday night 10 p.m.' [3 Apr. 1909], Princeton.
[74] Davidson to Richards, 27 Jan. 1909, Princeton.
[75] Davidson to Richards, 16 Jan. 1909, Princeton.

and I shall—shall'.[76] Three days later he had completed 'Song for the Twenty-Fourth of May'. 'I hope Dr. Harris [*sic*] will get Elgar to set my song to a thundering good diatonic tune, and let it be for all time our Imperial Anthem', he wrote.[77] He was hopeful that he would get a good sum for it—40 to 50 guineas had been mentioned. He even talked of going to London. When Maggie encouraged him he began to find excuses—he had no clothes, no boots. As in the past, his final answer was a grimly stoical, 'We've got to go on.' His regular income at this time was less than £4 a week, but his expenses left him no money to spare for anything except an occasional cigar.

He was delighted in February by a piece of gossip about Douglas. It came to him in a letter from Sandy to his mother. The story being told in the London publishing circles was that Douglas had called at Heinemann's, canvassing for advertisements for the *Academy*, and had been seen by the partner of the firm, as Heinemann was not available. In writing afterwards to Heinemann, Douglas expressed regret that he had not seen Heinemann himself but only a mere publisher's clerk. He received an immediate answer, again from the partner, who expressed regret that Lord Alfred Douglas had not called but only a mere advertising canvasser. Davidson took great delight in repeating the story to Richards.[78]

His moods fluctuated, but by March he seemed less depressed than he had been during the autumn and winter. By Tuesday, the 23rd he had his new collection of poems ready for delivery. That day he wrote some reader's reports and made up two parcels. Maggie thought that he had posted both that day. This was to contribute to the confusion that followed. About half-past six that evening he got ready to go to the post office. He was in good spirits and wrote out instructions for his 'ideal dinner' on a porcelain menu tablet before leaving the house. It read:

> Crème aux Pommes de Terre
> Boeuf à la Schottishe
> Du Pain

[76] Davidson to Richards, 23 Feb. 1909, Texas.
[77] Davidson to Richards, 2 Mar. 1909, Princeton. Davidson announced its completion to Richards, 26 Feb. 1909, NLS.
[78] Davidson to Richards, 1 Feb. 1909, Texas.

Choufleur au Gratin
De l'Eau
Pouding de Riz.

He laughed about the bad handwriting which he explained by saying he had been writing all day.

Davidson was seen after that by several people. He arrived at the post office and mailed the parcel to Carlton Street. From there he went to the Star Hotel and ordered a single whisky and a cigar. The telegraphist at the Western Union Cable office, Mr Kiddie, saw him leave the hotel smoking his cigar, and turn in the direction of his house. At that point all trace of him disappeared. He usually took an evening stroll along the promenade, so he was not missed at home. But when he failed to appear by 10 o'clock that night, Maggie began to worry. She went to sit with a family of neighbours, the Astons, while Menzies and the Aston boy went to look for Davidson. The two youths searched the town and the esplanade in the direction of Mousehole, his favourite walk, but there was no sign of him. Maggie was anxious that he might have suffered a heart attack or had an accident. A month before he had walked absent-mindedly over a four-feet raised pavement common in the district and had injured himself.[79]

The next morning Maggie sent telegrams to Sandy and Richards in London to see if he had turned up there. Neither had heard from him, but the parcel he had sent the previous evening had been delivered to Richards's office that morning. At 3.41 p.m. that afternoon Maggie telegrammed Richards again to learn that only one parcel had arrived.[80] At that point Richards advised Maggie to report her husband's disappearance to the police. The police who came to the house suspected that he might have committed suicide and asked her to look for a suicide note. She found the handwritten will addressed to her in his desk, but the date at the top of the page—14 August—reassured her, and she stopped reading.[81]

A missing-person's notice went out to the chief constables of Cornwall, Devonshire, and Dorset as well as to some of the main

[79] *Daily Mail* (27, 29 Mar. 1909).
[80] Telegrams to Richards, 10.50 a.m., 3.41 p.m., 6.05 p.m., 24 Mar. 1909, Princeton.
[81] Sandy Davidson to Richards, 9 Apr. 1909, Princeton.

towns in England and Scotland. On Thursday night, two days after his father had vanished, Sandy took the story to the *Daily Mail*: the news broke in the London papers the next morning. In Cornwall itself policemen had been issued with a description and the coast guard at Penzance instructed to be on the look-out around Mount's Bay. There was a proposal to dredge the dock, but there had been a strong wind from the sea since Tuesday, and it was felt that if Davidson had fallen into the water, the body would have been washed up on the beach. One other possibility had been eliminated: the five passengers who had travelled by the only train that had left Penzance on Tuesday night had all been identified.

Belatedly, the police ordered a complete search of the district. A party retraced Davidson's favourite walk to Newlyn Paul and Mousehole returning by the shore and examining every possible place where an accident might have happened. They found nothing. Sandy tried to persuade the head constable at Penzance, Superintendent Kenyon, to extend the search, but Kenyon argued that if Davidson had walked into Land's End district or towards Morvah he could have fallen down a disused shaft where a whole army of searchers would never find him. *The Times* expressed dismay at the conduct of the search in an article 'Where is John Davidson? Is he alive?' Richards also thought the police 'extremely supine' and wrote to the chief constable of Cornwall to complain.[82]

The cost of a more extensive search in those days had to be met by the family. Sandy learned from his father's bank manager at Wood Green, Mr Ridgway, that his father's account was £12 overdrawn, and that £7 was still owing on the rent. His father's quarterly pension money was due on 1 April, but it seemed likely in the circumstances that payment would be delayed.[83] Richards had managed to sell 'Song for the Twenty-Fourth of May' to the *Daily Chronicle* for 25 guineas, and there was still 10 guineas owing from the *Westminster Gazette*, but the editor was reluctant to send it as he felt that Davidson was probably alive. In desperation Sandy turned to the *Daily Mail* which agreed privately to bear the expense of the search in return for exclusive interviews with the family.

[82] R. Middleton Hill, chief constable of Cornwall to Richards, 8 Apr. 1909, Princeton.
[83] Sandy Davidson to Richards, 27 Mar. 1909, Princeton.

There was to be a disparity in the days that followed between the newspaper's energetic support for the search and its feature stories about the disappearance, which hinted that Davidson had either abandoned his family or committed suicide.[84] The family seemed naïvely unaware of this. In the Monday edition (29 March 1909) Maggie was quoted as saying:

He certainly liked to be alone, although he was the kindest and tenderest of husbands and fathers. He would say to me, 'If I were rich I would buy three houses—one for you, one for me and one for the boys.'

The article then reported that no importance was attached to the fact that Davidson's revolver was missing but concluded by quoting from the 'sad epilogue' of *Mammon and His Message*. An earlier report on Saturday 27 March had concluded an interview with Menzies in a similar way with lines from Davidson's 'Epilogue—The Last Journey'.

Maggie herself was now convinced that he had fallen into the water and drowned. But hopes were suddenly raised when four witnesses came forward claiming to have seen Davidson in the neighbouring town of Hayle on Thursday, two days after his disappearance. Sandy motored the seven miles that afternoon in the company of two reporters from the *Mail* and the *Chronicle*, but an all-out search of the town produced nothing. They were about to give up when reports came in of further sightings of Davidson at Cabis Bay, near Hayle, that afternoon and at St Ives where a man answering his description booked on to the 4.25 p.m. train for London Paddington. The passenger had asked if he might leave the train at Truro and re-join the 10 o'clock train that night for London. Sandy wired the news jubilantly to Richards.[85] But at Truro the trail again went cold, and Davidson was not among the passengers who arrived at Paddington Station at 3 p.m. on Tuesday morning.

There were to be other sightings. A ship's steward called Willis, who knew Davidson by sight, claimed to have seen him in Truro that morning. Sandy set off again with the journalists to question him. According to Willis, Davidson had recognized him and had tried to avoid him, but Willis had followed him to the station where he heard Davidson book to Falmouth. He

[84] *Daily Mail* (30 and 31 Mar. 1909).
[85] Telegram, Sandy Davidson to Richards, 12.20 p.m., 30 Mar. 1909, Princeton.

described him as not looking as he used to and wearing clean boots. Sandy became convinced that Willis was telling the truth and concluded that his father was in rooms somewhere. This seemed to be confirmed when he found a barber who claimed that a man answering his father's description had come to the shop the day before. Unfortunately, the barber who had shaved him had gone to St Austell. Sandy took down the barber's address in St Austell and telephoned the police there asking them to check the story. He decided to stay in Truro that night in case his father turned up there again.[86]

The reporters had reached their own conclusion. A week had now passed since the disappearance. For them the circus was over. The reporter from the *Mail* moved on to Bath. The man from the *Daily Chronicle* returned to London promising Sandy he would report the details of the search personally to Richards. At Coulston Terrace the neighbours were taking turns to bring Maggie her meals and make her eat something. She was convinced that he had drowned, but when J. M. Barrie, an old acquaintance of their London days, generously sent a cheque for £100, she suggested to Richards that they offer some of the money as a reward for information.[87] Richards placed a brief notice in the London newspapers on 1 April displaying a photograph of Davidson and announcing a reward of £20. It advised that no one was to lay 'violent hands on Mr. Davidson in the anxiety to secure the reward, since his mind may be in such a state that the occurrence of anything of that kind would have disastrous consequences'. Readers were recommended to have Davidson followed if they saw him, while they tried to get a medical man or a policeman.[88] In Penzance Sandy arranged for a reward bill to be printed for display in police stations and shop windows throughout Cornwall. It described Davidson as:

Aged 51 years; height about 5 feet 5 ins; stout build; dark complexion; full round pale face; brown piercing eyes; dark hair, moustache, and imperial tinged with grey; bald on top of head; has a varicose vein in left leg, and a mark where a wart has been recently removed from first finger on left hand.

[86] Sandy Davidson to Richards, 1 Apr. 1909, Princeton.
[87] Mrs Davidson to Richards, 'Wed. mor.' [31 Mar. 1909], Princeton.
[88] Richards's instructions for the notice are in a letter to 'Dear Sir', 31 Mar. 1909, Princeton.

Dressed when he left home in a blue serge suit, dark overcoat, bowler hat, and black buttoned boots.

Davidson always carries one eyeglass, is well known as a literary man, walks very quickly, and has the appearance of a Frenchman.

It is feared that he may be suffering from some loss of memory, or some ill may have befallen him.[89]

The reward prompted a retired inspector of the City Detective Force, Charles Bryan, to offer his services as a private detective for £1 5s. 6d. a day plus travel expenses.[90] It also resulted in futher sightings, including one from a woman who claimed she had sat opposite 'to a very similar face' in the London Underground about the time of Davidson's disappearance.[91] But after talking to the reporter from the *Chronicle* Richards had developed a theory of his own. The family was in a state of feverish suspense when Richards's letters hinted that he knew the truth. Maggie and Sandy prepared to leave Penzance at once for London. But in the end Maggie was too exhausted to travel. Sandy was to be thankful for this later when he heard further news from Richards, for he found Richards's theory—that Davidson had deserted them—insulting and utterly ridiculous.[92] Maggie was equally bewildered when Richards's letter was read to her on Saturday night. She had scarcely slept since the disappearance and was close to nervous collapse. She wrote at 10 o'clock that night in distress: 'Of course we had differences of opinion—but we had no two ideas in common— that's how we got on so well—I simply let him do what he liked.' Then in tearful recrimination: 'I was no good to him—except— to see that his creature comforts were as good as I could get. . . . The awful strain on me has not been lessened by your letter . . . I shall never see him again. I'm as certain as that I'm writing this, that he fell into the sea, which has not as yet given up its dead.' By Sunday morning she was able to complete the letter more resolutely: 'My own belief is that he is drowned, and has been washed out to sea where he will never be found. I would rather think that than what you have tried to make

[89] Reward bill, Princeton.
[90] Charles Bryan to Richards, 1 Apr. 1909, Princeton.
[91] Miss J. L. Benecke to Richards, 1 Apr. 1909, Princeton.
[92] Sandy Davidson to Richards, 4 Apr. 1909, Princeton.

me believe. Don't think I'm angry—I'm past [it] or anything else.'[93] Sandy kept her in bed that day. She was too weak to write and had to dictate to Sandy a letter in which she confidently dismissed Richards's theory as a fabrication of the man from the *Chronicle* and his friends. She had spoken to her neighbour, Mr Aston:

he is convinced that so far no one saw my husband after he was seen to leave the Star Hotel. Mr Aston says that knowing my husband fairly well and also his physical condition it is impossible for him to be living unless he is housed in some institution, and if that were so we should have some intimation of it through the police or the press.[94]

This made sense, as Davidson had only about £2 in his pocket when he disappeared.

That day Sandy and Menzies followed up a final hopeful lead when a Mrs Penrose of Lamorna, further up the coast from Mousehole, claimed to have seen a man answering Davidson's description walking backwards and forwards on the path near her house the previous Wednesday. She had recognized Davidson from the photograph in the Penzance papers and described his manner as abstracted as 'he walked as far as the nearest stile, and back again several times'.[95] This sounded like their father, but like the other sightings and theories it fell to the ground. Sandy himself began to doubt all the evidence and decided on Saturday 10 April to return to work the following Tuesday, exactly three weeks after his father's disappearance. He now accepted the possibility that his father was dead. 'One feels so absolutely helpless', he wrote to Richards.[96]

In one last effort to solve the mystery, Sandy got in touch with Sir Arthur Conan Doyle, an old friend of his father, to ask his opinion. From the evidence of the missing revolver, and the subsequent discovery that two catridges were also missing from the house, the creator of Britain's most famous detective suggested that suicide was the only theory which fitted the case, although when he learned about the unfinished trilogy, he conceded that it was a strong point in favour of Davidson still

[93] Mrs Davidson to Richards, 'Sat. Night 10 p.m.' [3 Apr. 1909], Princeton.
[94] Mrs Davidson to Richards (dictated to Sandy Davidson), not dated [4 Apr. 1909], Princeton.
[95] Quoted in *Cornish Telegraph* (8 Apr. 1909), 8.
[96] Sandy Davidson to Richards, 7 and 9 Apr. 1909, Princeton.

being alive.[97] But back in Penzance, Menzies had made a discovery that supported Conan Doyle's grimly logical conclusion.
Going through his father's papers again on Thursday the 15th,
Menzies found one of the two parcels that his father had made
up on the day of his disappearance.[98] It contained the manuscript of his last collection of poems, with the following prefa-
tory note:

The time has come to make an end. There are several motives. I find
my pension is not enough; I have therefore still to turn aside and
attempt things for which people will pay. My health also counts.
Asthma and other annoyances I have tolerated for years; but I cannot
put up with cancer.

An undated letter to his agent A. P. Watt read: 'This will be my
last book. Please forward it to Grant Richards and arrange with
him upon the usual terms. I have appointed Grant Richards my
literary executor to account to you, and to my heirs.'

   Maggie was prostrate. The significance of those last moments
took on a new meaning—the talk of the 'ideal meal'; the nervous humour about the shaky handwriting; the whisky and cigar
at the Star Hotel. She contacted Sandy and Richards in London
and asked them what to do. 'Surely, surely, my husband must
have been out of his mind to do this', she wrote to Richards on
Saturday morning. And then: 'I must be brave for my two's boy's
[sic] sakes.'[99] The two men had met at 6 o'clock the previous
night at Richards's house in Roland Gardens to prepare a statement for the press. Maggie saw a copy on Saturday evening and
panicked when she read that it was the belief of the family that
the poet had 'in a moment of acute depression made an end of
his life'. She asked Richards if it was too late to withdraw the last
statement and perhaps even suppress the details of his death.
She had once heard Davidson talk of how the suicide of
Addison Bright, the editor of the *Theatre* in the 1890s, had been
hushed up. 'Would it be compounding a felony to do so', she
asked. 'If it is to hurt his honour why do it! In his will he gives
me his insurance which I won't get if this is published. Then I
suppose the pension is also forfeited.' She did not believe that

[97] Sandy Davidson to Richards, 16 Apr. 1909, Princeton.
[98] Menzies Davidson to Richards, 15 Apr. 1909, Princeton.
[99] Mrs Davidson to Richards, 'Saturday Morning 8.10' [17 Apr. 1909], Princeton.

the poems would 'add to his fame either'.[100] There was an anxious exchange of telegrams between Richards and Coulston Terrace. A telegram from Menzies at 5.20 p.m. on Saturday assured Richards that nobody in Penzance except himself and his mother knew about the discovery.[101] But any plan they may have had to suppress the truth was forestalled unexpectedly on Sunday when *Lloyds Weekly* announced in its latest news box in blue ink: 'Mr. John Davidson the poet has committed suicide.' The source turned out to be the Penzance correspondent for the *Daily Chronicle* who had guessed the truth.[102]

The following day Davidson's will appeared in *The Times* together with an obituary notice. The will, written in August, appointed Richards his literary executor and imposed two stern injunctions:

No word, except of my writing, is ever to appear in any book of mine as long as the copyright endures. No one is to write my life now or at any time; but let all men study and discuss in private and in public my poems and plays, especially my Testaments and Tragedies.

He ordered that the manuscripts of his seven unpublished plays and adaptations, which included 'Lancelot' and 'The Game of Life', should be destroyed along with all his other unpublished writing, including his letters. The will concluded: 'I hope to live to finish my Testaments and Tragedies; but I may have to die before, and at any moment now, for reasons that concern myself alone.'[103]

The mystery of Davidson's disappearance was not completely solved by his final messages. The family could find no evidence that he had been suffering from cancer. The treatment he had been receiving from his doctor had been for haemorrhoids. Richards decided to place a notice in the *Lancet* calling on the doctor who might have treated Davidson recently to come forward. He received no response, and one must assume that Davidson simply had a morbid delusion that he was suffering from the disease. He had recently burned away a

[100] Mrs Davidson to Richards. 'Saturday Afternoon' [17 Apr. 1909], Princeton.
[101] Telegrams from Menzies Davidson to Richards, 5.20 p.m., 17 Apr.; 9.35 a.m. and 12.19 p.m., 18 Apr. 1909, Princeton.
[102] Richards to Robert Donald, 18 Apr. 1909, Princeton.
[103] Davidson to Richards, 14 Aug. 1908, Princeton.

sebaceous cyst from his scalp by applying nitric acid to the growth.[104]

The main problem was the absence of proof of death, which meant that Maggie had to prove her widowhood through the courts before the insurance could be paid, or even the portion of the civil pension due at the time of his disappearance. This could take years. Her sons could not support her. Sandy's salary was only £88 a year, while Menzies made about £1 a week as a chauffeur for a local businessman. Immediate rescue came in the form of a Royal Bounty Grant of £100 from the prime minister, the result of the efforts of Lane and William Watson.

Maggie was surprised at how few letters and telegrams of sympathy she received, but Richards told her that people 'hesitate to intrude themselves on sorrow' and that she could judge what people thought from the amount that was being written about Davidson in the papers. But he warned her: 'In reading them remember that they were written by people who are parts of the machine which your husband was always trying to destroy.'[105] She saw William Watson's letter in *The Times* on 26 April which accused the press and the public of causing Davidson's death by putting too many demands on the poet. 'His blood is upon us', Watson wrote.[106] It sparked a fierce debate on the situation of the poet in a commercial age. The *Academy* remained unrepentant about its attacks on Davidson and denied responsibility for his death, dismissing Watson contemptuously as another pensioner of the Liberal party.[107] Watson's final response came in a letter to *The Times* on 12 May in which he stated that Davidson was a greater poet than Otway or Chatterton and prophesied that one day his case would be ranked with theirs as instances of English dullness and inhumanity.[108] Three days later Filson Young wrote angrily from New York to tell the readers of the *Saturday Review* that Davidson had been hounded out of life neither by poverty nor public neglect but by the indifference of his fellow men of letters.[109] Many

[104] Information from Menzies Davidson, in J. Benjamin Townsend, *John Davidson: Poet of Armageddon* (New Haven, Conn., 1961), 454.
[105] Richards to Mrs Davidson, 26 Apr. 1909, Princeton.
[106] William Watson to the Editor, *The Times* (26 Apr. 1909), 10.
[107] 'The Murder of John Davidson', *Academy*, 76 (8 May 1909) 54–5.
[108] Watson to the Editor, *The Times* (12 May 1909).
[109] Young, 'The Truth About John Davidson', 623–4.

agreed with him, among them Davidson's old friend at the War Office, Arthur Legge, who condemned the mediocrity and self-satisfied dogmatism of anonymous reviewers towards 'the unhappy man of genius'.[110] By then Maggie had stopped taking the notices. She moved back to London to be with Sandy, taking a house at Thornton Heath. Menzies stayed on in Penzance. On 31 May her sister-in-law Effie applied on her behalf to the Royal Literary Fund. The regulations concerning widows were altered to make her eligible to apply for an award, and on 19 July she received a grant of £200.[111]

Fleet Street, and Other Poems appeared in June. Maggie and Sandy had wanted a commercial success, but the reviews made unhappy reading.[112] The poetic advancements and innovations of the final poems—with their fusion of rural and urban imagery, their modernist juxtapositions, and freer verse forms—bewildered most contemporary reviewers. For the *Times Literary Supplement*, Davidson's final poems illustrated the 'suicidal futility' of pure negation.[113] Even for those favourably disposed to Davidson's poetry, the last poems seemed to have strayed further into the strange jargon of scientific and literary slang—'Davidsonese'—which had 'swallowed up his singing voice'.[114]

With the reception of *Fleet Street, and Other Poems*, the final chapter of Davidson's life and work seemed to have closed. The general public soon forgot about him. In literary circles, his death had been overshadowed by that of Swinburne who had also died that spring. But to some admirers Davidson continued to matter, like the 17-year-old Hugh MacDiarmid then about to take his first anxious steps as a poet, and the young Harvard men like T. S. Eliot who discovered Davidson's poetry at this time. Some people refused to accept that Davidson was dead. Marie Corelli, who had sent supportive and sympathetic letters to Maggie after Davidson's disappearance and thought herself 'somewhat of a psychist', believed that he had disguised himself and gone away.[115] A youthful Rupert Brooke had similar fan-

[110] Arthur E. J. Legge, Letter to the Editor, *Saturday Review* (29 May 1909), 689.
[111] Correspondence File 2529, Royal Literary Fund, 31 May 1909, BL.
[112] Sandy Davidson to Richards, 9 July 1909, Princeton.
[113] 'John Davidson's Last Poems', *Times Literary Supplement* (15 July 1909), 260.
[114] *Star* (19 June 1909), 2.
[115] Marie Corelli to Mrs Davidson, 19, 20, and 22 Apr. 1909, Princeton.

tasies that autumn while holidaying in Cornwall with Dudley Ward, Margery and Bryan Olivier, and Bill Hubback. Describing a delightful cliff top walk to Jacques Raverat, he wrote:

The world was before us, sun, rain, wind, and road, and each other. We were filled with joy and youth and ecstacy. We talked as we ran and swung along, of Davidson—quoted (you know it?)
                    Out of time and out of all
                    While others sing through sun and rain
                    'Heel and toe, from dawn to dusk,
                    Round the world and home again.'
We were the 'others' then. We should die, as he had died; and there'd be others . . . and others . . .

Had he died? we wondered . . . I drew a picture of the poet, married, with grown up sons, hampered, driven to write, poor, worried, fettered, walking out one day from it all, changing his name and appearance and facing the world anew, reborn, tasting every drop of life with the keen sense of myth and freshness and the added relish of experience.[116]

That was in early September. Davidson had been missing for five months.

EPILOGUE

At about 5 p.m. on Saturday, 18 September, Orlando Humphreys and James Harvey Lawson were fishing in a punt about half a mile off Mousehole when they saw gulls hovering over an object in the water. It came towards them on the tide from the direction of Carn Dhu. When they were alongside they saw a decomposed body dressed in a dark overcoat with a gull sitting on it. They towed the body towards Mousehole Harbour where the local policeman, PC Wells, was sent for. The body was laid on a stretcher and Wells and other villagers carried it up through the village to a toll house above Penlee Point on the road to Penzance.[117]

[116] Rupert Brooke to Jacques Raverat, *Letters of Rupert Brooke*, ed. Geoffrey Keynes (London, 1968), 193–4.
[117] The account that follows is based on John Penwith, 'A Poet's End', in his *Leaves from a Cornish Notebook* (Penzance, [1950]), 36–9, and contemporary newspaper reports.

It was now dusk. Menzies was sent for, and in the dim lantern light of the hut he identified the clothing on his father's remains, and also a pipe—a plain straight-stem briar—found in one of the pockets. Another pocket contained a packet of Boardman's tobacco, his father's favourite, a bone paper knife, and a silver matchbox. The inquest was arranged for Monday afternoon in the United Methodist Church at Mousehole. Menzies gave evidence about his father's disappearance, including details of the missing revolver and cartridges. Then the inquest heard the testimony of Dr Millar, the examining physician. He believed that the state of decomposition of the body was consistent with it having been in the sea for about six months. He had found a round cavity in the right temple and another larger hole exactly opposite, consistent with a bullet being fired close to the forehead, but the condition of the body made it impossible to say with certainty that the man had shot himself. There was also evidence of a fractured skull caused by a severe blow, but again Millar could not say whether this had been caused by a stone or a boat's keel. The general opinion was that the body had become moored near where it was discovered, and so had not come ashore or been washed out to sea. The coroner, Edward Boase, spoke sympathetically of the nervous strain of the literary life, but as there was insufficient evidence of suicide, a verdict of 'Found Dead' was returned.

Suicide was a subject which had a particular fascination for the young men of Davidson's generation as they sought to break with the Victorian past. For the doctor in Hardy's *Jude the Obscure*, the suicide of Father Time 'is the beginning of the coming universal wish not to live'. Davidson himself from very early on had considered the possibility of suicide, which forms one of the recurrent themes of his writings. In *Smith* it is presented in characteristically Romantic terms as a dramatic gesture of contempt towards a world hostile to youth and art; in 'Lammas' it is the result of hereditary degeneration and the survival of the fittest; by the time of the 'Testaments and Tragedies' it is the supreme prerogative of the man of will. Davidson's own suicide is consistent with his desire to desacrilize the world. In the end, one could argue, it became the only way to kill God. His life in any case may not have seemed worth prolonging. At the time of his death, he had no money in the bank, and his debts were mounting. His health was failing, and the poetry for which he had sacrificed his well-being was generally despised. To many, Davidson's end suggested comparison with Chatterton's, 'Oh! damnable land! Land of scorn! be cursed forever!' But his last acts suggest a quieter, less dramatic mood. Suicide is generally viewed as the abnormal act of a depressed and unstable person, but suicide is chosen by about 1 person in 10,000 for a variety of motives, and, as is well known, increases fairly regularly with age. As is often the case, Davidson prepared his death quietly, hiding his intentions from his family. It was a private, solitary act, although for his friends and admirers his death was seen, perhaps with some justice, as a rebuke to the world that survived him.

Davidson's body was placed in a plain pine coffin with a plate inscribed, 'John Davidson, died March 23, 1909, aged 52'.[118] He had wanted to be buried at sea, and it was decided to bury him off the coast of Cornwall between Mousehole and Newlyn at 5 o'clock in the morning on Tuesday, 21 September. When the fishermen of Mousehole got to hear of this they objected on the grounds that the body might be trawled up by their nets. Charles Tregenza, a representative of the county council, and Mr Blewett, the harbour master, sent urgent telegrams to Gladstone, who was then Home Secretary, asking for permission to go ahead. Gladstone's answer came at midnight; he disapproved 'of any course other than burial in ordinary way, or cremation in accordance with law'. But when Sandy telegraphed again asking to bury his father seven miles out to sea, permission was given. However, the fishermen of Mousehole continued to object, and it was decided that the body should be taken out from Penzance.

On Tuesday morning the coffin was taken to Penzance harbour in an open hearse. It was then transferred to a ship's boat and towed out by the steam launch *Nora*. The vicar of Newlyn, the Revd J. S. Patrick Fagan, was on board with Sandy and Menzies, Vaughan T. Paul, a Cornish photographer, and four others. The ship steamed slowly out of the harbour shortly before midday with the flag lowered at half-mast. The people

[118] On 23 March 1909, the day of his disappearance, Davidson was in fact 19 days short of his 52nd birthday.

who had gathered on the pier stood bareheaded as she passed. Fishermen in the bay stopped at their work and lifted their caps. Ten miles out the *Nora* stopped. The Revd Fagan read the burial service and spoke in tribute of the poet's life and work. Then in calm waters, lit by brilliant sunshine, the body of John Davidson was committed to the sea.

Select Bibliography

JOHN DAVIDSON'S WORKS

For a check-list of Davidson's contributions to journals, see John A. Lester, 'John Davidson: A Grub Street Bibliography', The Bibliographical Society of the University of Virginia (Charlottesville, Va., 1958).

Poetry and plays

Diabolus Amans: A Dramatic Poem (Glasgow, 1885).
Bruce: A Drama in Five Acts (Glasgow, 1886).
Smith: A Tragedy (Glasgow, 1888).
Plays (Greenock, 1889); reissued as *Scaramouch in Naxos: A Pantomime, and Other Plays* (London, 1890).
In a Music-Hall and Other Poems (London, 1891).
Fleet Street Eclogues (London, 1893).
Ballads and Songs (London, 1894).
Plays (London, 1894).
A Second Series of Fleet Street Eclogues (London, 1896).
For the Crown (London, 1896); translation of François Coppée's *Pour la Couronne*.
St George's Day: A Fleet Street Eclogue (London, 1896).
New Ballads (London, 1897).
Godfrida: A Play in Four Acts (London, 1898).
The Last Ballad and Other Poems (London, 1899).
Self's the Man: A Tragi-Comedy (London, 1901).
Testament, No. I. The Testament of a Vivisector (London, 1901).
Testament, No. II. The Testament of a Man Forbid (London, 1901).
Testament, No. III. The Testament of an Empire-Builder (London, 1902).
A Rosary (London, 1903); essays and poems.
The Knight of the Maypole: A Comedy in Four Acts (London, 1903).
A Queen's Romance (London, 1904); adaptation of Victor Hugo's *Ruy Blas*.
The Testament of a Prime Minister (London, 1904).
Selected Poems (London, 1905).
The Ballad of a Nun (London, 1905).
The Theatrocrat: A Tragedy of Church and Stage (London, 1905).
Holiday and Other Poems (London, 1906).
God and Mammon: The Triumph of Mammon (London, 1907).

God and Mammon: Mammon and His Message (London, 1908).
The Testament of John Davidson (London, 1908).
Fleet Street and Other Poems (London, 1909).
Poems by John Davidson, ed. R. M. Wenley (New York, 1924).
Poems and Ballads, ed. R. D. Macleod (London, 1959).
John Davidson: A Selection of his Poems, ed. Maurice Lindsay, with a preface by T. S. Eliot, and an essay by Hugh MacDiarmid (London, 1961).
The Poems of John Davidson, ed. Andrew Turnbull, 2 vols. (Edinburgh and London, 1973).

Prose

The North Wall (Glasgow, 1885).
Perfervid: The Career of Ninian Jamieson (London, 1890); included in the same volume is the story 'The Pilgrimage of Strongsoul and Sanders Elshander'.
The Great Men and a Practical Novelist (London, 1891); short stories, and a new retitled edition of *The North Wall.*
Persian Letters, by Charles Louis, Baron de Montesquieu, trans. and introd. John Davidson. 2 vols. (London, 1892).
Sentences and Paragraphs (London, 1893).
A Random Intinerary (London, 1894).
Baptist Lake (London, 1894).
A Full and True Account of the Wonderful Mission of Earl Lavender (London, 1895).
Miss Armstrong's and Other Circumstances (London, 1896).
A Rosary (London, 1903); essays and poems.
The Man Forbid and Other Essays, ed. E. J. O'Brien (Boston, 1910).

In Collaboration with C. J. Wills

Jardyne's Wife (London, 1891).
Was He Justified? (London, 1891).
His Sister's Hand (London, 1892).
Laura Ruthven's Widowhood (London, 1892); authorship attributed.
An Easy-Going Fellow (London, 1896).

SECONDARY SOURCES

For a comprehensive bibliography of writings about John Davidson, see Mary O'Connor, 'John Davidson: An Annotated Bibliography of Writings About Him', *English Literature in Transition,* 20. 3 (1977), 112–74.

FINEMAN, HAYIM, *John Davidson: A Study of the Relation of his Ideas to his Poetry* (Philadelphia, 1916).

MACLEOD, R. D., *John Davidson: A Study in Personality* (Glasgow, 1957).

MILLARD, KENNETH, *Edwardian Poetry* (Oxford, 1991).

O'CONNOR, MARY, *John Davidson* (Edinburgh, 1987).

TOWNSEND, J. BENJAMIN, *John Davidson: Poet of Armageddon* (New Haven, Conn., 1961).

TURNBULL, ANDREW, 'Introduction', *The Poems of John Davidson*, 2 vols. (Edinburgh, 1973), xiii–xxxiv.

Index